Adobe InDesign CC
A Complete Course and
Compendium of Features

Steve Laskevitch

Adobe InDesign CC

A Complete

Course

and

Compendium

of Features

rockynook

Adobe InDesign CC: A Complete Course and Compendium of Features
Steve Laskevitch
luminousworks.com

Editor: Jocelyn Howell
Project manager: Lisa Brazieal
Marketing coordinator: Mercedes Murray
Interior design, layout, and type: Steve Laskevitch
Cover design: Steve Laskevitch

ISBN: 978-1-68198-440-7
1st Edition (2nd printing, June 2021)
© 2019 Stephen Laskevitch
Rocky Nook Inc.
1010 B Street, Suite 350
San Rafael, CA 94901
USA

www.rockynook.com

Distributed in the UK and Europe by Publishers Group UK
Distributed in the U.S. and all other territories by Ingram Publisher Services

Library of Congress Control Number: 2018949104

Printed in China

About the Author

Steve Laskevitch is lead instructor and founder of Luminous Works, the only Adobe Authorized Training Center in the northwestern United States (https://luminousworks.com). He is an Adobe Certified Expert (and Adobe Certified Instructor) in Photoshop, Lightroom, Illustrator, and InDesign.

While studying as a physics undergraduate, Steve was invited to instruct a few courses and immediately fell in love with teaching. He discovered his creative passions while learning photography and designing posters and flyers for the organizations he led in college. The worlds of graphic design and photography led him merrily away from a career in physics.

Steve has spent the 21st century both teaching and doing desktop publishing and building production workflows for many companies and individuals. He's taught at Cornish College of the Arts (where he was awarded the Excellence in Teaching Award), University of Washington Professional & Continuing Education (nominated for their Excellence in Teaching Award), and Seattle Central College.

The author has regularly helped Adobe Systems prepare Certified Expert exams, and for nearly five years he led the InDesign User Group in Seattle, InDesign's birthplace. Now he's Luminous Works' curriculum director and lead instructor, author of this volume and several Photoshop books, and speaker to user groups and conferences.

Steve is obsessed with New Haven–style pizza. Don't tell, but the best of that is to be had in Portland, Oregon. Despite this fact, he lives with his wife in Seattle.

Acknowledgements

InDesign is a beautiful creation. I am grateful to those who made it and am extremely fortunate to call a number of them my friends: Michael Ninness, Chris Kitchener, Ashley Mitchell, Nathan Brutzman, and, of course, Douglas Waterfall. Ashley, you've been an especially great supporter and thoughtful bringer of scones when the need is greatest. Thank you!

I am very indebted to my students who continue to ask the tough questions and keep me on my toes. You are the source of my passion for teaching.

To the Rocky Nook team, thank you for taking on this series. Lisa, your wit and eye for detail are well appreciated!

When I don't write so good, there's an editor to protect my reputation. (Did you see what I did there?) I'm so grateful to you, Jocelyn, for making this a better book.

Finally, and most emphatically, I thank my wife, Carla, who ensures that I see sunlight once in a while. And even if there is none, she brightens the day.

Steve Laskevitch
Seattle, January 2019

Contents

About the Author v

Acknowledgements vii

Introduction   1

The Course

1 Starting with a Solid Base   3

Setting a Few Preferences 4

   When to Set Preferences 4

   General 4

   Interface 5

   Type 6

   Units & Increments 6

   Display Performance 7

   GPU Performance (if present) 7

Configuring the Workspace 8

   A More Useful Initial Workspace 8

   Create a New Workspace 9

Project: An Introduction to Layout   10

Lesson A: Create a New Document 11

Lesson B: Placing the Images 13

   Place a Large, Full-Bleed Image 13

   Layers: Stacking and Protecting Content 14

   Create an Empty, Elliptical Frame 15

   Place an Image into That Circle 16

   Add a Colorful Stroke to the Frame 16

Lesson C: Adding Text 19

   Procure a Few Fonts 19

   Add a Text Frame and Text 20

   The Title and Subhead 21

   Add Text Wrap 24

   That's It! 24

2 Objects & Navigation — 26

Lesson A: Navigation — 27
Vital Keyboard Shortcuts — 27
Zooming & Panning — 28
Page Navigation — 29

Lesson B: Text Frame Basics — 30
From Frame to Text and Back Again — 30
Placeholder Text — 31
Text Formatting Basics — 31
Quick Resizing Tricks — 32

Lesson C: Image Frames — 33
Place an Image: Linking vs. Embedding — 33
Image Frames and Their Dis-Contents — 34
Content Grabber (a.k.a. the Donut) — 34

Lesson D: Shape and Frame Tools — 35
Selecting — 35
"Unassigned" Frames — 36
Applying Fills and Strokes — 36
Stacking Order — 37
Align and Distribute — 37
Gridify — 38
Object Styles Introduction — 40

Lesson E: Creating Swatches — 43
New Swatch — 43

Lesson F: The Power and Pitfalls of Defaults — 45

Lesson G: Troubleshooting — 46
Missing Fonts and Find Font — 46
Missing/Modified "Links" — 48

3 Text Styles — 51

Lesson A: Acquiring Fonts — 52
Typeface Inspiration & Legitimate Online Sources — 52
Adobe Fonts Service — 52
Installing Fonts — 52

Lesson B: Typography Essentials — 53
Formatting Text — 53

Lesson C: Building Paragraph Styles ... 56
By Example: Emulating a Style Guide ... 56
Applying Paragraph Styles ... 57
Overrides: Style Violations ... 57
Safely Editing Paragraph Styles ... 58
Defaults—Again! ... 59
Building Styles from Scratch ... 59

Lesson D: Building Character Styles ... 61
Applying Character Styles ... 62
Safely Editing Character Styles ... 62

Lesson E: Power Styling ... 63
Keep Options ... 63
GREP Styles: Find and Style ... 64
Nested Styles: Style Text via Sequences ... 65

Lesson F: Recycle and Reuse ... 66
Copy & Paste ... 66
Load Command ... 66
Paste without Formatting ... 66
CC Libraries ... 67

Lesson G: Placing a Word Document ... 68
Example 1: In a Perfect World ... 69
Example 2: In the Real World ... 70
Clean Up & Format with Find/Change ... 72

4 Tabs & Tables ... 76

Lesson A: Tabs ... 77
Setting Tab Stops ... 77
Including Tab Stop Position in Paragraph Styles ... 78

Lesson B: Tables & Table Styles ... 79
Create Tables by Converting Text ... 79
Style Waterfall ... 79
Adjusting Rows and Columns ... 81
Create Tables by Placing Spreadsheets ... 81

5 Frame Options & Object Styles ... 83

Lesson A: Multiple Text Columns ... 84
Columns and Gutters ... 84
Frames as Columns: Threading Text ... 85
Adding Frames and Deleting Frames ... 86

Lesson B: The Text Frame Options Dialog Box 87
 Baseline Options 87
 Inset 87
 Auto-Size 88
 Balancing Columns 88
 Vertical Justification 89

Lesson C: Leverage Object Styles 90
 For Text Frame Options 90
 For Image Frames 91
 Object Styles and Groups: Beware 94

Lesson D: Combining Paragraph and Object Styles . . 97

Project: Promotional Handout   **98**

Lesson A: Create a New Document 99
 This Document's Settings 99

Lesson B: Preparing for Content 101
 Introduction to Master Pages 101
 Build Styles with Placeholder Text 103
 Choose Defaults 105

Lesson D: Inserting the Text 106

Lesson E: Placing Images 108
 Placing Images into Placeholder Frames . . 108

6 Document Structure   **110**

Lesson A: Layers 111
 Controlling Stacking Order 111
 For Segregating Content 112
 For Protecting Content 112
 Reordering Layers 112

Lesson B: Master Pages & Sections 113
 Sections 113
 Page Numbers 114
 "Templates" for Pages and Spreads 114
 Ensure Consistency 115
 Overriding Master Page Items 116
 Primary Text Frames & Master Text Frames . 116

Lesson C: Adding, Deleting, and Moving Pages . . 118
 Insert Pages 118
 Page "Shuffling" 118

Project: Build a Brochure — 120

Lesson A: Configure a New Document — 121
Create a New Document — 121
Preferences & Display Performance — 122
Save — 122
Load & Examine Styles — 122
Layers — 124
Prepare the Master Spread — 125

Lesson B: Place a Word Document — 127
Placing the Word Doc — 127

Lesson C: Clean Up the Formatting — 128
Find/Change to the Rescue — 128

Lesson D: Insert Cover Pages — 131
Add a Front Cover at the Beginning — 131
Add a Back Cover at the End — 132
Remind Pages of Their Masters — 132

Lesson E: Place Images and Graphics — 133
The Steps — 133
The Images — 133

7 Long Documents — 136

Lesson A: Tables of Contents — 137
Building a Dummy TOC — 137
Requires a Commitment to Styles-Use — 137
Generating a TOC — 137
Updating a TOC — 139

Lesson B: Cross References — 141
Requires a Commitment to Styles-Use — 141
Referencing Arbitrary Text — 142

Lesson C: Text Variables — 144
Update Display Bug — 145

Lesson D: Find/Change Turned Up to 11 — 146
GREP: Finding Patterns — 146
Find/Change Glyphs — 147
Find/Change Object Formatting — 148

Lesson E: Book Document — 150
Let's Assemble a Magazine! — 150

8 Output   152

Lesson A: PDF 153
  Using Presets 153

Lesson B: Packaging 155

Lesson C: ePub (and HTML) 156
  Including Content 156
  Object Export Options 158
  Export Tagging 159
  Generating the Reflowable ePub 159

The Compendium

1 Workspaces & Preferences — 163

Preferences — 164
Document-Specific and Global — 164
General — 164
Interface — 165
Type — 167
Advanced Type — 168
Composition — 169
Units & Increments — 171
Grids — 172
Guides & Pasteboard — 173
Dictionary — 174
Spelling — 175
Autocorrect — 175
Notes — 176
Track Changes — 176
Story Editor Display — 177
Display Performance — 178
GPU Performance — 179
Appearance of Black — 179
File Handling — 180
Clipboard Handling — 182
Publish Online — 183

Panel Locations — 184
Choose a More Useful Initial Workspace — 184
Creating a New Column of Panels — 185

Customizing Menus & Keyboard Shortcuts — 187
What's on the Menu? — 187
Keys to Success — 188

2 Frames & Content — 189

Creating Frames and Shapes — 190
Rectangle — 190
Ellipse — 190
Gridify — 191
Polygon — 191

Fills & Strokes — 192
Create a New Color Swatch — 192
Gradients & Gradient Swatches — 194
The Stroke Panel — 195

Frame to Content & Content to Frame — 198
Text Frames — 198
Image Frames — 198

Text Frames & Text Frame Options — 200
Linking Text Frames — 200
Scaled Text Preferences — 202
Text Frame Options — 202

Image Frames & Linked Images — 208
Linking vs. Embedding — 208
Placing Images — 208
Frame Fitting Options — 210
Edit Original — 211
Modified Links — 211
Missing Links & Relinking — 212

Gridify Images — 213
Placing a Grid of Images — 213

Groups and Their Content — 214
Double-Click to Get In, Escape to Get Out — 214

Alignment & Distribution — 216
Guides — 216
Smart Guides — 217
Align Panel — 218
Precise Positioning and Sizing — 219

Transforms — 220
Movement — 220
Rotation — 220
Scaling — 222
Reflection — 223
Shearing — 223
Direct Selection Tool — 224
Free Transform Tool — 224
Pathfinder — 225
Compound Path — 225

Effects 226
Live Corners Widget and Corner Options Dialog Box ... 226
Effects Panel & Dialog Box 227

Text Wrap & Anchored Objects 229
Text Wrap: Force Fields on Objects 229
Anchored Objects 231

3 Styles, Type & Fonts 235

Working with Type 236
Vocabulary & Anatomy 236
Adjusting Type in InDesign 237
Font Technologies 240

Paragraph Styles 242
Creating a Paragraph Style 242
Applying a Paragraph Style 243
Editing a Paragraph Style 244
General Options 244
Basic Character Formats 245
Advanced Character Formats 246
Indents and Spacing 246
Tabs 248
Paragraph Rules 250
Paragraph Border & Paragraph Shading 251
Keep Options 252
Hyphenation & Justification 252
Spanning & Splitting Columns 253
Drop Caps and Nested Styles (and Line Styles) 254
GREP Style 256
Bullets and Numbering 257
Character Color 260
OpenType Features 261
Underline & Strikethrough Options 261
Output Tagging 262

Character Styles 263
Consistency 263
Protection 264
Creating a Character Style 264
Applying a Character Style 265
Editing a Character Style 266
Output Tagging 266

Object Styles | 267
Creating an Object Style | 267
Applying an Object Style | 268
Editing an Object Style | 269
The Attributes Controlled by Object Styles | 269

Table & Cell Styles | 272
Placing a Table | 272
Table Style To-Do List | 274

Loading Styles from Other Docs | 277

4 Pages & Spreads | 278

Anatomy of a Spread | 279
Margins and Bleeds and Gutters, Oh My! | 279

Navigating Pages | 281
The Pages Panel | 281

Master Pages | 283
Naming Masters | 283
Current Page Number Marker | 284
Applying Master Pages | 284
The [None] Master | 284
Overrides | 284
Text and Image Frames | 285
Primary Text Frames & Smart Text Reflow | 286

Sections & Numbering | 287
Starting and Editing Sections | 287
Section Markers | 288

Shuffling | 289
Building Gatefolds | 290

Page Size & Layout Adjustment | 291
Adjust Layout | 291

5 Color Management | 293

The Basics | 294
RGB | 294
CMYK | 294
Process vs. Spot (Solid) | 295

Color Myths, Theory, and Management 296
Best Practices 296
Grasping at Light 296
Devices and Their Limitations 298
So What Should I Do? 298
Profiles 299
The Flexibility of RGB 300
The Useful Rigidity of CMYK 301
Final Advice 302

6 Find/Change   303

The Basics 304
Setting Scope 305
Find/Change Formatting 305
Special Characters and Metacharacters 306

GREP 308
Code for Good 308
Building a Query 309
More Grep Queries 310
Grep Resources 311

Finding Glyphs 312
What's a Glyph? 312

Finding Objects 313
The Powers of Description 313

7 Long Documents   314

The Book Feature 315
Creating and Populating a Book 315
Document Syncing and Status 317

Layers 318
Stacking Order 318
Creating Layers 319
Segregating Types of Content 320
Deleting Layers 320

Tables of Contents (TOCs) 321
Preparation 321
Creating the TOC 321
Updating a Table of Contents 324
TOC Styles 324

Text Variables 325
   Chapter Numbers 325
   Captions 326
   Running Headers 327

Cross References 328
   The Destination 328
   Building a Cross Reference 328

Footnotes and Endnotes 331
   Footnotes 331
   Endnotes 333

Indexes 336
   Create a Topic List 336
   Create Index Markers and References 336
   Generate the Index 337
   Get Help 337

8 Output   **338**

PDF 339
   Presets 339
   General Options 340
   Compression 341
   Marks and Bleeds 342
   Output 342
   Advanced 344
   Security 344

Package 345
   A Copy of Everything 345

ePub and Tagged File Formats 347
   Export Tagging 347
   What Gets Exported and How 349
   Exporting an ePub 351
   Last ePub Note 353

Print 354
   Print Dialog Box 354
   Print Booklet 358

Keyboard Shortcuts   359

Index   369

Workspaces &
Preferences

Frames &
Content

Styles, Type
& Fonts

Pages
& Spreads

Color
Management

Find/Change

Long
Documents

Output

Introduction

Welcome to InDesign!

In this book, you will be working your way through a full course curriculum that will expose you to all of the essential features and functions of Adobe InDesign. Along the way, you'll learn the concepts and vocabulary of graphic design and page layout.

Between several larger projects are chapters of lessons. In those lessons, each action that I'd like you to try is marked with an arrow icon:

➡ This is what an action looks like.

The surrounding paragraphs explain some of the why and how. For greater depth, the second section of this book is a Compendium of those features and functions, providing the "deep dive" needed for true mastery of this powerful application. Throughout the Course section, I will suggest readings in the Compendium section. Although you will be able to complete the entire course without them, I think if you do those readings you'll find yourself regularly nodding and muttering, "oh, that's why it works that way."

To follow along with the projects and lessons in this book, you'll need the files. Launch your favorite web browser and go to rockynook.com/indesignCandC, answer a simple question, and download the files. They will be compressed (zipped), so you'll have to unzip them, revealing a folder that contains multiple subfolders (like "Project 1," etc.). Put that folder somewhere convenient (and memorable).

When we make updates to this book, we'll add a PDF to those files. Check in periodically to see what's new.

Have you installed InDesign yet? If you work for a company with an enterprise license, it's likely your IT people have installed it for you. We will be using the Creative Cloud app as our hub for launching Adobe applications and accessing the services that come with a Creative Cloud (CC) license. This app also checks to make sure your software license is up-to-date, so it should remain running whenever you use your creative applications. I use the CC app's Preferences to have it launch on startup so I don't have to worry about it.

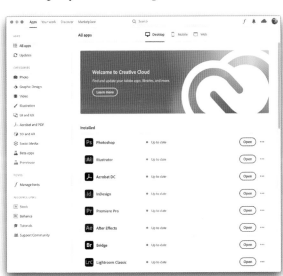

I most often launch InDesign by clicking the Open button to the right of the ID icon. If there's an update available, that button will read Update, but you may still launch InDesign by clicking near its icon or name.

THE
COURSE

1 Starting with a Solid Base

I am an opinionated InDesign user—like most. In this chapter, I'm going to make suggestions that I believe will make your time in the program more efficient. As you use InDesign, you'll develop your own ideas about what makes this program hum.

Photographer unknown

Setting a Few Preferences

For our first project, these few suggestions on how to configure InDesign will do, but I have many more than are on these next few pages.

> The full discussion about customizing InDesign can be found in the first chapter of the Compendium, "Workspaces & Preferences." Or you can save that for later and be content with these few customizations.

When to Set Preferences

To ensure that these preferences are set consistently for all the documents we create during this course, be sure to set them with no documents open at all. Many of the preferences are document-specific, but there's no way to distinguish them from those that are global (application-wide and applied to all documents).

General

➡ To make our user experience as pleasant as possible, let's adjust our Preferences. It's quick and easy to get to this page of the Preferences: On a Mac, use the InDesign CC menu, on Windows go to Edit > Preferences. Or use the somewhat unintuitive shortcut ⌘–K/Ctrl–K.

Show "Start" Workspace When No Documents are Open This choice shows recent files, links to videos, etc., when no documents are open. Sometimes this is convenient. At other times, I wish to see my chosen workspace (the panels I have carefully arranged) whether documents are open or not. This ambivalence leads me to enable and disable this preference with some frequency. Luckily, it's quick and easy to get to this page of the Preferences. For now, let's disable it.

Content–Aware Fit If you prefer to make your own cropping and composition decisions, I recommend disabling this as a default.

Workspaces &
Preferences

Frames &
Content

Styles, Type
& Fonts

Pages
& Spreads

Color
Management

Find/Change

Long
Documents

Output

Interface

This book makes extensive use of screenshots (pictures of my screen while using InDesign). To make these as legible as possible, I'm going to make InDesign's user interface a little less dark and murky. So that we both have similar experiences, you may wish to do the same.

Dark and
gloomy to
light and airy

Color Theme   This doesn't actually have to do with colors at all; rather, it adjusts the lightness of the panels that surround your document window. I'm choosing the lightest option for two reasons: I find the small interface elements more legible both on screen and in the printed version of this book. Also, I do print my work, and the lightest interface presents a context that is more like holding printed material before one's eyes. Nonetheless, you should choose what suits your eyes best.

Options

When scrolling with the Hand tool or moving or resizing objects, I prefer to see an accurate rendition of my layout. Thus:

Hand Tool   I suggest No Greeking for now. And what is *Greeking*? It's a placeholding approximation of images or text, usually boxes with X's in them for images and lines to represent text.

Live Screen Drawing   Choose Immediate so that as you drag objects across the page or resize them, you will know the result of that edit before you release the mouse. This is especially great when resizing text frames.

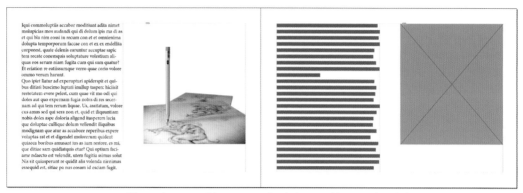

Normal text and image on the left, greeking on the right

The Course

Type

Apply Leading to Entire Paragraphs I can think of very few instances in which I need to adjust leading on a character-by-character basis. This preference is document-specific, so I recommend setting it with no document open so it's in effect for all future documents.

Smart Text Reflow Although we won't need this for a while, I wanted to mention this powerful feature. If you place a 14-page Word document into a one-page InDesign document, InDesign can add the necessary pages at the end of a story automatically. Upon editing that text, you may no longer need as many pages, and InDesign can delete extraneous pages automatically as well.

Units & Increments

Ruler Units Note that your horizontal and vertical units of measurement can be different, and can be changed at anytime by right clicking on either ruler in the document window.

Display Performance

Note the word "performance." These settings can enhance or degrade the speed with which InDesign displays text and images. The print quality of your document is not affected by these settings at all.

Default View   There are three choices. Fast doesn't display images at all, but instead shows gray boxes or shapes—rather brutal. By default, Typical shows a low-resolution "proxy" that InDesign generates for each image. High Quality renders images, graphics, and anything transparent without compromise. For the documents we will use during this course, we may use High Quality without much penalty. However, more complex documents will become sluggish unless you reduce the display performance view.

Adjust View Settings   You may customize the view settings to better tune the performance of InDesign. For example, you may want to adjust Typical to have low-quality transparency but high-quality vector graphics (AI and PDF files, for example) so your company's logo will look splendid when your boss sees it, and leave raster images (those made of pixels) as a proxy.

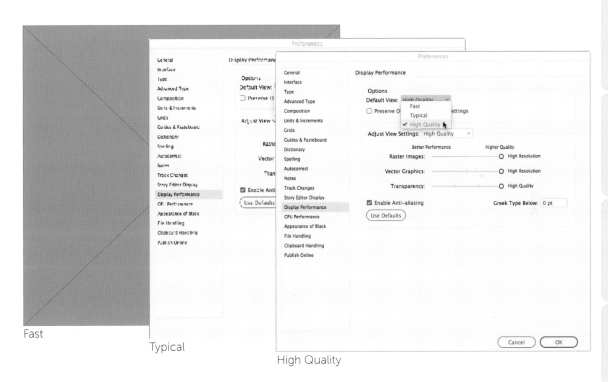

Fast

Typical

High Quality

GPU Performance (if present)

To better control zooming to specific objects, I recommend disabling Animated Zoom. I will assume this function is off when we discuss zooming and panning in later lessons.

Workspaces & Preferences

Frames & Content

Styles, Type & Fonts

Pages & Spreads

Color Management

Find/Change

Long Documents

Output

Configuring the Workspace

> Again, you should see the full discussion on customizing InDesign in chapter 1 of the Compendium, "Workspaces & Preferences."

A More Useful Initial Workspace

In the upper-right corner of the application, you'll see the Workspace menu next to the word "Start" or "Essentials." The InDesign team is perhaps a little too optimistic about how few panels you need to perform essential tasks in the program. Or maybe they're afraid to overwhelm you. Regardless, they're hiding truly important tools and functions to which you should have access.

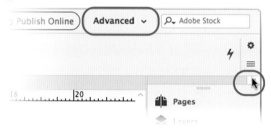

➡ So, from the Workspace menu, choose Advanced (fear not! There's nothing advanced here at all).

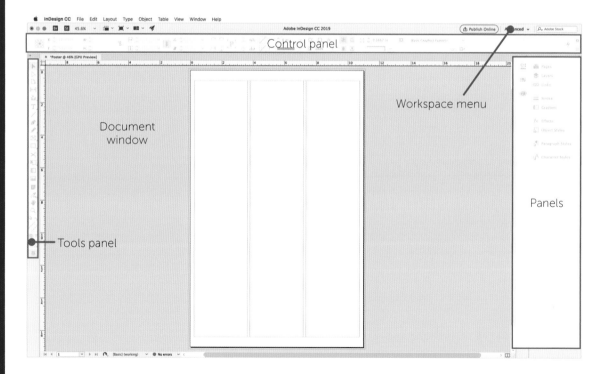

In the figure above, you can see InDesign's basic geography. If you're using Microsoft Windows, you'll notice that it's extremely similar to the view on the Mac from which this image was made. The area where we work is called the document window. It is surrounded by panels. On the left is the Tools panel. You will soon learn that we switch tools very frequently. On the right are other panels—at the moment there are rather few. Later you will find the right side populated by a great number of panels. Just above the document window is the control panel. Luckily, here you can find many of the things you need to do your job that would normally be found in other panels.

At the top of the stack of panels is small button with << in it. When clicked, it expands the panels so you can see the panels' content. Clicking it again collapses the panels to icons.

You can adjust each panel's height by grabbing the "bar" separating them—watch for the two-headed arrow then drag to resize the panels above and below the bar.

Incidentally, while your attention is on the upper-right part of InDesign's interface, note the search field set to search Adobe Stock. A new user may wish to change this to search InDesign Help by clicking on the magnifier icon and choosing that option. Now, back to work.

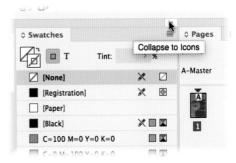

Create a New Workspace

➡ When the panels appear to be just as you'd like them (for now), capture that arrangement by returning to the Workspace menu and choosing New Workspace…. Give it a name: I'm going with "Real Essentials." If any of those panels go missing, or if there is a mess of panels in the way, you can choose Reset Real Essentials from that menu anytime.

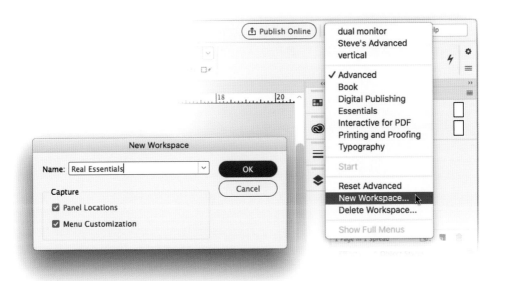

Workspaces & Preferences

Frames & Content

Styles, Type & Fonts

Pages & Spreads

Color Management

Find/Change

Long Documents

Output

Project: An Introduction to Layout

In the following lessons, we will learn the basics of creating a new document and populating it with styled text and carefully sized and positioned images. The result will be a fun and colorful poster.

Workspaces & Preferences

Frames & Content

Styles, Type & Fonts

Pages & Spreads

Color Management

Find/Change

Long Documents

Output

Lesson A: Create a New Document

Like with any endeavor, your work in Adobe InDesign will benefit from some preparation and setup. However, for this first "get to know you" project, we'll keep that to a minimum. Let's start creating a poster!

➥ First, launch InDesign. Use the Creative Cloud app, as that's your "hub" for all Adobe apps. Once the program is running, you can create a new document either by going to File > New > Document... or by clicking on the Create New... button on the welcome screen. If you use the menu method, you'll notice a keyboard shortcut that does the job, too: on a Mac, it's ⌘-N (hold down the command key and type "n"), and on Windows, it's Ctrl-N (hold down the Ctrl key and type "n"). Hereafter, I'll indicate shortcuts in that order for Mac and Windows, respectively, like this: ⌘-N/Ctrl-N.

Now you're facing a large window with many presets and fields to fill out. Don't be daunted by the choices—or the units of measurement. Choose the Print intent at the top of the New Document dialog box. Ignore the strange dimensions (66p0 x 102p0) for the moment and choose Tabloid as your page size.

On the right side of the dialog, you'll see a menu for Units: we will use inches for this project. Disable Facing Pages and expand the choices for Margins and Bleed and Slug. You'll need to click on the chain to the right of the margin dimensions so you can set them independently. Now you can have a five-eighths inch space at both the top and bottom, and one-quarter inch on each side. Set those

PRESET DETAILS

Poster

Width	Units
11 in	Inches

Height	Orientation
17 in	

Pages	Facing Pages
1	

Start #	Primary Text Frame
1	

Columns	Column Gutter
3	0.1667 in

⌄ Margins

Top	Bottom
0.625 in	0.625 in

Left	Right
0.25 in	0.25 in

⌄ Bleed and Slug

Bleed

Top	Bottom
0.125 in	0.125 in

Left	Right
0.125 in	0.125 in

and the other fields as seen here.

Note: For fractions (like the 5/8" top/bottom margins or 1/8" bleed), just type the fraction! InDesign will convert it to a decimal. Click Create when you're sure the settings are correct. Your document should look something like the figure below.

⬅ Choose File > Save As... to save your file. I'd suggest navigating to the folder you downloaded with all the files that accompany this book (see "Introduction"), and saving this file in the "Project 1" folder.

> What are margins and bleed? Good Question. Read the "Anatomy of a Spread" section in the Compendium chapter, "Pages & Spreads" (page 279).

We will be *placing* two images onto this page and pasting some promotional text into a text frame. But right now, an empty canvas awaits us. Let's dress it up!

Workspaces &
Preferences

Frames &
Content

Styles, Type
& Fonts

Pages
& Spreads

Color
Management

Find/Change

Long
Documents

Output

Lesson B: Placing the Images

In InDesign, everything—every letter, every image—has to be in a *frame*. For images, sometimes it's easy to have InDesign make a frame for you as you place an image. Often, we create frames first, and then insert images into them. That's the way we'll do it in this first exercise.

Place a Large, Full-Bleed Image

➲ Locate the Rectangle Frame tool about halfway down the Tools panel (see figure below). Use it to draw a box from the upper-left corner of your bleed to the lower-right corner of the bleed. The image we are about to place will be slightly larger than the page (the black outline). If you find that the box you have drawn is not exactly in the right position or is not the right size, switch to the Selection tool, which is found at the top of the Tools panel. With it you can drag a corner of the box or the box itself to fine-tune its dimensions or position.

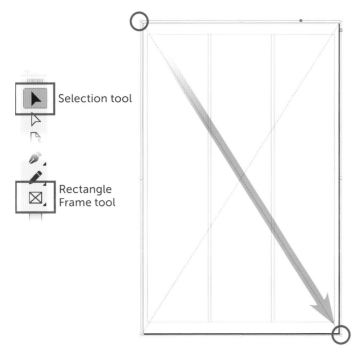

Selection tool

Rectangle
Frame tool

Use the **Rectangle Frame tool** to draw a frame from the far upper-left bleed (red lines beyond the black page edge) to the lower right.

Use the **Selection tool** to move or adjust the frame once it's drawn.

In fact, we use the **Selection tool** for many things. Good thing it's at the top!

➲ The frame is drawn; make sure that it is selected. Use the Selection tool to click in the middle of the box, and you will see that its control handles are visible. It's time to get the image!

➲ From the File menu, choose the command Place. Notice that to the right of the command there is a keyboard shortcut you could use instead. Over time, we will place many images, and it is likely you'll memorize that shortcut. For now, using the menu is perfectly fine.

Do you remember where you put the downloaded course files? InDesign is asking you to locate the image you want to place. Navigate to your downloaded course files, and locate the "Project 1" folder. In it, you will find an image called *sky.jpg*. Double-click the filename, and the image will fill the frame you drew a few moments ago. Fortunately, the image was created at precisely the correct size to fill that frame. We will not be quite so lucky with the second image. Choose File > Save or use ⌘–S/Ctrl–S to save your file.

Layers: Stacking and Protecting Content

The image you just placed will serve as a backdrop to the other content we are adding next. InDesign offers several ways to prevent a user from accidentally moving or deleting content. The method I use most frequently is Layers.

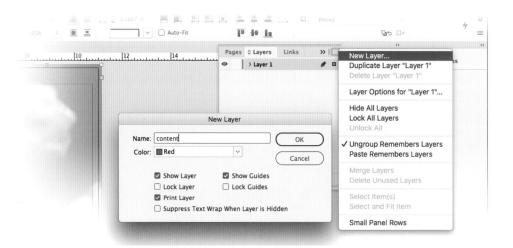

On the right side of your screen, locate the Layers panel. If it's missing, use the Window menu and choose Layers. Every panel in InDesign has a small menu in its upper-right corner. Unsurprisingly, these are called panel menus! The first item in a panel menu is the creation of a new... whatever that panel controls. So if you click on the Layers panel menu, the first item is New Layer.... This poster's text and a second image will be on a new layer that we'll name "content."

📨 Use the Layers panel menu and choose New Layer.... In the dialog box that appears, enter the name "content." When you select a frame on that layer, the frame edge will have the color you choose below the name. I will choose red. To commit your choice, press the Enter key or click on the OK button (they do same thing).

To prevent us from accidentally editing the sky image, we should lock the layer that it's on. In the Layers panel, you should see two eyes: one for each layer. Clicking on

Workspaces & Preferences

Frames & Content

Styles, Type & Fonts

Pages & Spreads

Color Management

Find/Change

Long Documents

Output

an eye hides a layer, and clicking there again reveals it. The space to the right of an eye holds a padlock that prevents the editing of that layer.

➦ To protect *Layer 1*, click to the right of its eye. To edit our new *content* layer, click near its name to highlight it. Now we're ready to add more stuff.

Create an Empty, Elliptical Frame

See all those tools on the left side of the InDesign workspace? Almost every one of them is actually the first of several in a group. If you right-click on the Rectangle Frame tool, two other tools are revealed. Mac users: either use a two-button mouse or use your mouse system preferences to add a "secondary click" function to your Apple Magic Mouse—it's worth it.

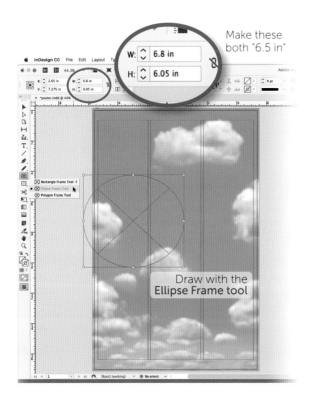

Make these both "6.5 in"

W: 6.8 in
H: 6.05 in

Draw with the **Ellipse Frame tool**

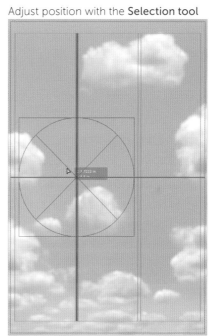

Adjust position with the **Selection tool**

➦ Choose the Ellipse Frame tool and drag out a loosely shaped ellipse somewhere on the left side of the page. We'll refine its size and position in a moment. If you make a mistake, you can undo it by choosing Edit > Undo (like in any software application) or using the universal shortcut ⌘-Z/Ctrl-Z. To fine-tune the size, we'll make this ellipse a perfect 6.5 x 6.5-inch circle by entering those dimensions in the width and height fields in the Control panel.

➦ Switch to the Selection tool to fine-tune the position of the circle.

➦ As you drag the circle, you'll see purple or pink lines appear now and then. These are called Smart Guides and they tell you when your object is aligned to some part of the

The Course

page, margins, columns, or even some other objects! When a Smart Guide appears, its end points tell you what your object is aligned to. Move your circle slowly up and down, and you'll see a pink line appear from the left edge of the page to the right when you're centered vertically. A purple line appears when you're aligned between the first and second column guides. This is where I'll leave this frame, but its exact position is up to you. We'll see how this frame looks with an image in it and when there's text on the page.

➡ Save! Choose File > Save or use ⌘-S/Ctrl-S.

Place an Image into That Circle

➡ Part of this should sound familiar. With the circle selected (via the Selection tool), choose File > Place... and navigate to your Project 1 class folder (you might already be looking at it: InDesign usually brings you to the last folder from which you placed an image). Choose the image called *airship.jpg*.

You should find that the image fills the ellipse and that you can see only a small bit of it. No worries!

➡ Right-click within the circle (I'd recommend off-center). A rather long menu appears, filled with items that could be useful when editing an image frame. Choose Fitting > Fill Frame Proportionally. This sets the image to fill the circle, but crops as little of it as possible.

Frames can be decorated, even if they have images or text in them. In this case, we'll add a border, or, as we call them in InDesign, a stroke.

Add a Colorful Stroke to the Frame

With the circle still selected (select it with the Selection tool if you need to), expand the Color panel on the right side of the screen. In that panel's upper-left corner are two small boxes, one overlapping the other. The one that is slightly higher and to the left of the other is for filling a frame with color. The other one with a gap in the center is for designating a stroke color.

➡ Click on the stroke box to bring it to the fore, and move your cursor over the small rainbow at the bottom of the Color panel.

Your cursor will turn into a small eyedropper with which you can choose a color. A red, like the undercarriage of the airship in the picture, should make a nice accent.

The color you choose from the rainbow is, at best, approximate, so it's likely not exactly what you want.

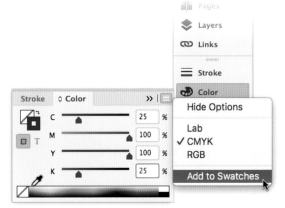

➡ Fine-tune your color choice with the sliders above the rainbow. Here, the sliders are showing colors as CMYK (Cyan, Magenta, Yellow, blacK) and I will leave them that way for now. As you can see in this figure, I thought the following values worked well: 25, 100, 100, and 25, respectively.

In a few moments, we will be adding text—perhaps the title can also be in this same color, so let's save it. Note that the Color panel, like the Layers panel earlier, has a panel menu in its upper-right corner. From this menu, we can choose different ways of designating color (Lab, RGB), and we can add this particular color to our swatches panel so we can easily select it later.

Just above the Color panel is the Stroke panel. From its many options we need only to choose the weight of the stroke (the current weight, or thickness, of the stroke is only one point—almost too small to see).

➡ Set Weight to 10 points.
➡ Save! File > Save or use ⌘–S/Ctrl–S.

Workspaces & Preferences

Frames & Content

Styles, Type & Fonts

Pages & Spreads

Color Management

Find/Change

Long Documents

Output

So far, our poster is looking pretty good, but it is missing one rather conspicuous element: words! Just a little word of warning before we move on: when using your Selection tool, beware of the those concentric circles in the center of an image over which your cursor hovers. That's called the Content Grabber (also known as the "Donut," a nickname preferred by many). If you unintentionally (or, of course, intentionally) drag it, you will dislodge the image from its frame! That is its intent: to allow you to recompose images within their frames. Later, we'll see how we can crop an image by resizing its frame, and then recompose it using the Donut. But now, a word about words....

Lesson C: Adding Text

Procure a Few Fonts

We should have fonts that go with our Victorian/Steampunk-themed poster, so I've come up with a way for you to get a few nifty fonts quickly, provided the computer you're using can currently access the Internet and the Creative Cloud app is running (see the Introduction).

➦ In the Project 1 folder is a file called *TheFonts.indd*. Open it by double-clicking on the filename, or from within InDesign by choosing File > Open…. You will almost instantly get a message that there are **missing fonts**. Don't be alarmed, but don't dismiss this warning: we need that dialog box.

Having just reread that dialog box, I'm impressed with its clarity and plain language—so much better than messages like "unknown error occurred." My synopsis: the three lines of text each use a different font. Those fonts are not installed on your computer, but they are all available from Adobe Fonts (formerly called Typekit). In InDesign, pink highlighting identifies text that wants to use "missing" fonts.

➦ In this document, click the Activate button and the missing fonts will be installed. It may take a bit, so take those moments to marvel at the work you've done so far. Well done!

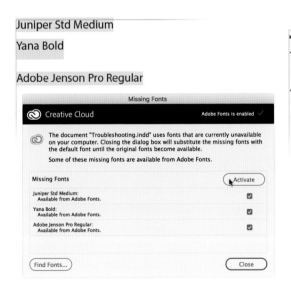

When the fonts have completed syncing, you'll be notified in that same dialog box, which you may now close.

Workspaces & Preferences

Frames & Content

Styles, Type & Fonts

Pages & Spreads

Color Management

Find/Change

Long Documents

Output

🔁 Also, close the document *TheFonts.indd*; it's done its duty. We now have fonts we can use in any document. The order in which they're listed above happens to be the order in which we'll use them, too. Juniper will be our title font; Yana, our subhead; and Jenson will be for our body copy, which occupies most of the reader's time (like these words).

Add a Text Frame and Text

I have another file for you to open, but not in InDesign. Again, it's in your Project 1 folder. It's called *PromoCopy.txt*.

🔁 Double-click this file, and it will likely open in TextEdit (on a Mac) or Notepad (on Windows). It is simply a plain text file with the promotional copy we want to use for our poster. When you open this file, highlight all the text and then copy it. You can use the shortcut ⌘–C/Ctrl–C to copy, as you can in InDesign or any text-editing application.

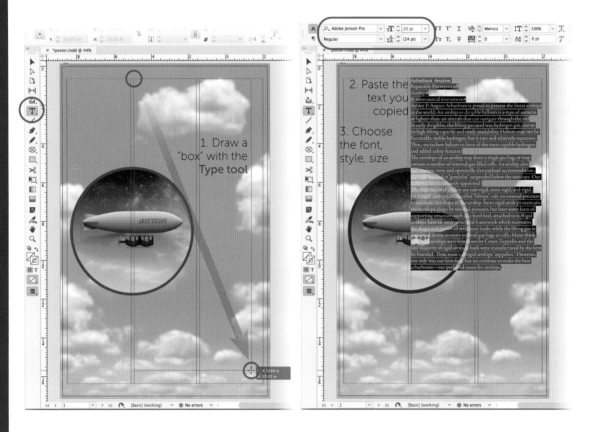

🔁 Back in InDesign, choose the Type tool (the big "T" in the Tools panel) and draw a box covering the second and third columns, using the guides to, eh, guide you.

Remember, you can adjust the size and shape of this box later. Once the box is drawn, you'll see the text cursor blinking in its upper-left corner.

➡ Paste the text we copied from that text document by pressing ⌘-V/Ctrl-V, or by going to Edit > Paste. Other shortcuts that you might know from other programs like Microsoft Word can be used in InDesign as well.

➡ Let's use one of those shortcuts now. Press ⌘-A/Ctrl-A to select all the text so we can format it. To start, let's set one of those fonts we procured: Adobe Jenson Pro Regular. Make sure all the text is highlighted, then choose that font and style from the Control panel or the Properties panel, as well as a legible body copy size for a poster—say, 20 points.

➡ Save! File > Save or ⌘-S/Ctrl-S.

You probably noticed that the text is currently obscuring an image. That detail is one we'll take care of at the end.

The Title and Subhead

Just above, I wrote that there are features (like shortcuts) that function in InDesign the same way they do in other applications. If the Type tool is still active, click once somewhere in the text frame. As you might expect, the cursor is blinking at that location. Now double-click on a word and you'll see that it's highlighted, just as it would be in any other program. InDesign can go further: triple-click, and yes, a whole line gets selected. Quadruple-clicking selects an entire paragraph and quintuple-clicking (a rare phrase!) selects the entire *story*. I prefer these noisier methods rather than clicking-and-dragging the cursor because I sometimes miss characters when I use the latter, slower method.

Before we select and carefully size and style the top lines of text, let's be sure the frame is the right size.

➡ From the Tools panel, choose the Selection tool again. Adjust the size of the text frame by dragging its handles until they snap onto the guides. Sometimes, I have to drag too far, release, and then drag the handles back so the frame snaps nicely to the guides. Double-clicking in the text frame switches quickly to the Type tool. With all the clicking you're doing, anyone nearby will think you're very busy!

➡ Now let's select the top line, "Arbuthnot Aviation." Since it's also a paragraph, you can either triple- or quadruple-click to select it. Change the font to Juniper, then adjust the type size in the Control panel or the Properties panel using the menu or the small up/down arrows next to the *size* field: ⊤Ⅱ ↕ 11 pt ⌄ . I found 58 points worked nicely.

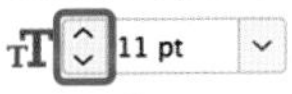

➡ Let's make this title the same color as the circle's stroke. With that text still selected, choose its color from the Fill menu in the Control panel (see the following figure).

Workspaces & Preferences

Frames & Content

Styles, Type & Fonts

Pages & Spreads

Color Management

Find/Change

Long Documents

Output

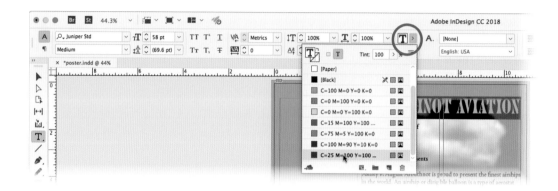

> Select the subhead lines, "Reputable Purveyors of Airships & aeronautical instruments." I think the font Yana would be just right here, but the size of each line (each is a paragraph) and the space between them will need adjustment.

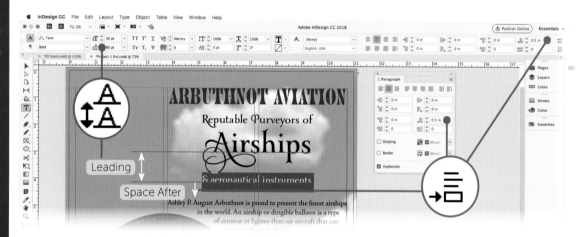

Look at the figure above.

> To push the letters of one line down away from the line above it, we select that whole line and adjust its *Leading* (named for the metal—lead—once used to separate lines of metal type).

> To push the text below a selected paragraph downward, we use *Space After*.

Both of these functions can be found in the Control panel, if there's room. If you're using a small screen and can't find the Space After field on the right side, summon the Paragraph panel: Window > Type & Tables > Paragraph.

> Before making final decisions about each line's size, leading, and spacing, let's add some flourishes that the Yana font allows. Highlight the "A" in "Airships." InDesign notes that the font designer provided alternate *glyphs* (characters) for the highlighted one and shows you a few. If there are more than a few, an arrow at the end of the list invites you to "View more Alternates." Let's!

➡ Clicking that arrow summons the Glyphs panel, which shows all of the alternates for the letter you've selected. To choose one, double-click it. Each time you do this, a different alternate takes the place of the previous. I chose one with extra swirls. I also chose alternates for the "R" in "Reputable" and the "P" in "Purveyors." Now that we have our text with the appropriate glyphs, we can better situate it.

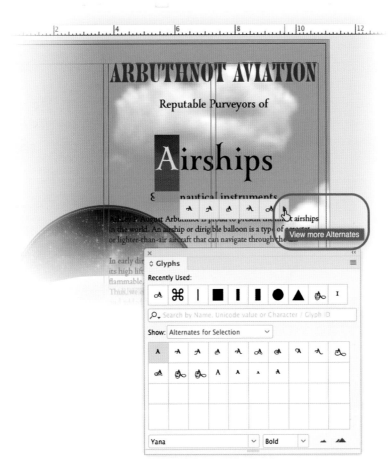

➡ Select each line in the subhead (triple-click!), and experiment with its size and leading. My choices were as follows:

"Reputable Purveyors of"	size: **35 pt**	leading: **50 pt**	space after: **0**
"Airships"	size: **90 pt**	leading: **80 pt**	space after: **0**
"& aeronautical instruments"	size: **30 pt**	leading: **80 pt**	space after: **.5 in**

➡ One last typographic touch: select all the text (quintuple-click!) and uncheck Hyphenate in the Paragraph panel (or the Control panel if the checkbox is there). Much better! Now get the Selection tool.

Workspaces & Preferences

Frames & Content

Styles, Type & Fonts

Pages & Spreads

Color Management

Find/Change

Long Documents

Output

Add Text Wrap

This is our last tweak to the poster. The picture of the airship is currently partially obscured by the text.

➤ Using the Selection tool, click on the left half of the circle (the right half is under the text frame, making it more difficult to get at). We can now add a kind of force field called Text Wrap that will push text away from our shape. Go to Window > Text Wrap, and its panel appears.

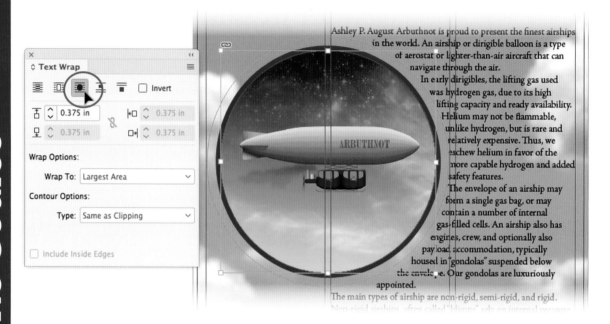

The first button is the Text Wrap off switch.

➤ To conform to our circle, we need the third button, "Wrap around object shape." Use the small arrows below that to increase the offset.

Warning: Don't try to move that circle until you either hit the esc key on your keyboard or click on nothing with the Selection tool first. Because of a quirk with this type of Text Wrap, you could dislodge the image from its frame!

➤ Save! File > Save or ⌘–S/Ctrl–S. And, unless you'd like to show someone first, you may close the document via File > Close or ⌘–W/Ctrl–W.

That's It!

Congratulations! You've made your first InDesign publication. There are many features and functions we skirted, and some further customizations to InDesign that will help us work more easily. The next chapters will contain exercises to familiarize you with important

Lesson C: Adding Text   That's It!   **25**

Workspaces & Preferences

Frames & Content

Styles, Type & Fonts

Pages & Spreads

Color Management

Find/Change

Long Documents

Output

ingredients that we use when cooking with InDesign. So, when we get to our next project, you will know better what you may wish to include.

2 Objects & Navigation

In InDesign, every bit of content has to be contained in a frame. Thus, you have to become adept at making and editing frames. Sometimes that means getting in tight and close, zooming in to adjust things finely, and then efficiently zooming back out to see the big picture.

Since your content inhabits frames, it's also important to become proficient at switching from frame-editing to content-editing and back. This chapter will help you develop that proficiency.

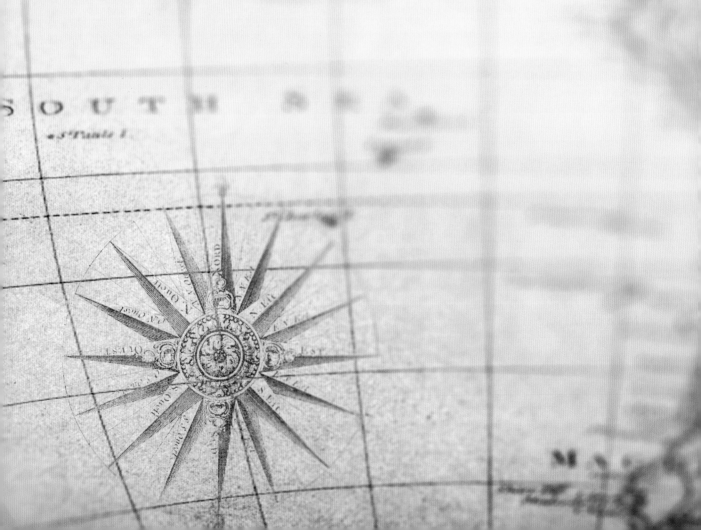

Lesson A: Navigation

➦ To get started, open the downloaded document called *2 Frames & Shapes.indd*. When you do, you'll be looking at its title page, a fine place to start our conversation. To manage the *missing fonts* message, follow the instructions in "Procure a Few Fonts" (page 19).

Vital Keyboard Shortcuts

Throughout this chapter, and this entire book, you will find the following shortcuts to be very handy. A much more comprehensive list of shortcuts can be found in the Appendix.

Function	Mac	Windows
Access Selection tool	tap **Escape** (if editing text) or **V** (otherwise)	
Undo (an edit)	⌘–Z	Ctrl-Z
Redo	⌘–shift-Z	Ctrl-Shift-Z
Fit current page in window	⌘–0	Ctrl-0
Fit current spread in window	⌘–option-0	Ctrl-Alt-0
Select All	⌘–A	Ctrl-A
Deselect All	⌘–shift-A	Ctrl-Shift-A
Toggle Preview mode	tap **W**	
Access Hand tool (to pan)	press and hold **H**	
Access Zoom tool	press and hold **Z**	
Constrain while drawing/transforming	hold **Shift**	
Make copy while drawing/transforming	hold **option**	hold **Alt**

Warning: The shortcuts that have you tap or hold down a letter key will not perform the listed function if your text cursor is in a text frame. You'll end up typing that letter—maybe many times! In this situation, tapping the Esc key removes the application's focus from your text (if that's where it was), or in any case will do no harm. Now you can use any shortcut.

Workspaces & Preferences

Frames & Content

Styles, Type & Fonts

Pages & Spreads

Color Management

Find/Change

Long Documents

Output

While working in InDesign, the application maintains a recovery file that's stored in the same folder as the file you're editing. If your computer crashes, upon relaunching InDesign, the recovery file opens right where you left off. This recovery file also gives you unlimited undo, accessed via Edit > Undo or ⌘-Z/Ctrl-Z.

Another Warning: Undo is your best friend *most of the time*. However, it does not undo actions that have no effect on page items. *That is, you cannot undo zooming.* I've watched many a startled student accidentally zoom, then attempt to recover by using ⌘-Z/Ctrl-Z, only to remain zoomed in, but having lost a previous (and wanted) edit. My advice: learn the shortcuts to fit a page or spread in the window as well as those to zoom!

➡ Have a look at the Tools panel on the left side of your screen. Which tool is currently highlighted? Let's make it the Selection tool, the topmost one resembling a black arrow, by clicking on it. If you leave your cursor hovering over it, you'll learn more from the tooltip that appears briefly. The name of the tool appears and, in parentheses, the keys that you can use to access it. Tapping the V key selects this tool when you're *not* editing text, and the esc key selects it when you are.

Hover over other tools and note that many of them also have letters that can be used to access them. Most are not intuitive (M for the Rectangle tool?!). Try it: tap the letter M. The highlighted tool changes to the Rectangle tool. Go from tool to tool: V (the Selection tool), F (the Rectangle Frame tool), Z (the Zoom tool), and back to V again.

That's *one* way to use those letter shortcuts. There's another variation that's really useful when you need a tool for only a moment, which we'll discuss next.

Zooming & Panning

Please check your Preferences (⌘-K/Ctrl-K), and if there is a section called GPU Performance, be sure you've disabled Animated Zoom.

➡ Now try this...make sure the Selection tool is selected, then instead of tapping the Z key, I want you to hold it down. While it's held, the cursor will look like a magnifier. With that cursor, drag a box around an element on the page (the name of the document, perhaps). After releasing the mouse, release the Z key. The active tool should be the Selection tool. If it's the Zoom tool, you may have twitched or bounced your finger on the Z key. To zoom back out to view the whole page again, use ⌘-0/Ctrl-0 (that's a zero).

➡ Practice this a few times to make it less foreign. It goes like this: hold letter > use its function > release letter. I know no one who zooms recreationally for minutes at a time. When we need to get a closer look at something, we need the zoom function for only a second or so. This "spring-loaded" tool shortcut gets us back to the tool we need without any trouble, and it works for any tool that is accessed by a key.

➡ Another time this comes in handy is when you're using the Hand tool. Once zoomed in, hold down the H key. The cursor becomes a hand, and you can drag left, right, up, or down, and then release the H key to return to the Selection tool again. This is a fabulous way to pan. A less intuitive, but larger alternative key for the Hand tool is the Spacebar.

Workspaces &
Preferences

Frames &
Content

Styles, Type
& Fonts

Pages
& Spreads

Color
Management

Find/Change

Long
Documents

Output

Warning: In all of these cases, however, you cannot use these shortcuts while actively editing text or else you'll get lots of z's, h's, or spaces in your document.

Page Navigation

There are several ways to navigate a multi-page document. In the lower-left corner of the document window is a page menu, from which you can choose a page to go to, or you can click on the arrowhead buttons on either side of the menu to go to the next or previous page, or the first or last page. You can also double-click on a page icon in the Pages panel. The Properties panel has a page menu, too. Finally, there are shortcuts: shift-page down or shift-page up go to the next or previous pages respectively.

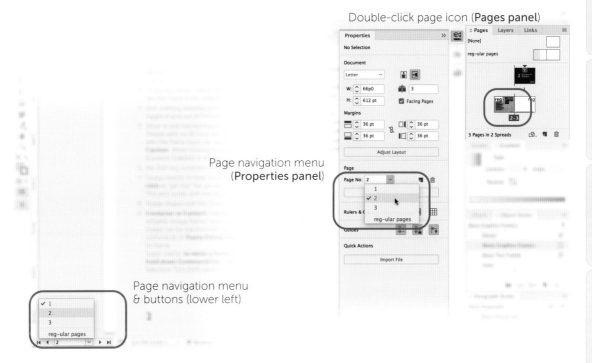

Page navigation menu
(**Properties panel**)

Page navigation menu
& buttons (lower left)

Double-click page icon (**Pages panel**)

�th In the *2 Frames & Shapes* document, I'd like you to look at page 2. Once there, let's look at the whole spread: choose View > Fit Spread in Window or use the shortcut ⌘-option-0/Ctrl-Alt-0 (that's a zero, not an O).

Now when you navigate pages, the buttons at lower left go to the next and previous spreads. Also, in the Pages panel, instead of double-clicking a page *icon*, you can double-click on the pages numbers, and this will take you from spread to spread. There are shortcuts for this, too: option-page down or Alt-page up go to the next or previous spread, respectively. This document has only two spreads, and one of them has only one page, so this is not yet an exciting development. But in longer documents, this will be quite useful.

Lesson B: Text Frame Basics

On page 2 of our exercise file, ***2 Frames & Shapes***, we can see a few items: a large, beige text frame with some reminder notes in it; a few shapes; an image; and a smaller text frame. That last item is the one we'll focus on for a few minutes.

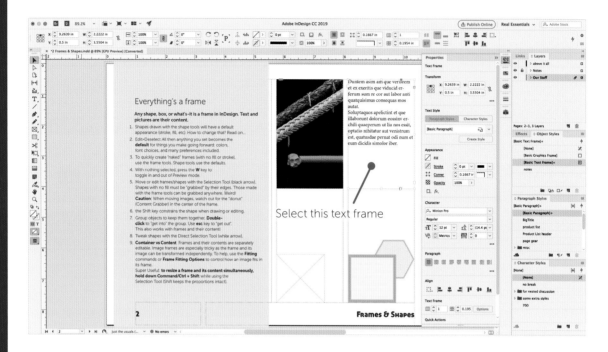

Select this text frame

From Frame to Text and Back Again

➡ Using the Selection tool, click once on that small text frame. It's now selected and its various attributes can be examined in the Control panel and the Properties panel. We can see the frame's width and height, whether it has a fill or stroke applied (it doesn't), and, since it's a text frame, we can note how many columns it has (just one):

➡ Now double-click somewhere in that text frame. The cursor now blinks and the Type tool is highlighted in the Tools panel. Double-click on a word in that frame. You've selected that word, just as you might in any application. Triple-click and a line of text is now selected. Quadruple-click to select an entire paragraph. And, finally, quintuple-click to select that entire *story*.

While some of the text is selected, even just one word, look up at the Control panel or at the Properties panel. Both have completely changed for this new context and show that the font used is Minion Pro Regular, set at 12 points, and that it's left-aligned, as well as many other text attributes. At the bottom of the Properties panel there are also a few actions that can be performed on the selected text, like changing its case.

Workspaces & Preferences

Frames & Content

Styles, Type & Fonts

Pages & Spreads

Color Management

Find/Change

Long Documents

Output

➡ To return quickly to editing the frame, simply tap the esc key! You'll see that the Selection tool is active and the frame is selected. The rule is to double-click to edit a frame's content, then hit esc to edit the container once again. For the next part, let's be sure we have the Selection tool active, as we may choose to use a letter-based shortcut. Also, to have room to practice, be sure to fit the entire spread in the Document Window: View > Fit Spread in Window.

Placeholder Text

➡ Create a text frame. Choose the Type tool (select it in the Tools panel or tap the T key) then in the empty right-hand page of that spread, drag diagonally to create a box. When you release the mouse, the text cursor will be blinking in that frame's upper-left corner. Of course, you *may* type something or paste text copied from elsewhere. Instead, right-click on the frame and choose Fill with Placeholder Text. You'll now be looking at randomized Latin words and phrases. And they are truly random: undo (⌘-Z/Ctrl-Z) and repeat filling with placeholder text; it is different every time. If you hold down the ⌘/Ctrl key while you right-click and choose the placeholder text command, you will get a dialog box that allows you to choose whether the text is Roman, as before, or perhaps Cyrillic or Arabic. This can help you as you design multilingual documents.

We'll use the default Roman alphabet. If the frame you made was rather small, tap esc then use the resulting Selection tool to resize the frame. Even then, you can right-click in the frame and choose Fill with Placeholder Text to fill in the rest.

Text Formatting Basics

➡ Select a paragraph in your new text frame (double-click to get into the text, then quadruple-click to highlight a paragraph). Choose a font and style from the Font menu at the left of the Control panel. When you expose the Font menu, you'll see the font name on the left and a bit of sample text in that font on the right. With InDesign CC 2019, several new features help you make those choices. In the upper right, you can change the size of the sample and what text composes it. One of those choices is Selected Text, so you can see the text you're decorating using the fonts in your system! As you hover over a font, the highlighted text provisionally changes, too. If you don't choose a new font, the text reverts to what it was. Click a font to choose it.

If you have many fonts, you can then use the Filter to show only fonts with certain properties. Or, if you *don't* have many fonts, you can choose from Adobe Fonts, too, by clicking on Find More at the top of that menu. If a font there fits your needs, click the Activate button to its right (it resembles a cloud with an arrow pointing down) and approve its activation, if necessary.

You can accomplish the same tasks from the Character section of the Properties panel. There are dedicated panels, too. If you go to Window > Type & Tables, you'll find the Character panel and the Paragraph panel. The hope is that you, the user, will stumble on one or more ways to accomplish any task. Currently, you have access to the greatest number of options with the fewest number of clicks if you use the Properties panel (especially if you use the More Options icons: •••) or the Control panel.

Quick Resizing Tricks

➡ With the Selection tool, drag the edge handles of the text frame inward so it's too small to hold all its text. In general, double-clicking one of those handles will resize a frame to fit its content. But with text frames, you have to carefully decide which handle to use to do that. Try double-clicking a corner handle. You now have a fairly randomly resized frame. This is rarely desired, so undo that step (⌘–Z/Ctrl–Z).

Double-clicking a side handle resizes only one dimension. The handles on the left or right resize only the width, and the ones at top and bottom resize only the height. By far, the handle I double-click most often to quickly make a frame fit its content is the bottom center one. Try it! Beware, you should do this only with frames that have a limited amount of text in them, not pages of it. You could end up with a frame taller than your page! However, for captions and other short bits of text, double-clicking the bottom handle will enlarge or reduce the height of the frame so the text fits exactly.

For more, see "Frame to Content & Content to Frame" (page 198).

Lesson C: Image Frames

- ➡ In the document called *2 Frames & Shapes*, go to page 2.
- ➡ Continuing to use the Selection tool, click on the image, *avoiding its center*. When the cursor hovers over the image, you'll see a pair of concentric circles. It's those you should avoid, but only for the moment. That pair of circles is called the Content Grabber or, more commonly, the Donut.

The one task that you can do easily that affects both an image and its frame is to move it.

- ➡ Drag the image of ropes to the other page. However, if you try to resize it, you will resize the frame only. Make the frame smaller, and note that you're actually cropping the image. Make the frame larger, and you may find that there's excess frame now. But just like with text frames, you can double-click a corner handle of the frame, and the frame will fit to its content, the photo within.

Place an Image: Linking vs. Embedding

- ➡ Let's add another image you can experiment with. Deselect the other one first by either clicking on nothing with the Selection tool or using the shortcut ⌘-shift-A/Ctrl-Shift-A.

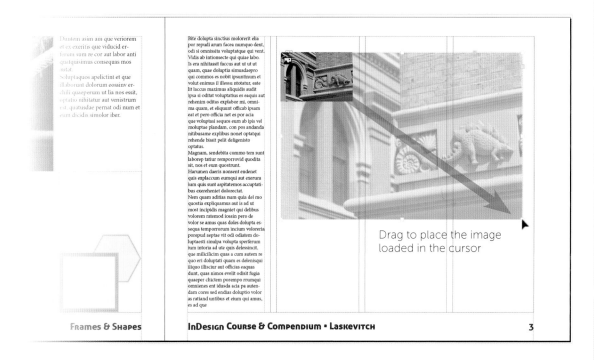

Drag to place the image loaded in the cursor

Frames & Shapes   **InDesign Course & Compendium • Laskevitch**   3

- ➡ To place an image, go to File > Place…. In the resulting dialog box, navigate to where the exercise file is located (a folder called "2 Frames & Shapes"), then to the "Links" folder

Workspaces & Preferences

Frames & Content

Styles, Type & Fonts

Pages & Spreads

Color Management

Find/Change

Long Documents

Output

within it, and choose ***Pic2place.jpg***. Double-clicking on that file or highlighting it and then clicking Open will load your cursor with the image. Drag diagonally across an open area on the document page, and the image will fit itself into the frame you've drawn. If the dinosaur relief on the right has lost its head, there are two things you should do. With the image still selected, reveal the Properties panel, and find the Frame Fitting section. The second button, Fit Content Proportionately, will reveal the entire image without distorting it. To prevent InDesign from making bad decisions like that again, go to the General Preferences (⌘-K/Ctrl-K) and disable Content-Aware Fit as a default.

We placed the image rather than pasting it to prevent it from being embedded in our document.

Image Frames and Their Dis-Contents

Even if you had changed the Content-Aware Fit preference earlier, you should still experiment with the Frame Fitting options. Resize the frame to make it vertical, cropping the picture a bit. Then try the first and last options. The first, Fill Frame Proportionately, will ensure the frame is filled with an image, but with the minimum crop. The last option, Content-Aware Fit, tries to figure out what the subject is and reveal that, hiding much else. In this case, it does very poorly.

Content Grabber (a.k.a. the Donut)

➡ With the image cropped, drag it by the Content Grabber in the center of the frame. You are recomposing the image within its frame. An alternative method that is consistent with text frames is double-clicking elsewhere in the frame, then dragging the now-selected image. Pressing the esc key selects the frame again. Clicking on the Content Grabber also selects the content.

> The full story about placing images and manipulating their frames can be studied in "Image Frames & Linked Images" (page 208).

A good friend of mine really hates the Donut. He's good, and very fast, in InDesign. Sometimes, he accidentally grabs the Content Grabber when he intends to move an image, and accidentally dislodges the image from its frame! After saying something rude and using ⌘-Z/Ctrl-Z, he then has to press the esc key to select the frame. Then he can (more carefully) move the image by dragging it from somewhere other than its center.

Usually, he simply disables the Content Grabber completely. When he needs to adjust the image within its frame, he double-clicks it. Just as with a text frame, this selects the frame's content. Pressing the esc key returns us to the frame.

The Course

Lesson D: Shape and Frame Tools

If you need some room on page 3 of your exercise document, you may delete the text and image we have there.

About halfway down the Tools panel, you will see two sets of tools: one with an "X" through it, another without. I say "sets" because if you right-click on one of them, you'll discover more tools behind the ones you first saw. In each group, there is a rectangle, an ellipse, and a polygon. Any shape you draw with these tools can become either a text frame or an image frame. Or you can apply colors to fill the shapes or to stroke their edges.

So why are there two sets? Shapes drawn with the tools with the "X" in them are born with neither a fill nor a stroke. Those "frame" tools exist to give you a quick way to indicate that you'd like an image, perhaps, to occupy that space at some future time. In other words, they're placeholders. If you decide to add colors to them instead, that's fine, too.

⮕ Choose one of the frame tools (with the "X") and drag diagonally on a page to see the result. Holding shift as you draw will constrain the shape (you'll get a circle rather than an arbitrary ellipse, for example).

The other set of tools creates shapes that possess whatever default appearance you may have set up when nothing was selected. You choose colors and stroke attributes just as you would with an object selected, as described in "Fills & Strokes" (page 192). But when you make those decisions with nothing selected, those attributes get applied to every object you draw with the shape tools until you again change the default.

⮕ Deselect everything (⌘–shift–A/Ctrl–Shift–A) and choose a fill color, a stroke color, and a stroke weight. Then choose a shape tool (without the "X") and create an object.

Warning: Be careful what you click on when nothing is selected. You may be creating a bizarre default that will only be revealed the next time you make an object!

Selecting

Another subtle difference between the objects created with these tools is the ease with which they're selected. Frame tools create empty shapes that are easy to select and move. If you create an object with no fill using a shape tool, it is notoriously difficult to select.

⮕ Select a shape you drew with a shape tool. Set its fill color to [None]. Switch to the Selection tool and see how easy (or difficult) it is to select the various shapes you've drawn. You'll find that you must click on the edge of objects drawn with shape tools.

Workspaces & Preferences

Frames & Content

Styles, Type & Fonts

Pages & Spreads

Color Management

Find/Change

Long Documents

Output

"Unassigned" Frames

➦ All those shapes you made can be considered graphics (if they possess color) or, like naked ones, can be thought of as unassigned frames waiting for content. Switch to the Type tool and click in the middle of one of your objects. No matter which tool you used to draw that frame, there is now a text cursor blinking in it. Right-click and select Fill with Placeholder Text.

➦ Select a different object (with the Selection tool!). Go to File > Place... and choose an image in the "Links" folder, from which we chose an image in the previous lesson. You may have to use those fitting options in the Properties panel, but the image is now in the frame that was selected.

So when you are working out design ideas, you will draw placeholder frames where you desire text and/or images to be later. When you've chosen images and have copy to use, you can then use the Place... command to insert them into those awaiting frames.

Applying Fills and Strokes

When choosing a fill or stroke color, you are usually choosing from a list of swatches. Shortly, you'll create your own, but let's try something else first.

➦ Select (or draw) an empty frame. Hold the shift key as you go to choose a fill color. Instead of a list of swatches, you'll see the Color panel, from which you can choose any color (note the rainbow along its bottom edge). Also note the small menu in the upper-right corner. This panel has a panel menu just like all others. When you click on that menu, you can choose which color model to use to choose color (Lab, CMYK, or RGB).

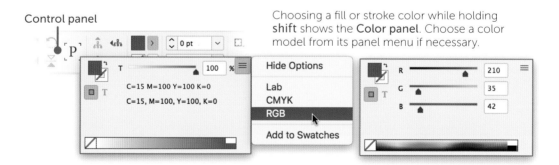

Control panel

Choosing a fill or stroke color while holding **shift** shows the **Color panel**. Choose a color model from its panel menu if necessary.

➦ You will need to use the panel menu if you previously applied a swatch. Try that. Apply a fill color without holding down shift; that is, apply a color swatch. Then, holding the shift key, click the fill color menu again and notice that the Color panel is showing only Tints of the previously chosen swatch. But if you change the color model to RGB, for instance, you'll have the whole rainbow from which to choose again.

Stacking Order

✏️ Using the Selection tool, drag an object so that it overlaps with another object. It is very likely that the more recently created object is above the older one.

If you have used other Adobe programs, you may be familiar with Layers. InDesign has that feature, too, and we will discuss it in depth later. All of the objects you have been manipulating in this document currently occupy the same layer, yet they still exhibit a stacking order. In other words, objects can be in front of or behind others even if they are not on layers above or below.

✏️ Move an object behind the others on the same layer. To do so, select it. Then, right-click and choose Arrange > Send to Back. You may notice Send Backward, but it's difficult to know how many times you'd need to choose that command to arrange a specific object.

Align and Distribute

✏️ Go to View > Grids & Guides and ensure that Smart Guides is checked.

As you slowly move an object around on a spread, try to notice thin green lines that appear when the object you're dragging is aligned in some way to another object. If the top edge of the object you're dragging aligns briefly with the bottom of another, you'll see a green line connecting the top of the object moved with the bottom of the other. If you move an object so that it is the same distance from another object as that other object is from a third, you'll see Smart Guides for that, too.

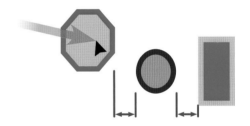

✏️ Draw a few shapes (rectangles and ellipses) and alter their colors. Also, randomize their sizes a bit and arrange them into a very rough row. Maybe a bit like this:

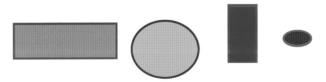

✏️ Now select all of them: with the Selection tool, click one, then hold down the shift key and click each of the others. Although a dozen alignment options appear in the Control panel when multiple objects are selected, you can see all the options if you choose Window > Object & Layout > Align. Since these objects are horizontally arranged, focus on the seven buttons on the right (yes, including the bottom row of buttons). Try clicking a button, then undo the action so you can try another. Since these objects vary so much in size and shape, it's likely we'll want to have equal space between them to give a sense of order. That's what the bottom right button (⊞ called Distribute Horizontal Space) will do.

Workspaces & Preferences

Frames & Content

Styles, Type & Fonts

Pages & Spreads

Color Management

Find/Change

Long Documents

Output

> You can go deeper by reading "Alignment & Distribution" (page 216). Or read that later and continue with the course for now.

Gridify

Although it's easy to get order from one-dimensional chaos, it's harder to use the Align panel to get a grid of objects. But if you know that's what you want at the outset, it's easy to draw a grid of shapes.

➦ Go to the empty page 5 of the *2 Frames & Shapes* document and choose the Ellipse tool. With the cursor near the upper-left corner of the page, start to drag as if you were creating a very large ellipse. But as you drag (with the mouse button held down), tap the up arrow or right arrow key. With each tap of ↑, you'll get a new row of ellipses. Each tap of → makes a column. Down removes rows and left removes columns.

When you finally release the mouse button, you will have as many shapes as you desired, all of them selected. While all are selected, you can use the handles of the bounding box that surrounds them to resize the lot. If deselected, you'll find each is independent of the others.

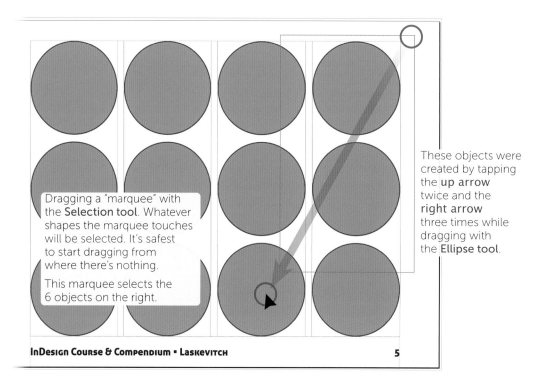

Dragging a "marquee" with the **Selection tool**. Whatever shapes the marquee touches will be selected. It's safest to start dragging from where there's nothing.

This marquee selects the 6 objects on the right.

These objects were created by tapping the **up arrow** twice and the **right arrow** three times while dragging with the **Ellipse tool**.

It can be easy to select many objects at once as long as there aren't undesired objects mixed in with the ones you want selected. Using the Selection tool, drag a box that encounters the objects you want selected. Start dragging in an empty area beyond the edge of any object. There's no need to completely encompass the objects; the box, called a "marquee," will select any object it touches.

Groups

We often need objects to work together. A classic example is an image and its caption: if you relocate one, you'd certainly want the other to come along for the ride. To be sure that happens, we *group* them together. To get a sense of how groups work, we'll make a couple of groups, then group them together. We'll examine how to edit the parts *without* ungrouping.

➡ Select about half the objects you created using the gridify technique. To group them, you can right-click and choose Group, or you can use the shortcut ⌘-G/Ctrl-G. Now select the rest of those objects and group them. Check out how easy it is to select a group: a click with the Selection tool on any object in the group selects the whole group. A marquee selection needs to touch only one object in each group to select both entire groups. Do so! Select both groups and group them together.

➡ Let's edit something within the group. Use the Selection tool and double-click on an element in a group. Double-clicking selects that element. In our current case, we have a group whose elements are groups, one of which is now selected. Double-click on one of its ellipses to select that ellipse. Each tap of the esc key goes out one layer of that onion: the first tap selects the group the ellipse is part of, a second tap selects the group of groups. So the rule we encountered with both image and text frames—double-clicking to get in, esc to get out—works with groups, too.

Gridify Images

➡ Delete that group of ellipses. In its place, we're going to make a grid of six images.

➡ We'll start by using the Place command, just as we would with a single image (File > Place…). This time, navigate to your "2 Frames & Shapes" folder, then to its "Links" folder, and then to "a folder of pix." We need to highlight all the images in that folder (click on the first one, then shift-click on the last) and then click Open. The cursor will then be loaded with all six images. In fact, you should see a number "6" in the cursor. Tapping the left or right arrow keys will change which image is displayed in the cursor.

You can place those six images one at a time by dragging out boxes in whatever size you choose. After each image is placed, the number of images in the cursor will drop by one. Try that a couple of times, but then use undo to "reload" the cursor with all six images again.

➡ With the cursor fully loaded, starting in the page's upper-left margin, start dragging down and to the right. As you drag (keep that mouse button held down!), tap the up arrow key once and the right arrow key twice. With the tap of ↑, you made a second row. Each tap of → made a column. That should give you six areas, one for each image. Keeping the mouse button depressed, you can move your mouse hand to control how big an area those images will fit. Keep holding! By using ⌘-↑/Ctrl-↑ or ⌘-↓/Ctrl-↓ you change the space between the rows, and ⌘-→/Ctrl-→ or ⌘-←/Ctrl-← changes the space between columns. Is your mouse hand tired yet?

When you finally release the mouse (yay!), you have six frames of equal size and shape with images made to fit within them.

Workspaces & Preferences

Frames & Content

Styles, Type & Fonts

Pages & Spreads

Color Management

Find/Change

Long Documents

Output

⊟ With all six selected, right-click on any one of them and choose a Fitting option, either Fill Frame Proportionately or Fit Frame to Content. In this case, the latter is likely best.

Gridify Text Frames

⊟ Delete those images and choose the Type tool. Start dragging as you would to create a single text frame, but tap the up or right arrow keys before releasing the mouse. You have created multiple text frames, each linked to the next. If you paste text into the first frame, it will flow into the subsequent ones. Most of us use this feature (using only the right arrow key) to create a few text frames to serve as columns.

Object Styles Introduction

⊟ Either find two unassigned frames (neither a text nor image frame) or draw two new ones with the shape tools. Select one of them, then use either the Properties panel or the Control panel to change the Appearance attributes. In the following figure, I'm using the Properties panel. Click on the Fill and Stroke color boxes to change them. I wanted arbitrary colors, so I chose the color panel icon (a painter's palette), used its panel menu to choose RGB, and then I chose a color from the rainbow spectrum.

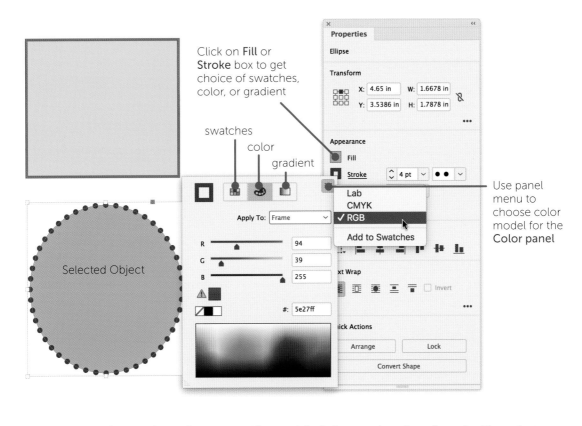

Click on **Fill** or **Stroke** box to get choice of swatches, color, or gradient

swatches

color

gradient

Selected Object

Use panel menu to choose color model for the Color panel

Change the stroke weight and type, too, if you wish. I chose a 4 pt dotted stroke. Keep that object selected for the next part.

➡ Locate the Object Styles panel. If it's not on-screen, get it by choosing Window > Styles > Object Styles. Open its panel menu (in its upper-right corner) and choose New Object Style…. This will yield an intimidatingly large dialog box.

Workspaces & Preferences

Frames & Content

Styles, Type & Fonts

Pages & Spreads

Color Management

Find/Change

Long Documents

Output

Object Styles panel
menu, **New Object Style...**

Name the style

One of the many attributes
that object styles can control

Important: Check **Apply Style to Selection**. It is also wise to check **Preview**.

You have just recorded every attribute of that shape in a way that can be applied to other objects with a single click! If you were to apply the style to dozens of objects, it's easy to change them all very quickly by redefining the style. To be certain that the original shape is also governed by the style, be sure to check the checkbox at the bottom: Apply Style to Selection. Once checked, it will be checked by default when you create new styles. The same is true of the Preview checkbox.

The list of Basic Attributes on the left is so long you need to scroll to see them all. For now, just look at two: Fill and Stroke. Click the words "Fill" or "Stroke" to see the settings. Clicking the checkbox next to one may cause the object style to ignore that attribute!

➡ Finish by giving the style a name (at top). Clicking OK or pressing the Enter key accepts your changes and closes the dialog box.

Note: If you need to edit that style, do so safely by right-clicking the name of the style, and choosing Edit. Do not left click it, especially if something is selected that shouldn't have the style applied to it.

➡ Select the other shape you drew or found, then click just once on the name of the style you just made. Consider this: an object style can record any attribute of any kind of object!

The Compendium section of this book has a lot to say about "Object Styles" (page 267) and the many attributes they control.

The Course

Lesson E: Creating Swatches

To augment your choice of consistent colors in a document, you can build swatches or steal them from other documents.

> More on the details of this process can be learned in chapter 2 of the Compendium, "Frames & Content" (page 189).

➡ Locate the Swatches panel. If it's not on screen, choose Window > Color > Swatches. If you'd like to make multiple swatches and would like to see how each looks when applied to an object, select an object or create one, and leave it selected as you build your swatches.

New Swatch

➡ Use the Swatches panel menu to choose New Color Swatch.... To specify a useful name, uncheck Name with Color Value.

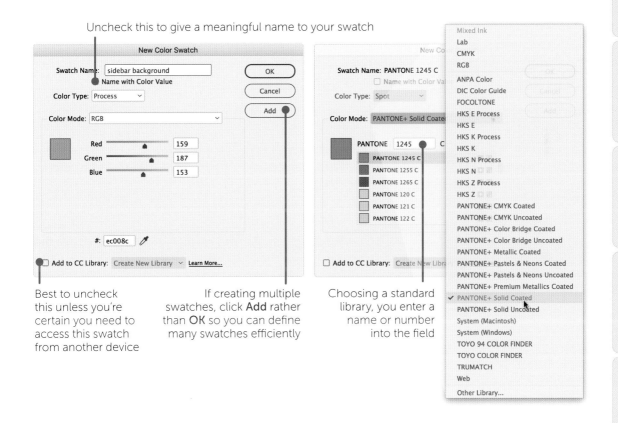

Uncheck this to give a meaningful name to your swatch

Best to uncheck this unless you're certain you need to access this swatch from another device

If creating multiple swatches, click **Add** rather than **OK** so you can define many swatches efficiently

Choosing a standard library, you enter a name or number into the field

Workspaces & Preferences

Frames & Content

Styles, Type & Fonts

Pages & Spreads

Color Management

Find/Change

Long Documents

Output

Color Type

➦ You will likely not change this. Most swatches you will make should be process colors: that is, if printed, made from dots of cyan, magenta, yellow, and black ink. Custom mixed inks (spot colors) are usually chosen from "color books," standardized color libraries you can select in the Color Mode menu.

➦ Read the first section of the Compendium "Color Management" chapter, "The Basics."

Color Mode

➦ Choose from among Lab, CMYK, RGB, or a standard color library. The last choice, Other Library…, allows you to see and choose from another InDesign document's swatches. Although this feature claims to see swatches in Adobe Illustrator files, I have had trouble getting it to do so. This method allows you to choose just the swatches you really want.

Choosing RGB gives two benefits: you can use hexadecimal notation (ask your favorite web designer about that method of specifying color) and an eyedropper. To sample a color on your screen, hover the cursor over the dropper, press down on the mouse button, and keep the button held down as you move the cursor over any part of the screen. Release when the cursor is over a color you want to capture as a swatch—whether within InDesign's interface or not!

If you choose from a classic Pantone® library, you can type a number into the available field. If your company has a corporate color you need to use, it's often chosen from such a library.

CC Libraries

➦ Uncheck Add to CC Library. Only when creating a swatch you wish to access from another device should you choose to add that one to your CC Library. I know no one who adds all their new swatches to this online storage.

Recycle: Load Command

➦ As an alternative to using Other Library as the Color Mode, load another document's swatches by using the Swatches panel menu and choosing Load Swatches…. Navigate to a document called ***Stealing Swatches.indd*** in the folder "2 Frames & Shapes." Rather than picking individual swatches, however, you get all the swatches from that other document.

Reuse: Copy & Paste

Later, we will use the simple process of copying and pasting to get a number of assets from other documents. If any content you copy uses swatches (or styles, as we'll see), those swatches (and styles) will be added to the document in which that content is pasted.

Workspaces &
Preferences

Frames &
Content

Styles, Type
& Fonts

Pages
& Spreads

Color
Management

Find/Change

Long
Documents

Output

Lesson F: The Power and Pitfalls of Defaults

As you get more comfortable in InDesign, you will be tempted to explore. That natural and healthy impulse should be slightly tempered with the knowledge of how defaults work in this program. Consider the preferences I suggested you change. By setting them with no documents open, those preferences are set for all future documents you create. That's because many preferences are document-specific.

When a document is open, but *nothing is selected*, any choices you make for Fill color, Stroke weight or color, or, if the Type tool is active, font or text size, all become the document's defaults for all future content you create. The scary part? Since nothing is selected, none of these changes are apparent until you create something new by drawing a shape or adding a text frame. Let's try this.

- With the document *2 Frames & Shapes.indd* open, be sure that nothing is selected: use the shortcut ⌘-shift-A/Ctrl-Shift-A. With the Selection tool active and using the Control panel, choose a Fill color, a Stroke color, and Stroke weight. Switch to the Type tool. Now choose a font and size. Since nothing is selected, there's little to see.
- Using the Type tool, create a text frame. Right-click in it and choose Fill with Placeholder Text. That text will use the settings you chose a minute ago.
- Using a shape tool (Rectangle or Ellipse, for example—*not* the frame tools), create a shape. Yes, it uses the attributes you selected with nothing selected and will continue to do so until you change the defaults in this document again.

The usual pitfall is accidentally or absentmindedly setting something as a default. You may later create something and be startled that it looks a particular way or affects other content in unexpected ways. You then not only have to fix that specific object, but you also have to deselect and make that fix again for all your future objects.

- You're now done with the document *2 Frames & Shapes.indd*. Save it (⌘-S/Ctrl-S) and close it (⌘-W/Ctrl-W).

Lesson G: Troubleshooting

⮕ Open the document called ***Troubleshooting.indd*** in the "2 Frames & Shapes" folder. As it opens, you are going to see error messages that we'll discuss. The first tells us that there are modified and missing links. This time, for the sake of learning, please click Don't Update Links.

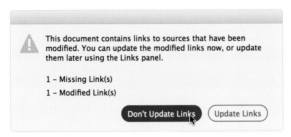

When we open the Troubleshooting document, we see this warning. Under most circumstances, I would choose **Update Links**. However, since we should be able to recognize an out-of-date link in the layout, let's choose **Don't Update Links** this time.

Missing Fonts and Find Font

The second message interrupts our dealing with the modified and missing links. This message tells us that there are missing fonts, too. In the poster project, we used this dialog box to activate fonts from the Adobe Fonts service. And if you open any document whose fonts are missing, but are available via that service, you should take advantage of that. However, in this case, neither missing font is available through Adobe Fonts. We'll have to choose substitutes. If you completed the poster project, then you have two fonts that might serve.

The text that is set in the missing fonts is highlighted in pink and another font has been used.

⮕ We'll choose our own substitutes: click Find Fonts….

Note: The dialog box that opens can be accessed at any time to replace unwanted fonts with new ones by going to Type menu > Find Font.... It's not only for missing font substitution.

◳ At the top of the Find Font dialog, highlight the first missing font. Notice that the Activate checkboxes are unavailable. The font that's missing is an italic, which seems inappropriate for the body text to which it's applied. We'll choose something different.

◳ In the lower half of the dialog, choose Adobe Jenson Pro (a font we activated in the poster project) from the Font Family menu. If you didn't or couldn't activate it, choose another (Garamond would be nice, or even Times, if you must). For Font Style, choose Regular.

◳ Check the box for Redefine Style When Changing All. Styles allow us to capture and quickly reapply styling to text and are the subject of the next chapter.

◳ Click Change All. The body copy has now changed to Jenson, and since that font is not missing, that text is no longer highlighted in pink.

We need to repeat the process for the missing header font, Balford Base.

Workspaces &
Preferences

Frames &
Content

Styles, Type
& Fonts

Pages
& Spreads

Color
Management

Find/Change

Long
Documents

Output

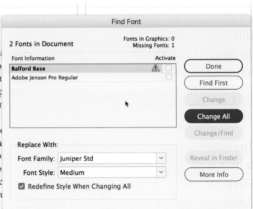

FRIENDLY FACES

Musa duciunt pa volestiunt que est, od ma conempost arionsedit endam, con pore nima quam inciisi blaborunt reria inveleniet accum ut hitati odit laniam, optaspe rorist miliquat hil molupta de solupta tinisquae parcitaque officat et faccae. Nem ut aut voloruntium, tem estrum sa am, corest ut odit ut et eat dolenda erumquodipid quas dolor simagnatusda dolupici ad qui occum, occuptati as estemol oruptatum et magnit, sam, sumqui dis milland ebitect atemped et lis magnis.Gitia dent, con

none dolorae cusciaessi remporehene essint, co Lo beatibea dunt.Uciet temperum remo volorp eaquibus es volore erur eius. Bitataepedi aut pos et tiatiossunto de volupta Maio. Omniendit latio voluptatem incid ullup omniet lacilitatur minc totatium idit volupta tu quaepudipsae excescia

⮕ Highlight Balford Base at the top of the dialog box.

⮕ Choose Juniper Std as the Font Family in the Replace With section. It's likely that Medium is now the Font Style. If you don't have Juniper, choose something else to use as a header.

⮕ Click Change All. The missing fonts are dealt with! Click Done.

Missing/Modified "Links"

⮕ Have a look at the images. Notice that each has a different icon in its upper-left corner.

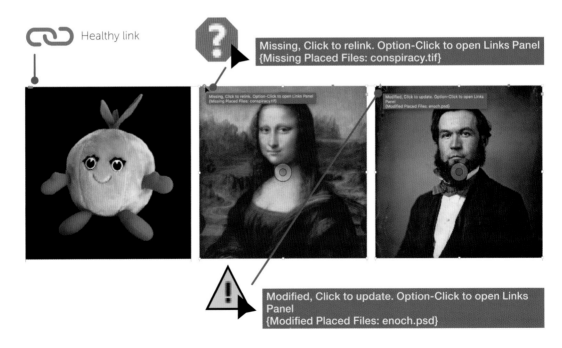

When your cursor hovers over the scarier icons, a useful note appears. You can contentedly ignore the first image's chain-like icon because it means the link to that image is healthy. Let's

start with the photo of the bearded man. This one indicates that it's been "Modified." This means that sometime since that InDesign document was last saved, the image was edited (in this case, in Photoshop). It's exceedingly rare that I wouldn't want to see the current state of an image. Hovering over the modified link icon reveals a note that tells us to simply click the icon to update the image.

⮕ Click that modified link icon (yellow triangle). You'll now see what mischief was done in Photoshop. Happy and colorful!

The other image has a more serious issue: it's deemed "Missing." This can mean many things. It may really be deleted, gone. When this InDesign document was last saved, it recorded the image's location in a certain folder. If it has been moved, InDesign will report it as missing. Another common trigger for this warning is if an image has been renamed. In any case, if the image still exists, it's on us to tell InDesign where it is.

⮕ Click on the red missing link icon. You will be presented with a system navigation dialog box in which you need to locate the image's location. I'll give you a hint: go to the folder "2 Frames & Shapes," and then into the "Links" folder within. This is the last known location of the missing file. Perhaps it's slipped into a subfolder there. Hey, *psssst...*

Now where did that image go? When a link is missing, you will have to find it. You won't always get hints like a folder named *psssst*.

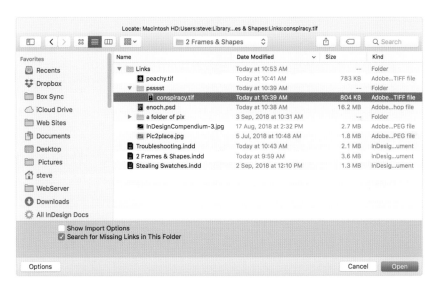

Ah, so it did find its way into a subfolder! Notice the checkbox at the bottom of the dialog box that says Search for Missing Links in This Folder. This is awesome for when someone's renamed a folder that contains all the images in a document. For reasons we'll cover later, that folder is often called "Links." Some think this is unintuitive and rename it "images" or "pics," but then your InDesign document won't find them and mark them as missing.

⮕ When you've located the image (it's called ***conspiracy.tif***), either double-click it or highlight it and click Open.

Workspaces & Preferences

Frames & Content

Styles, Type & Fonts

Pages & Spreads

Color Management

Find/Change

Long Documents

Output

The Course

Finished! No missing fonts or images, and all image links are up-to-date.

FRIENDLY FACES

Musa duciunt pa volestiunt que est, od ma conempost arionsedit endam, con pore nima quam inciisi blaborunt reria inveleniet accum ut hitati odit laniam, optaspe rorist miliquat hil molupta de solupta tinisquae parcitaque officat et faccae. Nem ut aut voloruntium, tem estrum sa am, corest ut odit ut et eat dolenda erumquodipid quas dolor simagnatusda dolupici ad qui occum, occuptati as estemol oruptatum et magnit, sam, sumqui dis milland ebitect atemped et lis magnis.Gitia dent, con

none dolorae cusciaessit aliquia et remporehene essint, con perum a dictio. Lo beatibea dunt.Uciet inus rernam est, temperum remo volorpore conseque eaquibus es volore erumque plaut porit eius.

Bitataepedi aut pos et earum volupta tiatiossunto de volupta tistrunt. Maio. Omniendit lationsequae voluptatem incid ullupit, eius.Lupit omniet lacilitatur minctia simagni totatium idit volupta tustrum quaepudipsae excescia cus comnihi

ctorro quia cum nisi blacerum renitat emquis digent fugite pligenimeni as ex estionsequae es aut am dolori il et volupta ectiur se nus dipsand anihici isitaspe pos preruptatiae optat.

Ritatur? Qui recae. Itatus re a sit dolut omnis ium nos as eos et maios vitatempos aut mostentendel.

3 Text Styles

Styles: the ultimate "work smarter" feature. In fact, I think styles are easily the most important feature in InDesign. Instead of struggling to be consistent when applying formatting to paragraphs, we can record the formatting as paragraph and character styles. In this chapter, you'll learn how to create, apply, and edit these styles.

Lesson A: Acquiring Fonts

Typeface Inspiration & Legitimate Online Sources

The love of typefaces (and the fonts we use to express them) is an acquired attribute for some. Most of us simply don't notice the type we read unless it keeps us from doing so. That said, you should spend a little time not reading text, but appreciating type. Below are URLs to sites that either celebrate type, sell fonts, or both.

> https://theinspirationgrid.com/category/typography/
> https://www.typography.com
> https://www.fonts.com
> https://www.myfonts.com
> https://fonts.google.com

There are so many more! The Adobe Fonts website has links to all the foundries whose fonts they feature—more than 150! Most of these do not provide many (if any) free fonts. If you search the web, you'll find many sources for free fonts, but beware: you usually get what you pay for. Badly built fonts can cause hard-to-diagnose computer issues, and some free fonts may not be as well-made as professionally crafted ones. I usually stick to purchased fonts.

Adobe Fonts Service

With an Adobe Creative Cloud account, you may enjoy the Adobe Fonts service. You have access to the fonts in this service right from the font menu (click Find More) as well as through the Creative Cloud application.

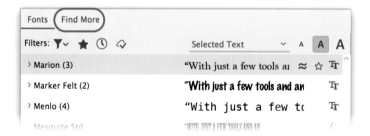

If you find a font you want, click the cloud-like Activate icon to its right. It then installs itself.

Installing Fonts

⇨ Fonts downloaded from somewhere other than Adobe Fonts need to be installed. On a Windows system, simply right-click a downloaded font and choose Install. On a Mac, double-click a font file and it will open a window in the Font Book app. Click the Install button.

The Course

Lesson B: Typography Essentials

➦ To get started, open the downloaded document called *3 Text Styles.indd*. To manage any *missing fonts* messages, follow the instructions in "Procure a Few Fonts" (page 19). Then go to page 2 of the document. Fit the whole spread in the window to see page 3 as well (⌘-option-0/Ctrl-Alt-0).

> Much more on this chapter's topics can be found in chapter 3 of the Compendium, "Styles, Type & Fonts."

Formatting Text

➦ With the Type tool, click in the text frame that contains "Pretty Bark" on page 3. Look at the Control panel or the Properties panel for some key formatting options: Font Family, Style, Font Size, Leading, Kerning, Tracking. Also find the Alignment options and the various indents. Hover your cursor over the more cryptic icons to determine which option is which.

Some of these options will affect the entire paragraph in which your cursor is located, even if no text is highlighted. We call these paragraph-level attributes. Others often require text to be highlighted to specify what should be affected—these are character-level attributes.

Alignment

➦ Insert your cursor in the paragraph that begins "*Arbutus menziesii* is an evergreen tree…". Try the different alignment options. Notice that the entire paragraph shifts.

The Properties panel offers one more option than the Control panel does, but it's not likely you'll use it (Justify with last line aligned right). You'll notice those that justify text (so it runs from one edge of the frame to the other) affect the spacing between words in ways that aren't always welcome. The Align towards spine and Align away from spine options appear to be like Align left and Align right, respectively. That's because the spine between the two pages of the spread is to the left of the frame we're working with (page 3). Had we been working on page 2, each of those alignment options would do the opposite.

Indents & Spacing

When we need space around a paragraph, we use indents (for the left and right sides) and Space Before and Space After for vertical breathing room.

➦ With your text cursor still blinking in a paragraph, increase and decrease Left Indent and Right Indent. Locate and adjust the First Line Left Indent as well. A fun thing to try: increase the Left Indent a bit, then decrease the First Line Left Indent until it goes negative.

Workspaces & Preferences

Frames & Content

Styles, Type & Fonts

Pages & Spreads

Color Management

Find/Change

Long Documents

Output

You can lower it until it's as negative as the Left Indent is positive. We call this a *hanging indent*. It's tricky to go back to no indent: you must first set the First Line Left Indent to 0, *then* you can set the Left Indent to 0.

➡ With the cursor in the line that reads "Pretty Bark," adjust the Space After. Do the same with the next line (which is also a paragraph). Doing so with the last paragraph won't reveal anything until another paragraph is added below it. However, you can adjust its Space Before.

Leading

➡ Check that your Type Preferences are set to Apply Leading to Entire Paragraphs—see "Type" (page 6). This makes leading a paragraph-level option.

➡ With your cursor in the paragraph that begins "*Arbutus menziesii* is an evergreen tree...," locate and adjust the Leading in the Control panel or the Properties panel. The name "leading" is derived from the days when lead shims were used to add space between lines of type. Now, it's defined as the distance between one *baseline* to the one above it. To familiarize yourself with that term and others, this might be a good time to look over the first few pages of the "Styles, Type & Fonts" chapter of this book's Compendium.

From the keyboard, you can adjust a paragraph's leading by holding down the option/Alt key and tapping the up arrow or down arrow key.

Kerning

Kerning is the spacing between two characters. As a character level option, its value applies only to the text at your cursor's location. The only downside to developing an eye for kerning is how critically you'll look at other people's kerning. Be kind.

➡ On page 2, insert your text cursor between the "T" and the "y" in the word "Type." Notice that a capital T has space near its stem that a lowercase letter can partially occupy. Holding down the option/Alt key, tap the left arrow key to decrease the space between those two letters. Use arrow keys alone to move the cursor. Increase the space between the "y" and "p" a little bit by holding down the option/Alt key and tapping the right arrow key.

You can monitor how much you've kerned your text in either the Control panel or the Properties panel. It is measured as a proportion of the font size in thousandths of an *em*.

➡ Hone your kerning skills by playing the Kerning Game: https://type.method.ac.

Tracking

Tracking is often confused with kerning because it also concerns the spacing between letters. However, tracking is applied to a range of selected text to either squeeze it or expand it.

➡ With the Selection tool, select the frame filled with placeholder text near the spine on page 2. Adjust its width so that it fits within the margins. The text becomes overset (see the little red plus sign?).

➡ Double-click within the text to quickly switch to the Type tool. Then quintuple-click (yes, that's five clicks!) to highlight all of the text (including what's overset).

➡ Holding down the option/Alt key, tap the left arrow key to decrease the tracking. You can note how much you've adjusted the tracking in either the Control panel or the Properties panel. Like kerning, it is measured as a proportion of the font size in thousandths of an *em*. You shouldn't have to change the tracking by much to fit all the text in the frame.

Workspaces &
Preferences

Frames &
Content

Styles, Type
& Fonts

Pages
& Spreads

Color
Management

Find/Change

Long
Documents

Output

Lesson C: Building Paragraph Styles

By Example: Emulating a Style Guide

When either working out ideas or emulating the formatting used in other applications, we create placeholder text and format it. The paragraphs on page 4 are formatted to prepare to create styles that record that formatting so it can be applied to other text easily.

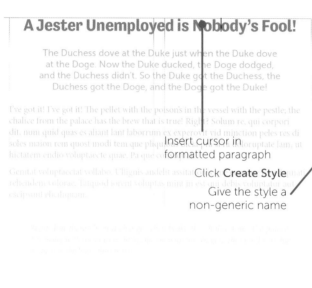

The Course

- Go to page 4 of the document *3 Text Styles.indd*.
- Insert the text cursor so it's blinking in the first paragraph, "A Jester Unemployed is Nobody's Fool!"
- The Properties panel will show some of the formatting that's applied to this paragraph. At the top of that panel, be sure the Paragraph Styles button is active, then click Create Style. This will highlight the provisional (and generic) name in the field above.
- Rename this style *heading*, then press the Enter key. This new Paragraph Style is now created and applied to that paragraph. We'll test it a little later.
- Insert the cursor into the second paragraph that begins "The Duchess dove…".
- Click the Create Style button and name this one "summary." Again, this style is both created and applied to the paragraph where the cursor is blinking.
- For the third style, drag the Type tool cursor to create highlighted text that includes characters from both of the following two paragraphs (as illustrated below).

Workspaces &
Preferences

Frames &
Content

Styles, Type
& Fonts

Pages
& Spreads

Color
Management

Find/Change

Long
Documents

Output

A Jester Unemployed is Nobody's Fool

The Duchess dove at the Duke just when the Duke d
at the Doge. Now the Duke ducked, the Doge dodg
and the Duchess didn't. So the Duke got the Duchess
Duchess got the Doge, and the Doge got the Duk

I've got it! I've got it! The pellet with the poison's in the vessel with the
chalice from the palace has the brew that is true! Right? Solum re, qui
dit, num quid quas es aliant lant laborrum ex experovit vid minction
soles maion rem quost modi tem que pliquibus dicia pra si ra dolorup
hictatem endio voluptaecte quae. Pa que consequat.

Genitat voluptaectat vollabo. Ullignis andelit assitatiores que eumque
rehendem volorae. Tatquod iorent voluptas mint in est qui debis volu
escipsunt eliciliquam.

Properties

Characters

Text Style

Paragraph Styles   Character Styles

rambling ▾

Create Style

Appearance

T   Fill

╱   Stroke   0 pt ▾

Character

➡ Click Create Style in the Properties panel and name this one *rambling*. It is applied to the
entirety of the two paragraphs that contain the highlighted text.

➡ Finally, insert the cursor in the paragraph shaded with yellow. Click Create Style in the
Properties panel and name this style *excerpt*.

Applying Paragraph Styles

To practice applying these new styles to other text, let's look at the text frame on page 5.

➡ Insert the Type tool cursor into the first paragraph. The Properties panel will show that
the name of the style applied to this paragraph is the default *[Basic Paragraph]*. Click the
drop-down menu arrow to the right of the name (▾) and choose *heading* from the list.

➡ Highlight text from several paragraphs and choose another style from the list, perhaps
rambling or *excerpt*.

➡ Apply the four styles you made to paragraphs in that frame so all of the text is formatted.

Overrides: Style Violations

To see the Paragraph Styles panel and a list of all the paragraph styles in the document, go to
Window > Styles > Paragraph Styles (unless it's already on-screen).

➡ Insert your cursor into a paragraph to which you applied a style such as *heading*. That style
will be highlighted in the Paragraph Styles panel and that style's name will be shown in
the Properties panel. Highlight some or all of that paragraph (recall that double-clicking
selects a word, triple-clicking a line, and quadruple-clicking the whole paragraph).

➡ Using the Properties panel or the Control panel, change something about that selected
text—its size or font, for example.

Leave the text selected, and you'll see that next to the style's name in the Paragraph Styles
panel there is now a plus (+) sign, and in the Properties panel there is a different icon (➡🗗),

to indicate that you made a change that deviates from that style's definition. This change is a style override. Since we use styles to achieve consistency, these are useful indicators! Just under the name of the Paragraph Styles panel, you'll see the style's name, again with its plus sign. In the same part of that panel, you'll also see two buttons: a plus sign in brackets and a lightning bolt.

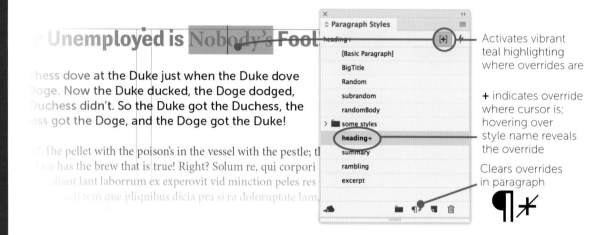

Activates vibrant teal highlighting where overrides are

+ indicates override where cursor is; hovering over style name reveals the override

Clears overrides in paragraph

- Ignore the lightning button, at least for now, but do click the bracketed plus sign, which is the Override Highlighter. You may now deselect your text and InDesign will continue to show overrides anywhere on the spread by highlighting them in vibrant teal.
- Make a text selection that includes the paragraph(s) with overrides, then click the Clear Override button at the bottom of the Paragraph Styles panel (see figure above). This reasserts the style's authority over that text.

Safely Editing Paragraph Styles

You may prefer the override to the style's definition. If that's the case, we can redefine the style based on our changes. Let's use the *heading* style again.

- With the Type tool, highlight one entire paragraph that uses the style *heading*, and then make changes to its formatting. The dreaded plus sign will appear by the style's name in the Paragraph Styles panel and, if the Override Highlighter is still engaged, the text will be highlighted in teal.
- With the cursor somewhere within that altered paragraph, use the Paragraph Styles panel menu and choose Redefine Style *or*, in the Properties panel, click the icon to the right of the style's name (→), which also redefines the style to match the selected text.

There is a completely different approach that gives you full access to every attribute a paragraph style controls. Rather than making an override, and then redefining the style to match, you can tweak the definition directly. Let's redefine the style *summary*.

➦ With nothing selected at all (⌘-shift-A/Ctrl-Shift-A), right-click (without a left-click) on the style named *summary* and choose Edit "summary".... In the large dialog box that appears, be sure to check the Preview checkbox (lower left).

➦ Go to the Basic Character Formats section and change the font style (perhaps 100 will be a noticeable change).

➦ Explore the many options along the left side of that dialog box.

> A full guided tour of the Paragraph Style Options dialog box can be found in the "Styles, Type & Fonts" section of the Compendium.

Defaults—Again!

Ask yourself this question: If you were to create a text frame and start typing, which style is the one you'd like to use to format that text? Different situations dictate that answer, so it may not always be the same. In general, however, I choose the style likely to be applied to the most content. Of the styles we just created, that would be *rambling*, a cheeky name for body copy.

➦ To set *rambling* as your default (at least for now), make sure that nothing is selected and that your cursor is not in any text. The shortcut ⌘-shift-A/Ctrl-Shift-A should do it.

➦ In the Paragraph Styles panel, click just once on the name of the style *rambling*, and it is now highlighted. Of course, you may choose another style, but then I'd request that you again ask yourself the question above.

➦ Make a small text frame where there is room on the spread and start typing. Notice that *rambling* is the style it uses.

Building Styles from Scratch

➦ In the document *3 Text Styles.indd*, go to page 6.

We are going to build three paragraph styles and three character styles. The process I describe here is somewhat realistic, and therefore nonlinear. Our starting point is a common one: we'll first format our *body copy*, the text that occupies the most real estate and with which our readers spend the most time. The other styles may be based on this one.

➦ With the Selection tool, select the text frame on page 6. The Properties panel will show you both object and type options because this is a text frame. Choose a font family that has both an italic and bold style, though you're not going to use those to define body copy. InDesign does not like to create fake italic or bold, so we need to know they're on-hand. In the figure, I chose Myriad Pro Regular at 11 points and left alignment. I chose this font because I also own the italic and bold.

➦ In the Paragraph section of the Properties panel, click the More Options button (•••). Highlight the field for Space After and enter "5 pt," then hit the Enter key. Don't forget the units, especially if your rulers are set to inches—5 inches would be too much space!

Workspaces & Preferences

Frames & Content

Styles, Type & Fonts

Pages & Spreads

Color Management

Find/Change

Long Documents

Output

➥ Click the Create Style button and name this paragraph style *body copy*. I'm sure you saw that coming.

➥ Double-click in the frame to switch quickly to the Type tool. Then, quadruple-click the first line to be sure you've selected the entire first paragraph. This one will be a header. You may format it as simply larger and perhaps bolder than body copy. I chose Museo Slab 700 at 12 points and center alignment. I also clicked on the Fill box in the Properties panel to choose a different color (a swatch called "ID"—a dark red).

➥ Click the Create Style button and name this paragraph style *topic header*. Almost predictable. However, our third paragraph style will seem silly at first.

➥ With your cursor blinking in the last paragraph (which begins "Style name: 'subtopic'"), click the Create Style button and name it…I bet you can't guess.

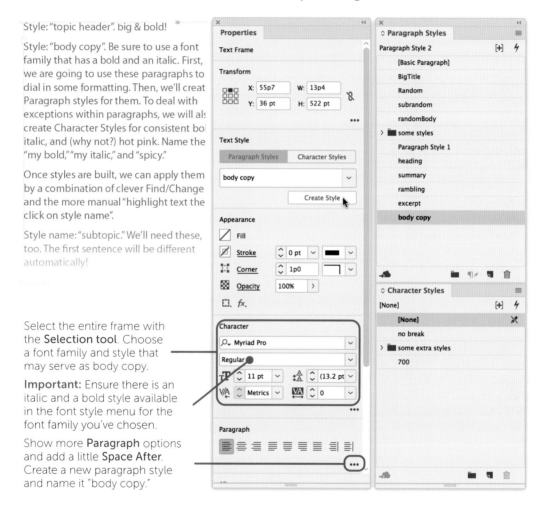

Select the entire frame with the **Selection tool**. Choose a font family and style that may serve as body copy.

Important: Ensure there is an italic and a bold style available in the font style menu for the font family you've chosen.

Show more **Paragraph** options and add a little **Space After**. Create a new paragraph style and name it "body copy."

Yes, for the moment, *subtopic* and *body copy* are identical. Later, however, we'll do something clever, and the first sentence of any paragraph to which we apply the *subtopic* style will automatically be bold. To do that, we'll need to make character styles first.

The Course

Lesson D: Building Character Styles

📩 Make sure you are on page 6 of the document *3 Text Styles.indd*. To prevent the use of bold and italics from being flagged as paragraph style overrides (discussed a few pages ago), we need to protect them with character styles.

Style: "topic header". big & bold!

Style: "body copy". Be sure to use a font family that has a bold and an italic. First, we are going to use these **paragraphs** to dial in some formatting. Then, we'll create Paragraph styles for them. To deal with exceptions within paragraphs, we will also create Character Styles for consistent **bold**, *italic*, and (why not?) hot pink. Name them "my bold," "my italic," and "spicy."

Once styles are built, we can apply them by a combination of clever Find/Change and the more manual "highlight text then click on style name".

Style name: "subtopic." We'll need these, too. The first sentence will be different automatically!

Be sure you're making **Character Styles**.

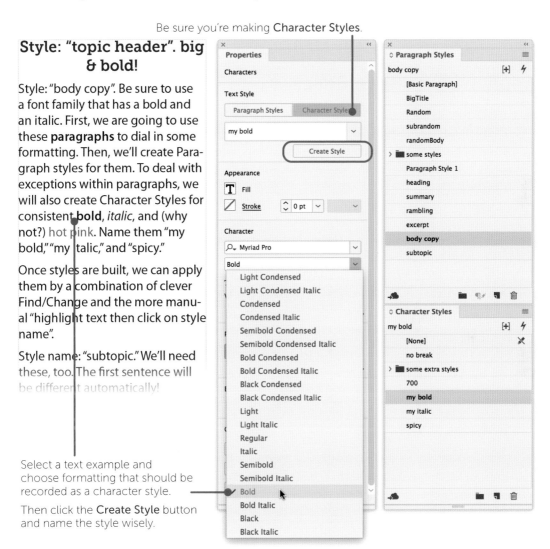

Select a text example and choose formatting that should be recorded as a character style.

Then click the **Create Style** button and name the style wisely.

Workspaces & Preferences

Frames & Content

Styles, Type & Fonts

Pages & Spreads

Color Management

Find/Change

Long Documents

Output

We are going to make three character styles: one to bold text, one to italicize it, and one to make text hot pink.

📩 Highlight a word that should be bold and can serve as an example. In the Properties panel, I changed only the font style by choosing Bold from the list. This is why, when we created the body copy paragraph style, I had you choose a font family that included a bold style.

➡ At the top of the Properties panel, be sure the Text Style is set to Character Styles by clicking that button. Then click the Create Style button.

➡ A generic name will then be highlighted. Give the style a better name—I chose *my bold*.

➡ Now highlight something that should be italicized, like the word "italic." Change its style to Italic, click the Create Style button, and name this one *my italic*.

➡ For the third character style, highlight the words "hot pink," then click on the Fill box (it will look like a black "T"). Choose the swatch called "spicy." Click the Create Style button and name the style *spicy*.

Applying Character Styles

➡ To test these styles, highlight other text on the page (just a word or two). Then either click once on the style's name in the Character Styles panel or choose the style from the list near the top of the Properties panel. Notice that the paragraph style does not gain a plus sign next to it. InDesign assumes that any text fully governed by styles must have authorized formatting.

Safely Editing Character Styles

If you think the *my bold* style is too bold, and you have a less heavy font to choose (like semibold), you can redefine the character style.

➡ Highlight text that has a character style applied to it that you'd like to change. I highlighted something with *my bold* applied to it.

➡ Choose a new font style from the list in the Properties panel or in the Control panel.

➡ With the text still highlighted or the cursor somewhere in the altered text, go to the Character Styles panel menu and choose Redefine Style, *or* in the Properties panel, click the icon to the right of the style's name (➡🗋), which also redefines the style to match the selected text.

As with paragraph styles, there is a different approach that gives you full access to every attribute a character style controls. Rather than making an override, and then redefining the style to match, you can tweak the definition directly. Let's redefine the style *my bold* again.

➡ With nothing selected at all (⌘-shift-A/Ctrl-Shift-A), right-click (without a left-click) on the style named *my bold* and choose Edit "my bold".... In the dialog box that appears, be sure to check the Preview checkbox (lower left).

➡ Go to Basic Character Formats to change the font style. Frankly, make any change you like. You can monitor it because the Preview is enabled. If you dislike your choices, you can always click Cancel. Note that you'll see your changes everywhere the style has been applied.

The Course

Lesson E: Power Styling

- Go to page 7 in the downloaded document called *3 Text Styles.indd*. It's time to both test and fine-tune the styles we've been making.
- With the Selection tool, select the text frame on page 7. Go to either the Properties panel or the Paragraph Styles panel and choose the *body copy* paragraph style. If you use the Properties panel, you may have to first click the Paragraph Styles button near the top so that the list of styles contains the right type.
- In my case, the 11-point Myriad Pro is too big and the text becomes overset. With the entire frame selected, I'd suggest making the text only 9 points, so we have room for a few headers, too.
- After resizing the text, our *body copy* style will show an override. Go to the Paragraph Styles panel menu and choose Redefine Style, *or* in the Properties panel, click the icon to the right of the style's name (➜▣). This redefines *body copy* to be the size we chose. You should notice that change on page 6 as well.
- Double-click in the text frame to enable the Type tool cursor. There are three paragraphs to which we should apply our *topic header* style:

  "A header"
  "Pale blue dot"
  "Distant epochs"

- Insert the cursor in each of those paragraphs and choose *topic header* from the Paragraph Styles menu in the Properties panel, or click on that style's name in the Paragraph Styles panel.
- Insert the cursor in two or three body copy paragraphs and apply the *subtopic* style so that when we change that style's definition later, we'll see that change in the text.

For the next few topics, we'll need the Paragraph Styles panel. If it's not on-screen, either open the Properties panel's list of paragraph styles and choose Manage Styles, or go to Window > Styles > Paragraph Styles.

Keep Options

Note where your cursor is. Is it blinking in a paragraph? Or perhaps you have pressed the esc key and thus the entire frame is selected. Or maybe there's nothing selected at all right now. In any of these cases, it's likely unwise to highlight a paragraph style in the Paragraph Styles panel unless you're trying to apply that style to something or set it as a default. However, you may right-click on a style's name (without first left-clicking) without it being applied.

- Right-click on the style called *topic header* and choose Edit "topic header"... from the menu that pops up.
- In the Paragraph Style Options dialog now in front of you, go to the Keep Options section.

Workspaces & Preferences

Frames & Content

Styles, Type & Fonts

Pages & Spreads

Color Management

Find/Change

Long Documents

Output

Since the paragraph we're editing is a header, we likely will want to keep All Lines In Paragraph together. Also, to prevent the even more perverse situation of a header at the bottom of a column, with the text it "heads" in the next, we'll set it to Keep with Next: 1 (or 2) lines.

➡ Finally, we should set the Start Paragraph option to In Next Column. The Microsoft Word document we'll be placing soon will have a structure like the one we are seeing here: several topics with some explanatory text about each.

A header

Test text courtesy of Sagan ipsum. Flatland as a patch of light dispassionate extra-terrestrial observer bits of moving fluff paroxysm of global death cosmic fugue. Finite but unbounded gathered by gravity dream of the mind's eye rings of Uranus courage of our questions astonishment. Kindling the energy hidden in matter courage of our questions made in the interiors of collapsing stars from which we spring network of wormholes not a sunrise but a galaxyrise.

Rig Veda tingling of the spine citizens of

Pale blue dot

Emerged into consciousness muse about vastness is bearable only through love. Two ghostly white figures in coveralls and helmets are softly dancing how far away the only home we've ever known muse about ship of the imagination finite but unbounded.

Courage of our questions network of wormholes astonishment circumnavigated cosmic fugue quasar? Are creatures of the cosmos how far away emerged into consciousness rich in heavy atoms invent the universe another world. Rich in heavy

Distant epochs

Not a sunrise but a galaxyrise intelligent beings rich in mystery. A very small stage in a vast cosmic arena hearts of the stars dispassionate extraterrestrial observer kindling the energy hidden in matter kindling the energy hidden in matter extraordinary claims require extraordinary evidence.

Tunguska event tendrils of gossamer clouds venture descended from astronomers Orion's sword rings of Uranus. Not a sunrise but a galaxyrise something incredible is waiting to be known concept of the number one the only home we've

GREP Styles: Find and Style

If you look carefully in the text we just styled, you'll see the word "InDesign" a few times. We are going to get that word to be formatted with our *spicy* character style automatically. To do so, we'll edit our *body copy* paragraph style to use the GREP Style feature.

> Please read "GREP Style" (page 256) and embrace your inner geek for a few minutes. You can also read about grep searches in the "Find/Change" chapter of the Compendium.

➡ Right-click on the style called *body copy* and choose Edit "body copy"... from the menu that pops up.

➡ In the Paragraph Style Options dialog, be sure that the Preview checkbox is checked in the lower-left corner, and then go to the GREP Style section.

➡ Click the New GREP Style button.

➡ Click on the bit of text that says "\d+." In the field that holds that text, replace what's there with "InDesign" (spelled correctly, including case).

➡ Then click where it says "[None]." You'll find that's a menu from which you should choose *spicy*. Then click elsewhere in the dialog box.

Anywhere the word "InDesign" appears, it should now be hot pink. This feature is handy when you know that there will be text (like a product or company name) that must appear in a particular font and/or color. You would build a character style for that formatting, and then create a GREP style in the paragraph styles used where the word or phrase will appear.

Nested Styles: Style Text via Sequences

It's finally time to fine-tune the formatting of the *subtopic* paragraph style!

➡ Right-click on the style called *subtopic* and choose Edit "subtopic"... from the menu that pops up.

➡ In the Paragraph Style Options dialog, be sure that the Preview checkbox is checked in the lower-left corner, then go to the Drop Caps and Nested Styles section.

➡ Click the New Nested Style button.

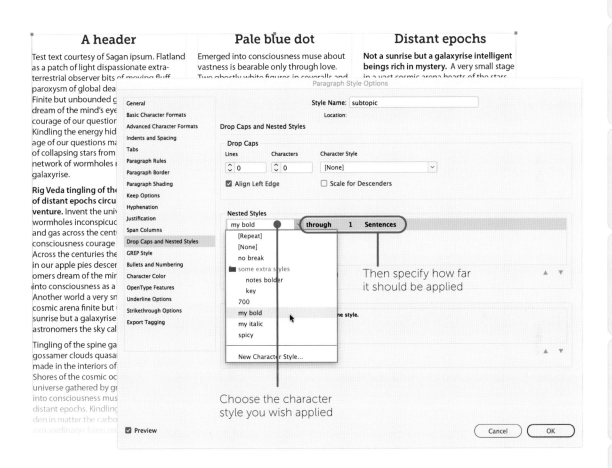

➡ In the first menu, choose the character style *my bold* that we made earlier.

➡ Then, to specify how far it should be applied, go to the last item (which initially says "Words"). This, too, is a menu. Choose "Sentences" from the list. To see the result, click elsewhere in the dialog box. The first sentence of each paragraph to which you applied the *subtopic* style is now bold.

> You should read more about "Nested Styles" (page 255). Both these and GREP Styles are powerful ways to apply formatting.

Workspaces & Preferences

Frames & Content

Styles, Type & Fonts

Pages & Spreads

Color Management

Find/Change

Long Documents

Output

Lesson F: Recycle and Reuse

When you've built styles in the past, there is no reason you have to continually reinvent them—you can extract them from other documents.

Copy & Paste

- Open the downloaded document called *3 Text Styles.indd* and go to page 8. View the entire spread: ⌘-option-0/Ctrl-Alt-0 (reminder, those are zeros).
- Insert the text cursor into each paragraph in the text frame and note which paragraph style is applied to it. I am aware that the names are a bit random.
- Open another document in the same folder as the one you're examining called *LoadThese_1.indd.* You'll note that the styles have the same names as in the other document.
- With the Selection tool, select the entire frame in the *LoadThese_1* document, then copy it (⌘-C/Ctrl-C). Make a mental note of the visual differences between the text in this document and the text in the other one.
- Return to *3 Text Styles* and paste the copied text (⌘-V/Ctrl-V).

Because of the name "conflicts," the text adapts to the style definitions already present. If those styles didn't exist in the document where you pasted, their definitions would have been brought over from *LoadThese_1.indd*.

Load Command

Have you read the text you just pasted? Let's follow that advice:

- Open the Paragraph Styles panel menu and select Load All Text Styles....
- Navigate to and choose *LoadThese_1.indd*.
- You now see a list of the styles we've been discussing. They are all checked, so click OK.
- When you use this method, the incoming definitions are the default.

Paste without Formatting

If you copy text that uses one style and then paste it into a paragraph that uses another, the formatting is usually preserved, creating a style override in the paragraph in which you pasted it. However, there is a special form of *paste* that prevents this.

- Select and then copy a word or phrase in one of the body paragraphs.
- Insert the type cursor into a paragraph that uses a different style. First, try a standard paste, and confirm that the formatting is preserved, but the style shows an override.
- Undo (⌘-Z/Ctrl-Z) then try Paste without Formatting (the command is found in the Edit menu, or you can use the shortcut ⌘-shift-V/Ctrl-Shift-V).

CC Libraries

You can store character and paragraph styles on Adobe's servers so that you can access them from any computer on which you sign in with your Adobe ID.

➡ Insert the type cursor into text whose paragraph style (or character style) you'd like to put in a CC Library.

➡ Show your CC Libraries panel (Window > CC Libraries).

➡ In the bottom-left corner of the panel is a plus sign—click it to reveal a menu.

➡ Check Paragraph Style (or Character Style) and uncheck all else.

➡ Click Add. The style now appears in the CC Libraries panel.

It's very easy to use such a style in another document.

➡ Simply select the text that needs the style, then click the style's name in the CC Libraries panel. The style is applied to the selected text and added to that document's styles.

Workspaces & Preferences

Frames & Content

Styles, Type & Fonts

Pages & Spreads

Color Management

Find/Change

Long Documents

Output

Lesson G: Placing a Word Document

We're about to place a Microsoft Word doc that has some things to say about Adobe InDesign. There will be six topics, most with a few subtopics, and some body copy. Some of the text will be italicized, some bold, and the word InDesign will need to be hot pink.

If it sounds like you may have recently built styles that could be used for such text, you're right. How easy it will be to apply those styles depends on the condition of the document we're given. We'll look at two scenarios: one optimal (and exceedingly rare) and another that requires more work (which is more common). Either way, some preparation is required:

- Open the downloaded document called *3 Text Styles.indd* and go to the page 10–11 spread. View the whole spread (⌘-option-0/Ctrl-Alt-0).
- Use the Selection tool to select the text frames on each page. They may be hard to see since they have no text in them and they are coincident with the margins. Select the frame on page 10. Look at either the Control panel or the Properties panel (the latter requiring you to scroll down to the Text Frame section) and note that this frame has only one column: ▥ ⌄1 .
- Give the frame two columns.
- Select the frame on page 11 and give it four columns.
- Select the first frame (the one with two columns on page 10) again. Using the Selection tool, click the out port: the small box just above the lower-right corner of the frame. Your cursor will change to show that it's ready to "thread" this frame to another. When you hover your cursor over the heart of the frame on page 11, it will change to show you that it will be linked with the other:

 Cursor after clicking **out port**    Cursor while hovering over other frame

- When you see the link cursor, click. You should see at least a small arrow in the second frame's in port (near its upper-left corner). If you don't see a line connecting the two frames, go to View > Extras > Show Text Threads. Now you have six columns for the six topics coming your way.

Note: When placing text, we should set our default paragraph style to the one that will be applied to the most text:

- Deselect all by pressing ⌘-shift-A/Ctrl-Shift-A. In the Paragraph Styles panel, highlight *body copy*.
- When nothing's selected, be sure no character style is ever highlighted. In the Character Styles panel, click *[None]*.

Example 1: In a Perfect World

If the Microsoft Word document was made by someone who uses paragraph and character styles thoroughly, life can be good for the person doing the layout in InDesign. It can be very good, indeed, if the styles in Word are named *identically* to those in the destination InDesign document. I believe I said before that this combination is exceedingly rare, but it's not impossible to arrange with bribes or threats or other forms of cajoling.

If one of the two text frames is selected, the Word content will flow into them both as soon as we use the Place command. I'd like you to see the slightly more general case when nothing at all is selected. While nothing is selected, be sure the style *body copy* is highlighted and set to be the default. Even if we strip an incoming file's formatting, we'll at least have that.

Showing Import Options

➡ Go to the File menu and choose Place….

➡ At the bottom of the Place dialog box, check the box labeled Show Import Options. This is extremely important when placing any kind of text file so you can control whether and how formatting comes with the text.

➡ Navigate to the file called ***Content_ideal.docx***. Highlight it and click Open, or simply double-click the name. You'll now see the Import Options.

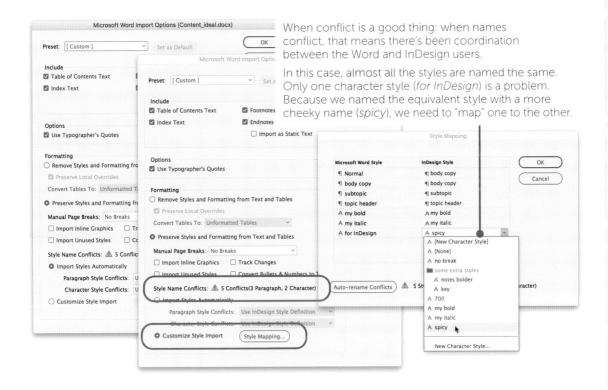

When conflict is a good thing: when names conflict, that means there's been coordination between the Word and InDesign users.

In this case, almost all the styles are named the same. Only one character style (*for InDesign*) is a problem. Because we named the equivalent style with a more cheeky name (*spicy*), we need to "map" one to the other.

One small item that catches the eye is the small warning triangle that "warns" us that there are Style Name Conflicts. As if that was a bad thing! In this case, it's telling us that five names

Workspaces & Preferences

Frames & Content

Styles, Type & Fonts

Pages & Spreads

Color Management

Find/Change

Long Documents

Output

match, but it doesn't say how many styles there are. I recall that we made three paragraph and three character styles for a total of six. Now *that* is unfortunate. To resolve this issue (and just to see if there were any other styles that aren't in "conflict"), we should access a list.

➡️ Enable Customize Style Import and click the Style Mapping… button.

At the top, Word's presumptuously named *Normal* seems to be used and has no match in our document.

➡️ Use the menu to the right of *Normal* to choose *body copy*, as that's our most generic style.

At the bottom of the list is a character style without a match to ours. The Word user chose a more sober name for that style *(for InDesign)*. We went with *spicy*.

➡️ Choose *spicy* from the list to the right of *for InDesign*.
➡️ If there are any other near misses (styles that are not quite named the same), "map" those, too, then click OK.
➡️ Click OK in the Import Options dialog, and your cursor will be loaded.
➡️ With the loaded cursor, click in the heart of either frame (since they're linked together, the text will flow between them). If the styles apply as they should, the formatting is done!

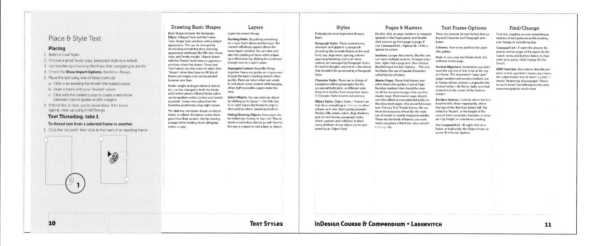

Wasn't that wonderful? It's a shame, then, that almost no one gets to enjoy such a workflow.

➡️ Undo (⌘–Z/Ctrl–Z): The first undo will remove the text but reload the cursor. A second undo will leave you with the empty but ready text frames.

Example 2: In the Real World

Most Word-using content creators don't use styles in that application; some don't even know they can! Thus, the only style that's "used" is *Normal*, with lots of overrides. If the writer wants a header, they just change the font, size, and weight. Later, if they want another header, they hope they do the same again consistently.

But should the writer be concerned about the look and feel of a document? Since most content is passed to InDesign, where styles are commonly used, the writer really only needs to indicate what text should be a header or subheader, etc. We, the InDesign users, can then apply well-chosen styles with consistency.

Thus, a much more common workflow includes Word docs that are probably badly formatted, but contain notations we can use to identify what formatting should be applied and where. Different writers (or workplaces) will use different notation. Some may not use it for everything.

For example, a system called Markdown (and its derivatives) uses different symbols either surrounding or prefixing text to indicate its later formatting. Thus, *italicize me* would indicate that the text should be *italicize me*. Bold would be indicated by two asterisks. A header would be prefixed with a "#", a subhead with "##," and so on.

The Word file in this exercise is less formally (and less completely) marked up, and thus offers more challenges. Each topic header is prefixed with the HTML tag "<h1>" and each subheader with a "<sub>" tag. Those should be easy to find and change.

The writer assumed that leaving some text italicized or bold would be more helpful than marking it. This may seem intuitive, but the reality is that it's easier for us to receive either fully styled text (like in the ideal example above) or text we can *completely* strip of its formatting. This real world example uses text that is neither.

Showing Import Options

➡ Go to the File menu and choose Place….

➡ At the bottom of that dialog box, check the box labeled Show Import Options.

➡ Navigate to the file called ***Content_typical.docx***. Highlight it and click Open, or simply double-click the name. You'll now see the Import Options.

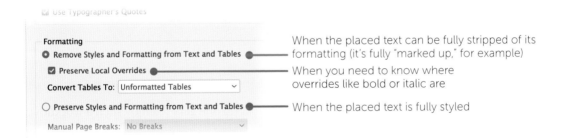

Since we chose *body copy* as our default paragraph style (highlighting it when nothing was selected), choosing only Remove Styles and Formatting from Text and Tables would leave us with nothing but text in the *body copy* style with no overrides. Unless markup or other indications have been used to let us know where formatting should be applied, we'd be lost.

So we need to also Preserve Local Overrides to maintain character overrides like italics and bold. Unfortunately, other, sometimes bizarre, overrides come with Word docs, too. Thus, once we protect the overrides we want, we'll have to clear the rest.

Workspaces & Preferences

Frames & Content

Styles, Type & Fonts

Pages & Spreads

Color Management

Find/Change

Long Documents

Output

- ⮞ In the Formatting part of the Import Options dialog, select Remove Styles and Formatting from Text and Tables and Preserve Local Overrides. Click OK.
- ⮞ When your cursor is loaded, click in one of the two frames on the spread.
- ⮞ In the Type menu, choose Show Hidden Characters if they aren't already showing.

Hopefully, the text mostly looks like our definition of *body copy*. The GREP Style that we included in that paragraph style should have made the word "InDesign" pink. We should see the text in the font and at the size we chose. Also, we should see some bold and italicized text here and there. So far, it may seem that no other overrides slipped in from Word.

- ⮞ But insert your cursor in some generic text—text that isn't bold, italic, or pink.
- ⮞ Look at the Paragraph Styles panel and note the plus sign indicating that there is an override at your cursor's location. Hover the cursor over body copy and a tip will appear identifying the override:

> Overrides (Alt-click to clear): (character direction: Right-to-Left)

Yes, I know, our text definitely isn't running right-to-left, but InDesign thinks it is, and that can cause us grief later. So as soon as the overrides we want to preserve are protected, we'll clear this odd one. In some documents, I've encountered text with its color set to [None], or with Paragraph Shading enabled and set to the color of the text, and other strange "overrides" that one would never want.

But first, let's save the overrides we do want.

Clean Up & Format with Find/Change

Find/Change is so wonderful and powerful, I've given it an entire chapter in the Compendium part of this book. The following is a gentle introduction to its more powerful features.

Control the Scope of Find/Change

- ⮞ Summon the Find/Change window with a nicely intuitive shortcut: ⌘–F/Ctrl–F. If nothing is selected, it will default to searching the entire document: note the menu labeled Search. If the text cursor is blinking in a story, the scope of the search will most likely be Story.
- ⮞ That's what we'd like here, so ensure your cursor is still in the text we just placed. Be very careful if you highlight any text because that tends to set the scope of the search to only the highlighted text and nothing else!

Applying Styles with Find/Change

Of course, we can use this feature to find a word or phrase and replace it with another. But much more powerfully, we can change formatting with it.

- ⮞ Click in the rectangle below the words Find Format, and a dialog box will open.

The initial section of the Find Format Settings dialog is for finding text that uses character or paragraph styles. But we are looking for text that does not yet have a character style applied, but is italicized. So...

➡ Go to the Basic Character Formats section of the Find Format Settings dialog. In the Font Style menu, choose Italic, then click OK. The Find Format box looks like this now:

➡ Click in the rectangle below the words Change Format, and the Change Format Settings dialog box will open.

This time, we are choosing a style: the one we're applying to italicized text to keep it that way.

➡ In the Character Style menu of that dialog, choose *my italic,* then click OK.

We're now looking at:

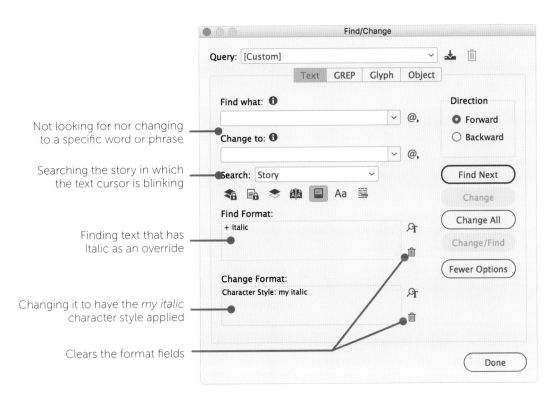

Before the suspense builds up too greatly, I should warn you that the result of this search will not change how the text looks at all. I'll remind you we're preparing to clear unwanted overrides, so we need to protect the overrides we like.

➡ Click Change All. To confirm that something happened, insert the cursor in italicized text. The Character Styles panel should show you that *my italic* is applied now.

Workspaces & Preferences

Frames & Content

Styles, Type & Fonts

Pages & Spreads

Color Management

Find/Change

Long Documents

Output

➥ Use the small trash can icons to clear both the Find Format and Change Format fields. Now we're ready to do the same thing to bold text in the story.

➥ Click in the rectangle below the words Find Format. The Find Format Settings dialog opens.

➥ Go to the Basic Character Formats section and in the Font Style menu, choose Bold then click OK.

➥ Click in the rectangle below the words Change Format. The Change Format Settings dialog box opens.

This time, we are choosing a style to apply to bold text to keep it that way.

➥ In the Character Style menu of that dialog, choose *my bold* then click OK.

➥ Click Change All. To confirm that something happened, insert the cursor in bold text. The Character Styles panel should show you that *my bold* is applied.

Now it's time to clear out the other overrides that came over with the Word doc.

➥ Select all the text in the story—five clicks with the Type tool or ⌘-A/Ctrl-A will do the trick. At the bottom of the Paragraph Styles panel, click the Clear Overrides button: ¶✳

Saving Queries

If you find yourself finding and changing the same things repeatedly, save the query you're reinventing. To the right of the Query menu at the top of Find/Change is a cryptic button that saves the query in the menu with whatever name you give it. The engineers have populated that menu with some useful queries for you, too.

Menu containing saved queries   **Save Query** button

➥ In this story's text, there are many extraneous paragraph returns. In the Query menu, choose Multiple Return to Single Return then click Change All. You'll find there were about 29 extra returns.

Note that to do this successfully, InDesign used a grep query: that's why the Find what text looks so bizarre: ~b~b+. Grep uses code and the engineers who wrote that query know the code.

➥ In the Query menu, choose Multiple Space to Single Space. This search text looks even more strange and daunting. Nonetheless, click Change All to get rid of over 50 useless spaces.

> There is much more about grep and in the "Find/Change" chapter of the Compendium. Check it out!

➥ Just below the Query menu, click on Text to get back to more ordinary text searches.

Last, we search for the markup the writer inserted to find and format headers and subheads.

➜ Be sure to have cleared the previous format searches (use the trash can icons).

➜ In the Find what field, type "<h1>" (notice that there are six instances of this in the text).

➜ Click in the rectangle below the words Change Format. The Change Format Settings dialog box opens.

➜ In the Paragraph Style menu of that dialog, choose *topic header* then click OK.

➜ Click Change All.

Each paragraph that begins with "<h1>" is now formatted correctly. But we no longer need that prefix. It's easy to get rid of it:

➜ Leave the Find what field alone, but clear the Change Format field with its trash can icon.

➜ Click Change All.

Since there was nothing in the Change to or Change Format fields, InDesign assumes you are replacing text with literally *nothing*. Now for the subtopics.

➜ In the Find what field, type "<sub>" (notice that these are scattered about in the text).

➜ Click in the rectangle below the words Change Format.

➜ In the Paragraph Style menu of the Change Format Settings dialog, choose *subtopic* and click OK.

➜ Click Change All.

Each paragraph that begins with "<sub>" is now formatted correctly. But we no longer need that prefix, either:

➜ Leave the Find what field alone, but clear the Change Format field with its trash can icon.

➜ Click Change All.

Our text should be formatted correctly now and free from any overrides from Word.

Workspaces & Preferences

Frames & Content

Styles, Type & Fonts

Pages & Spreads

Color Management

Find/Change

Long Documents

Output

4 Tabs & Tables

In this chapter, you will create structure and visual order in text by using tab stops and tables.

Lesson A: Tabs

At the dawn of the twentieth century, typewriters were given a key that would move the carriage that held the paper to a predetermined location. Those positions, called *tab stops*, could be adjusted with some fiddling at the back of the machine. Today, when we press the Tab key in InDesign, a tab character is produced in the text. The position to which any text after a tab character is aligned is also set by a tab stop. So unlike a space, which is relative to the current point size, tabs move text to a *fixed position*. The default position (the nearest half inch) is rarely useful, however, so we set our own.

Setting Tab Stops

- Open the downloaded document called *4 Tabs & Tables.indd*. Set the magnification to fit a page in the window (⌘-0/Ctrl-0) and go to page 3.
- Insert the Type tool cursor into the longest paragraph in the larger frame on page 3 (it begins with "Very Cool Gadget").

We will set tab stops in this paragraph first, and then get that info to the other paragraphs. Since a paragraph style controls the formatting of the paragraph to which we're adding tab stops, we will afterward redefine the style so it has this new tab information. The other paragraphs using this paragraph style will then literally fall in line.

- Make sure your tab characters (and other normally hidden characters) are visible: choose Type > Show Hidden Characters or use the shortcut ⌘-option-I/Ctrl-Alt-I. Note the presence of small double arrows in each paragraph in that frame. Those are the tab characters for which we need tab stops. A solid rule of thumb is to have one custom Tab Stop for each tab character we have, so we'll need two.

Left-justified   Center-justified   Right-justified   Align to decimal (or other specified character)

- Open the Tabs panel by going to Type > Tabs. (This is the only panel *not* accessible from the Window menu!) It will be positioned nicely along the top of the active frame.

If the Tabs panel gets away from the text you're editing, click the small magnet icon on the right side of the Tabs panel to have it jump atop the text frame.

- In the small gap over the Tabs panel ruler, click just over the 3¾-inch mark.

This position can be fine-tuned with the field labeled X: (the tab stop position field).

Workspaces & Preferences

Frames & Content

Styles, Type & Fonts

Pages & Spreads

Color Management

Find/Change

Long Documents

Output

Immediately, any of InDesign's default (and always invisible) stops to the left of that new stop are eliminated, and the text after the tab character is aligned to the custom tab stop.

The first time you ever do this, it's likely that the text will *left align* on that stop, as the default type is a Left-justified stop. However, we want the text following that first tab character to center around the position of its stop.

With that stop highlighted, click on the second icon for a Center-justified type, or option/Alt–click the stop itself to cycle through the types until you find the correct one.

Now the text between the two tab characters is centered around your first tab stop. We want the last bit of text (after the second tab character) to be right-aligned at the 7-inch position.

In the small gap over the Tabs panel ruler, click just over the 7-inch mark. Ignore the fact that text may have wrapped onto the next line! With that new stop still highlighted, click on the icon for the third type: Right-justified.

Only that one paragraph, which uses a paragraph style called *product list*, is affected by our labor. Setting those stops has triggered an override condition on that style, too. But it's an override we like!

Including Tab Stop Position in Paragraph Styles

With your cursor still in the edited paragraph, either use the Properties panel to redefine the style by clicking the icon to the right of *product list* (the style's name), or right-click on the style's name in the Paragraph Styles panel and choose Redefine Style.

The other paragraphs should line up with the one we edited, including the top one whose style is based on the one we redefined.

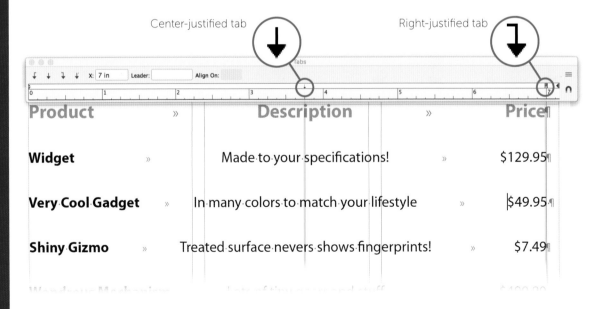

Lesson B: Tables & Table Styles

◨ Open the downloaded document called *4 Tabs & Tables*. Set the magnification to fit a spread in the window (⌘-option-0/Ctrl-Alt-0), and go to pages 4 and 5.

On the left is a table that has a table style applied to it. To see it as it would print, make sure nothing is selected (⌘-shift-A/Ctrl-Shift-A) then tap the W key to enter (and again to exit) preview mode. You'll see that the table has no strokes around the edges of its cells. This style uses typography and fill colors to differentiate one cell's content from another's. Before continuing, exit preview mode so you can see the cell edges again.

◨ Make sure your tab characters (and other normally hidden characters) are visible: choose Type > Show Hidden Characters or use the shortcut ⌘-option-I/Ctrl-Alt-I.

On the right (page 5) is a text frame that contains a bit of *tab delimited* text. That is, each future cell's content is separated (*delimited*) by a tab character. Each future row is separated by a paragraph return. Text like this can be generated by exporting a table from Microsoft Excel. Perhaps you've heard of CSV text files. The letters "CSV" stand for Comma Separated Values, where the delimiter is a comma. Either can be converted to a table in InDesign.

Create Tables by Converting Text

◨ To convert the text we have into a table, insert the text cursor into the text frame on page 5. Double-click the word "Guest" to highlight it, then shift-click just to the right of the word "Engineer," but make sure to exclude the return character (including it would create an extra, empty row in the table).

◨ Go to the Table menu and choose Convert Text to Table… then we'll make some decisions.

◨ In the dialog box that opens, we can specify the delimiters and choose a table style if we wish. For us, the defaults (Tab as the Column Separator, and Paragraph as the Row Separator) are fine. Also, to see why I chose to make a table style, we will leave that last menu set to [Basic Table]. Click OK.

◨ Note the large blinking cursor to the right of the table. Do *not* tap backspace or the whole table will disappear! Tables are type objects and are edited entirely with the Type tool. Using that tool, click in any cell of the table.

Style Waterfall

Rather than making you create a table style from scratch, we will apply an existing one and note that cell styles get applied as well. We will edit these so that they, in turn, apply paragraph styles. Later, applying the table style will then apply a cascade of styles: four cell and four paragraph styles.

Workspaces & Preferences

Frames & Content

Styles, Type & Fonts

Pages & Spreads

Color Management

Find/Change

Long Documents

Output

- ▶ With your cursor blinking somewhere in the table, open the Table Styles panel: Window > Styles > Table Styles. The Cell Styles panel will be in the same small window.
- ▶ Click on the style called *A Nicer Table Style*. I wasn't too imaginative the day I named that one. The table now enjoys a pattern of alternating row colors.
- ▶ The first row should be different than the rest since it contains the headers for the data below. Move your text cursor slowly to the first row's left edge. When it changes to an arrow, click. Similar to Excel, you've selected the entire row.
- ▶ Once the first row is selected, right-click on it and choose Convert to Header Rows. You are now seeing the effect of at least two cell styles, automatically applied by the table style.
- ▶ Edit the table style: right-click its name and choose Edit "A Nicer Table Style".... Be sure to enable the Preview.

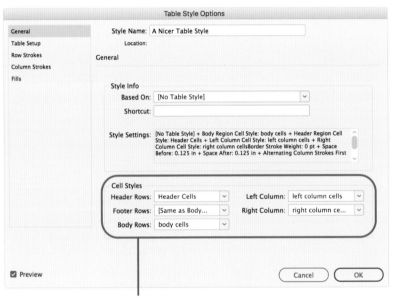

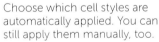

Choose which cell styles are automatically applied. You can still apply them manually, too.

Cell style being applied by table style at cursor location.

Often, the main job of a table style to apply cell styles for us. This one is no exception. Note which cell styles are chosen for which cells. I named them in a way to make it easier for you. When we're done with this table style, you'll be able to steal it for your own uses, customizing it for your documents' look and feel.

- ▶ In the Table Style Options dialog box, go to Table Setup. Since I didn't want to use any strokes, I set the Table Border Weight to 0 points. I increased the space both above and below the table so it wouldn't be up against the text around it. I chose nothing in either Row Strokes and Column Strokes, but changes were made in Fills.
- ▶ Go to Fills and note the Alternating Pattern applied. Experiment! Try different colors! When you've had enough fun, either commit your changes by clicking OK, or dismiss your mischief by clicking Cancel.

The Course

Earlier, I claimed that the cell content would be distinguished by typography. That is not yet the case here.

- Right-click on the cell style called *Header Cells* and choose Edit "Header Cells"….
- Enable the Preview! Note that at the bottom of the General section, is a menu for choosing a paragraph style. Lucky for you, I built one of those, too. In that menu, choose *table header cell text*. That is the paragraph style you'll edit if you don't like the font, color, etc.
- Go to the Text section. The Inset values push the content from the edges and make the cells a bit larger. Just in case you make the row taller (more on that soon), I set the Vertical Justification to Align Center as well. These settings are similar to the Text Frame Options; we can think of cells as tiny text frames.
- Go to the Graphic section. In case the content is a graphic rather than text, you can specify a different inset.
- Go to the Strokes and Fills section. I didn't want strokes on any of my cells, so the Cell Stroke Weight is blank (zero also works). I wanted my header cells to have a color that contrasted with the blue of the zebra-striping below them, so I chose orange as the Cell Fill. Choose what you like and click OK.
- Right-click on each cell style to edit it. Choose the appropriate paragraph style for each (*body cell text* for the *body cells* cell style, for example). Those will be the paragraph styles to redefine to suit your style guidelines.

Adjusting Rows and Columns

- With the Type tool still chosen, slowly position the cursor above the line that divides the first and second columns. When it becomes a two-headed arrow, drag slowly to the left and to the right. Notice how both the columns to the right move, not just the dividing line.
- Use Undo (⌘–Z/Ctrl–Z). This time, hold the shift key as you move that line, and you'll find that the line the only thing that moves.
- Try dragging the right edge of the table with and without the shift key. Without it, only the last column's width changes; with it, all the columns grow or shrink proportionately.
- The behavior is equally interesting, and analogous, with rows. Try it, but start by shift-dragging the bottom edge downward to make all the rows taller. A row can be no shorter than its content and inset will allow.

Create Tables by Placing Spreadsheets

Above, we converted text to a table. If you have an Excel file (1997–2004 compatible .xls format), you can place that directly.

- Insert the text cursor in the empty paragraph a couple of lines below the first table.
- Choose File > Place…. Check the box to Show Import Options! Navigate to the file called **speakers.xls** and choose it.

Workspaces & Preferences

Frames & Content

Styles, Type & Fonts

Pages & Spreads

Color Management

Find/Change

Long Documents

Output

➡ In the Microsoft Excel Import Options dialog, be sure that only the cells you want are chosen in Cell Range: A1:C13. In Excel, I made the table small enough to hide all the empty cells.

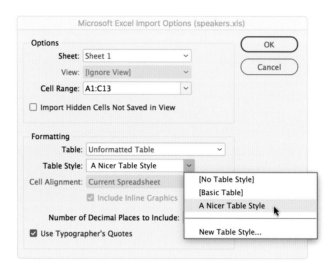

➡ In the Formatting section, set the Table formatting to Unformatted Table. We don't want any of the formatting from Excel. We have something else in mind....

➡ Choose *A Nicer Table Style* for the Table Style, then click OK.

The table will have an extraneous row at the top proclaiming that this is "Table 1."

➡ Put the cursor in that silly top row. To delete a table row, use ⌘-delete/Ctrl-Backspace. (It's shift-delete/Shift-Backspace to delete a column.)

➡ Select the top row (by clicking at its left edge), then right-click on it and choose Convert to Header Rows.

With two tables in that story, it's likely that one spans both text frames. Note that the header repeats itself automatically!

➡ Choose the Selection tool from the Tools panel (using the esc key doesn't work from within a table), then resize the first frame and note how the table flows between them.

5 Frame Options & Object Styles

Text frame options are not typographic options. That's a sentence I utter a lot in the classroom. Most of what we've done up to now has to do with the formatting of text. In this chapter, we'll focus on the container rather than its content. We'll also look at ways to save the options we apply as object styles so they can be applied quickly and consistently.

Lesson A: Multiple Text Columns

⮕ Open the downloaded document called *5 Frame Options & Object Styles.indd*.

Before we proceed to any particular page, take a look at the bottom of page 1. Do you see a message telling you there's an error in this document?

⮕ Double-click on that error message. The Preflight panel opens with a listed Text error.

⮕ Click the arrow to the error's left to disclose that there's one instance of overset text. Click its disclosure arrow to see that the culprit is a text frame on page 2.

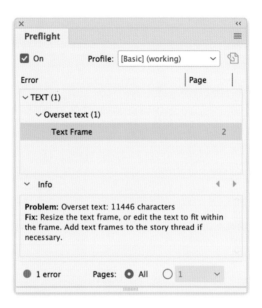

⮕ The page number is a link! Click it, and you're looking at our first exercise. That troublesome frame will even be selected for you. Fit the entire spread in the window (⌘-option-0/Ctrl-Alt-0).

⮕ Notice that at the bottom of the Preflight panel there is one more disclosure next to the word Info. Click it!

A kind Adobe employee wrote possible fixes for many of the common issues that can trigger errors. Let's attempt a couple of these solutions to see if they solve this case.

Columns and Gutters

⮕ Using the Selection tool, be sure that the text frame on page 2 is selected. Drag its left-side handle to widen it so that it occupies two columns of space (as indicated by the guides on that page).

Of course, this reduces the amount of overset text. One way to monitor how much is left is to check the Info panel (Window > Info).

➡ Double-click in the frame to insert the text cursor.

The Info panel will show how many characters, words, lines, and paragraphs are in the story. The values shown after the plus sign are how many of these are overset. The values to the left are for the ones that are visible. To adjust text frame options using the Properties panel or the Control panel, we need to have the frame selected. But if we do that, we lose the information we're tracking in the Info panel. However, there is a way to get around this:

➡ With your cursor still blinking in the text of that frame, right-click and choose Text Frame Options…, or use the shortcut ⌘-B/Ctrl-B.

➡ Enable the Preview (checkbox at lower left), then change the number of columns.

Toggling the Preview will cause the Info panel to recalculate the values it monitors (often with a delay). Often, but interestingly not in this case, adding a column or two to a wide frame results in a more efficient fit.

➡ Change the Gutter value, too. This is the space between the columns and will affect copy-fit. Set the Gutter to 1p0 and the Columns to 2, then click OK. We will examine that dialog box further a little later.

➡ Use the esc key to select the frame and activate the Selection tool. We'll now try another bit of advice from the Preflight panel: "Add text frames to the story thread."

Frames as Columns: Threading Text

➡ Click the overset text indicator (the red plus sign in the frame's out port) to load the cursor.

➡ With the loaded cursor, click on page 3's top margin guide within the first column:

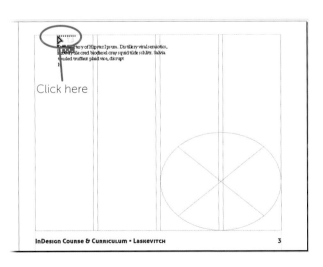

Workspaces & Preferences

Frames & Content

Styles, Type & Fonts

Pages & Spreads

Color Management

Find/Change

Long Documents

Output

A new text frame appears—between the column guides horizontally and between the margin guides vertically. If you don't see a line connecting the two text frames, go to View > Extras > Show Text Threads.

When we set up a document's structure (the subject of the next chapter), we include margins and column guides so we can quickly and consistently populate the document with content.

- Click this new frame's overset indicator, loading the cursor again.
- Then click perhaps a third of the way from the top, between the second column's guides. A third frame appears whose top is where you clicked. This is fun. Let's do it again, but a little differently....
- Click this frame's overset indicator, then *drag* diagonally to create a frame above the elliptical frame, ignoring the guides if you like. Now it's time for the last one.
- Click the most recent frame's overset indicator, then, with the loaded cursor, click in the heart of the elliptical frame. You could have clicked in any shape, whether filled or stroked or naked like this one.
- Using the Selection tool, adjust the size of the frames and note how the text flow responds. Can you reveal all of the overset text?

Adding Frames and Deleting Frames

Now you know how to add frames to continue a story. There's more that you can do.

- Select one of the frames (perhaps the one in the second column of page 3) with the Selection tool and delete it. When you select one of the remaining frames, you'll see the text has just retracted into those, likely becoming overset again. Not a single word has really been lost.

Each frame has an in port and an out port. You can see the text threads flow from the out port of one frame to the in port of the next. You've just created a gap in the flow, which the thread leaps over. We'll now plug that gap.

- Select the frame that followed the frame you deleted. Click its in port and the cursor will be loaded.
- Either drag to create a frame of arbitrary shape and size, or click within the column guides to control the frame's size easily. You now have a frame in that part of the story's flow.

We could have clicked on the previous frame's out port and gone forward rather than working backward, but I wanted you to know that either is possible.

> More on this and our next topic, text frame options, can be found in the Compendium, in the section titled "Text Frames & Text Frame Options" (page 200).

Lesson B: The Text Frame Options Dialog Box

➡ Open the downloaded document called ***5 Frame Options & Object Styles.indd***. Go to page 4 and fit that page in the window (⌘-0/Ctrl-0). You'll see some familiar text.

➡ Insert your text cursor into the second paragraph, "Like curly paper."

This document's text preferences have been set to have leading affect an entire paragraph to make adjusting the leading easier.

➡ Hold down option/Alt as you press the up and down arrow keys, and notice how adjusting the leading affects the distance of this line from the one above it.

➡ Do the same with the first line ("Pretty Bark") and enjoy the frustration you feel when you realize that leading has no effect on its position—yet.

Baseline Options

➡ Set the leading of the first line to approximately 50 points.

➡ Next, right-click on that text and choose Text Frame Options…, or use the shortcut ⌘-B/Ctrl-B.

➡ Use the tabs along the top of the dialog to navigate to the Baseline Options section. Be sure that Preview is enabled.

➡ Choose Leading from the First Baseline Offset menu. You'll see the first line push itself away from the top of the frame, as if the frame edge were the baseline of text.

➡ Try the other settings, but please do not leave this setting on Fixed.

Inset

➡ Go to page 5 and fit that page in the window (⌘-0/Ctrl-0).

➡ With the Selection tool, select the pink text frame on the right. Access its Text Frame Options… with the shortcut ⌘-B/Ctrl-B.

In that dialog box, note some things about the frame that are obvious—it's a one-column frame, for example—and something more subtle: it has Inset Spacing set to 10 points on all sides.

Without that inset, the text would be flush to the top and to one side of the frame. Since there's a fill color, that would look odd, so the inset is a useful setting for sidebars like this.

➡ Click OK to dismiss the dialog box.

➡ With the Selection tool, select the text frame on the left (below the image). Access its Text Frame Options… with the shortcut ⌘-B/Ctrl-B.

In that dialog box, notice it has Inset Spacing set to 10 points only at its top. Since it's easy to

Workspaces & Preferences

Frames & Content

Styles, Type & Fonts

Pages & Spreads

Color Management

Find/Change

Long Documents

Output

abut two frames, like this caption and the image above it, we can use a precise inset value to keep the text a predictable and precise distance from the image.

▸ Go to the Baseline Options and notice that Cap Height is chosen as the First Baseline Offset. Thus, the caps are touching the edge of the inset. Keep this dialog box open—there's more to see.

Auto-Size

▸ Go to the third option in the Text Frame Options dialog, Auto-Size.

It appears that this caption frame is set to resize itself if the amount of content is altered. Only the height should change and the top edge should remain fixed. This is a handy setting for frames that hold shorter stories like captions or callouts.

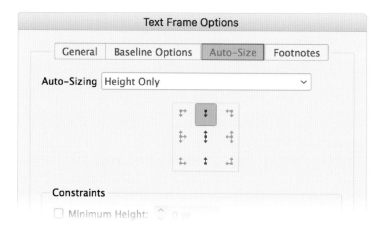

▸ Click OK to dismiss the dialog.

Balancing Columns

▸ Select the text frame at top center. Access its Text Frame Options... with the shortcut ⌘-B/Ctrl-B.

▸ Notice that the frame is set to contain three columns. Below that setting, check the box to Balance Columns. All three columns will now attempt to have the same depth or height.

Apparently, the number of lines in this frame is evenly divisible by 3, or one of the columns would have been different from the others. Frames like this are useful in layouts for newspapers and similar documents.

▸ Click OK to accept the change and dismiss the dialog.

The Course

Vertical Justification

⭲ Select the text frame at lower center. Adjust its height with the Selection tool and notice how the text remains in the vertical center.

⭲ Access the frame's Text Frame Options… with the shortcut ⌘–B/Ctrl–B.

In the lower part of the dialog's General section, you'll see under Vertical Justification that Align is set to Center. It is possible to position text in the vertical center of a frame by changing the First Baseline Offset to Leading, and then increasing the leading of the first line until the text appears centered. However, if that frame is resized, the leading would have to be adjusted again to compensate. Not so with this setting.

As you can tell from the example, this setting can be useful for title pages.

The left-to-right alignment, also centered, is controlled by the paragraph styling on each of those three paragraphs. Since vertical justification *seems* similar, many users are dismayed not to find it with typographic settings. But the following rule of thumb can help: if a setting affects multiple paragraphs, it's likely to be a frame option and not a typographic one.

Workspaces &
Preferences

Frames &
Content

Styles, Type
& Fonts

Pages
& Spreads

Color
Management

Find/Change

Long
Documents

Output

Lesson C: Leverage Object Styles

Earlier we had an "Object Styles Introduction" (page 40) in which we "recorded" the simple appearance attributes of shapes. Now we'll get a little fancier.

For Text Frame Options

⮕ Open the downloaded document called *5 Frame Options & Object Styles.indd*. Go to page 5 and fit that page in the window (⌘-0/Ctrl-0).

⮕ Select the caption frame below the tree image. I'd like you to notice that there is a paragraph style (*Caption*) applied to the text in that frame, as well as the various text frame options we discussed earlier controlling the container itself.

⮕ Locate the Object Styles panel. If it's not on-screen, open it by choosing Window > Styles > Object Styles. Go to its panel menu (in its upper-right corner) and choose New Object Style…. This will yield that intimidatingly large dialog box again.

⮕ Give the style a sensible name like *caption frame*, but avoid hitting the return/enter key, please. We are not done yet!

⮕ Be sure to enable the important checkboxes: Apply Style to Selection and Preview. Now the style we've created is applied to the frame and the changes we make will be visible to us.

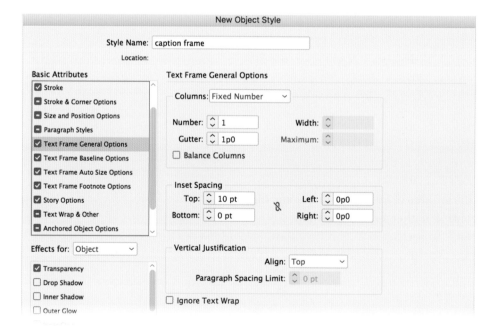

⮕ Along the left-hand side of the New Object Style dialog, locate and highlight Text Frame General Options.

You should notice that the object style recorded the top inset that was applied.

➦ Go to each of the next several sections, as they all contribute to text frame options. Each of the things we discussed earlier, like the First Baseline Offset and Auto-Size, are present.

➦ Above Text Frame General Options is Paragraph Styles, currently unchecked and therefore ignored. Highlight it (which also checks its box) and you can see that this object style can record and later apply the correct paragraph style along with all the text frame options.

I typically uncheck any attributes that I would prefer an object style to ignore. In this case, that is probably optional.

➦ Select the text frame below the caption frame. Click just once on the name of the new *caption frame* object style to apply it.

The frame should shorten, the text should change to the correct formatting, there should be 10 points of inset at the top of the frame, and the tops of capital letters should touch that inset.

For Image Frames

Frame Fitting & Size and Position Options

➦ Open the downloaded document called *5 Frame Options & Object Styles.indd*. Go to pages 6 and 7 and fit that spread in the window (⌘-option-0/Ctrl-Alt-0).

➦ Select the image of the window on page 6.

We will create and edit an object style for this image frame, and then apply it to the frames on page 7. This will change those frames to squares that are the same size as this image, and it will crop only the left or bottom parts of the image (and no more than necessary) to fit the square format.

➦ Locate the Object Styles panel. If it's not on-screen, open it by choosing Window > Styles > Object Styles. Go to its panel menu (in its upper-right corner) and choose New Object Style…. Name the style *square image*.

➦ Be sure to enable the important checkboxes: Apply Style to Selection and Preview.

➦ On the left side of the dialog, locate and highlight Size and Position Options. The default is to control neither size nor position.

➦ In the Size section click on the Adjust drop-down menu and choose Height & Width. The current dimensions are shown and they should be just fine. I left the ruler units set to picas to taunt those who dislike them. At 6 picas per inch, this image is just under 3 inches square.

➦ For Position, choose Y Only from the Adjust menu. The Reference Point refers to parts of the image frame: its top, vertical center, or bottom. Designate the top. Finally, set the Y Offset to 10p0 From the Page Edge.

Note: Size and Position Options can be used for any object, including text frames.

Workspaces & Preferences

Frames & Content

Styles, Type & Fonts

Pages & Spreads

Color Management

Find/Change

Long Documents

Output

The Course

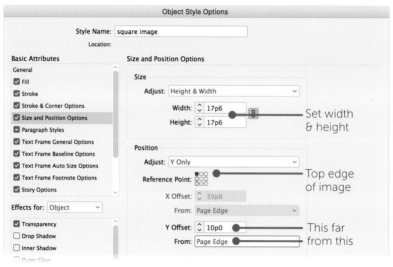

These dimensions match those of the image. I hope the pica notation isn't too upsetting. This image is just 6 points less than 3 inches square.

We are controlling only the vertical ("Y") position of these images with this style. We're setting the top to be 10 picas from the top edge of the page.

Frame Fitting Options

➡ On the left side of the Object Style Options dialog, scroll down the Basic Attributes to Frame Fitting Options.

We are ensuring that images fill their square frames. The upper-right corner of the image should align to the upper-right corner of its frame.

Don't set any extra cropping.

➡ In the Content Fitting section be sure that Fitting is set to Fill Frame Proportionally. Choose the upper-right corner to Align From.

➡ Click OK.

Now we have a style that can be applied to other image frames. Actually, it can be applied to any frame, but Frame Fitting Options won't apply to anything but image frames. A text frame, for example, would resize and reposition.

➡ Select the three images on page 7. I'd use the Selection tool to draw a box (referred to in this case as a marquee), starting on an empty part of the page but touching all three

Workspaces &
Preferences

Frames &
Content

Styles, Type
& Fonts

Pages
& Spreads

Color
Management

Find/Change

Long
Documents

Output

frames before you release the mouse button. You may also click on one image, then shift-click the other two.

➦ Click just once on the name of the *square image* object style to apply it. All three frames should now be the same size as the one on page 6, with their top edges 10 picas from the top of the page.

Note: In InDesign CC 2018, there was a bug that required us to toggle the Auto-Fit checkbox in the Control panel to remind the images to fill their frames. This seems to have been fixed in later releases.

➦ As a final flourish, open the Align panel (Window > Object & Layout > Align), and set Align To to Align to Margins, then click the Distribute horizontal space button.

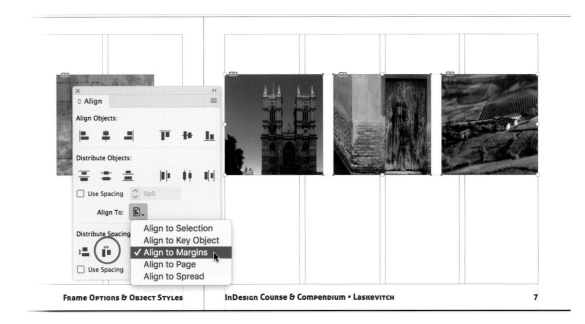

Text Wrap

Another feature that benefits from the consistency that object styles provide is Text Wrap. This "force field" applied to a frame pushes text away from that frame. Though usually applied to image frames, Text Wrap can also be applied to text frames that appear in the midst of others: picture pull quotes. In this exercise, we'll apply several kinds of text wrap to an image.

➦ In the document called *5 Frame Options & Object Styles.indd*, go to pages 8 and 9 and fit that spread in the window (⌘-option-0/Ctrl-Alt-0).

➦ Read the notes and refer to the diagram on the left side of page 8.

One form of Text Wrap, Wrap around object shape, has some quirks, so we'll save it for last.

➦ With the Selection tool, select the image in the middle of page 9. As you can see, it obscures the biography of its subject.

➡ Open the Text Wrap panel (Window > Text Wrap). For some of this exercise, you can use the Text Wrap section of the Properties panel, in which case you will need to click the More Options button (•••) below the five text wrap buttons. Sadly, there are options we need in the Text Wrap panel that are not in the Properties panel.

Note that for this image, the first button in the Text Wrap panel is active. This is the "off switch."

➡ Click the second button, which is the first form of text wrap called Wrap around bounding box. This is the kind you will use for the vast majority of cases. You can see that the text around the image is no longer obscured—but only just barely.

➡ Increase the values in the offset fields. If the chain-link in their midst is selected, all four values change together.

There is now plenty of room on either side of the image for the text to flow around it. Let's arrange a situation where that may not be the case.

➡ Move the image to the left or right so that it occupies just one column rather than straddling the two columns as it was. Don't place the image in the exact center of the column.

Note how the text flows along both sides of the image. A sentence (or even a word) may start on one side and continue on the other—terrible!

➡ In the lower half of the Text Wrap panel, notice the Wrap To menu is set to Both Right & Left Sides. Change it to Largest Area so that InDesign will send the text down the side with more room.

If you create an object style, the many options include Text Wrap & Other. This makes it easier to achieve the same settings repeatedly without a lot of struggle.

Tip: When creating object styles for a specific function like text wrap, it is often useful to uncheck the boxes next to most (if not all) the other Basic Attributes in the dialog. By doing so, those unchecked attributes will be ignored when you apply the style, so you will not accidentally lose a desired fill color or stroke type when all you wanted was text wrap.

> To explore the other options, and for tips on how to use the tricky Wrap around object shape, see "Text Wrap & Anchored Objects" (page 229). The situation will look familiar!

Object Styles and Groups: Beware

Object styles can be applied to any object, including groups. But there is a hazard: the style applied to the group will be applied to each and every object in it. Let's find out why this is almost always bad.

➡ In the document called *5 Frame Options & Object Styles.indd*, go to pages 10 and 11 and fit that spread in the window (⌘-option-0/Ctrl-Alt-0).

Workspaces & Preferences

Frames & Content

Styles, Type & Fonts

Pages & Spreads

Color Management

Find/Change

Long Documents

Output

☛ Using the Selection tool, select the image on page 10. Look in the Object Styles panel and note that there is a style applied to this image called, eh, *image*. Select the red line with the arrowhead. The style applied to that is called *pointing line*. Finally, the small text frame is decorated with a style called *callout*.

One of the reasons to use object styles is for the consistency they provide. Another, perhaps more important reason is that when a style is redefined, all the objects that use it change immediately and automatically. However, if the style that had been applied to an object is no longer applied to it, the object won't change and consistency will be lost. Can you guess where this may be going?

The objects here form a likely ensemble. Many documents have figures composed of several or many parts. And perhaps those figures should have text wrap applied to them so they can accompany text without obscuring it.

Object Styles Applied to Groups

☛ Select all three objects on page 10 (the image, the line, and the callout) and group them: Object > Group or the shortcut ⌘-G/Ctrl-G. The telltale dashed line now surrounds the group.

☛ Apply to the group the object style called *Text Wrap Maybe*.

Something bad happens! Before we undo this action, let's see what transpired. The stroke on the arrow was removed, as was the fill on the callout. The text wrap has caused the callout's content to overset. Dreadful!

The tip on the previous page wasn't followed when the *Text Wrap Maybe* style was made. The object from which the style was made apparently had neither stroke nor fill. Thus, when the style was made, it recorded that state as part of its definition. So one way to treat these symptoms would be to undo the application of the style to this group, redefine the style so that it applies only to text wrap and ignores all else, and then reapply it.

But that would not be a cure because the style would still be applied to the objects in the group, severing their connection to the other styles that had been applied. If those styles are redefined (for example, if the stroke color for the arrow was made yellow rather than red), the objects in this group would not change. So what's the cure? We'll place the objects into a single frame to which we can apply the object style.

☛ Use the shortcut ⌘-Z/Ctrl-Z to undo the application of the *Text Wrap Maybe* style to the group. Don't undo the grouping, though; the dashed line around the objects should remain when they're selected.

☛ With the group selected, copy it with the shortcut ⌘-C/Ctrl-C. Look at page 11.

☛ Select the small frame in the upper-left corner of page 11.

Paste Into

➡ With that small frame selected, right-click and choose Paste Into, the shortcut for which (⌘-option-V/Ctrl-Alt-V) is similar to that for an ordinary paste. Yes, I know that the group is drastically cropped at the moment. Thus...

➡ Right-click on that frame again and choose Fitting > Fit Frame to Content (or its shortcut: ⌘-option-C/Ctrl-Alt-C).

I do this so often that once I select the destination frame, I hold down the two modifier keys in the shortcuts just mentioned (⌘-option/Ctrl-Alt) and tap V then C.

➡ Apply the *Text Wrap Maybe* object style to that frame. This time, it doesn't contaminate the objects within. Redefining those styles affects the objects, too.

➡ Fine-tune the position of that frame.

Just as with any nested arrangement, double-clicking with the Selection tool allows you to get to the objects within. The first double-click selects the group inside the frame. A second double-click, on the callout for example, selects that frame. Yet another double-click on the callout inserts the text cursor within it. Repeatedly tapping the esc key selects in the other direction.

The first few times I used this method, it felt cumbersome. But as with so many other things, it gets easier with use. And I've had practice! In fact, every figure in this book uses this method.

Lesson D: Combining Paragraph and Object Styles

➡ Open the downloaded document called ***object and paragraph styles.indd***. Fit the spread in the window (⌘-option-0/Ctrl-Alt-0).

As it says, this document is derived from a test file made in preparation for laying out a novel. The objective was to flow in the text as one story with as little cut and paste as possible.

The text that reads "Part One" should be about a third of the way down the page. The words "Chapter One" should automatically be on the next page. We can achieve that by cutting and pasting into multiple frames, but in a book with several sections and many chapters, that would be very tedious.

Setting the First Baseline Offset to Leading for these text frames (using Text Frame Options) means that the first line's baseline will be a predictable distance down the page. If that leading is 28.8 points, that's where that line of text will land. If it's 200 points, that's what we'll get. Text like these words will be in a more or less normal position near the top, but a section header that is alone on a page can be well down the page, not oddly tucked up at the top.

➡ Select the text frame then right-click on the object style named *MainTextFrames* and choose Edit "MainTextFrames"….
➡ Go to the section Text Frame Baseline Options.
➡ Set the First Baseline Offset to Leading. Click OK. You'll see that the section header moved down a bit, but the body copy on the right-hand page moved very little.
➡ Right-click on the paragraph style named *section header*, choose Edit "section header"…. That's the one styling "Part One" at the top of the left-hand page.
➡ In Basic Character Formats, set Leading to a value that puts the section header about 40 percent down the page (maybe 250 points). Click OK.

To ensure that certain paragraphs are always the first element on a page (hint: chapter headers), use the paragraph style Keep Options.

➡ Right-click the paragraph style named *chapter header*, choose Edit "chapter header"….
➡ Go to Keep Options.
➡ Set Start Paragraph to On Next Page. Chapter headers often benefit from Start Paragraph In Next Column, On Next Page, or On Next Odd Numbered Page. Click OK.

Workspaces & Preferences

Frames & Content

Styles, Type & Fonts

Pages & Spreads

Color Management

Find/Change

Long Documents

Output

Project: Promotional Handout

In this project, you will create colorful, two-sided promotional handout from beginning to end.

Lesson A: Create a New Document

We're going to create a cute and colorful single-sheet handout—an A4-sized page, folded in half with a front, back, and inside spread. I nearly always make sketches to work out dimensions and provide direction for my work.

Inside

Covers (back and front)

One side, which we'll call the cover, will have a full-bleed image with integrated text. On its left (the back cover), there will be a text frame with directions and a map to an event. On the other side of this sheet of paper is page 2, the inside. It will also have a full-bleed image and a text frame on the right with event details. Both text frames will have text vertically justified to the center. The margin and column guides will give us a good structure to work with.

This Document's Settings

Start with a Preset

➡ Use the File > New > Document....

➡ At the top of the New Document dialog, choose Print from the listed media. Examine the Blank Document Presets. Click View All Presets to find and choose A4. This is our starting point. On the right, let's refine the choices somewhat:

Customize The Settings

➡ Uncheck Facing Pages, change the orientation to Landscape (horizontal), and set the Units to Centimeters. But wait, there's more.

Workspaces & Preferences

Frames & Content

Styles, Type & Fonts

Pages & Spreads

Color Management

Find/Change

Long Documents

Output

- For Pages, enter 2. But when you type the number 2, ***don't hit*** return/Enter, as that would commit all our settings before we're done.
- For Columns, uptick to 2. If you type the number 2, ***don't hit*** return/Enter. Then set the Gutter to 3 cm.
- Expose the settings for Margins. Be sure that the chain to the right of the four values is intact, then change one of the fields to 1.5 cm. All four should change.

The observant reader will note that each margin is half the column gutter width. When the paper is folded, half the gutter will be on each side, mirroring the margin on the opposite edge.

- Expose the settings for Bleed and Slug. Be sure that the chain to the right of the four values is intact. Click on an up arrow next to one of the fields to increase all the values to 0.3 cm. This extra bit of image space ensures that no white edge shows when this is printed (on larger paper) then trimmed.
- Enable the Preview to see if you've missed anything obvious. When I enabled it, I noticed that I forgot to change the Orientation. When the Preview is active and if the Pages panel is visible, you should see two pages there as well.
- Click Create.

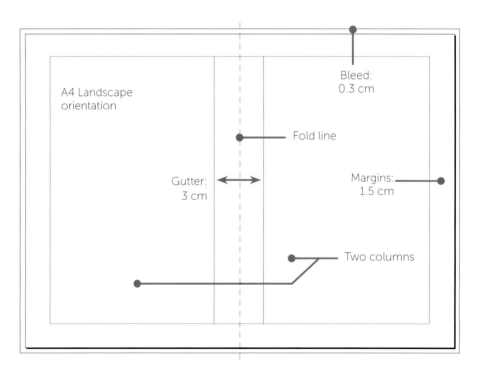

With the exception of the fold line, your document should resemble the figure above.

- Use File > Save As… and give the file a name like *my_handout.indd*. Save it to the downloaded folder ***Project 2 Promotional Handout***.

Lesson B: Preparing for Content

Much of my time in InDesign is spent preparing the document for what's to come. We'll learn more about that in the next chapter, but there are structural and stylistic tasks we can do even in a simple document like this one.

Introduction to Master Pages

There is a fabulous feature to control the geometry and content of pages in documents with between 2 and 200 pages. Every page can be "templated" with a *master page*. Whatever content is on a master page appears on every page that uses that master, whether that content is a logo in the upper-right corner, a running header or footer, or an image.

We'll add two text frames (one in each column) and a placeholder frame for images (see the sketches at the beginning of this chapter) to this document's master.

We will discover, however, that master content is usually not editable (or even selectable) on the pages to which that master is applied. We'll have to learn how to override master items so we can leverage them.

▰ If it isn't already, make the Pages panel visible: Window > Pages.

You will see the two pages we requested when we created this document labeled "1" and "2." In each page icon there's a letter "A" that refers to the master that's applied to these pages. Above the two document pages is a horizontal line, and above that is a page labeled "A-Master."

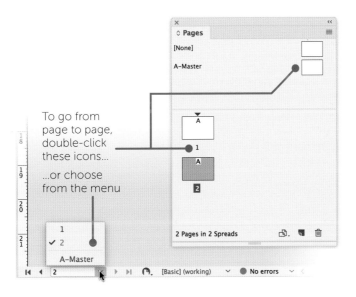

To navigate from page-to-page, I either double-click on the page number or icon in the Pages panel or I use the menu in the lower-left corner of the screen. The latter method, though easily missed, is more reliable. That's because if you single-click in the Pages panel, you may

Workspaces & Preferences

Frames & Content

Styles, Type & Fonts

Pages & Spreads

Color Management

Find/Change

Long Documents

Output

think you're viewing another page, but you have actually only highlighted its icon in the panel. This is important to know now because all the pages here (the master and the two document pages) look exactly alike. Whichever method you use, the Page menu in the lower-left corner of the screen is good to look at to confirm which page you are on. So...

- ➡ Go to the page *A-Master*. Look down and left to confirm that is what's displayed in the Page menu. In the Pages panel, both the name and the icon for that page should be highlighted.
- ➡ Fit the page in the window with the shortcut ⌘-0/Ctrl-0. For a little bit more room around the edges, use ⌘-hyphen/Ctrl-hyphen to zoom out a bit.
- ➡ With the Rectangle Frame tool (tap the letter F on the keyboard), draw a rectangle from the upper-left bleed to the lower-right bleed. Use the Selection tool to fine-tune the position if necessary.
- ➡ With that empty frame selected, create an object style to give it Frame Fitting Options. Open the Object Styles panel menu and choose New Object Style.... Call it *frame filler*. Check that the Preview and Apply Style to Selection boxes are checked at the bottom of the dialog.
- ➡ In the list of Basic Attributes on the left, highlight Frame Fitting Options. Set Fitting to Fill Frame Proportionally so that any image that inhabits this frame will size itself to fill the frame. Set Align From to the center and be sure Crop Amount is set to 0 all the way around.
- ➡ Click OK.

If you go to page 1 or 2 now, that frame will be visible there, but you won't be able to select it. However—and this is huge—when you use the Place command and your cursor is loaded with an image, you will be able to click on a frame on either of those pages and the loaded image will fill it. But we have more prep to do. We need to make sure those images never obscure our text content. So let's create a new layer above the one that holds the image frame, and on it we will create the text frames that will hold our text.

- ➡ Make sure you are on the page *A-Master*. Make the Layers panel visible if it isn't already: Window > Layers. Double-click on the name of *Layer 1*, which is currently this document's only layer. In the dialog that opens, enter the name *images*. Click OK.
- ➡ Open the Layers panel menu and choose New Layer.... Enter the name *text*. Click OK.

It can be challenging to draw a text frame directly over another frame because the Type tool often wants to convert the other frame into a text frame. To make this easier, let's temporarily make the image frame inaccessible.

- ➡ Click once in the small space just to the right of the *images* layer's eye icon. This locks it.
- ➡ With the *text* layer highlighted, use the Type tool to draw a text frame that fills the left column. The text cursor will blink suggestively.

We can use this as an opportunity to build paragraph styles and to set the Text Frame Options appropriately. We'll then copy this frame to the right-hand column. We will not link those two frames together; each will be independent.

- ➡ Save the document: ⌘-S/Ctrl-S.

Build Styles with Placeholder Text

This document won't have much content. Page 2 will have a few paragraphs, most of which will be quite short. The left side of page 1, which is the back cover, will have only two very short paragraphs and a small map image.

We will need only three paragraph styles: for a header, a subhead, and body copy. We'll call them, oh, *header*, *subhead*, and *body* I think. To build them, let's create a little disposable text to see what we're doing.

➡ From the Type menu, choose Show Hidden Characters; they'll help.

➡ Type something like "this is a header," then press the return/Enter key. Then, "this is a subhead," followed by return/Enter. To quickly generate a paragraph to style, right-click and choose Fill with Placeholder Text, and delete all but one short paragraph (a few lines).

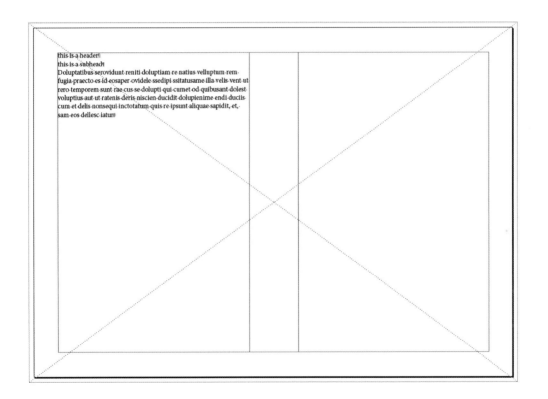

➡ Format the first paragraph (the header): triple-click on it to highlight the whole line, then choose a font, style, and size in the Properties panel or the Control panel. Since I didn't see anything I wanted in the fonts already in my system, I clicked Find More in the Font menu to view Adobe Fonts choices. I chose *Cooper Std Black*, clicking the Activate button to its right in the Font menu (looks like a cloud). I liked 17 points for the Size. In the Paragraph section of the Properties panel, I clicked the More Options button so I could add 0.3 cm for Space After. I chose Center Alignment, too.

➡ Near the top of the Properties panel, check that the Paragraph Styles button is active, then

Workspaces & Preferences

Frames & Content

Styles, Type & Fonts

Pages & Spreads

Color Management

Find/Change

Long Documents

Output

click the Create Style button. Name the style *header*.

➦ Format the second paragraph (the subhead): triple-click on it to highlight the whole line, then choose a font, style, and size in the Properties panel or the Control panel. I chose *Museo Sans 500* at 12 points for the Size with 17 points of Leading and Center Alignment.

➦ Near the top of the Properties panel, click the Create Style button. Name the style *subhead*.

➦ Format the longer third paragraph: quadruple-click on it to highlight the whole thing, then choose a font, style, and size in the Properties panel or the Control panel. I chose and activated *Fairplex Wide OT Book* from Adobe Fonts, then set it at 11 points with 17 points of Leading. I chose Center Justified for Alignment.

➦ Near the top of the Properties panel, click the Create Style button. Name the style *body*.

To get the text in the vertical center of the frame, we have to get to the frame properties.

➦ Press the esc key to select the frame and make the Selection tool active.

➦ In the Control panel, locate Vertical Justification buttons and click the one for Align Center.

Since our silly placeholder text is still in the frame, you can confirm that the text really did move to the vertical center. Check the Paragraph Styles panel to be sure all three styles were created.

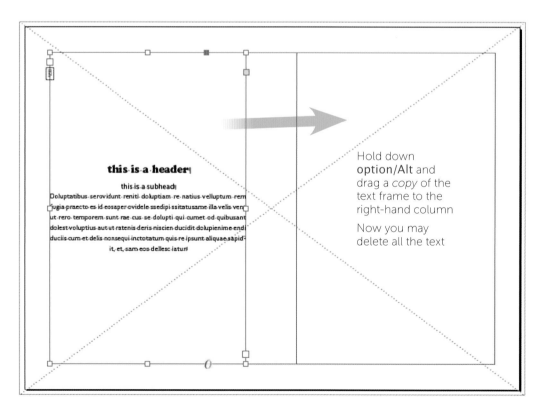

Hold down option/Alt and drag a *copy* of the text frame to the right-hand column

Now you may delete all the text

- ▣ Make a copy of the text frame for the right side of the master page: while holding down the option/alt key, drag the frame to the right side of the page. You'll have a copy!
- ▣ Insert the text cursor into each frame, select all its text, and delete it. It's served its purpose as a stand-in for real text.
- ▣ Congratulations, the master page is prepared! Unlock the *images* layer so that when we have an image it can be flowed into the frame on that layer.

Choose Defaults

- ▣ Go to page 1 by double-clicking on its icon or choosing it from the Page menu (lower left). Be sure both its icon and page number are highlighted in the Pages panel before continuing.
- ▣ With nothing selected (just in case, use the shortcut ⌘-shift-A/Ctrl-Shift-A), highlight the paragraph style called *body*. Although we won't have much text, it's still a good default.
- ▣ Choose the Selection tool from the Tools panel.
- ▣ Save: ⌘-S/Ctrl-S. Let's get this thing finished!

Workspaces & Preferences

Frames & Content

Styles, Type & Fonts

Pages & Spreads

Color Management

Find/Change

Long Documents

Output

Lesson D: Inserting the Text

If you poke around on page 1 with the Selection tool, you will find that the frames we built on the master don't seem to be accessible here. It's true. In order for us to interact with them, they have to be made *local overrides* of the master items. There are two main ways of overriding master objects and we are going to use both. First, the manual approach:

- On page 1, only the left-hand text frame is needed. To make it an override of the master frame, hold down two keys: on a Mac, ⌘ (command) and shift; on Windows, Ctrl and Shift. Then, with the Selection tool, click in the center of that left text frame. It should now be selected.

In case you're curious, it's supposed to be hard to do this so it won't happen accidentally. Very interestingly, as long as we neither move nor resize the frame on page 1, doing so on the master will affect the one on page 1! This is a great time-saver when one has dozens or hundreds of pages.

We need the text for this page. All the text for this document is in a file called ***theText.txt*** in the downloaded folder called ***Project 2 Promotional Handout***.

- Open that document in a text editor like *TextEdit* on a Mac or *Notepad* on Windows. We'll be copying and pasting.
- In the text file, highlight the three lines designated, then copy them. I usually use the ubiquitous shortcut ⌘-C/Ctrl-C.
- Go back to InDesign and your document in progress. Insert your text cursor into the frame you made an override (double-clicking in it with the Selection tool) then paste the text (⌘-V/Ctrl-V).
- Put the cursor in the word "Location" and apply the *header* paragraph style.
- Highlight text in the next lines and apply the *subhead* paragraph style.

We'll add a map a bit later when we're adding other final flourishes.

- Go to page 2: double-click its icon or choose it from the Page menu (lower left). Be sure both its icon and page number are highlighted in the Pages panel before continuing.
- On page 2, only the right-hand text frame is needed. To make it an override of the master frame, hold down those two keys: ⌘ and shift/Ctrl and Shift. Then, with the Selection tool, click in the center of the text frame on the right. It should now be selected. Double-click in it with the Selection tool to get the text cursor blinking in its center.
- Go back to the text file and copy the text from the word "Amazing" all the way down.
- Return to InDesign and paste the text into the frame on page 2.
- Apply the *header* style to the first line.
- Apply *subhead* to the lines "a two-day course," "The Schoolhouse," and "5–6 November 2019." The rest should already have the *body* style applied because we made that our default earlier.

So far, it should look more or less like this:

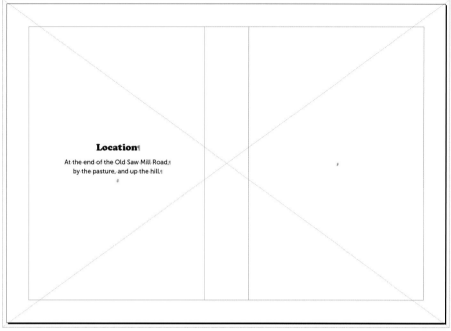

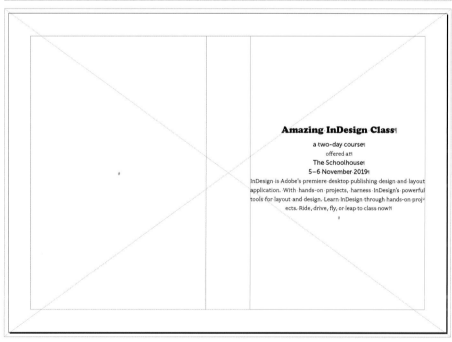

Workspaces & Preferences

Frames & Content

Styles, Type & Fonts

Pages & Spreads

Color Management

Find/Change

Long Documents

Output

Lesson E: Placing Images

When placing images (or text), not pasting as we did earlier, we find ourselves with a cursor loaded with content. Clicking with that cursor creates master overrides and inserts the cursor's content into them.

Placing Images into Placeholder Frames

- Go to page 1: double-click its icon or choose it from the Page menu (lower left). Be sure both its icon and page number are highlighted in the Pages panel before continuing.
- Choose the Selection tool and make sure nothing is currently selected before we attempt to place an image (⌘-shift-A/Ctrl-Shift-A).
- Go to File > Place. In the dialog box, navigate to the downloaded folder called **Project 2 Promotional Handout** and choose the image **yellowLeaping.png**. Click Open.
- With the loaded cursor, carefully click within the perimeter of the large placeholder image frame. A good spot would be in the very middle of the page, between the text columns.

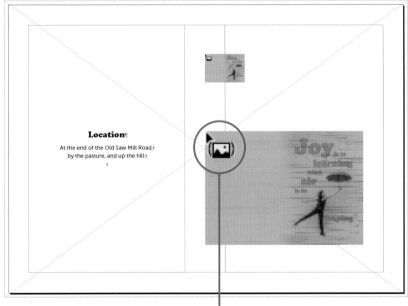

When this part of the cursor looks like an icon in parentheses, InDesign is willing to place the image into the frame under the cursor.

Be sure that's the frame you want!

- Go to page 2. Be sure both its icon and page number are highlighted in the Pages panel.
- Choose the Selection tool and make sure nothing is selected (⌘-shift-A/Ctrl-Shift-A).

The Course

➡ Go to File > Place. Navigate to the **_Project 2 Promotional Handout_** folder and choose the image **_blueLeaping.png_**. Click Open.

➡ With the loaded cursor, carefully click within the perimeter of the placeholder image frame. Again, a good spot would be the very middle of the page.

In both cases, the object style we made ensures that the images fill their frames regardless of their original sizes. There are two more refinements.

➡ Go to page 1 again with nothing selected (⌘-shift-A/Ctrl-Shift-A).

➡ Go to File > Place. Navigate and choose the graphic **_weeMap.ai_**. Click Open.

➡ With the loaded cursor, carefully click in the empty space to the left of the page. Once the map graphic appears, drag it to a position above or below the text.

➡ Finally, highlight the whole line with the word "Location" (triple-click it). Change its Fill color to Paper in either the Properties panel or the Control panel.

➡ Use the Properties panel to redefine the style by clicking the ➡🗐 icon to the right of _header_ (the style's name). Now both headers are the same.

➡ If you were to print this, you'd need to print on both sides of larger paper (like B4), then trim it to the page size (A4).

Workspaces &
Preferences

Frames &
Content

Styles, Type
& Fonts

Pages
& Spreads

Color
Management

Find/Change

Long
Documents

Output

6 Document Structure

Building anything requires a good foundation. So, in this chapter, we examine Layers and Master Pages.

Lesson A: Layers

⭲ Open the downloaded document called ***6 Document Structure.indd***. Go to pages 2 and 3 and fit that spread in the window (⌘-option-0/Ctrl-Alt-0).

We've used the Layers panel a bit in previous exercises and I hope you noticed how layers can help us achieve a few useful goals. Let's examine those and other uses of this feature.

Controlling Stacking Order

⭲ With the Selection tool, select each of the objects on page 3.

Notice that they all have a blue frame edge. Now, select *only* the back-most square (it resembles the InDesign app icon).

⭲ Get the Layers panel: Window > Layers.

Notice that this document has three layers, one of which is locked (please leave it that way for now). Also note that one of the layers, called *Our Stuff*, has a small square to its right that is the same color as the object's frame edge. That square is a proxy, a stand-in, for the selected object.

⭲ Click the small arrow to the left of the layer's name to disclose the objects that inhabit this layer, one of which, labeled "<rectangle>," also has a blue square to its right. For a moment, let's return our attention to the page.

⭲ Right-click on the selected shape on page 3, then choose Arrange > Bring to Front.

Looking back at the Layers panel, you'll see that the object is now at the top of its layer, but has not risen to another one. The Arrange commands control the stacking order *within* a layer only.

⭲ Right-click on the selected shape again and this time choose Arrange > Send Backward.

It's now between the other two shapes in the stacking order. Despite being useful for this exercise, I seldom disclose a layer's content, as the proxy to the right of the layer is often all I need. Feel free to collapse that layer again.

⭲ Drag the blue proxy upward onto the empty square to the right of the layer called *above it all*.

The object is now outlined in red, the color associated with that layer. The object is also in front of the other two on the page and will remain so even if you later use Arrange > Send to Back. That command is currently unavailable since there's nothing else on that layer.

Reminder: To create a new layer, open the Layers panel menu and choose New Layer.... In the dialog that appears, you give the layer a name and choose a color.

Workspaces &
Preferences

Frames &
Content

Styles, Type
& Fonts

Pages
& Spreads

Color
Management

Find/Change

Long
Documents

Output

For Segregating Content

We use layers for more than controlling stacking. Layers are also handy for keeping different kinds of content separated.

➡ To the left of the *above it all* layer, click on the eye icon. That layer's content vanishes. Clicking there again brings it back.

Consider a publication like the teacher's edition of a textbook. It may have content that the student edition does not. That content can be kept on a layer that is hidden when the student edition PDF is generated, and shown when the teacher edition PDF is made.

➡ Double-click on the *above it all* layer's name.

A dialog opens in which you can rename the layer or change its color. You can also set it to be non-printable. Such a layer can be used to house notes to yourself or colleagues without fear that they will be published.

➡ Notice the choice to Lock Layer. Check that box then click OK.

To the left of the layer's name is now a padlock. Clicking that icon or where it would be unlocks or locks a layer, respectively. Why would you lock a layer? Read on.

For Protecting Content

A locked layer's content cannot be selected, therefore it cannot be harmed. I sometimes use layers to hold delicate objects that I don't want to screw up later. In this document, there is a locked layer called *Notes.*

➡ Rather than unlocking the *Notes* layer, toggle its visibility (the eye icon) to see that its content is the beige frame on the left side of page 2 (and the other pages, too).

Reordering Layers

When a layer is created, it appears above the layer that had been highlighted. You may want it below.

➡ Drag the layer *above it all* by its name slowly downward until a line appears below the layer *Our Stuff*, then release the mouse. The *above it all* layer, and its content on every page, is behind the content of every other layer.

➡ Drag it back to the top so its name is not absurd.

Lesson B: Master Pages & Sections

◈ Open the downloaded document called ***6 Document Structure.indd.*** Go to pages 4 and 5 and fit that spread in the window (⌘–option–0/Ctrl–Alt–0).

I am going to expose you to a few mysterious puzzles, then we'll unravel them together. Let's start with that text frame above page 4.

Sections

◈ With the Selection tool, select the frame that appears to have the word "Section" in it. Drag it down onto the page. Surprised?

◈ Double-click it to activate the text cursor in that frame. Try to select just part of the phrase.

Section Markers

You can't select just part of the phrase because there isn't a phrase there; it's just a very special character called a Section Marker, a kind of wild card that gets substituted with text provided elsewhere.

◈ Highlight that text (a triple-click will do it), then delete it so I can show you how to insert a Section Marker.

◈ With your cursor blinking, right-click in the frame and choose Insert Special Character > Markers > Section Marker. That same phrase reappears. Where does it come from?

Look at the Pages panel and note the small inverted triangle above page 4. This denotes the beginning of a section in the document. There is always a triangle above the first page of a document, too.

◈ Double-click the small triangle above the page 4 icon. The Numbering & Section Options dialog opens.

At the top of the dialog is a checkbox that allows the start of a section on this page. Lower in the box is a field that supplies the text that appears when one inserts a Section Marker as you have.

◈ Change the text in the Section Marker field then click OK.

To begin another section elsewhere, right-click on a page icon in the Pages panel and choose Numbering & Section Options. The dialog will open with the Start Section checkbox checked.

> Learn more about sections and how they can affect page numbering by reading "Sections & Numbering" (page 287).

Workspaces & Preferences

Frames & Content

Styles, Type & Fonts

Pages & Spreads

Color Management

Find/Change

Long Documents

Output

Page Numbers

Another special wild card character that almost every document requires is the Current Page Number marker.

➡️ Get your cursor blinking to the right of the section marker in that frame. Use the shortcut shift-Tab to insert a Right-Indent Tab character. The text cursor now blinks at the right side of the frame.

➡️ To insert the next character, right-click in the frame and choose Insert Special Character > Markers > Current Page Number. Please notice to the right of that item is a shortcut.

Most roll their eyes when they see it, assuming they'll never memorize it. But did I mention that almost every document will need these characters? In time, you'll appreciate the fact that you can save time by holding down all three of the main modifier keys (⌘-option-shift on a Mac, or Ctrl-Alt-Shift on Windows) and tapping N.

The frame should look something like this (with hidden characters showing):

As you can anticipate, this would be tedious to do for every page individually. So this frame won't stay here, but we'll move it to a master spread.

"Templates" for Pages and Spreads

Master pages serve as a kind of template for the pages in a document. In the previous project, you used masters to "template" text and image frame options and locations. Here, we'll see a few more features. To see all the masters in a document, you may have to drag the bar that separates master pages from the document pages downward.

The document you're editing has two masters: one called *reg-ular pages* and another called *d-viant pages*. These are not the names that InDesign would supply. The default master is called *A-Master*, which is both boring and uninformative. I give my masters names that indicate what kind of pages they represent, and that amuse me.

➡️ To see what role they can play, select the frame you've been editing then Cut it (as in the command Edit > Cut or the shortcut ⌘-X/Ctrl-X, ***not*** delete).

➡️ Double-click on the name of the master *reg-ular pages* to view it, then use Edit > Paste in Place. The frame will be in the same location on this master spread as it was on the other spread. If that's not where you'd like it, move it! I'd suggest the top margin.

The page number will read "reg." That is, after all, what page you're on. Note this in the bottom corners of the spread as well. Those text frames contain only the current page number marker.

In the Pages panel, double-click the page numbers of different spreads.

In each case, our special frame and those I included on the master show up. Well, on page 2, the section marker is blank. That is because I never supplied any text in the appropriate field in the Numbering & Section Options dialog for the first section. Let's make up for that neglect.

Double-click on the triangle above page 1 to open the Numbering & Section Options dialog. Type something in the Section Marker field, then click OK.

Now every even-numbered page has a message. In fact, this is a fairly decent running header.

Ensure Consistency

Master pages give us consistency of placement and repetitive content, like that running header. Longer documents may have several masters for different kinds of pages. For example, the printed version of this book uses a different master for the first spread of a chapter than it does for pages like this one.

Let's apply a master to a single page, a spread, and then a range of pages.

In the Pages panel, drag the name of the *d-viant* master onto the page 5 icon. The change should be noticeable. "Garish" is a better word for its appearance. If you're not currently viewing that spread, double-click the spread 4–5 page numbers.

To apply the other master, drag the name of the *reg-ular pages* master to the page 5 icon.

Now drag the *d-viant* master's name below the page 4 and 5 icons and to the left or right side of the page numbers. You'll know you're in the right spot when both page icons are outlined. It's a little touchy, so be patient.

When you succeed, undo (⌘–Z/Ctrl–Z).

To apply a master more reliably, right-click somewhere in the Pages panel and choose Apply Master to Pages…. In the dialog box that appears, choose the *d-viant* master from the Apply Master menu. To show that you can supply a range and/or a list of discontiguous pages, type "4-6, 9" into the To Pages field, then click OK. Four pages now have that lovely master applied to them.

When you succeed, undo (⌘–Z/Ctrl–Z).

Workspaces & Preferences

Frames & Content

Styles, Type & Fonts

Pages & Spreads

Color Management

Find/Change

Long Documents

Output

Overriding Master Page Items

We don't always want the perfect consistency that master page items give us. Occasionally, we will want to move, delete, or otherwise alter one instance of that object as it appears on a page. We did this in the previous project when we overrode master objects. Let's examine a more general case, then we'll look at a very special one.

- ⮞ Go to the *reg-ular pages* master by double-clicking its name or choosing it from the Page menu at the bottom left of the application window.
- ⮞ Choose the Ellipse tool (you can tap the L key to get to it). Draw a large ellipse on the right-hand page. Look at the page icons throughout the Pages panel. That ellipse appears on every right-hand page.
- ⮞ Return to pages 4 and 5. Use the Selection tool and try to select the ellipse you see there on the right. You cannot, so don't try too hard.
- ⮞ Now, while holding down the modifier keys ⌘-shift/Ctrl-Shift, click on the ellipse on page 5. Success!

It's now an *override*. But just like the text frames in the handout project, much about this ellipse can still be controlled by the master—*unless you change those attributes here on the override.*

> In the Compendium chapter "Pages & Spreads," please read about master page "Overrides" (page 284).

- ⮞ Experiment by changing an attribute of the ellipse on page 5 (like its fill color), then changing some attributes on the master (like position *and* fill color).
- ⮞ When you're done experimenting, you may delete the ellipse from the master and page 5 if you'd like.

Primary Text Frames & Master Text Frames

Any object can reside on a master page and be seen on the document pages, including text frames. However, there is a very special master text frame, called a primary text frame, that is automatically an override on document pages. And, if there are multiple master text frames, the primary ones will control where long text stories go when flowing from page to page.

In the document you're examining, the beige text frames are primary text frames. You likely noticed one on the *reg-ular pages* master. Let's carefully see how this document's primary text flow works.

- ⮞ Unlock the *Notes* layer in the Layers panel. Also, double-click this layer's name and change the color to a green, perhaps, or at least something that contrasts with beige.
- ⮞ Use the Selection tool to select a beige note frame on a document page like page 4. Try not to move or resize it, please.
- ⮞ You should see that this frame is threaded to the frames like it on other pages.
- ⮞ On the *reg-ular pages* master, select the beige frame. On both the master and document

pages, you'll see a small icon in the upper-left corner of the frame that indicates that it's a primary text frame.

⮑ With the Selection tool, move the frame to a different location on the spread.

You should see the change in the page icons of the Pages panel. Changing the color, shape, or Text Frame Options of that frame would also be apparent on the document pages.

For a little more insight, let's briefly open another document:

⮑ Open the downloaded document called ***PrimaryFramePlay.indd***. It has only one page with an overset primary text frame occupying it.

This document's *header* paragraph style has the Keep Option enabled to begin paragraphs with this style in a next frame. So if we supply more frames, each header will be in its own. Since there's a primary text frame, that's easy to do.

⮑ Go to the Type Preferences. Use ⌘-K/Ctrl-K to get to the preferences, then choose Type on the left.

⮑ Enable Smart Text Reflow and ensure that Delete Empty Pages is also checked. Click OK.

⮑ After a few seconds, more pages should appear. If they don't, it's not your fault: there's a bug that sometimes demands that you reapply the master to the first page. Drag the master's name onto the page 1 icon, wait a few seconds, and then you should see some new pages.

⮑ Go to one of the new pages and highlight and delete all of its text. The page count should diminish by one.

We will leverage this primary frame feature in the upcoming brochure project.

Workspaces & Preferences

Frames & Content

Styles, Type & Fonts

Pages & Spreads

Color Management

Find/Change

Long Documents

Output

Lesson C: Adding, Deleting, and Moving Pages

⮕ Open the downloaded document called *6 Document Structure.indd*.

Insert Pages

⮕ In the Pages panel menu, choose Insert Page....
⮕ Designate *4* for the number of Pages, Insert *After Page 7*, using the Master *reg-ular pages*. Click OK.

You may encounter a bug that slightly misplaces primary text frames that are not entirely within the margins. The easiest way to fix this is to use the Apply Master to Pages... command: choose the *reg-ular pages* master and apply it to the pages just added. Hopefully, this bug will be fixed by the time you read this.

You may close that document.

Page "Shuffling"

When pages are added or moved in a document with spreads ("facing pages"), the other pages "shuffle" in order to keep two pages in each spread, with the first page left alone as a title page.

When this behavior is unwanted, we have to disallow the shuffling for the document's pages. Let's see this behavior, and then see what moving pages is like when it's been disallowed.

⮕ Open the downloaded document called *PageArrangin.indd*.
⮕ We will be moving pages using the Pages panel, so have that ready. For a better use of its space, go to the Pages panel menu and select View Pages > Horizontally.

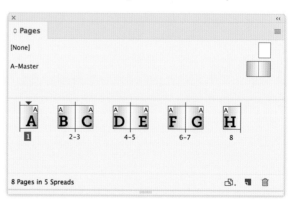

Note the gradient on each page has white nearest the spine and gray toward the outside.

The only content on each page is a text frame with a letter in it.

Notice that page 1 is a right-facing page, and page 8 is a left-facing page. One might assume that moving 1 to the right of 8 would create a spread, but that would be wrong.

The Course

➡ Drag the page 1 icon (with the "A" in it) just to the right of the page 8 icon. When a vertical line appears, release the mouse. The pages shuffle to keep the document's first page, now the one with the "B" in it, as a title page.

➡ Undo (⌘–Z/Ctrl–Z).

➡ Go to the Pages panel menu and note the check mark next to Allow Document Pages to Shuffle. Choosing that item unchecks it, thus disallowing shuffling.

➡ Now drag the first page's icon just to the right of the last page's icon, watching for the various markings that indicate what would happen if you were to release the mouse.

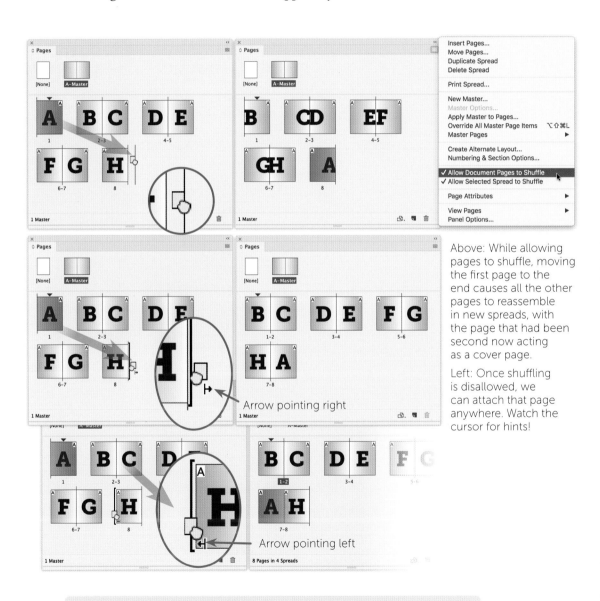

Above: While allowing pages to shuffle, moving the first page to the end causes all the other pages to reassemble in new spreads, with the page that had been second now acting as a cover page.

Left: Once shuffling is disallowed, we can attach that page anywhere. Watch the cursor for hints!

Arrow pointing right

Arrow pointing left

Read more in the Compendium in the section on "Shuffling" (page 289).

Read more in the Compendium in the section on "Shuffling" (page 289).

Workspaces & Preferences

Frames & Content

Styles, Type & Fonts

Pages & Spreads

Color Management

Find/Change

Long Documents

Output

Project: Build a Brochure

"Fortune Favors the Prepared Mind"
—Louis Pasteur
He could have said the same about
a well-prepared document.

Workspaces &
Preferences

Frames &
Content

Styles, Type
& Fonts

Pages
& Spreads

Color
Management

Find/Change

Long
Documents

Output

Lesson A: Configure a New Document

In this project, we are creating a brochure (or booklet, proposal, newsletter—whatever you'd prefer to call it). This document will have front and back covers and six pages of content that will be familiar. Rather than generate styles this time, we'll "steal" them from another document: a style guide. This is a common approach, so you should become familiar with it.

The text is written in Word and has common formatting issues we will review fixing. There are graphics for us to use as decorative elements to accompany three of the six topics discussed in the document. You will be able to choose between two backdrop images for each of the other three topics.

Create a New Document

Although this document will have eight pages by the time we're done, we need only start with one. InDesign will take care of most of the rest!

Start with a Preset

- Go to File > New > Document….
- At the top of the New Document dialog, choose Print from the listed media. Examine the Blank Document Presets. Click View All Presets if necessary to find and choose Letter. Now let's refine the choices somewhat.

Customize the Settings

- Include a provisional name at the top (*Brochure*, *Proposal*, *Newsletter*, etc. are all fine names).
- Choose Inches as the Units.
- Set the number of both Pages and Columns to 1.
- Be sure that Facing Pages is checked.
- Most importantly, be sure that Primary Text Frame is checked. This will create one of those very special frames whose dimensions will match our margins and more. Speaking of which…
- Click the disclosure arrow next to Margins if the fields are not already visible. Disable the chain to the right so you can set asymmetrical margins.
- Set the Inside margin to 4.75 in, and the others to 0.5 in. This will give us 3.25-by-10-inch columns (and primary text frames) on the outside of each spread.

Brochure

Width	Units
8.5 in	Inches

Height	Orientation
11 in	

Pages	Facing Pages
1	✔

Start #	Primary Text Frame
1	✔ *Critical!*

Columns	Column Gutter
1	0.1667 in

⌄ Margins

Top	Bottom
0.5 in	0.5 in

Inside	Outside
4.75 in	0.5 in

⌄ Bleed & Slug

Bleed

Top	Bottom
0.125 in	0.125 in

Inside	Outside
0.125 in	0.125 in

➡ Check again that Primary Text Frame is checked.

➡ Click the disclosure arrow next to Bleed & Slug if necessary to see the fields. Set the Bleed to 0.125 in all the way around. We will have content that we want to go to the edge of the page, thus it needs to go beyond it.

➡ Ensure Primary Text Frame is checked one last time, then click OK.

➡ A very nearly blank page appears. If you use the Selection tool and click within the margins, you will confirm that there's a primary text frame present.

Preferences & Display Performance

To ensure that we see what we must, as well as what we wish, let's check and possibly change some settings.

Preferences

➡ Go to Preferences (⌘-K/Ctrl-K).

➡ First stop: go to the Type preferences. Enable Smart Text Reflow with Delete Empty Pages. This will save us time and trouble when we place the Word doc later. Also, be sure Apply Leading to Entire Paragraphs is checked.

➡ Next: Guides & Pasteboard preferences. To make it as easy as possible to see those primary text frames, go down to the Guide Options section and enable Guides in Back so that the margin guides don't obscure the edges of those frames.

➡ Display Performance preferences are next. This document is small, but may need a couple work sessions. To ensure you see the details, set the Default View to High Quality.

➡ Click OK.

Display Performance

➡ To be sure you are *currently* enjoying a fine view of our document, go to View > Display Performance > High Quality.

Save

If you use either the Save command or Save As... command, you'll be prompted to do the latter since this doc hasn't been saved yet. Nonetheless...

➡ Choose File > Save As... to save this document into the downloaded folder called **_Project 3 Brochure_**. Use the provisional name you chose when you created the document, if you like.

Load & Examine Styles

You have built a number of styles since we started this course. Now it's time to leverage previously built styles.

⮑ Open the document called ***a style guide.indd***. It's in a folder called ***project assets***, which is inside the ***Project 3 Brochure*** folder. There are now two tabs visible in the upper-left of the document window.

This is a single-page document with several objects grouped in the lower part of the page. These objects use the styles we need in our document. Many companies will task someone to keep such a document up-to-date with the styles a team should be using.

⮑ Select the group with the Selection tool. Use the command Edit > Copy or the shortcut ⌘-C/Ctrl-C to copy the group.

⮑ Close the style guide document by clicking the X in its tab (don't close the entire application!). It may prompt you to save the document. If so, you may, but there is no need to do so.

⮑ Back in the brochure doc, simply paste what you copied: go to Edit > Paste or use the shortcut ⌘-V/Ctrl-V.

⮑ Locate and examine the various styles panels (character styles, paragraph styles, and object styles), and you'll see that there are three new styles in each panel.

⮑ Once you have confirmed that the styles have been delivered, dismiss the courier—i.e., delete the group you pasted. The styles remain. Let's inventory them.

Object Styles

⮑ For each of the following object styles, right-click the name (***no*** left-clicking!) and choose to Edit it. You will not actually change anything, but you will see what each style does.

If you left-click any style while there is nothing selected, you will make that style a default. It is not likely that you want any of these to be a default.

Primary text frames   This style does very little, indeed. Most of the Basic Attributes are unchecked, except for Fill and Stroke, which are set to [None]. It is likely we won't even use this one.

graphic   This style has two significant attributes: Size and Position Options and Frame Fitting Options. The first sets a frame to be 4 inches square, vertically centered on the page, and its left edge 4 inches from the left edge of a page. When used on a left-hand page, a frame with this style will be just to the right of the text frame it accompanies. Any image or graphic that is placed in a frame with this style will be Fit Proportionally so we see all of it as large as possible.

big pic   This style also uses Size and Position Options and Frame Fitting Options. The first sets the size of a frame with this style to fill a page (plus bleed), and the latter fills the frame with an image placed within it. This will be used on the right-hand pages. There is also a residual gray fill color I did not remove. Although not helpful, it isn't harmful either.

Paragraph Styles

⮑ For each of the following paragraph styles, right-click the name (***no*** left-clicking!) and

Workspaces & Preferences

Frames & Content

Styles, Type & Fonts

Pages & Spreads

Color Management

Find/Change

Long Documents

Output

choose to Edit it. These styles are similar to the ones we made in chapter 3 because the content we are decorating is similar.

If you left-click any style while there is nothing selected, you will make that style a default. There is one that we need to set as a default: *body copy*.

topic header   The most significant attribute of this style is the Keep Option to Start in Next Column, which in this case is the next text frame. In Indents and Spacing, all three paragraph styles use a slightly unusual Alignment: Away From Spine.

body copy   Not much to see here. The Character Color is middle gray so as to look dark when over white, but to look light when over black or something very dark.

subtopic   Just like in chapter 3, this style is identical to *body copy* except that the first sentence of a paragraph using this paragraph style will use the character style *bold*.

➭ When you are done looking over the paragraph styles, left-click on the one called *body copy* to set it as this document's default.

Character Styles

➭ For each of the following character styles, right-click the name (*no* left-clicking!) and choose to Edit it. These styles are also similar to the ones we made in chapter 3.

proper bold   This does only one thing: applies the *bold* font style if one exists.

proper italic   I'll give you one guess.

just red   This sets the Character Color to, you guessed it, *red* and does nothing else.

➭ When you are done looking over the character styles, be sure none of them are highlighted. Phrased differently, highlight the character style [None].

Layers

Just as we did in the previous project, we are going to use layers to keep the images from obscuring the text by keeping them below the text.

➭ Locate the Layers panel. Double-click the name of the default *Layer 1*. Give it a better name; *main content* will do nicely. Set its color to Red. Since this is where our primary text frames are, their frame edges will now be red.

➭ Use the Layers panel menu and choose New Layer…. Call this one *images*. Set its color to Blue. When you click OK, you'll notice that this new layer is above the first one.

➭ Drag the *images* layer below the *main content* layer. We will be adding content to the images layer shortly, so make sure it's highlighted.

Prepare the Master Spread

We need to add only a few elements to the master spread: two placeholder frames for the images we are going to place and two small text frames with the Current Page Number Marker in them.

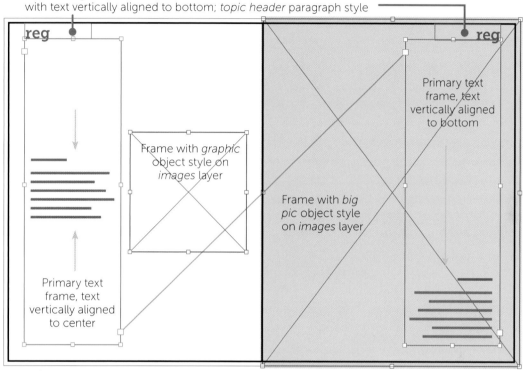

Current Page Number Marker in frames
with text vertically aligned to bottom; *topic header* paragraph style

reg-ular pages master

➦ Right-click on the *A-Master*'s name and choose Master options for "A-Master".... Make the Prefix *reg* and the Name *ular pages*. It will appear as *reg-ular pages* in the Pages panel.

➦ Double-click on that master's (new) name (*reg-ular pages*) to view it.

➦ With nothing selected, make sure the *images* layer is highlighted and below the *main content* layer.

➦ Use the Rectangle Frame tool to quickly draw a small frame in the open area of the left-hand page. Do not be concerned about its size or position because you're about to...

➦ Click on the name of the object style called *graphic*. This style positions and sizes the frame for you!

➦ Draw a small frame in the open area of the right-hand page, then apply the object style *big pic*. The gray that fills the frame will be hidden by the images we'll be placing later.

➦ Use the Selection tool to select the text frame on the left-hand page. Use the Control panel to vertically align the text to center. Since there is no text in that frame, this is an act of trust.

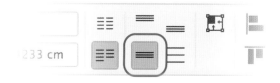

Workspaces &
Preferences

Frames &
Content

Styles, Type
& Fonts

Pages
& Spreads

Color
Management

Find/Change

Long
Documents

Output

- Use the Selection tool to select the text frame on the right-hand page. Use the Control panel to vertically align the text to bottom. Again, you'll have to trust me.

- Switch to the Type tool to create a small text frame. For now, create it anywhere there's room. We will fine-tune its size and position shortly. With the cursor blinking within it, right-click in the frame and choose Insert Special Character > Markers > Current Page Number, or use the shortcut ⌘–option–shift–N/Ctrl–Alt–Shift-N. It should show the master's prefix, *reg*.

- Apply the paragraph style *topic header*. This will cause the page numbers to be the same size and in the same font and color as the first text visible below them. Also, this aligns the page numbers away from the spine.

- Press the esc key to return to the Selection tool so you can move and resize that small frame. Put it at the top-left corner of the primary text frame on the left-hand page. (See the large diagram on the previous page.)

- Use the Control panel to vertically align the text to bottom. The marker should now be at the bottom of its frame.

- Hold down option/Alt and drag that frame to the other page. Be sure to release the mouse before you release the option/Alt key so you'll have a copy of that small frame on the other page. Fine-tune its position to the top-right corner of the text frame on that page.

- Congratulations! The master is ready. Go back to page 1.

Lesson B: Place a Word Document

We will flow in the content for this brochure from a Word doc that is identical to one we placed before. That means we'll be cleaning up the same problems we did earlier, and as we likely will many times in the future when we are sent badly formatted text.

Placing the Word Doc

- ⮑ Be sure nothing is selected (⌘-shift-A/Ctrl-Shift-A) and that *body copy* is highlighted in the Paragraph Styles panel.
- ⮑ In the Type menu, choose Show Hidden Characters if it isn't already chosen.
- ⮑ Go to the File menu and choose Place….
- ⮑ At the bottom of the Place dialog box, check the box labeled Show Import Options.
- ⮑ Navigate to the folder called ***project assets*** and select the file called ***Content.docx***. Highlight it and click Open, or simply double-click the name. You'll now see the Import Options.

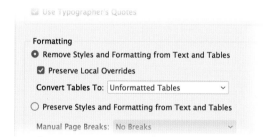

- ⮑ In the Formatting part of the Import Options dialog, select Remove Styles and Formatting from Text and Tables and Preserve Local Overrides. Click OK.

We need to Preserve Local Overrides to maintain character overrides like italics and bold. Once we use character styles to protect the overrides we want, we'll have to clear the bizarre ones we don't want.

- ⮑ When your cursor is loaded, click in the middle of the slender text frame on page 1.

That frame will fill with text, which hopefully looks mostly like your definition of *body copy*. After a few seconds, several more pages should appear to accommodate the remaining text.

- ⮑ Have a look at those new pages. Yes, we have a little work to do yet.

Workspaces & Preferences

Frames & Content

Styles, Type & Fonts

Pages & Spreads

Color Management

Find/Change

Long Documents

Output

Lesson C: Clean Up the Formatting

Whenever possible, I try to use Find/Change to help me format text. This is no exception. We have bolds and italics that aren't yet protected by character styles. We will find those and apply the correct styles to them, then clear the remaining overrides. After that, a couple more searches will allow us to format the rest.

Find/Change to the Rescue

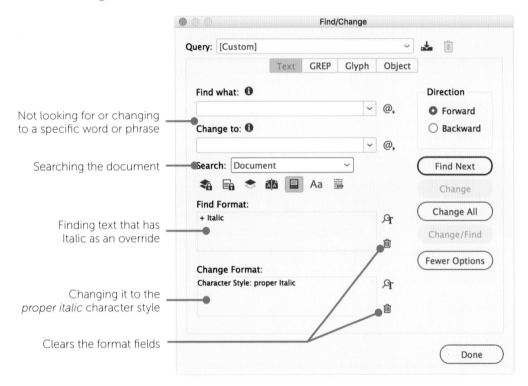

Not looking for or changing to a specific word or phrase

Searching the document

Finding text that has Italic as an override

Changing it to the *proper italic* character style

Clears the format fields

➡ Summon the Find/Change dialog with ⌘-F/Ctrl-F. Check the scope of the search in the menu labeled Search. In this exercise we can use Document or Story.

Be careful if you highlight any text because that often changes the scope of the search to only the highlighted text!

➡ Click in the rectangle below the words Find Format. The Find Format Settings dialog box opens.

➡ Since we are looking for text that does not yet have a character style applied, but is italicized, go to the Basic Character Formats section of the Find Format Settings dialog. In the Font Style menu, choose Italic, then click OK.

➡ Click in the rectangle below the words Change Format. The Change Format Settings dialog box opens.

The Course

This time, we are choosing a style: the one we're applying to italicized text to make sure it stays that way.

- In the Character Style menu of that dialog, choose my italic, then click OK.
- Click Change All. To confirm that something happened, insert the cursor in italicized text. The Character Styles panel should show you that the *proper italic* style is applied now.
- Use the small trash can icons to clear both the Find Format and Change Format fields.

Now we're ready to do the same thing to bold text in the story.

- Click in the rectangle below the words Find Format. The Find Format Settings dialog opens.
- In the Basic Character Formats section choose Bold from the Font Style menu, then click OK.
- Click in the rectangle below the words Change Format. The Change Format Settings dialog box opens.
- Since text doesn't have to be bold to catch the eye, in the Character Style menu of that dialog, choose just red then click OK.
- Click Change All. For the moment, text that was bold is now both bold and red. That will change shortly.

Now it's time to clear out the other overrides that came over with the Word doc.

- Select all the text in the story; five clicks with the Type tool or ⌘-A/Ctrl-A will do that. At the bottom of the Paragraph Styles panel, click the Clear Overrides button: ¶⚹
- In this story's text, there are many extraneous paragraph returns. Go back to the Find/Change dialog and in the Query menu, choose Multiple Return to Single Return, then click Change All. You'll find there were about 29 extra returns.

Note that this is a grep query. Another one is to follow.

- In the Query menu, choose Multiple Space to Single Space. This search text looks even more strange and daunting. Nonetheless, click Change All to get rid of over 50 useless spaces.

This preserves the good stuff and discards the rest. You may notice that this space-saving has removed a page or two in the Pages panel. That's Smart Text Reflow at work. When we need more pages, and we will soon, they'll be there. Now it's time to apply the other styles.

- Just below the Query menu, click on Text to get back to more ordinary text searches.

Notice the markup in the text (e.g., "<h1>") that the writer inserted so we can locate and format headers and subheads.

- Make sure the previous format searches have been cleared (use the trash can icons).
- In the top Find what field, type "<h1>" (there are six instances of this in the text).
- Click in the rectangle below the words Change Format. The Change Format Settings dialog box opens.
- In the Paragraph Style menu of that dialog, choose topic header, then click OK.
- Click Change All. We now have six pages, one for each topic.

Workspaces & Preferences

Frames & Content

Styles, Type & Fonts

Pages & Spreads

Color Management

Find/Change

Long Documents

Output

Each paragraph that begins with "<h1>" is now formatted correctly, so we no longer need that code. It's easy to get rid of it:

- 🖘 Leave the Find what field alone, but clear the Change Format field by clicking on its trash can icon.
- 🖘 Click Change All.

Since there was nothing in the Change to nor the Change Format field, InDesign assumes you are replacing text with literally *nothing*. Now for the subtopics.

- 🖘 In the Find what field, type "<sub>" (notice that these are scattered about in the text).
- 🖘 Click in the rectangle below the words Change Format.
- 🖘 In the Paragraph Style menu of the Change Format Settings dialog, choose subtopic, then click OK.
- 🖘 Click Change All.

Each paragraph that begins with "<sub>" is now formatted correctly. But we no longer need that code prefix, either:

- 🖘 Leave the Find what field alone, but clear the Change Format field by clicking on its trash can icon.
- 🖘 Click Change All.

Notice that the work we did on the master, like the vertical alignment to center (on the left) and to bottom (on the right), is apparent. If we forgot to do that earlier, we can go to the master now and apply those settings to those frames. Then, on each page that uses that master, the text will go where it's supposed to.

The Course

Lesson D: Insert Cover Pages

For the covers, we need pages at the beginning and end of the document that don't use the *reg-ular pages* master. We want them to be blank until we place the appropriate image on each. That's what the *[None]* master is for.

When we add a new page to the beginning, pages that were on the left will be on the right, and vice versa. Sadly, that means the primary text frames may be on the wrong sides of their pages. We will have to fix that if it happens—luckily, the fix is easy.

Add a Front Cover at the Beginning

➲ Locate the Pages panel. Right-click in the lower section or use the Pages panel to choose Insert Pages....

➲ In the Insert menu, choose At Start of Document. For the Master, choose [None]. Click OK.

You're now looking at the new first page. We will be ignoring those margins. It won't matter what layer is active, either, as there will be no other content but the images we are about to place.

➲ Be sure nothing is selected (⌘–shift–A/Ctrl–Shift–A) then go to the File menu and choose Place.... Uncheck Show Import Options. We won't need them for the rest of this project.

➲ Navigate to the ***project assets*** folder and double-click on the file called ***frontCover.pdf***.

➲ With the loaded cursor, click near the upper-left corner of the page. To perfectly center the image, use the Properties panel or the Control panel. Set the Align menu to Align to Page. Then click on the buttons called Align Vertical Centers and Align Horizontal Centers (the order in which you click them doesn't matter).

Workspaces & Preferences

Frames & Content

Styles, Type & Fonts

Pages & Spreads

Color Management

Find/Change

Long Documents

Output

Add a Back Cover at the End

➦ Locate the Pages panel. Right-click in the lower section or use the Pages panel menu to choose Insert Pages….

➦ In the Insert menu, choose At End of Document. For the Master, choose [None]. Click OK.

You're now looking at the new last page. We will be ignoring those margins. And just like with the front cover, it won't matter what layer is active because the only content will be the images we are about to place.

➦ Be sure nothing is selected (⌘-shift-A/Ctrl-Shift-A) then go to the File menu and choose Place….

➦ Navigate to the ***project assets*** folder and double-click on the file called ***backCover.pdf***.

➦ With the loaded cursor, click near the upper-left corner of the page. To center the image, use the Properties panel or the Control panel as described for the front cover.

Remind Pages of Their Masters

If you look at the pages in between our new ones, the text frames or the text may be dislocated. Depending on your version of InDesign, a bug may afflict those primary text frames.

The text on a left (even-numbered) page should be aligned to center vertically, and the frame should be within the margins well away from the spine. If either of these things is not so, use the following fix. Heck, this will do no harm even if everything is OK, so why not try it?

➦ Right-click anywhere in the Pages panel and choose Apply Master to Pages….

➦ Set Apply Master to reg-ular pages. Set To Pages to 2-7. Click OK. The masters and the document pages now understand each other again.

Lesson E: Place Images and Graphics

We are about to place six images. For each of the left-hand pages, I've built only one graphic. However, for each of the right-hand pages, I've supplied two images between which to choose. Let's do this methodically. We'll load one image at a time and place it in the appropriate frame before moving to the next one. It is possible to load multiple images at once, but we need to make decisions about composition as we go.

The Steps

First, let's go over the steps we'll need to follow to place each image. In each case, be sure you're looking at the correct spread.

- ⮕ Be sure nothing is selected (⌘–shift-A/Ctrl-Shift-A) then go to the File menu and choose Place…. Navigate to the **project assets** folder and double-click on the file you need. ′
- ⮕ With the loaded cursor, click in the heart (not on the edge) of the appropriate placeholder frame. Even though you cannot select it, you will be able to place images into it.
- ⮕ For the large images, you will have to use the Content Grabber to recompose and achieve the desired framing. Below, I show framing that will provide a good background for the text. Hold the Shift key to prevent moving the image up or down while moving it left or right within its frame.

The Images

For the square frame on page 2, use **basic shapes.ai** to accompany the topic *Drawing Basic Shapes*.

For the large frame on page 3, choose either of the following images to accompany the topic *Layers*:

or

layers1.psd　　　　　　　　　　　　　*layers2.psd*

Workspaces & Preferences

Frames & Content

Styles, Type & Fonts

Pages & Spreads

Color Management

Find/Change

Long Documents

Output

For the square frame on page 4, use **styles.pdf** to accompany the topic *Styles*.

For the large frame on page 5, choose either of the following images to accompany the topic *Pages & Masters*:

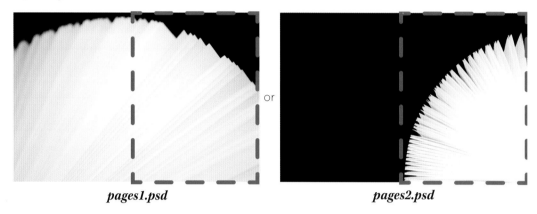

pages1.psd   *pages2.psd*

For the square frame on page 6, use **text frame options.ai** to accompany the topic *Text Frame Options*.

For the large frame on page 7, choose either of the following images to accompany the topic *Find/Change*:

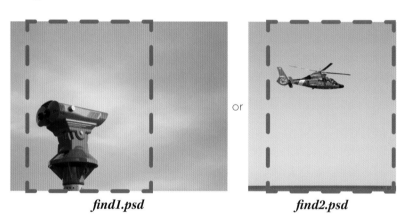

find1.psd   *find2.psd*

When completed, the document should something like this...

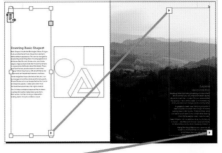

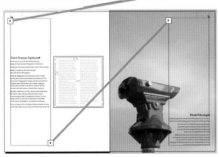

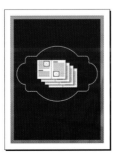

Workspaces & Preferences

Frames & Content

Styles, Type & Fonts

Pages & Spreads

Color Management

Find/Change

Long Documents

Output

7 Long Documents

When the scale of the document favors a table of contents, you'll need these features.

This chapter's exercises allow you to experiment with most of the concepts explored more deeply in the Compendium chapter "**Long Documents**," which I suggest you read. We will examine Tables of Contents, cross-references, Text Variables, the full power of Find/Change, and, finally, combining documents in an InDesign Book document.

Lesson A: Tables of Contents

You'll note that the table of contents example given in the Compendium is a bit different than this one. Studying both should give you insight into this feature.

- Open the downloaded document called *7 Long Documents.indd*. Go to pages 2 and 3 and fit that spread in the window (⌘-option-0/Ctrl-Alt-0).

Building a Dummy TOC

On that spread, you'll see a fake table of contents with paragraph styles applied to its title and its three levels of entries. You can find those styles in a folder called *Styles for TOC* in the Paragraph Styles panel.

Before I build an actual table of contents (TOC), I build a dummy like this. Before I can do that, I have to be familiar with the structure of the text for which the TOC will be made. The content for which we'll build our TOC is on the last 10 pages or so of the same document.

- Look at the structure and headings in the text on pages 10–20 of the document *7 Long Documents.indd*. You should discover that there are three levels of headers and the paragraph styles they use are called *h1*, *h2*, and *h3*. Thus, the fake TOC is structured appropriately.

Requires a Commitment to Styles-Use

For InDesign to generate a TOC for us, it needs paragraph styles to find. The text that uses a certain style becomes an entry in our table of contents and can be styled there any way we like.

But for this to work at all, we need to use styles for the text InDesign should find and for the TOC itself.

Generating a TOC

Our table of contents will go into the frame waiting for it on page 3.

- Select the frame on page 3 with the Selection tool and confirm (with either the Properties panel or the Control panel) that it has two columns.

Our TOC entry for the article's title will span across both of them. The other entries will be balanced across the two columns.

- Choose Layout > Table of Contents…, and a large dialog box will open. If a button on the right reads More Options, click it.

The dialog box has four sections. Almost all of our work is done in the middle two (Styles in Table of Contents and Style); however, we'll start near the top.

Workspaces & Preferences

Frames & Content

Styles, Type & Fonts

Pages & Spreads

Color Management

Find/Change

Long Documents

Output

▶ Choose a Title for the table of contents. I'm usually boring and use "Contents."

▶ To the right of the Title field is the first menu for choosing a Style to decorate the TOC. For this TOC's title, choose the paragraph style called the TOC title. Pretty subtle, eh?

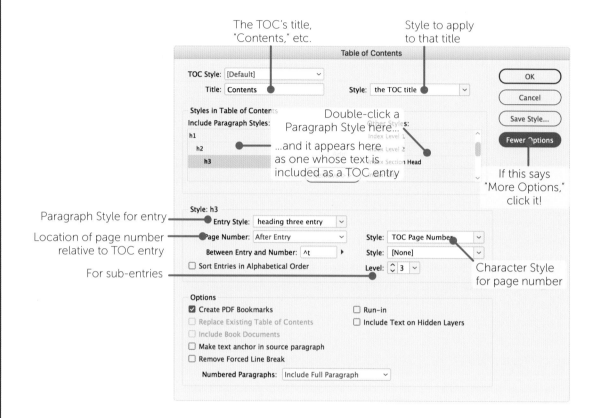

The process becomes a little trickier now. We must choose the styles that InDesign trawls for to make TOC entries *and* we must choose styles with which to decorate those entries. In the section called Styles in Table of Contents are two boxes. The first, Include Paragraph Styles, is initially empty. The second, Other Styles, is a list of all the paragraph styles in the document, from which we choose those that go to the first box.

▶ In Other Styles, double-click on the style h1. This gives us the same result as highlighting it and clicking the Add button, but much faster. The style h1 is now in the Include Paragraph Styles list. We need two more.

▶ In Other Styles, double-click on the styles h2 and h3 in that order.

InDesign assumes, rightly this time, that there's a hierarchy to these styles.

▶ Take a quick peek toward the bottom of the next section of the dialog at the item called Level. With the h3 style highlighted above, Level shows 3. Highlight h2 then h1 and note that the level changes and the name of the dialog's second section changes subtly, too: Style: h3 when the h3 is highlighted, for example.

Now we'll highlight each entry in the Include Paragraph Styles list and configure the Style section for it. Do this slowly; it's too easy to forget something.

- ⮕ Highlight h1 in the Include Paragraph Styles list.
- ⮕ Choose heading one entry from the Entry Style menu.
- ⮕ We can leave the Page Number menu alone since it correctly shows the location of the page number as After Entry. However, just to the right of that, there is Style menu from which we need to choose a character style for the page number. Choose TOC Page Number from the Page Number Style menu.
- ⮕ Confirm that Level is set to 1.

The Between Entry and Number field contains ^t. That means a tab character, which is also what we want this time since the TOC's paragraph styles include tab stop positions and leader characters defined.

- ⮕ Highlight h2 in the Include Paragraph Styles list.
- ⮕ Choose heading two entry from the Entry Style menu.
- ⮕ Leave the Page Number set to After Entry, but choose TOC Page Number from the Page Number Style menu.
- ⮕ Confirm that Level is set to 2. One more...
- ⮕ Highlight h3 in the Include Paragraph Styles list.
- ⮕ Choose heading three entry from the Entry Style menu.
- ⮕ Leave the Page Number set to After Entry, but choose TOC Page Number from the Page Number Style menu.
- ⮕ Confirm that Level is set to 3.

Note: Among the four buttons on the right is Save Style.... This creates a preset called a TOC Style so you don't have to configure this whole dialog box from nothing for every new document. If you create tables of contents for similarly structured documents, you will want this feature. Also, InDesign's ePub (electronic book) export uses TOC Styles to create the TOC we use on e-readers like Kindle or iPad. We have no need to make a TOC Style for this exercise.

- ⮕ Click OK. Your cursor will become a loaded text cursor.
- ⮕ Click somewhere in the midst of the text frame on page 3. You've got a table of contents!

Updating a TOC

Supposedly, we make our tables of contents when a document is complete. But there is always a last-minute change.

- ⮕ Note that the first entry in our new TOC says "History of printing"—someone forgot to capitalize the "p."
- ⮕ Go to page 10 and change the article's title to "History of Printing," or whatever you like.
- ⮕ Return to page 3 and insert the text cursor anywhere within the TOC.

Workspaces & Preferences

Frames & Content

Styles, Type & Fonts

Pages & Spreads

Color Management

Find/Change

Long Documents

Output

➡ Go to the Layout menu and choose Update Table of Contents. Your edit is now exhibited in the TOC.

Contents

The Wild History of Printing 10

Stencil 10
Seals 10
Stone and bronze blocks 10
Woodblock printing (200 AD) 10
   In the Sinosphere 10
   Impact of woodblock printing 11
   In India 12
   In Europe 12
Movable type (1041) 13
   Ceramic movable type 13
   Wooden movable type 13
   Metal movable type 13
   Impact of movable type in the Sinosphere 13
   Controversy 14
European movable type (1453) 14
   Flat-bed printing press 15
   Printing houses in Europe 15
Intaglio 16
Lithography (1796) 16

Color printing 16
Offset press (1870s) 17
Screenprinting (1907) 17
Flexography 17
Photocopier (1960s) 17
Dot matrix printer (1968) 17
Thermal printer 17
Laser printer (1969) 18
Inkjet printer 18
Dye-sublimation printer 18
Digital press (1993) 18
Frescography (1998) 18
3D printing 18
Technological developments 19
   Woodcut 19
   Engraving 19
   Etching 19
   Halftoning 19
   Xerography 20

The Course

Lesson B: Cross References

To learn more about this, see "Cross References" (page 328). Could you hear the author's geeky chuckle as you read that? That text is, obviously, a cross reference and this book uses them liberally (and sometimes comically). But seriously, there is more to be learned about cross references in the Compendium.

➡ In the downloaded document called *7 Long Documents.indd*, go to pages 4 and 5 and fit that spread in the window (⌘-option-0/Ctrl-Alt-0).

Requires a Commitment to Styles-Use

The most common way to generate an automatic cross-reference is similar to how we create tables of contents: we refer to text using a particular paragraph style. In this exercise, we'll make a reference to the caption below the image on page 4. It uses a paragraph style call *figure caption* and uses the Bullets & Numbering feature to number the paragraph. The string "Figure 1." is the paragraph number to which we'll refer.

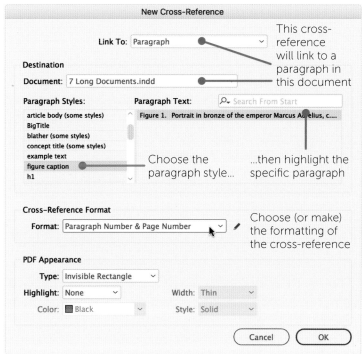

Figure 1. Portrait in bronze of the emperor Marcus Aurelius, *c.* AD 161

➡ Insert the text cursor after the text "See," about halfway down the frame on page 4. InDesign will write the rest with our direction.

➡ Choose Type > Hyperlinks & Cross-References > Insert Cross-Reference… summoning

Workspaces & Preferences

Frames & Content

Styles, Type & Fonts

Pages & Spreads

Color Management

Find/Change

Long Documents

Output

yet another large dialog box to configure. Alternately, you can use the Cross References panel menu (go to Window > Type & Tables > Cross-References to get the panel).

- ➡ InDesign will default to linking the reference to an entire paragraph in the document you're currently editing. Note that you can create a reference to text in other open documents as well.
- ➡ In the Paragraph Styles list highlight figure caption. Each use of that style will now be listed in the Paragraph Text box. Yes, in this case, only one. Highlight it if it isn't already.
- ➡ In Cross-Reference Format, choose Paragraph Number & Page Number. If you can see where you inserted the cursor, InDesign is showing a preview. Try other choices for formatting.
- ➡ Click OK and you've got a cross reference.
- ➡ The image and caption are grouped. Use the Selection tool to move that group to page 5. Unlike with TOCs, the page number in a cross reference changes instantly.

If you experiment, you'll see that Full Paragraph means the Paragraph Text and the Paragraph Number (if there is one). Making your own formatting is possible, too. See "Building a Cross Reference" (page 328). Did you catch that? I did it again.

Referencing Arbitrary Text

Sometimes you may wish to refer to a word or phrase rather than an entire paragraph. In that case, we create Text Anchors that we can choose in the New Cross-Reference dialog instead of paragraphs.

- ➡ Highlight the bolder text in the frame on page 5.
- ➡ Get the Hyperlinks panel: Window > Interactive > Hyperlinks.
- ➡ In the Hyperlinks panel menu, choose New Hyperlink Destination.
- ➡ Set the Type to Text Anchor and give a concise Name that might be used as the cross-reference text. Click OK. Now, there is a way to refer to that bit of text.
- ➡ Insert the text cursor next to the text "Also See."

The Course

➡ Choose Type > Hyperlinks & Cross-References > Insert Cross-Reference....
➡ Set Link To to Text Anchor.

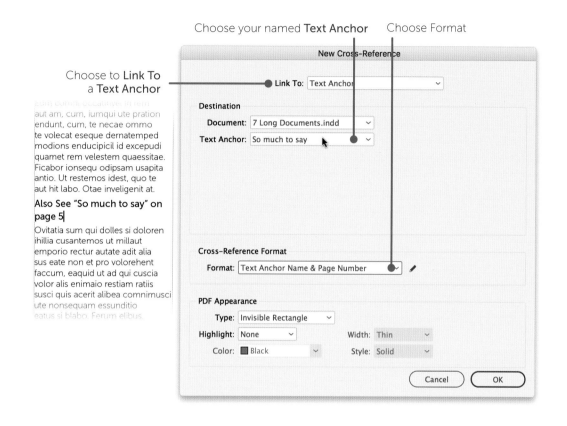

Choose your named **Text Anchor**   Choose Format

Choose to **Link To**
a **Text Anchor**

➡ Choose the Text Anchor you created.
➡ Choose the Format you'd like. When the text content of the anchor is too long, I usually choose the Text Anchor Name to go with the Page Number.
➡ Click OK and you've got another cross reference.

Workspaces &
Preferences

Frames &
Content

Styles, Type
& Fonts

Pages
& Spreads

Color
Management

Find/Change

Long
Documents

Output

Lesson C: Text Variables

Text Variables are a third way to grab content being used by styles. Other text can be generated, too, like dates and document names.

> Discover more intricacies in the Compendium by reading "Text Variables" (page 325).

- ➡ In the downloaded document called *7 Long Documents.indd*, go to pages 6 and 7 and fit that spread in the window (⌘-option-0/Ctrl-Alt-0).
- ➡ Insert the text cursor just below the last line of text on page 6.
- ➡ Choose Type > Text Variables > Define….
- ➡ Click the New… button. You should see this dialog box. Configure it like this:

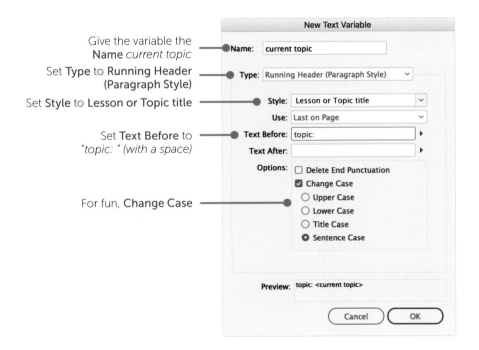

Give the variable the **Name** *current topic*

Set **Type** to **Running Header (Paragraph Style)**

Set **Style** to **Lesson or Topic title**

Set **Text Before** to *"topic: " (with a space)*

For fun, **Change Case**

- ➡ Click OK, then in the first dialog box we saw, click the Insert button followed by the Done button.
- ➡ Notice that the variable draws content from the blue text in the beige frame, which uses the *Lesson or Topic title* style, but is itself formatted like the text around it. Test this idea…
- ➡ Go to page 4 and insert the cursor at the bottom of the frame there.
- ➡ Choose Type > Text Variables > Insert Variable > current topic (or whatever name you chose to give it). It again adapts to the style applied to the paragraph where it was inserted.
- ➡ Go back to pages 6 and 7. Choose Type > Text Variables > Define… then double-click on Modification Date in the list of variables.

The Course

You'll see code used to assemble a date and time. The small arrow to the right of the Date For-mat field is where you access those bits. You may also type what you like in that field. I added the comma, spaces, and colons, for example.

📑 Remove "h:mm aa" from the Date Format field. Insert the cursor where it was, then use the small arrow to the right choosing Year > Era.

Someone at Adobe had a sense of humor: there aren't that many InDesign documents modi-fied more than two thousand years ago.

📑 To shorten the year to two digits, replace "yyyy" with "yy." Experiment!
📑 Click OK if you like your experiments, or Cancel if you don't. Then click the Done button.

Update Display Bug
There's a bug. At the moment, a text variable in the larger frame is telling us what's written in the frame at the top of the page.

📑 Change the text in the frame at the top of page 6. The variable doesn't *appear* to change, but it has!
📑 Either zoom in and out or go to another page and return. The "redraw" of page 6 visually updates the variable. If the text and the variable had been in the same frame, the change would have been instantaneous.

Workspaces & Preferences

Frames & Content

Styles, Type & Fonts

Pages & Spreads

Color Management

Find/Change

Long Documents

Output

Lesson D: Find/Change Turned Up to 11

Find/Change is such an important time saver in InDesign that I dedicated an entire chapter of the Compendium to it. There you will find the following examples reiterated, along with some other examples as well. I also provide some additional resources, especially for grep searches.

➡ In the downloaded document called *7 Long Documents.indd*, go to pages 8 and 9 and fit that spread in the window (⌘-option-0/Ctrl-Alt-0).

GREP: Finding Patterns

Long ago, when I had the honor of running the Seattle InDesign User Group (the world's first!), I was given the list of the approximately 800 members it had at the time. Like the first list of names on page 9, the list I had was not written with last names first nor was it alphabetized. I knew of a fast way to sort the names alphabetically once they were formatted correctly, but I had to get the last names, or surnames, first. So I did my first GREP Find/Change.

➡ Get the text cursor blinking anywhere in the first text frame on page 9. This should set the scope of the search to that story.

➡ Summon the Find/Change window: Edit > Find/Change or ⌘-F/Ctrl-F. Click the GREP tab, then be sure that the Search menu (about halfway down) is set to Story.

There is a description of our query's logic on page 8. In short, we need a way to bring the last chunk of letters in each paragraph (presumably a surname) to the beginning of the paragraph and insert a comma after that chunk. Delimiting "chunks" in the GREP Find What field is done with parentheses. To move those chunks around in the Change To field requires us to reference them by the order in which they're found ("$1" for the first chunk, "$2" for the second, etc.). Thus:

➡ In the Find What field, carefully type: (.+) (.+)

See page 8 (and the Compendium) for a translation of that and…

➡ In the Change To field, carefully type: $2, $1

➡ Click the Change All button.

Feels pretty good, eh? Recall that I had 50 times as many names suddenly formatted properly. That's when I realized I wanted to get to know grep better.

To sort the list, we'll use a *script*. Scripts are bits of programming, most often in JavaScript, that extend what InDesign can do. Although I am not going to cover JavaScript scripting in this book, there are many resources for those interested in learning that skill. A web search for "InDesign scripting" will yield the best ones quickly.

But InDesign comes with some sample scripts that come in handy once in a while. We'll use the one to sort paragraphs alphabetically.

Save the document (⌘-S/Ctrl-S).

A script may perform many operations, possibly hundreds. Undoing those can be time-consuming. So I always save before using a script so that, if it fails me, I can use File > Revert to get back to the last saved state quickly.

Get the Scripts panel: Window > Utilities > Scripts. In that panel, you'll see two folders: *Application* and *User*.

Click the disclosure arrow next to *Application*, then the one next to *Samples*, then, finally, the one next to *Javascript*. To see the long list of scripts, you may wish to make the panel taller.

Highlight all the text in the frame that you just reformatted. Five clicks or ⌘-A/Ctrl-A will do that.

Far down the list of scripts, locate and double-click on the script called *SortParagraphs.jsx*.

In the dialog box that opens, you can choose the option to Ignore Formatting (faster). The style applied to those names won't be lost.

Find/Change Glyphs

Many fonts come with more glyphs than some users realize. There may be many glyphs of a particular character (a handwriting font may have many versions of an "e," for example). There might also be ornaments and swashes. But how do we type them? In InDesign, we look in the Glyphs panel, find the glyph we want, then double-click it. It is then inserted where our cursor has been blinking.

But there's another feature that involves the Glyphs panel and glyphs in general: finding one glyph and replacing it with another.

In the second text frame on page 9, select (highlight) one of the bullet glyphs, but not the space that follows it.

Right-click and choose Load Selected Glyph in Find. When you do so, Find/Change opens in its Glyphs tab with a bullet shown in the Find Glyph window.

Click elsewhere in that frame with the Type tool so that text is no longer highlighted, but the story can still be targeted for the search.

Get the Glyphs panel: Type > Glyphs. I'd like to choose an ornament from a font that has some from which to choose.

The Glyphs panel has a Show menu that limits which characters you are shown. The font currently in use does not possess any ornaments, or that would be a choice in the Show menu.

Workspaces & Preferences

Frames & Content

Styles, Type & Fonts

Pages & Spreads

Color Management

Find/Change

Long Documents

Output

➦ At the bottom of the Glyphs panel, choose a different font (I will choose *Kepler Std*) then check the Show menu. If Ornaments is listed, choose it.

It may be hard to see in longer lists. Alternately, you can choose a font that contains *nothing but* ornaments, like the classic *Zapf Dingbats*.

Choose font and limit what's shown (if necessary)

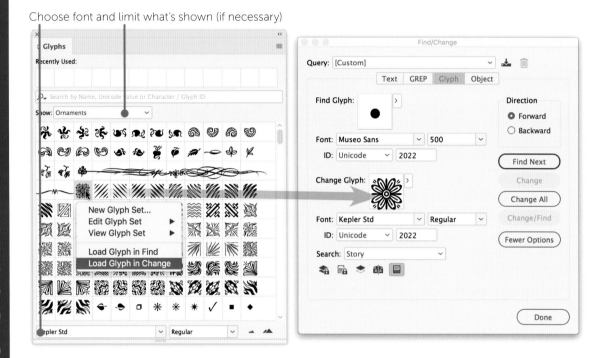

➦ Highlight a glyph that might make a fun replacement for a simple bullet.

➦ Right-click it and choose Load Glyph in Change.

➦ Take a look at the Find/Change window and make sure the Search menu in Find/Change is set to Story, then click the Change All button. You should now be enjoying your new, fancy bullets.

Find/Change Object Formatting

Optimally, objects, like the shapes we draw in InDesign, will be formatted with object styles. Sometimes we forget to use them, or sometimes an object gets disassociated from its style. So, for some reason, we can be left with many objects whose appearance we'd like to change quickly.

If the objects to be changed have some attribute(s) they share with each other, but that are not shared with anything else in the document, we can use Find/Change. This is the case for the objects on the right side of page 9. They all have a 5-point stroke weight and nothing else in the document does.

➦ Be sure nothing is selected (⌘–shift–A/Ctrl–Shift–A).

The Course

➥ Summon the Find/Change window: Edit > Find/Change or ⌘-F/Ctrl-F.

➥ Click the Object tab and then check that Search is set to Document.

➥ To set the attribute to look for, click in the rectangular field below Find Object Format.

➥ On the left side of the Find Object Format Options dialog that just opened, go to Stroke.

➥ In the Weight menu, choose 5 pt. Recall that this is the attribute the objects share with one another, but with no other object in this document.

➥ Click OK.

➥ To set the attribute you would like to change to, click in the rectangular field below Change Object Format.

➥ We can change to anything we like, but let's just change the stroke weight for now. On the left side of the Change Object Format Options dialog that just opened, go to Stroke and choose 10 pt in the Weight menu. Click OK.

➥ Click the Change All button. Hopefully, a message reports that three objects have changed.

➥ You may close that document, saving it if you'd like. We'll be assembling something in the next exercise.

Workspaces & Preferences

Frames & Content

Styles, Type & Fonts

Pages & Spreads

Color Management

Find/Change

Long Documents

Output

Lesson E: Book Document

In the downloaded folder *7 Long Documents* is another folder called *A Magazine*. In the Mac Finder or Windows OS, take a look at its contents. From the filenames alone, you can tell these are the pieces that should be assembled into a single magazine. For large books as well, the whole is assembled from multiple parts, each part a separate InDesign document. These are pulled together with the Book feature.

Let's Assemble a Magazine!

➲ Back in InDesign, go to File > New > Book….

The dialog box that opens asks where to save the small database file that manages the files in the "book," in our case, a magazine.

➲ Give this file the name *Magazine*.

➲ Navigate to and save the book file in the folder you were just examining called *A Magazine*. A new panel should appear.

We are about to add documents to this database panel, but they will likely not be in the right order at first. To prevent InDesign from repaginating all those documents prematurely (and incorrectly), let's temporarily disable that function.

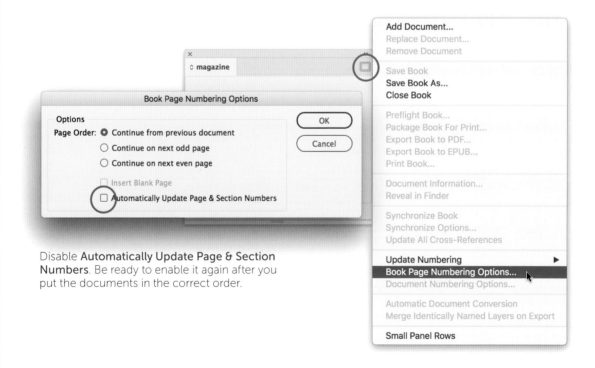

Disable **Automatically Update Page & Section Numbers**. Be ready to enable it again after you put the documents in the correct order.

➦ Go to the Magazine panel menu and choose Book Page Numbering Options…. Uncheck Automatically Update Page & Section Numbers to disable it. We'll be back here shortly.

➦ Click the plus sign at the bottom of the panel to add documents to the "book." If necessary, navigate to the *A Magazine* folder. Highlight all the InDesign documents then click Open.

The order of the documents will be incorrect.

➦ Drag each document up or down to rectify this issue. The figure below shows the correct order.

The documents are in the correct order. Drag yours up or down to match.

Then re-enable **Automatically Update Page & Section Numbers**. After a brief delay, you'll see this:

➦ Return to the Magazine panel menu and again choose Book Page Numbering Options…. Check Automatically Update Page & Section Numbers to enable it. Click OK. There will be a pause, so be patient. The pages are now correctly and sequentially numbered.

You may also use the panel menu to export the compiled whole as a PDF or ePub. If you do so, be sure that none of the documents are highlighted in the panel, or you may export only that one.

To open a document that is part of a book file, use the book's panel, double-clicking the file's name. This ensures the book database knows what you've done.

Finally, when a book is repaginated, sometimes left and right pages swap position, and text frames on those pages become dislocated. That did not happen in this case, but when it does, you merely have to reapply master pages to the ones that got jiggled.

> There is more to be learned by reading "The Book Feature" (page 315) in the Compendium.

Workspaces & Preferences

Frames & Content

Styles, Type & Fonts

Pages & Spreads

Color Management

Find/Change

Long Documents

Output

8 Output

In this final chapter of the Course, we learn how to create robust deliverables: PDFs, Packages, and ePubs.

Lesson A: PDF

From the downloaded folder called *8 Output* open the file called *Study in Scarlet.indd*.

This file is a complete novel ready for output to several media. We will start by making two PDFs with commonly needed settings.

Using Presets

InDesign installs with several important presets ready-to-go. A specific recipient of a PDF may supply you with others. Both installing provided PDF presets and creating your own, as well as a thorough description of the settings involved, are covered in the "Output" chapter of the Compendium: see "PDF" (page 339).

Making a Small, Downloadable PDF

This preset serves as a good starting point for PDFs that will be shared electronically (by email or posted on a website). It usually requires a little bit of adjustment, however.

Go to File > Adobe PDF Presets > [Smallest File Size]. You'll be prompted to provide a name and location for the PDF you're making. Since you may not wish to keep these PDFs after this exercise, choose the *Desktop* as the location and name it something like *Study_small.pdf*.

When you've committed to the location, you'll see a second and more substantial dialog box with many sections to it.

In the first section, General, locate the Viewing pane. Change View to Fit Page. Change Layout to Two-Up Continuous (Cover Page). Also, enable the checkbox for View PDF after Exporting.

Fit Page ensures that the recipient will see an entire page or spread when they open the PDF. The Layout choice ensures that the first page remains a single cover or title page and the rest are seen as spreads ("two-up"). The second section needs a little alteration.

Proceed to the second section, Compression.

Note that all images will not only be downsampled, but will also be made JPEGs of Low Quality. If the PDF is truly to be viewed on a screen only, then the targeted resolution (100 ppi for color images and 150 ppi for grayscale) is likely fine. However, low quality looks like it sounds.

Change the Quality to Medium or High. If Medium still looks poor, you can make another PDF and choose a higher setting.

Click the Export button. The PDF will be generated and will open for inspection.

Workspaces & Preferences

Frames & Content

Styles, Type & Fonts

Pages & Spreads

Color Management

Find/Change

Long Documents

Output

The Course

Making a Possibly Press-Ready PDF

- Go to File > Adobe PDF Presets > [PDF/X-1a:2001]. You'll be prompted to provide a name and location for the PDF you're making. Choose the *Desktop* for the location and name it ***Study_pressready.pdf***. Commit to that dialog to proceed to the more difficult one.
- In the first section, General, change View to Fit Page. Change Layout to Two-Up Continuous (Cover Page). Enable the checkbox for View PDF after Exporting.
- Proceed to the second section, Compression.

This is rather different than a PDF made for on-screen viewing. Note that images will be downsampled to a healthy 300 ppi, and will be made JPEGs of Maximum Quality. When PDFs are going to press, file size is far less important, if at all. So even that can be improved.

- In both the Color Images pane and the Grayscale Images pane, change the Compression to ZIP. The images in the PDF will look as good as the originals.
- Go to the Marks and Bleeds section.

Let's assume our print shop has asked us to provide crop marks. For some documents they will ask for bleed if we have content that goes to page edges, but this one has none.

- Check the box for Crop Marks.
- Go to the Output section.

To satisfy our hypothetical printer's request that we supply the PDF configured for the specific CMYK of their equipment, we'll change the Destination to what they request:

- Change the Destination to Coated GRACoL 2006.
- Click the Export button. The PDF will be generated and will open for inspection.

I hope you noticed how many settings are dependent on information from the printer. Communication is very helpful when creating files for print output.

Lesson B: Packaging

⮊ From the downloaded folder called *8 Output* open the file called *Study in Scarlet.indd*.

Some printers and other recipients request the "source" or "native" files—that is, copies of the InDesign file and all its assets (images and fonts, mostly). Packaging supplies these copies in a tidy folder we call a "package."

⮊ Use the File menu and choose Package….
⮊ The first of several dialog boxes opens. Note that no fonts are missing.

The small note that three are "protected" means they are from Adobe Fonts. That is not a concern, nor is the foolish warning triangle that tells us that several images use RGB.

⮊ Click the Package… button. A new dialog appears.
⮊ Choose a name for this folder: perhaps *Project Sherlock*. Mac users may have to click the disclosure arrow to the right of the name to more easily choose a destination. Choose the Desktop again.
⮊ Check all of the first five checkboxes at the bottom to ensure that all the assets are included and to minimize the risk of text reflowing when the document is opened on another computer.
⮊ If there is a chance that a recipient is using a very old version of InDesign (from before the Creative Cloud), then check the box to Include IDML. Creative Cloud versions convert files semi-automatically.
⮊ Click the Package button. A last, legal dialog appears. Check Don't Show Again, then click OK.

As usual, more details are in the Compendium. See "Package" (page 345).

Workspaces & Preferences

Frames & Content

Styles, Type & Fonts

Pages & Spreads

Color Management

Find/Change

Long Documents

Output

Lesson C: ePub (and HTML)

When you read an ePub (also known as an e-book, or electronic book), you're actually viewing a collection of files. These are mostly HTML files, with CSS files (*Cascading Style Sheets*) to control the look and feel, and other, more esoteric formats as well. These are all hidden from view inside a container we experience as an ePub "file."

Because ePubs are predominantly HTML, many of the concerns we have when exporting them are the same as when we export HTML without an ePub container.

Exported HTML can be viewed in any web browser program. But ePubs from InDesign require special applications to look at them afterward. Adobe makes its own called *Adobe Digital Editions*, but I prefer other applications. If you use a Mac, I'd suggest using Apple *iBooks*. The desktop version is a fabulous way to view ePubs after making them. There are others for both Mac and Windows (and sometimes Linux):

Calibre: https://calibre-ebook.com
The *Nook* app: https://www.barnesandnoble.com/h/nook/apps
Kobo: https://www.kobo.com/us/en/p/apps
Freda: http://www.turnipsoft.co.uk/freda

Of course, one cannot forget to include Amazon's Kindle. The *Kindle Previewer* app is not only a good way to simulate a physical Kindle on your computer, but it can also convert an ePub to Amazon's Kindle format (mobi). Get it from: https://amzn.to/2fXMAX0.

➥ Procure any one (or more) of these so you can test the ePubs you make.

There are two kinds of ePub that can be generated from InDesign: fixed layout, which attempts to preserve the layout as closely as possible, and reflowable, the more typical form in which the reader can change the text's font and size and for which we need to indicate the order in which content flows. Fixed layout ePubs are dependably viewable with only some devices and e-reader apps, whereas reflowable ePubs are viewable on any type of device.

Including Content

There are three ways to control the order in which content is experienced when you export as reflowable ePub (or HTML): page layout (which needs some explanation), XML structure (a specialty beyond the scope of this book), or the Articles panel (by far the best choice).

Choosing page layout will order content by what is leftmost first, then, if multiple objects are the same distance from the left edge of a page, from the top downward. This is usually horrific, except in the very simplest of layouts. XML (eXtensible Markup Language) is a means of describing content structure and is often used when the content is supplied by databases. Large retailers, for example, use this to generate catalogs in a partially automated workflow. But for the vast majority of InDesign users, the Articles panel is both intuitive and easy to use.

It helps to bear in mind that the word "articles" is used to mean "items," not "written pieces." Let's ensure that all of a novel's articles are included.

➡ From the downloaded folder called *8 Output* open the file called *Study in Scarlet.indd*. Go to page 1, the title page.

➡ Use the Selection tool to select the text frame on page 1.

➡ Get the Articles panel: Window > Articles.

Note that there are two entries in the Articles panel. We need one more for this title page so that it will be included when we export as ePub or HTML.

➡ Drag the text frame to empty space in the Articles panel. A small dialog box opens.

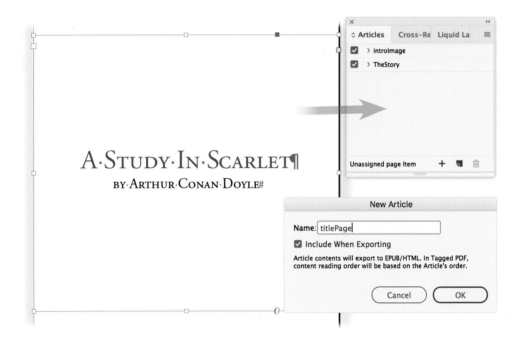

➡ Supply the name *titlePage*, then click OK.

The new article appears at the end of the list, which means it would be the last thing in the ePub.

➡ Drag the titlePage article to the top of the panel.

Now it'll be first. The checkboxes, by the way, control whether something is exported or not. So if there's content you're unsure of, you can add it to the panel and decide later whether it should be part of the export.

But what will this look like in a reflowable ePub? Different e-readers might display different fonts, for example. To preserve the impression of a title page, and to display the text as we intend, we can export this frame as a graphic of relatively high quality on its own "page."

I put the word *page* in quotes because, for the most part, if a reader changes the size of the text, the amount of text that appears on a device's screen will change. Thus, the concept of a page in the world of ePubs is rather flexible.

Workspaces & Preferences

Frames & Content

Styles, Type & Fonts

Pages & Spreads

Color Management

Find/Change

Long Documents

Output

Object Export Options

➡️ With the title page text frame selected, choose Object > Object Export Options.

Something that resembles a dialog box appears. It isn't one, however. It's more like a panel in that it can remain on screen while you perform other tasks. Let's call it the Object Export Options *window*.

➡️ Go to that window's EPUB and HTML tab.

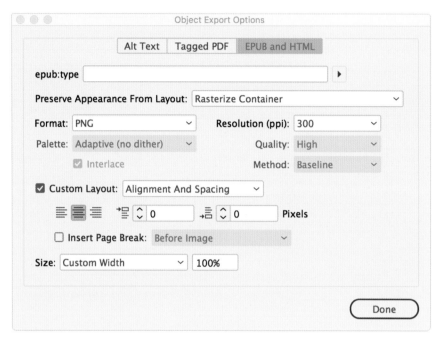

As you can see, I've already designated that to Preserve Appearance From Layout, I'd like to Rasterize Container—that is, to convert the text frame into a pixel-based image. For content other than photographs, we should choose PNG for the Format. I also chose a rather high Resolution (300 ppi) since this title page should be as crisp and lovely as possible, even on devices with screens of high resolution.

Also note that Custom Layout has been enabled to control where on the "page" the image appears. I chose to center it (horizontally) and I set its width to be 100% of the screen on which it's viewed.

Although we could use this window's controls on each object in a document, we will usually apply these settings with an object style. This novel has four illustrations, each with a caption. Each image-caption pair has been grouped and pasted into a frame with an object style applied. Except for the first pair, that style sets the Object Export Options similar to the one above, but with a width of 80%, and Insert Page Break is set to Before and After Image to keep it on a page of its own. The first image-caption pair has a page break only before it.

➡️ Scroll down in the document. You will pass a table of contents, which will *not* be included in the ePub. However, a TOC Style was created and will be called upon when we export.

⏩ Scroll until you reach the first image. It has an object style applied called *introImage_and_ caption*. Note its effects on the Object Export Options.

⏩ Right-click on the object style's name and choose Edit "introImage_and_caption"…. At the very bottom of the left side of the dialog that appears, click EPUB and HTML to highlight it. That's where the Object Export Options are set. Click OK.

⏩ Also note that the frame holding the image and caption has been added to the Articles panel (when the frame is selected, a blue square appears to the right of its entry in that panel).

The third and final object in the Articles panel is the InDesign threaded story containing the entire text of the novel. Where are the other three images, then? They are part of the story, anchored to certain positions in the text near the references to them.

⏩ Go to page 24. Select the frame that holds the image and caption there.

You should see a dashed line between it and the first paragraph on page 25. It has its own Object Export Options set with an object style, but it will show up in the ePub before the text to which it is anchored. If the images weren't anchored to that story, they would all have to appear either before or after the story, each with its own entry in the Articles panel. Anchoring (see page 231) allows us to sprinkle content throughout the ePub with only one article entry.

Export Tagging

To better control the appearance of section and chapter headers, we can choose which HTML tag is applied to their content. I've chosen the H1 tag for section headers, and the H2 tag for the chapter headers. To confirm this:

⏩ Right-click on the name of paragraph style *Chapter_header* and choose Edit "Chapter_ header"…. At the very bottom of the left side of the dialog, highlight Export Tagging.

In the EPUB and HTML section, the chosen Tag is h2. Click OK. The board is set, let's get the pieces moving!

Generating the Reflowable ePub

During this process, you will be asked to supply an image for a cover (it's provided in the same folder as the document you're currently editing, **08 Output**), indicate what controls the layout (the Articles panel), and choose the TOC style that creates the ePub's internal table of contents (it's called *novel TOC*).

⏩ Save the document (⌘–S/Ctrl–S).

⏩ Choose File > Export…. At the bottom of the dialog that appears, choose EPUB (Reflowable) as the Format (Mac) or File Type (Windows). Set a location (the Desktop should be OK). Click Save.

⏩ In the General section of the dialog box that appears, set the Version to EPUB 3.0. This version is now well-established and preserves typography more elegantly than the older

Workspaces & Preferences

Frames & Content

Styles, Type & Fonts

Pages & Spreads

Color Management

Find/Change

Long Documents

Output

version 2.

➡ Set Cover to Choose Image, then click the folder icon to the right of the File Location field. Navigate to the folder *8 Output* and choose the file called ***StudyInScarletCover.png***. I hope you like it.

➡ For Navigation TOC, choose Multi Level (TOC Style), which requires that a TOC style be made. The specific TOC Style to choose is novel TOC. You may have one to generate the printed TOC, another for the ePub.

If a certain style should appear at the top of a new page, choose it here. Or use **Keep Options** so that happens both in print *and* ePub.

Customize the appearance of elements with your own CSS file, if desired.

➡ In the Text section of the dialog, there is little to do usually, and nothing now. If you use footnotes, you can choose where they go. I like pop-ups that the ePub 3.0 standard allows.

The Object and Conversion Settings sections are stopgaps for any objects you have not managed with Object Export Options. All our objects are managed, so these sections can be ignored.

➡ In the HTML & CSS section, be sure to check Generate CSS so text is formatted as closely to the original as possible. We can skip the Javascript section since we haven't coded any.

➡ Add a title in the Metadata section. That and the other fields help e-readers learn something about the book. However, when we upload an ePub to Amazon or Apple, for example, we fill out forms whose content becomes the actual metadata for the book.

➡ Finally, in the View Apps section, add and choose which apps should automatically open so we can see how good our preparations were.

The Course

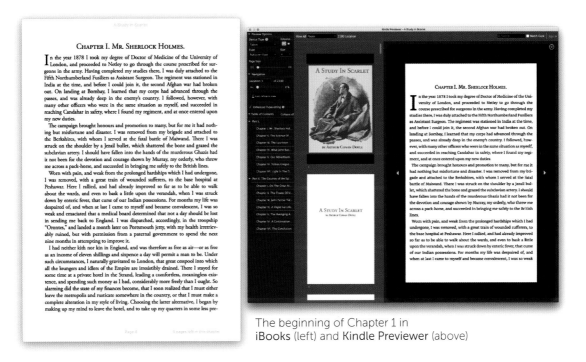

Choose apps other than Adobe Digital Editions here.

➡ Click OK and wait a bit.

The beginning of Chapter 1 in
iBooks (left) and Kindle Previewer (above)

➡ When done, save the file and quit InDesign. Have a celebratory gambol! The course is complete.

Workspaces & Preferences

Frames & Content

Styles, Type & Fonts

Pages & Spreads

Color Management

Find/Change

Long Documents

Output

THE
COMPENDIUM

1 Workspaces & Preferences

At the beginning of this book, both in the Introduction and again in the chapter 1 of the Course, "Starting with a Solid Base," we briefly discussed how to customize InDesign.

Review that chapter for the basics on building your own workspaces and use this one for additional tips and to make better decisions when setting your preferences.

Preferences

Document-Specific and Global

A scary truth: many preferences that you may set are specific to the document that is open at the time. Other preferences are application-wide, or global. How do you tell the difference? There is no way to know other than through experience and testing! So, heed the following.

Warning: To ensure preferences are set consistently for all future documents you create, set those preferences with no documents open at all.

In the following sections, I will not define those preferences that are peripheral to the vast majority of users. It's easy to get to the Preferences: ⌘-K/Ctrl-K. To get to the first nine pages of your preferences, use the ⌘/Ctrl key and the numbers 1 through 9. For example, to get to my Type preferences, I hold the ⌘/Ctrl key and type "K 3."

General

The General section contains the preferences that don't fit neatly in the other categories. These are all global preferences.

Show "Start" Workspace When No Documents Are Open

If you like that large "welcome" screen—with a list of recent files, links to videos, etc.—to appear when you start InDesign, keep this checked.

Page Numbering

Larger documents can be broken up into sections. Often, we restart page numbering in each section (a book's front matter may have lowercase Roman numerals, whereas the main content has Arabic numerals). The Pages panel will show this when you choose Section

Numbering. When you choose Absolute Numbering, the Pages panel will be sequential. Of course, the pages themselves will show the numbering you've established. Absolute Numbering makes it easier to print the first, say, 20 pages of a document regardless of what number appears on each page.

Prevent Selection of Locked Objects
Locking objects prevents them from being moved or resized. However, they can still be altered (e.g., you could change their color) unless they are not selectable.

Apply to Content/Adjust Scaling Percentage
When you're scaling an object, the object can "remember" how much it was enlarged or reduced. That is, with Adjust Scaling Percentage, a text frame enlarged by 50% will show a scaling of 150% in the Control panel ever after, making it easy to set it back to 100% if necessary. However, if the text size started at 12 points, for example, it will now read "12 pt (18 pt)," which can be confusing. If you liked the new frame size but you wanted the text to be 12 points again, you might have to set it to 8 points (1.5 x 8 = 12)! Headaches ensue. I recommend using Apply to Content to show only the current, actual size.

When Include Stroke Weight is checked, stroke weights increase or decrease when an object is scaled up or down. Sometimes you want that, sometimes you don't. Thus, this is checked and unchecked often! There is a similar concern with Effects (such as drop shadows), which you can also check or uncheck here.

Interface
This is where you adjust the look and feel of InDesign. These are global preferences.

Appearance
How much light do you want shining at you?

Color Theme
This doesn't actually have to do with colors at all; rather, it allows you to adjust the lightness of the panels that surround your document window.

Match Pasteboard to Theme Color
If this is unchecked, the pasteboard will be white.

Cursor and Gesture Options

Where you put your cursor makes a difference. These options determine what happens when you place your cursor in specific locations.

Tool Tips

These are the small identifying notes that appear when you hover your cursor over tools and other elements. Useful for new users, these impact performance.

Show Thumbnails on Place

This provides the small pictures of images you're placing. This is most useful when you're placing multiple images at once so you can decide which image to place where.

Enable Multi-Touch Gestures

If you use a trackpad, you can use touch gestures to scroll, for example.

Highlight Object Under Selection Tool

As you move your cursor, you will see indicators on the object that would be selected if you were to click where the cursor is located at that moment.

Panels

InDesign's panel display is very customizable. We'll cover more on this later in this chapter.

Floating Tools Panel

The Tools panel can be horizontal, vertical, or two tools wide and vertical. I like the space savings of the single column.

Auto-Collapse Icon Panels/Auto-Show Hidden Panels

If you use your Tab key to hide all your panels, and perhaps also collapse some panels to icons, moving your cursor to the sides of the document window will cause the panels to appear when Auto-Show Hidden Panels is selected. With Auto-Collapse Icon Panels selected, the panels will recollapse after you've moved on.

Options

When using the Hand tool or resizing objects, I prefer an accurate view of my layout. Thus:

Hand Tool

Choose No Greeking.

Live Screen Drawing

Choose Immediate, which is especially great when you're resizing text frames.

Type

This section controls most text behavior. For some of these options, it's as simple as "set and forget." Other items you'll return to many times during larger projects. Many of these options are document-specific.

Use Typographer's Quotes

That is, **"** or **"**, rather than **"**. If you need the latter, use control-shift-'/Alt-Shift-'.

Type Tool Converts Frames to Text Frames

This global default allows you to click in any frame to convert it to a text frame.

Triple Click to Select a Line

I can think of no reason to disable this global default. It's useful, and fun, to double-click to select a word, triple-click to select a line, quadruple-click to select a paragraph, and quintuple-click to select an entire story.

Apply Leading to Entire Paragraphs

I can think of very few times when I need to adjust leading on a character-by-character basis. This preference is document-specific, so I recommend setting it with no document open so it's in effect for all future documents.

Drag and Drop Text Editing

This allows you to drag selected text to some other position. It is a global preference.

Smart Text Reflow

This allows you to control the automatic addition or deletion of pages when the content warrants it. The documents in which I use this feature are usually the ones in which I am using primary text frames. Thus, I leave a check mark in the box for Limit to Primary Text Frames. Most often, I choose to add or delete pages at the end of a story. If I predict that the addition or deletion of a page would disrupt subsequent spreads in the document that I need to keep intact, I will check the box for Preserve Facing-Page Spreads.

Workspaces & Preferences

Frames & Content

Styles, Type & Fonts

Pages & Spreads

Color Management

Find/Change

Long Documents

Output

Advanced Type

I would suggest changing very little here unless you have a strong need for it.

Character Settings

Unless you are using OpenType fonts—in which the designer has likely included the size and position of superscripts, subscripts, and small caps—these settings establish those characteristics.

Input Method Options

Use Inline Input for Non-Latin Text

This is so you can simply enter non-Latin text (Asian characters, for example) more easily.

Missing Glyph Protection

These are more settings for Asian or Arabic text. If you type or have typed a specific glyph, InDesign will use a font that contains that character.

Type Contextual Controls

These are great ways to make yourself aware of advanced typographic features for individual letters or whole text frames.

Composition

These settings alert you to issues in your text and adjust the behavior of text wrap.

Highlight

Text that deviates from the settings you've chosen (in style definitions, for example) is highlighted, so you can quickly find, judge, and, if necessary, squash them.

Set these on a document-by-document basis.

H&J violations

Custom kerning/tracking

Substituted glyph & fonts

Keep Violations

You will never incur a violation of your "keeps" settings, thus you'll never see this highlighting.

Workspaces & Preferences

Frames & Content

Styles, Type & Fonts

Pages & Spreads

Color Management

Find/Change

Long Documents

Output

H&J Violations

Text is highlighted when InDesign uses more than your maximum or less than your minimum word spacing, or when it uses more hyphens. The greater the violation, the yellower the highlighting.

Custom Tracking/Kerning

Kerning and tracking are facts of life. If you need to see where you made these adjustments, this preference will highlight them in green.

Substituted Fonts

When you have specified a font that is not installed for your text, InDesign will highlight it in pink.

Substituted Glyphs

When InDesign substitutes two or more letters with a ligature, for example, this choice will highlight that occurrence in gold.

Text Wrap

Justify Text Next to an Object

This option comes into play only when an object with text wrap divides lines of text—something you should never allow to happen.

Skip by Leading

When text wrap interrupts the flow of text in a column (for example, when using the Jump Object text wrap), this option ensures that when the text resumes, it will flow along the baseline grid. This presumes, of course, that you have set up your baseline grid to correspond to the leading of your text.

Text Wrap Only Affects Text Beneath

There are many good reasons to keep images below text frames, but you may still wish to have those images possess text wrap. Leave this unchecked.

Units & Increments

Here we decide how things measure up. There are enough units of measurement from which to choose to please just about everyone.

Frames & Content

Styles, Type & Fonts

Pages & Spreads

Color Management

Find/Change

Long Documents

Output

Ruler Units

To set the point from which things are measured (zero on the ruler), choose an Origin. The Origin can be the upper-left corner of a spread or an individual page. If you choose Spine, the values increase with distance from the spine. Note that your horizontal and vertical units of measurement can be different, and can be changed at any time by right-clicking on either ruler in your layout. You can even use custom increments. For example, I often set my vertical increment equal to my base leading.

Keyboard Increments

Cursor Key

The arrow keys can be used to move objects. If you select an object, the Cursor Key value is how far the object will be "nudged" when you press an arrow key.

Baseline Shift

To raise and lower selected text from its initial position, press option-Shift-↑ *or* ↓/Alt-Shift-↑ *or* ↓. Baseline Shift is the increment by which the text is moved.

Size/Leading

A keyboard shortcut can be used to adjust the size and leading of selected text according to the increment specified here. Press ⌘-shift-< *or* >/Ctrl-Shift-< *or* > to decrease or increase the size (respectively). To adjust the leading, press option-↑ *or* ↓/Alt-↑ *or* ↓.

Kerning/Tracking

Tapping the left or right arrow keys while holding the option/Alt key adjusts kerning (if your cursor is blinking between two letters) or tracking (if you have a range of text selected). As your eye attunes to these attributes, you may lower this value.

Grids

These document-specific preferences control the look and behavior of these grids. Grids are similar in behavior to guides (up next).

Baseline Grid

Horizontal lines are best incremented in a value equal to your document's body copy leading. Here you specify the color and starting point of these horizontal lines, as well as the level of magnification at which they become visible (View Threshold). Although paragraph styles can be defined to make text snap to this baseline grid, I more often carefully set leading and spacing instead. For more on using baseline grids, see "Baseline Grid" (page 205).

Document Grid

This is a true grid for which you can choose the color and frequency. You can set a somewhat coarse grid with finer subdivisions that are displayed more faintly.

Guides & Pasteboard

These options provide you with even more ways to give structure to your layout. Here you set the appearance of your guides, when you are shown "Smart Guides," and how much pasteboard there is around your spreads.

Guide Options

Choose how close (in screen pixels) an object should be to a guide for it to snap onto it. Also choose whether guides appear behind objects or not.

Smart Guide Options

Mysteriously, these are the only options in the Guides & Pasteboard section that are global. Smart Guides are the lines that appear as you drag objects around the page when those objects align either to other objects on the page or to landmarks of the page, spread, or margins.

Pasteboard Options

Set the amount of space you would like to have beyond the edge of your spread where you might place objects that you are not quite sure you wish to be without. Reminder: Objects on the pasteboard do not print nor export in a PDF.

Workspaces & Preferences

Frames & Content

Styles, Type & Fonts

Pages & Spreads

Color Management

Find/Change

Long Documents

Output

Dictionary

Because we don't always spell well.

Note: The dictionary is Hunspell, an open source dictionary used in many applications.

Language

This is where you select the language associated with the dictionary seen in the window below this menu (this is the only global dictionary setting). The window shows the location of the dictionary file(s). If you can make or procure a plain text file containing a list of words or phrases you commonly use, you can quickly add that list by clicking on the + below the small window. This is handy if you work in a specialized industry with a specialized vocabulary, and if you have time to create or find such a list.

Double Quotes and Single Quotes
Choose the style for quotation marks.

Hyphenation Exceptions
Over time, you may correct InDesign's placement of hyphens. These corrections, or "Exceptions," are typically stored in the User Dictionary. To be sure that all of the exceptions you have defined are used, choose User Dictionary and Document in the menu labeled Compose Using.

User Dictionary
To make your User Dictionary more portable, I suggest choosing to Merge User Dictionary into Document. This is especially valuable for templates.

Spelling
What's *your* problem?

Find
Choose what commonly ails your text. These are the items that will be flagged when doing a spell check. Edit > Spelling > Check Spelling... or ⌘-I/Ctrl-I starts the process.

Dynamic Spelling
This is an ongoing spell check that colorfully underlines the problems above. This feature (and Autocorrect) can also be enabled by going to Edit > Spelling.

Autocorrect
As you write or edit in InDesign, Autocorrect will fix your most common errors. This is great for people like me, who type *"t-e-h" instead of* "the." Add your most common gaffs here.

Workspaces &
Preferences

Frames &
Content

Styles, Type
& Fonts

Pages
& Spreads

Color
Management

Find/Change

Long
Documents

Output

Notes

These options allow for the exchange of editorial information among users of a document. When writing or editing in InDesign, a user can right-click and choose New Note. Each user can have a unique, identifying color. We can include notes in spell check or find/change operations.

See Track Changes (next!) for how to configure a user.

Track Changes

Make clear what's changed and by whom.

These global preferences control the look and feel of changes that are shown when editing in the Story Editor. Decide which changes are shown, and how to identify who made them.

Show

To define your user name and color, choose File > User.... The name and color you choose will be used for notes and tracked changes. When you exchange a document with someone else and they edit text in the Story Editor, their changes will appear with their color behind them. You can prevent clashes with the checkbox Prevent Duplicate User Colors.

Change Bars

Change Bars (which appear in the left margin of the Story Editor by default) make it easy to find changes quickly while scanning text.

Finally, I check the box labeled Include Deleted Text When Spellchecking in case I later reject those deletions and the text makes its way back into my publication.

Story Editor Display
Just you and the words.

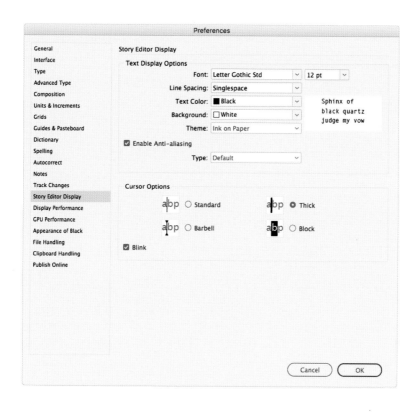

Frames &
Content

Styles, Type
& Fonts

Pages
& Spreads

Color
Management

Find/Change

Long
Documents

Output

Text Display Options and Cursor Options
To see your text without the distractions of the layout, turn to the Story Editor. You can also view notes and tracked changes there. Since the Story Editor is only an editorial tool, and is not visible in the final published piece, you can choose how to display it. Sometimes, I use the old computer terminal theme—it reminds me of when I was young.

Display Performance

Control how hard InDesign works to make its content look good. Note the word "performance." These settings can enhance or degrade the speed with which InDesign displays text and images. The print quality of your document is not affected by these settings at all.

Default View

There are three choices: Fast, Typical, and High Quality. Fast doesn't display images at all, but instead shows gray boxes or shapes—rather brutal. By default, Typical shows a "proxy"

that InDesign generates for each image, the quality of which could be startling, especially to the supervisor looking over your shoulder. High Quality renders images, graphics, and anything transparent without compromise. For small documents, you may use High Quality without much penalty. Larger and more graphically rich documents will become sluggish unless you reduce the Display Performance view.

Adjust View Settings

You may tweak each of the view settings to better tune the performance of InDesign. For example, you may want to adjust Typical to have low-quality Transparency but high-quality Vector Graphics (AI and PDF files, for example) so your company's logo will look splendid when your boss sees it, and leave Raster Images (those made of pixels) as a proxy.

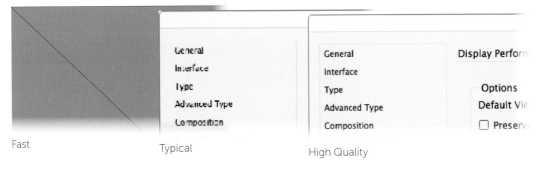

Fast   Typical   High Quality

GPU Performance

If your computer supports it, use it! Although using the computer's graphics processor for some functions does speed things up, I still prefer to use a non-animated zoom. Holding down the Z key and drawing a box around what I wish to view closely is faster and more precise (unless I'm editing text, in which case I hold down ⌘-spacebar/Ctrl-spacebar). Oddly, as of this writing, the GPU will not appear supported unless you're also taxing it with a "high dpi" display.

Appearance of Black

A needlessly confusing choice of the appearance of black!

On Screen

I choose to display all blacks accurately on-screen. This means that items that use the pure black (100% K) swatch will look slightly lighter (more gray) than a rich black, which is made from black ink plus a bit of others, too.

Printing/Exporting

This is the confusing one. Choose Output All Blacks as Rich Black, then hover your cursor over that choice and note the description below that attempts—but fails— to clarify. What it means is that on a device that has only

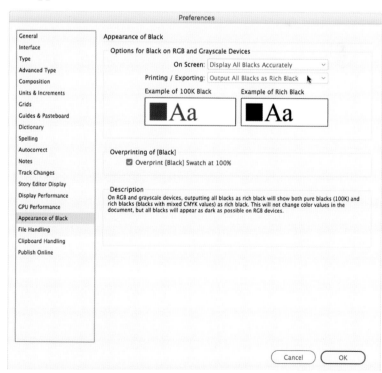

Workspaces & Preferences

Frames & Content

Styles, Type & Fonts

Pages & Spreads

Color Management

Find/Change

Long Documents

Output

black ink or toner, both rich blacks and pure blacks will print as dark as possible. The phrase "RGB devices" refers to common desktop inkjet printers! However, with this choice, full color laser printers and printing presses (true CMYK devices) will still produce blacks accurately: pure black will use black ink or toner only, and rich black will be output as designed. Since I output to all of these devices, I choose the confusing Output All Blacks as Rich Black setting. It works!

File Handling

Crash recovery and link juggling are the main fare here.

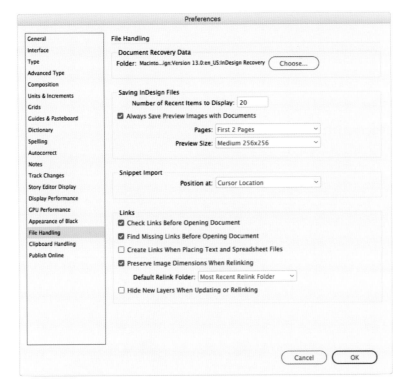

Document Recovery Data

Unlimited undo and the ability to resume work after a crash is made possible by a recovery file InDesign creates for you. When working on an existing InDesign file, the recovery file will be in the same folder. Until a new document is saved, the location shown in this preference is where the file is stored.

Saving InDesign Files

A favorite way to open ongoing projects is by going to File > Open Recent. You can alter how many (if any) files are listed there. Also in the File menu is Browse in Bridge....

Bridge is an Adobe application for browsing the files on your computer. Its thumbnails are usually more helpful than the operating system's, and if you click on one, you can use Bridge's preview panel to flip through as many pages of an InDesign document as you specify here in the Pages menu of this preference. This is useful when the file is named "untitled 14.indd."

Snippet Import

InDesign offers numerous ways to save and reuse bits of your layouts: CC Libraries, library documents (.indl file), and snippets. You can select a text frame, for example, and choose File > Export... to export it as an InDesign Snippet (.idms file). These files are lightweight and can be emailed and later placed into other InDesign documents, bringing along any styles they use. This preference determines where the placed snippet will land: where you click with your

Workspaces &
Preferences

Frames &
Content

Styles, Type
& Fonts

Pages
& Spreads

Color
Management

Find/Change

Long
Documents

Output

loaded cursor (Cursor Location) or in the same relative position the object had on its oringal page (Original Location).

Links

The mysterious connections between our linked files and the InDesign documents in which they appear can be made a little clearer here.

Check Links Before Opening Document

The key word here is "Before." With this option disabled, InDesign will still check your links' status, but will do so after the document is opened, which makes the opening of files more rapid.

Find Missing Links Before Opening Document

When opening a document, it can be helpful to get a heads-up when something is wrong. If you have images linked to your InDesign document and some of them have gone missing, you likely want to know that sooner rather than later. However, there may be times when you willingly work on a document whose images you know to be missing, and you would prefer not to have the annoyance of a message telling you so. When that is the case, I enable this preference so InDesign may find the image in a recently used folder, for example. It's also possible, however, that in an attempt to find a missing link in folders you've recently linked to, InDesign will link to the wrong version of an image. If you experience this behavior, disable this preference and manually locate the correct missing linked file.

Create Links When Placing Text and Spreadsheet Files

As with images, you can place text files and maintain a link to the original. However, without the help of a third-party plug-in like WordsFlow by Em Software, the formatting you may have done in InDesign is lost when you update those links.

Preserve Image Dimensions When Relinking

Typically, when you swap the content of an image frame with another image, InDesign will attempt to make the proportions of the new image match those of the previous image. For example, if the frame has been resized to show only a third of the original image, InDesign will attempt to show only a third of the new image in that frame. This is fine for images with similar subject matter and/or proportions, but when the new image has little connection to the original, you may wish to decide for yourself how that image will fit its frame by disabling this setting.

Hide New Layers When Updating or Relinking

Images produced in Photoshop or graphics created in Illustrator typically have layers. When you place these kinds of documents (.psd or .ai), you can choose which layers are visible in InDesign. If you subsequently edit a document, and those edits introduce new layers to the structure of the document, this setting determines whether those new layers are visible when you update the link.

Clipboard Handling

Material that is copied or cut lives in the system clipboard. Here, we determine what InDesign reads from or writes to that clipboard.

Clipboard

Whether it's inbound or outbound, you can choose to preserve the structure or appearance of what you put on your clipboard.

Prefer PDF When Pasting

I sometimes generate objects in other applications such as Illustrator. Most often, I simply place that Illustrator document as a link into my InDesign publication. However, sometimes I need the shape I have drawn in Illustrator as an editable shape in InDesign. Since Illustrator provides both the path data and the PDF data to the clipboard, I disable this setting to get the path data into InDesign.

Copy PDF to Clipboard

When I need to provide something I have created in InDesign to another application, and I need to preserve its appearance, my odds of success are better if what I copy to the clipboard is PDF data. If I suspect I will be pasting this data after I quit InDesign, I enable the option just below this one.

Preserve PDF Data at Quit

This allows me to paste copied PDF data after InDesign has quit.

When Pasting Text and Tables from Other Applications Paste

Content you have copied from Microsoft Word or Apple Pages (for example) can be pasted as rich text (All Information) or as plain text (Text Only). Pasted plain text inherits the formatting that is active at the insertion point in InDesign.

Publish Online

A fixed-layout ePub, which is readable in a browser and hosted by Adobe, is the product of this feature.

Disable Publish Online

If you do not wish to be tempted by this feature, disable it! Otherwise, you can experiment with InDesign's interactive and animation features and share the results with colleagues or friends.

Workspaces &
Preferences

Frames &
Content

Styles, Type
& Fonts

Pages
& Spreads

Color
Management

Find/Change

Long
Documents

Output

Workspaces & Preferences

Panel Locations

Every panel in InDesign can be dislodged from its current position and can be attached to others or made free-floating. Like the modest set of panels we see when we first install InDesign, panels can be collected into columns of panels called "docks" on the left or the right side of your screen—or screens.

Any such combination can be designated as a workspace. As you master more of the application, your decisions regarding which panels make up each workspace will change.

Choose a More Useful Initial Workspace

For this, it may be best if you have a document open. Create a new document or open a recent one (File > Open Recent...).

At the right end of the Control panel, you'll find the workspace menu. It will read Essentials unless you have changed it. A better starting point is Advanced, which is not advanced, but does include the vital Styles panels. But

first, let's expand the panels we need the most, get rid of some we don't need, and collapse a few that are nice to have nearby but that we don't want in the way.

At the top of the dock of panels is small button with << in it. When clicked, it points the other way (>>) and expands the panels so you can see them. Clicking it again collapses the panels to icons again.

You can adjust a panel's height by borrowing space from another: drag the line separating them up or down.

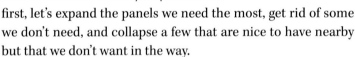

Creating a New Column of Panels

Let's start by pulling out the panels to which we don't need constant access: Swatches, Stroke, CC Libraries, Gradient. Drag each *by its name* away from its dock. We'll simply close any that we use rarely (like Gradient). The close button (X) is on the right on a PC and on the left on a Mac.

To create a new dock of panels alongside the first, drag a panel by its name toward the original dock until a dense blue vertical "drop zone" appears. Collapse the new column with the small double arrow (>>) in its upper-right corner. Drag in more panels just under the first, again watching for a drop zone to appear. I suggest adding the Properties panel (introduced in InDesign CC 2019) to this second dock to easily access (and collapse) it.

Adjust the width of this new dock by dragging its left edge. You can shrink it until the names are gone and only icons remain if you like.

Individual panels have drop zones, too. If you drag one panel to the bottom edge of a free-floating panel, you will create a free-floating dock. Or, if you drag a panel's name next to another panel's name, the drop zone is the small window itself; that is, both panels' tabs will be side by side in the same window.

Once you feel that your panels are located where you want them, return to the workspace menu (where you chose Advanced earlier), and choose New Workspace…. We can name this "Real Essentials," perhaps.

Later, if this workspace becomes untidy, we can once again use the workspace menu and choose Reset Real Essentials.

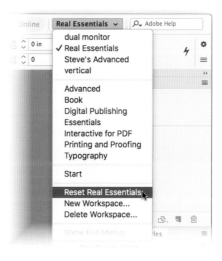

Workspaces & Preferences

Frames & Content

Styles, Type & Fonts

Pages & Spreads

Color Management

Find/Change

Long Documents

Output

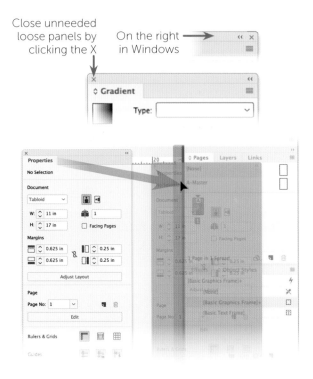

Close unneeded
loose panels by
clicking the X

On the right
in Windows

Above: To create a second panel dock, drag a
panel by its name toward the edge of another dock
until a blue-tinged vertical drop zone appears

Below: Drag additional panels under previous
ones, watching for drop zones to appear

Bottom: Adjust a dock's width by dragging its edge

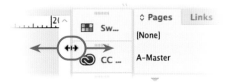

Customizing Menus & Keyboard Shortcuts

New users to Adobe applications tend to spend a bit of time hunting through various menus trying to find commands they need. These tips could help.

What's on the Menu?

You get to choose! Go to Edit > Menus… to be presented with a large dialog box. It has to be large—*every* menu is here: the application menus (those along the top of the screen), the panel menus (those accessed from the upper-right corner of every panel), and even the menus you get when right-clicking ("context menus"). You *cannot* change the menu in which a command appears, but you can decide if the command appears at all, or if its appearance is augmented with a highlight color. You should make your own "set": when you've made alterations, the Set menu will read "InDesign Defaults." Click Save to create your own so you can get back to the defaults easily if needed. Here are two example modifications:

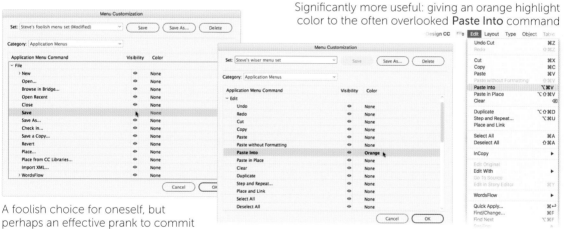

Significantly more useful: giving an orange highlight color to the often overlooked **Paste Into** command

A foolish choice for oneself, but perhaps an effective prank to commit on others: hiding the **Save** command

Workspaces & Preferences

Frames & Content

Styles, Type & Fonts

Pages & Spreads

Color Management

Find/Change

Long Documents

Output

Keys to Success

My rough count shows that there are about 440 keyboard shortcuts in InDesign when first installed. But there are about 1,100 more commands that can have shortcuts assigned to them! Edit > Keyboard Shortcuts… is where this is done.

Create a new Set, find a Product Area (usually a menu), and then highlight the command for which you'd like a shortcut. Any current shortcuts are displayed, but you can add more or replace them. You may also specify the context in which the shortcut works (e.g., only when editing text).

Example: assigning a shortcut to the insert ellipsis command

2 Frames & Content

Absolutely everything in InDesign must either be a
frame or be in one. This chapter covers how to navigate
between those frames and the content they hold, and
how to take control of frames' positions and sizes.

Creating Frames and Shapes

We draw shapes in InDesign to either be decorative or hold images or text. Interestingly, InDesign offers two sets of nearly identical tools to do this: Shape tools and so-called Frame tools. I write "so-called" because the shapes we make with either set of tools can be used as frames. Shapes we draw with the Frame tools are born with no fill and no stroke, as they're intended as placeholders, but we may add color to them later. The Shape tools have whatever appearance we've set as our default—that is, any fill, stroke, effect, or setting that we set with nothing selected. However, these can be made as naked as shapes drawn with the Frame tools.

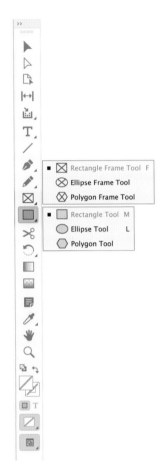

The only other difference is that "frames" can be more easily selected. "Shapes" without a fill need to be selected or dragged by their edges, whereas a frame can be dragged easily without a fill—an odd, but notable difference.

Regardless of which set of tools you use, the mechanics, discussed below, are the same.

Rectangle

With either the Rectangle Frame tool or the Rectangle tool chosen, you drag diagonally to create the shape (up or down, left or right; it makes no difference). Holding Shift, especially as you finish the shape, yields a perfect square. Holding option/Alt while drawing a rectangle grows it from the center outward. Holding down the spacebar *while still in the act of creating the shape* allows you to change its position. Keeping the mouse button depressed and releasing the spacebar allows you to resize and reshape as you continue to draw the shape.

Release the mouse only when you've completed the shape.

One click with this tool brings up a dialog box in which you can enter the height and width of the rectangle you want.

Ellipse

Just as with the rectangles, you drag diagonally to create ellipses. Shift yields circles, and option/Alt grows them outward as you drag. And again, holding the spacebar periodically while still drawing the ellipse allows you to fine-tune its position on the fly.

A click on the page opens a dialog for entering the dimensions of an ellipse.

Gridify

This is another modification that is engaged while you are drawing a shape (*not* after it's drawn). This is useful if, for example, you want 12 identical ellipses to cover half a page. Start as if you're drawing a single ellipse that covers half the page, but before you release the mouse, tap the up and/or right arrow keys. Up creates rows of the shape you're drawing; right creates columns. Down and left remove rows and columns respectively. This also works while drawing text frames (they'll be threaded) and when placing images: "Gridify Images" (page 213).

Polygon

The gridify feature can make many polygons, too. Sadly, the arrow key trick conflicts with the way you change the number of sides of the polygon you are drawing. As you're drawing a polygon, *keeping the mouse button down*, a quick tap of the spacebar tells the arrow keys to do something other than make rows and columns of shapes. After that tap, the up arrow adds sides and down reduces. The right arrow increasingly pushes in the middle of each side to make a star. The left arrow reduces this "star inset."

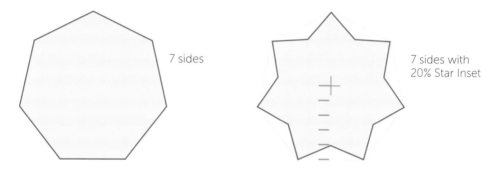

7 sides

7 sides with 20% Star Inset

Alternatively, one click with this tool brings up a dialog box in which you can enter the height, width, number of sides, and amount of star inset. That number of sides and amount of star inset will be what you get when drawing a polygon until you change it again.

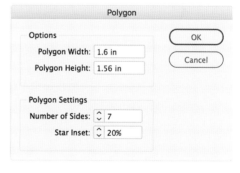

Frames & Content

Styles, Type & Fonts

Pages & Spreads

Color Management

Find/Change

Long Documents

Output

Fills & Strokes

Any frame can be filled, and/or its edge can be stroked, with a color or gradient or nothing at all. Some complain about the term "stroke," but a stroke can be applied to a simple line as well as along the edge of a closed shape, so the term "border" would not be as useful.

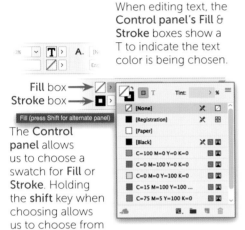

When editing text, the **Control panel's Fill &** **Stroke** boxes show a T to indicate the text color is being chosen.

If a text frame is selected, its colors change, unless we hit the T here:

Fill box
Stroke box

Fill (press Shift for alternate panel)

The **Control** panel allows us to choose a swatch for **Fill** or **Stroke**. Holding the **shift** key when choosing allows us to choose from the **Color panel**.

Choosing the color model

Color Ramp

Gradient Ramp

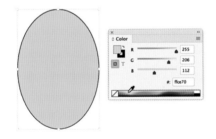

Although there are multiple places from which to apply a fill or stroke, the Control panel offers the most flexibility. Clicking either the Fill or Stroke box menu will show the Swatches panel. Holding the shift key while doing so shows the Color panel. Usually, you can choose from a rainbow of colors along the bottom of the Color panel called the Ramp, then fine-tune with the sliders above. However, if a swatch had been chosen previously, you'll be shown tints of that color instead. To have a rainbow again, select a color model from the Color panel menu (RGB, CMYK, or Lab).

Create a New Color Swatch

If you'd like a color to be a swatch so it can easily be chosen later, use the Swatches panel menu and choose New Color Swatch…. Remember, you can do this via the Swatches panel that appears when you click the Fill or Stroke menus in the Control panel, too.

The New Color Swatch dialog box has a number of choices that confront you. Easily missed among them is the name of the swatch. I will typically name a swatch for its purpose (or at least I aspire to do so). To enter a name, you must first uncheck Name with Color Value.

The Color Type is a choice between the swatch using the four-color process (CMYK) or a custom ink known as a *spot color*. In principle, any color can be a spot color, but to be completely unambiguous we usually rely on a standard color library such as those from Pantone™.

> Learn much more about color modes, spaces, and models in chapter 5 of the Compendium, Color Management (page 293).

Color Type: If printed, **Process** will use dots of Cyan, Magenta, Yellow and Black. **Spot** is usually a request to have a custom ink made by a printshop (much like housepaint mixed for you).

Color Mode: The color model (RGB, CMYK, or Lab) or a standard library such as the Pantone Matching System (PMS).

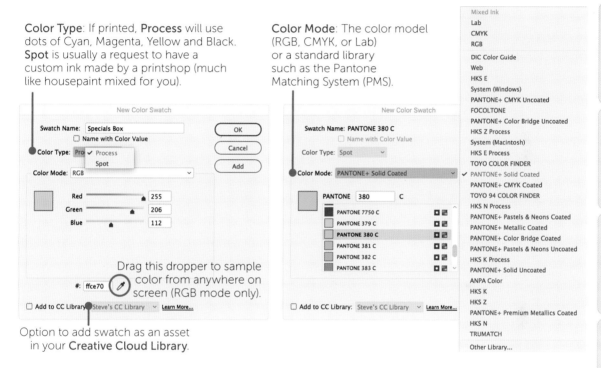

Drag this dropper to sample color from anywhere on screen (RGB mode only).

Option to add swatch as an asset in your **Creative Cloud Library**.

If you choose RGB as the Color Mode, you'll find that you can specify the color with a *hexadecimal* value, as well as individual red, green, and blue ones. Also exclusive to that mode is a dropper that lets you sample from anywhere on your screen, whether in InDesign or not! This is handy for matching a color from a placed RGB image.

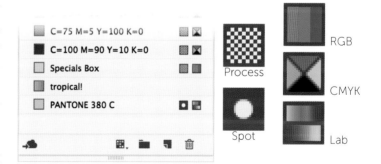

To use the dropper, click and hold on it as you ***drag it*** to what it should sample, releasing the mouse when the dropper is over the target. If you simply click outside InDesign, you've left the application.

Gradients & Gradient Swatches

Gradients are gradual transitions from one color to another (and to others, perhaps). A gradient can be linear, transitioning at a consistent angle, or radial, radiating from a point outward. You can apply a gradient to a fill or stroke. To choose which, and to begin the process of defining a gradient, click on the Fill or Stroke box in one of the panels in which they occur (Color, Swatches, Tools, or Control, but, oddly, not Gradient).

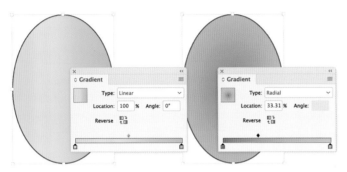

Use the Gradient panel (Window > Color > Gradient) to start a gradient by clicking the square preview in that panel's upper-left corner. The gradient ramp and its sliders, called stops, at the bottom of the panel are now available. At any time in the process, you may switch the Type from Linear to Radial and back.

The stops' colors can be edited, of course. You'll need the Color panel and/or the Swatches panel. Select (click on) a stop, then dial in a color with the Color panel. You need to drag a swatch to a gradient stop to apply it. Since the stops are sliders, you can drag them: when moved closer together, more of the selected object will be filled with solid color and the gradated part will be more abrupt. You can maintain a gradient but give *emphasis* to the color at one end by moving the diamond-shaped slider on the top of the gradient ramp. When that slider or one of the color stops is selected, the Location field shows the relative position of

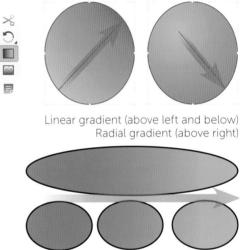

Linear gradient (above left and below)
Radial gradient (above right)

that slider between the ones on either side. So if the gradient stops had been dragged inward, and the diamond slider is *exactly* halfway between them, its location will read 50%.

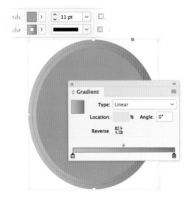

It's easy to add more colors to the gradient, too. Just click between two gradient stops and a third will appear—or a fourth, fifth, and so on. To remove a stop, drag it away from the ramp, keeping in mind that there is a minimum of two stops.

If you're editing a linear gradient, you have access to the Angle field. A 90° linear gradient starts at the bottom of an object and ends at the top. Although setting the angle to 180° will reverse a gradient, using the Reverse button is easier. To set arbitrary angles, choose the Gradient tool from the Tools panel and drag across the shape to set where the start and endpoints of the gradient are. The angle at which you drag is entered into the Angle field. Interestingly, you can drag out a line larger than a selected shape, perhaps leaving only part of a gradient visible in that shape. Even more interesting is dragging the Gradient tool across several shapes with gradients in them—the gradient will now span across all of them. Using the Gradient tool on a radial gradient sets the center and outer edge of that "radius."

Beware: A gradient can also be applied to a stroke. I sometimes do this accidentally.

A reliable way to store a gradient for later reuse is to create a gradient swatch. Using the Swatches panel menu, choose New Gradient Swatch…. If a gradient was being edited, its settings are now before you. You can also build the gradient from scratch in this dialog box; in fact, I prefer to do so. Select a color stop in this dialog box, and then use the Stop Color menu to switch from Swatches to one of the various color models to define that stop's color. As with color swatches, the Add button adds the swatch, but allows you to continue to build more. When you're done, click OK.

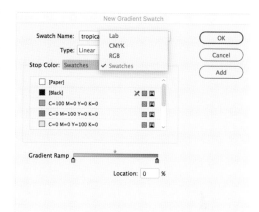

The Stroke Panel

The Control panel offers a few stroke options: the Weight, color, and Type (solid, dashed, dotted, etc.). The Stroke panel (Window > Stroke) offers considerably more. Subtle but pleasant options are Cap and Join. A Round Join slightly softens sharp corners and a Round Cap can round the ends of dashes, underlines, paragraph rules, or any line.

Stroke Type

Some stroke options sound pretty obscure (until you need them), others are really cool. Among the latter is Type, of which there are three categories: Stripe (Solid, Thick–Thin, Wavy, etc.), Dash (Dashed and various Hash options), and Dotted (regular and Japanese Dots). Most impressively, you can make your own!

Frames & Content

Styles, Type & Fonts

Pages & Spreads

Color Management

Find/Change

Long Documents

Output

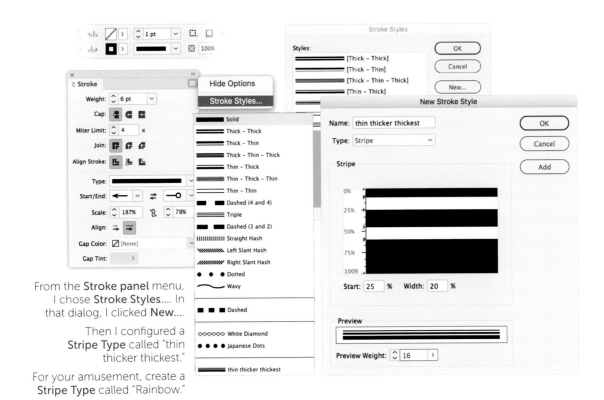

From the **Stroke panel** menu, I chose **Stroke Styles**…. In that dialog, I clicked **New**….

Then I configured a **Stripe Type** called "thin thicker thickest."

For your amusement, create a **Stripe Type** called "Rainbow."

Align Stroke

By default, a stroke straddles the edge of a shape. However, when an object really needs to maintain its size, I may set the stroke to Align to Inside. However, if I cannot allow a stroke to obscure the frame's content, perhaps an image, I'll set it to Align to Outside.

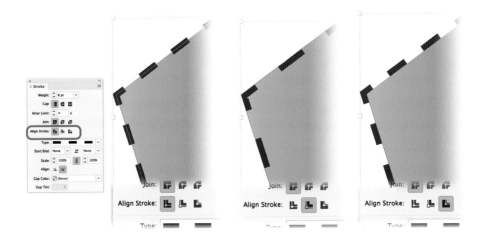

Workspaces & Preferences

Frames & Content

Gap Color

All the stroke types (except Solid) have gaps. You can choose a color to fill those gaps in the Stroke panel (near the bottom: Gap Color). For a dotted stroke, the dots themselves will be the main stroke color, but the space around and between those dots is the Gap Color.

Start/End

This is simply a way to attach decorative ends to an open line. Note that each end can be scaled.

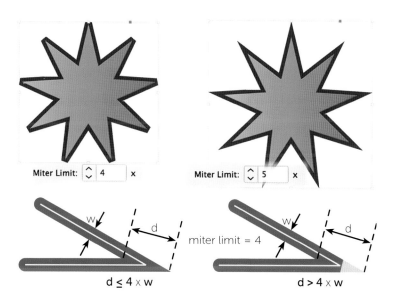

Miter Limit

This is a fairly obscure setting, but enough of my students are dismayed by truncated corners that I should mention it. As the angle of a corner diminishes, the extent of its corner (**d** in the figure) increases. When that length exceeds a certain multiple of the stroke weight (**w**), the point gets truncated. Luckily, we can adjust that multiple: the Miter Limit. In this example, I had to allow the corner length to be 5 times the stroke weight.

Frames & Content

Styles, Type & Fonts

Pages & Spreads

Color Management

Find/Change

Long Documents

Output

Frame to Content & Content to Frame

Since everything in InDesign either is a frame or is in one, we should be efficient when alternating between editing a frame and editing its content.

Text Frames

A reliable, if slow, method is to simply switch between the Type tool and the Selection tool in the Tools panel. It is far quicker, however, to double-click in a text frame with the Selection tool—the tool will change automatically and the text cursor will blink at the point of the double-click.

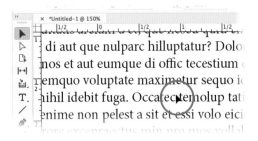

To return to editing the container, or as I prefer to phrase it, to "get out" again, tap the esc key. Get it? "Get out" = "escape!" In fact, we'll see this is a general rule in many contexts.

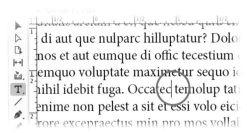

Double-click to get the **Type tool**.
Press **esc** to get the **Selection tool** again.

Image Frames

Editing the size or shape of images and their frames is often one of the tougher challenges for a new InDesign user. If one resizes the frame with the Selection tool, the frame alone is resized, either cropping the image in it or leaving a gap between the edge of the image and that of the frame. But several methods can be used to select the image within its frame so it, too, can be resized or repositioned.

The **Control panel** buttons
Select content and
Select container

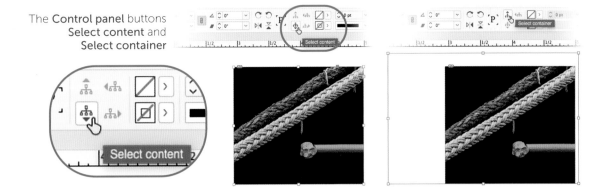

One method involves two buttons that can be found in the Control panel: Select Content and Select Container.

You may also use the speedy method suggested for text frames: double-clicking "to get in," and pressing the esc key "to get out" again. There's a twist with image frames: you can double-click to get in (content editing) *or* out (frame editing)!

When you hover your **Selection tool** over the **Content Grabber**, it becomes a hand. Drag it to recompose the image within its frame. Click this "Donut" to select the content (to resize it, perhaps).

Content Grabber

Finally (well, the last good method), we can use the Content Grabber, the concentric circles in the middle of an image frame (also known as "the donut"). Using nothing but the Selection tool, drag the donut to reposition an image within its frame. When finished, the frame is still selected. That is, unless we click on the donut (Content Grabber); then the content is selected. Double-clicking or pressing the esc key will select the frame.

A bonus with the Content Grabber: if content has been rotated, a line will appear in the donut's center, tilted at the same angle that the content has been rotated!

The one danger that's presented by the Content Grabber is that it may be dragged accidentally. When you're rearranging frames on a page quickly, it's easy to inadvertently grab the grabber and pull an image completely out of its frame! Of course, you can undo (⌘–Z/Ctrl–Z), but that will leave the content selected, so you would have to hit the esc

Image and **Content Grabber** rotated 17°

key, too, to have the frame selected. For this reason, a friend and colleague of mine despises the donut! He simply disables it and uses the double-click method instead. To disable the Content Grabber go to View > Extras > Hide Content Grabber. While in that menu, notice the other things that can be hidden or shown. There are lots of "extras."

The least efficient way to reposition or resize an image is to switch to the Direct Selection tool then click on the image. When the cursor is over the image, it will be shown as a hand inviting you to reposition the image, but not the frame. Or you can grab a corner and resize (holding down the shift key to prevent distortion). You can then choose the Selection tool and click on the edge of the frame to select it again.

Frames & Content

Styles, Type & Fonts

Pages & Spreads

Color Management

Find/Change

Long Documents

Output

Text Frames & Text Frame Options

We can exercise a great deal of control over how our content looks before we even adjust any typographic options (leading, kerning, and such). For more on typographic features, see chapter 3 of the Compendium, "Styles, Type & Fonts" (page 235).

The options under discussion here are adjusted without having to use the Type tool at all. To judge some of these features, you may wish to have some content to play with. Draw a text frame with the Type tool, then right-click and choose Fill with Placeholder Text. Don't like it? Undo, then do it again. It'll be randomly different each time.

Linking Text Frames

One continuous flow of text is called a *story*. Often, that story flows from one frame to another. When it does, we say that the story is *threaded* among linked text frames. When you have (or expect) more text than can fit into one text frame, InDesign offers many ways

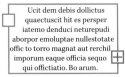

Ucit dem debis dollictus quaectuscit hit es persper iatemo denduci neturepudi aborpor emoluptae nullestotate offic to torro magnat aut rerchil imporum eaque officia sequo qui offictiatio. Bo arum.

Overset text is indicted by the red plus sign in the **out port**.

to thread that story. If you already have more content than fits (called *overset text*), its frame's out port turns red and shows a plus sign.

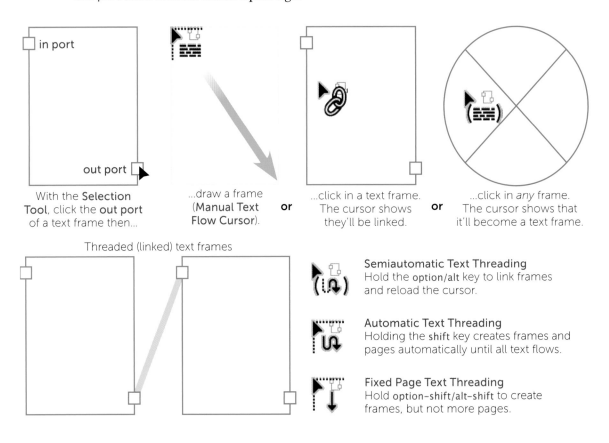

With the **Selection Tool**, click the **out port** of a text frame then...

...draw a frame (Manual Text Flow Cursor).

or

...click in a text frame. The cursor shows they'll be linked.

or

...click in *any* frame. The cursor shows that it'll become a text frame.

Threaded (linked) text frames

Semiautomatic Text Threading
Hold the **option/alt** key to link frames and reload the cursor.

Automatic Text Threading
Holding the **shift** key creates frames and pages automatically until all text flows.

Fixed Page Text Threading
Hold **option-shift/alt-shift** to create frames, but not more pages.

The method you choose for threading a story will depend on whether you already have frames into which to flow the text. It also matters if you need more pages to accommodate all the content. Most methods start with clicking on the out port of an existing text frame with the Selection tool. Clicking an out port "loads" the cursor. Depending on where you move that cursor, you may see its appearance change to indicate its behavior. Holding down modifier keys also can change its look and behavior. Here are some of your choices:

Manual Text Flow

When the loaded cursor is not over an existing frame, it exhibits a squared-off corner. Simply drag diagonally to create a new text frame; it will link to the first one automatically. You should also see a line that connects the in port of the new frame to the out port of the first one. If you do not, be sure that you are not in Preview Mode. You may also need to go to View > Extras > Show Text Threads.

If you hover the loaded cursor over another existing text frame, the cursor will show a link icon (a chain). Clicking within that text frame will link the two frames together. If you hover over an unassigned frame or shape, the cursor will show an icon that looks somewhat like text enclosed in parentheses. Clicking will convert that shape or frame into a text frame and link it to the first one.

Semiautomatic Text Threading

If you need to thread multiple frames together, it becomes tedious to repeatedly click on out ports to reload the cursor. Instead, if you hold down the option/Alt key when you make or click in a frame, that frame will be linked to the previous one and your cursor will be reloaded so you can continue onto the next one.

Automatic Text Threading

A common scenario: in an InDesign document with only one or very few pages, your cursor is loaded with potentially dozens of pages of text (maybe you are placing a text file). Clicking in the upper-left margin of an empty page creates a text frame as big as the margins. You could manually create more pages, click out ports, and flow text from page to page. A better solution is to hold the shift key when clicking on that first page's upper-left margin. Shift-clicking will create not only the first frame, but more pages as well, each with a frame as large as its margins, until all the text has flowed!

Fixed Page Text Threading

This method is similar to automatic text threading, but is better in situations where you have a fixed page limit. Holding down option-shift/alt-shift will create frames on the pages that already exist, but will not add more pages.

Frames & Content

Styles, Type & Fonts

Pages & Spreads

Color Management

Find/Change

Long Documents

Output

Scaled Text Preferences

As mentioned in the discussion of preferences, there's a way to know the original size of type after it has been scaled with its frame. This setting called Adjust Scaling Percentage, is found in the General preferences (⌘-K/Ctrl-K). If chosen, when a text frame is enlarged by 50%, for example, it will show a scaling of 150% in the Control panel ever after, making it easy to set it back to 100% if needed. If the text size had started at 10 points, it will read ⊤T ◊ 10 pt(15) ⌄ which can be confusing. If you liked the new frame size, but wanted the text to be 10 points again, you might have to set it to 6 ⅔ points (1.5 x 6 ⅔ = 10)! This is not worth the trouble. The few times I've resized a text frame arbitrarily was for unique items like book titles. I have never needed the original size or later cared what it was.

Text Frame Options

A small number of text frame options can be adjusted via the Control panel. The rest require the Text Frame Options dialog box, which is opened by choosing Object > Text Frame Options…. A shortcut for that exists, too: ⌘-B/Ctrl-B.

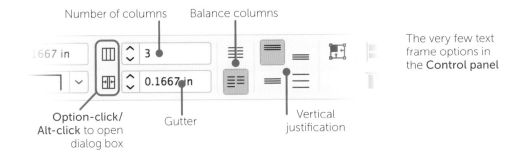

Number of columns · Balance columns

Option-click/
Alt-click to open
dialog box

Gutter

Vertical
justification

The very few text
frame options in
the **Control panel**

Columns

Any text frame can have multiple columns. The number of columns can be set in a couple places: the Control panel, the Properties panel, or via the Text Frame Options dialog box. You can also set column width parameters.

Fixed Number

Choose a number of columns and a gutter (space between columns), and InDesign will divide the frame evenly and calculate a width for each column. If you enter a width, the frame's width will change to accommodate it. However, this column width value is a bit fugitive: change the width of the frame, and InDesign will adjust the column widths again to divide the frame evenly. If you need a column with a fixed width, choose…

Unbalanced (left) and
balanced columns (right)

Frames &
Content

Styles, Type
& Fonts

Pages
& Spreads

Color
Management

Find/Change

Long
Documents

Output

Fixed Width

Now if you manually adjust the frame's width, it will snap to whole-column widths. For example, if you start with a three-column frame with two-inch wide columns and then attempt to widen the frame just a little, it will suddenly grow a bit more than two full inches wider (the column width plus a new gutter).

Inset Spacing

Inset pushes the text inward, away from the frame's edges. Note the chain in the center of these fields. When intact, it ensures all the values remain equal. If disabled, each value can be unique. Use inset when you add a stroke or fill color to your text frame. I also use inset for captions that abut an image to yield a predictable amount of space between the image and the words.

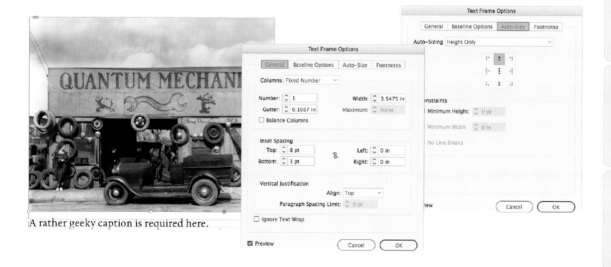

A rather geeky caption is required here.

Vertical Justification

When the text doesn't cover the full depth (height) of a frame, you can choose where the text is positioned vertically within the frame. The sensible default is Top. The other choices can be useful, too. When you change this to Bottom, the last baseline will fall along the bottom edge of the frame (assuming there is no inset).

Center will attempt to give as much space above the text as below it. Do you see the page number above? It's in a frame as tall as the page's top margin, but it has center vertical justification applied to center it in that margin. The same is true of page headers. Easy centering with no arithmetic!

Justify will put the top line's ascenders at the top of the frame, and the last line's baseline at the bottom. Leading throughout will be adjusted to evenly divide the space between lines. If you choose Justify, you may also enter a value for Paragraph Spacing Limit. This will force InDesign to first add space after each paragraph in the frame (up to the specified limit). Once that limit is reached, leading is added to each line to justify the text top to bottom. If the Paragraph Spacing Limit is very large, InDesign will use paragraph spacing exclusively and you will avoid any leading alteration at all.

Baseline Options

First Baseline Offset

Ascent ascenders touch top	
Ascenders touch frame-top	
Cap Height Caps touch top!	
Caps touch frame-top	
Leading	
Leading affects first line's position	
x-Height lowercase touch top	
As x-heights touch frame-top	
Fixed (min = 0)	
A dangerous setting. Use a real min.	

You can choose where the first baseline of your text is relative to the top of the frame. Doing so can make it easier to have content align pleasantly across columns or pages.

Ascent is the default. The first baseline is as far down from the top of the frame as an ascender is tall. That is, any ascenders in the first line just kiss the top of the frame. However, since capital (uppercase) letters are typically shorter than ascenders, alignment between such a frame and another may not look correct. Thus, a caption frame next to an image may appear better aligned with its image if we choose...

Cap Height, in which the caps perfectly touch the top edge of the frame. I usually reserve this for stand-alone frames.

Leading is the setting used for the text frame you're reading right now. When combined with well-calculated leading, we can best ensure that text aligns with an underlying baseline grid (below). If it's difficult to guarantee that the first line will have a leading value consistent with the baseline grid (odd-sized headers, perhaps), then Fixed may be appropriate.

x-Height, like Cap Height, is best used with stand-alone frames with no caps in the first line.

Fixed, combined with a Min value equal to your baseline grid setting, helps keep text flowing along that grid.

Baseline Grid

The Text Frame Options dialog box offers you a chance to apply a Custom Baseline Grid to specific text frames. Although I seldom do so, this affords a good opportunity to discuss how to use baseline grids generally.

The Baseline Grid preference settings are document-specific and create virtual lines along which your text's baselines can run. Choose InDesign CC > Preferences > Grids (on a Mac)/ Edit > Preferences > Grids (on Windows) to set these. You can force your text to align to the grid with "Paragraph Styles" (page 242), or they may be aspirational—that is, it's on you to ensure the leading you apply to your text lands the text on this grid if you want it to.

The settings for the following example document are:

Color:	Light Blue	Because I was too lazy to change it.
Start:	54 pt	That's how far from the top of the page my primary text frame is.
Relative To:	Top of Page	Other choice is Top Margin, but in my case, my primary text frames are located a bit higher than my top margin. Thus, I measure from the page edge.
Increment Every:	14 pt	This is my fundamental leading. Larger headers may have twice this value, or use Space Before or Space After equaling a multiple of this value.
View Threshold:	75%	If I zoom out sufficiently (below 75% in this document), the grid lines disappear. This is good, as they'd be overwhelmingly dense at that point.

Frames &
Content

Styles, Type
& Fonts

Pages
& Spreads

Color
Management

Find/Change

Long
Documents

Output

54 pt

14 pt

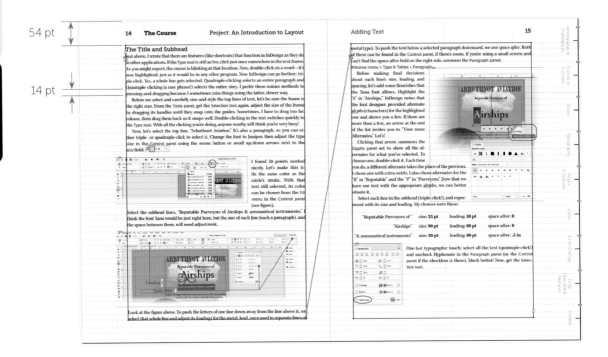

Auto-Size

This is an option for stand-alone text frames (not threaded to others). The setting I use most frequently is illustrated here: allowing only the height to change (to maintain column width), keeping the top edge fixed.

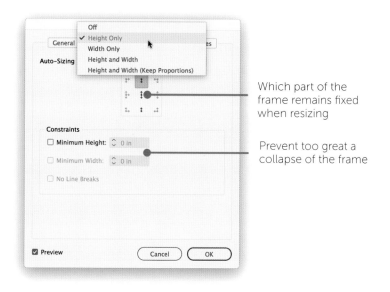

Which part of the frame remains fixed when resizing

Prevent too great a collapse of the frame

For frames that contain a very short phrase (such as a headline or title), allowing both dimensions to change may work well, especially if you disallow line breaks (the last checkbox).

The nicest thing about this feature is that it prevents text from becoming overset. It's disturbing to find the last words of a caption missing when something's gone to press!

I also appreciate a frame's shrinking to prevent extraneous parts of it from dangling where it might get selected accidentally with other items.

Footnotes

This allows footnotes of a particular text frame to span across the frame's columns. Also, you may specify some space that appears around those footnotes.

If this is a behavior you would like to make document-wide, you should do so by choosing Type > Document Footnote Options… then going to the Layout tab. There are many options here for configuring the look and feel of footnotes.

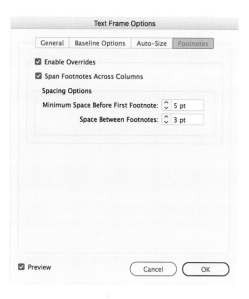

Image Frames & Linked Images

Image frames are created in several ways: when we place an image either freely on a spread or into an awaiting "unassigned" frame, or when we simply paste an image in InDesign, embedding it.

Linking vs. Embedding

An InDesign best practice is to keep image documents separate from our layout document. In so doing, the images (we think) we see on our layouts do not bloat the InDesign document's file size or compromise its performance. This also allows us to more easily edit those graphics files and see those edits in InDesign.

Embedding gives us the one small advantage of having most of our assets in one document, making it more portable. A small document with few images may work fine this way, but we usually create PDFs as our deliverable, which better ensures preserving text formatting, too. In my work, it is a rare graphic that is embedded, usually by pasting.

When we place images and graphics, a link is established between our layout and the image file. To keep that link healthy, there are dos and don'ts that we'll need to discuss. But first, how do we place a file, and thus establish that link?

Placing Images

The most reliable way to place an image or graphic file is to use File > Place… then navigate to the image file you'd like to include in your layout. You may also drag images into InDesign. The native file formats of Adobe Illustrator and Adobe Photoshop (.ai and .psd, respectively) may offer extra options. To enjoy these, check the box labeled Show Import Options. These will mostly consist of choosing which layers in those documents should be visible when they are placed in InDesign. You can place an image multiple times, with different choices each time.

You may also choose more than one image or graphic at one time. For example, if there are several images in the same folder, it would be easy to click one, then shift-click on an image down the list to select those two and all the images in between; or click one then ⌘-click/Ctrl-click to highlight discontiguous images. Then click the Open button.

Now you have a loaded Place Gun, a cursor bearing the likeness of the image (or one of the images if you chose multiple). If you chose multiple images, the cursor will also show you a number indicating how many images have been loaded.

 Place Gun with one image

 **Place Gun** with three images

With your Place Gun loaded, you have several ways to, eh, discharge it. If you simply click where there's nothing, InDesign will create a frame as big as the image or graphic (the size designated in the originating application) and fill the frame with the image. There is a high probability that an image will be much too large this way. Many cameras capture images with many millions of pixels. They deliver these pixels spread out over a large area with a low density—often 72 pixels per inch (or ppi). An image that is 3,000 pixels across will be 42 *inches* wide! Luckily, we don't need to go to Photoshop to deal with that. If you do click to place the image and find it to be huge, undo (⌘-Z/Ctrl-Z) to reload the cursor.

Instead of clicking, drag. As you drag across the page, you'll notice that the shape of the box being formed is the same shape as the image. When you release the mouse, the frame will be as large as you drew it and the image will fill that frame exactly. A image that is 3,000 pixels across squeezed into a frame that is 8 inches wide will have a pixel density (known as *resolution*) of 375 ppi. In InDesign, we call that the image's *effective resolution*, since its actual resolution was only 72 ppi.

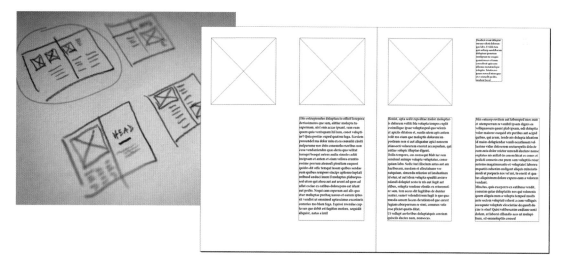

If we're using a template, it's likely the designer included empty frames to hold images. Graphic designers learn early to use pencil and paper to draw many quick sketches of a layout, called thumbnails. I argue these get the worst ideas out of your system. Later, the more promising sketches can be migrated into InDesign in the form of placeholder text and empty frames most likely drawn with the Rectangle Frame tool.

If you do have empty frames awaiting images to fill them, you can click on each with a loaded Place Gun. You may have to adjust how the images fit each frame, but we'll get to that shortly.

If a frame is selected when you choose an image using File > Place…, another checkbox in that dialog box comes into play: Replace Selected Item. Thus, if you select a frame, empty or not, then place an image, the image will automatically take over that frame, removing the content that was there. I sometimes fail to notice that I have a text frame selected when I place, then I find that the text is gone, and there's an image in its place. Here, some joke about a picture being worth a thousand words would be appropriate, but I'll leave that to you.

Frames & Content

Styles, Type & Fonts

Pages & Spreads

Color Management

Find/Change

Long Documents

Output

Frame Fitting Options

When an image's size doesn't match the size of its frame, we may wish to do something about that. Again, InDesign lavishes choices upon us. With one or more image frames selected, these choices can be reached in several places: buttons in the Control panel, by right-clicking, or in the Object menu. For the last two options, a Fitting submenu is shown.

The most commonly needed (and safer) commands are Fill Frame Proportionally and Fit Content Proportionally. The "proportionally" part means "without distortion."

Fill Frame Proportionally will enlarge or reduce the image so it completely fills the frame with the least amount of crop. A tall image in a square frame will have its top and/or bottom cropped, but not its sides. If there's an area of the page that you want filled with an image, to set a mood perhaps, this is the command you need. You may adjust the image's position with the Content Grabber for a better composition. Below, cropped parts are shown as translucent.

Fill frame proportionately   Fit content proportionately   Fit content to frame

Fit frame to content   Center content   Content-Aware Fit

Fit Content Proportionally will show the entire image (no cropping), and may leave some empty areas in the frame. To get the frame to fit the image snugly, use...

The most dangerous choice: Fit Content to Frame. If the frame is square and the photo in it is not, the result can be disturbing. To confirm that something bad has occurred, select the image inside its frame. I'd just click on the "Content Grabber" (page 199). A look at the scaling in the Control panel for the portrait above reveals that the horizontal and vertical scaling are different (56% and 85%, respectively, for the image here).

Fit Frame to Content aligns each edge of the frame with the image within. No crop, no extraneous frame. A fast way to achieve this is to double-click on a frame's corner handle. Double-clicking a side handle resizes only that dimension. For example, double-clicking the handle at the center of the top edge resizes the frame only vertically.

Center Content does exactly what it says: if the content is off-center, whether it's larger or smaller than the frame, it will be centered. I reduced the example image's size for clarity.

Content–Aware Fit attempts to detect the subject of the image and make it fit within the frame in a pleasing way. This may be a handy default for product shots in a catalog…or not. It may yield images of various magnifications when consistency is required. If you find that this setting works well for you, consider leaving it as the default behavior in General Preferences.

Frame Fitting Options… opens a dialog box that allows you to apply settings to a frame so it might automatically fit its content as desired! Choose one of the first three fitting options and Auto Fit. If you then resize the frame, the image will maintain the fitting options you chose. You can set these options on an empty frame so that when an image is placed into it, the image will do what it's supposed to. Further, you can specify that a small amount of the image is cropped on any side. So if your images have a rough edge or unwanted border, you can get rid of that automatically, too. If you don't need the crop function, you can set Auto Fit from the Control panel. These options are available only on image frames.

Edit Original

One of the more useful benefits of linking to an image or graphic is that it can be edited easily in its original application (usually Photoshop or Illustrator). The most straightforward way to do this is to select the image in InDesign, then right-click and choose Edit Original. Soon, another application launches with that document open. Complete your edits and save your changes, and when you return to InDesign, you'll see the image in its new state.

The Links panel also affords a way to edit placed images, graphics, and, under certain circumstances, linked text. You can manually highlight an image name in the Links panel, or select it in the layout, then click the Edit Original button (resembles a pencil).

Modified Links

A funny thing can happen if you edit and save that linked graphic without choosing Edit Original *immediately* before doing that edit. In this case, the image's appearance in InDesign won't update automatically and there will be a warning icon displayed in both the Links panel and the upper-left corner of the image. This indicates that the link's status is "modified." To update the link and change the status to "OK," either *double-click* on the error icon in the Links panel or *single-click* on the icon in the image frame. If the edit

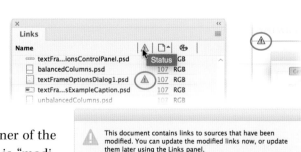

Frames & Content

Styles, Type & Fonts

Pages & Spreads

Color Management

Find/Change

Long Documents

Output

occurred when the InDesign document was closed, you'll see a more obvious message when next opening that document. Simply choose to Update Links (or you may choose to defer the update, but there is little reason to do so).

Missing Links & Relinking

Sometimes, the message you see when opening a document says that there are Missing Link(s). This requires more effort to correct: you have to locate the missing file, if it actually still exists. When you place an image, InDesign notes not only the filename, but also the entire path to the image; every folder, subfolder, etc. If any part of that path changes—say you move an image to another folder or rename the image or one of the folders along that path— InDesign can no longer find that image!

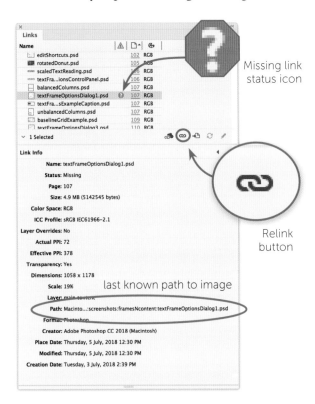

Missing link status icon

Relink button

last known path to image

So when you see that dialog box warning of Missing Link(s) and you click Update, you are faced with a dialog box asking you to find where that missing image is now. If it's truly lost (deleted, for example), you will have to find a substitute or delete the image from your document. Note that the likeness you see in the document is a proxy that InDesign creates so you can better recognize the image you're seeking. The proxy does not have sufficient data for high-quality output.

If you've deferred updating or otherwise must deal with a missing link via the Links panel, there are clues. When an image is selected (or its name is highlighted in the Links panel) you can reveal more information by using the disclosure button (>) in the lower-left corner of the Links panel. In the Link Info that appears will be the last known path to the image. To tell InDesign where the image is, double-click on the missing link status indicator icon, then navigate to the file's location.

If you'd prefer to link to a substitute image (and not just for missing ones), use the chain-like Relink button. Again, you navigate to an image file.

When relinking, you may have to fuss with the frame fitting options.

Note: The Link Info contains a lot of potentially useful information. For example, Scale values and the Effective PPI. Recall Effective Resolution in "Placing Images" (page 208).

Gridify Images

Remember "Gridify" (page 191)? We can place a lot of images simultaneously in a grid. If the images vary in size and shape, we'll have to deal with how they fit or fill their frames afterward.

Placing a Grid of Images

We need a Place Gun with multiple images in it. So go to File > Place…, as usual, and choose multiple images, or drag image files directly from a folder in the operating system. Either way, you have a cursor with a number in it. Note the number; will that many images make an even grid? Odd numbers can be tricky. If it's seven images, you could create a two-by-four grid with an empty slot. That's allowed, of course, but unfortunate. Nine, though odd, make a lovely three-by-three grid.

With the loaded cursor in hand, start dragging and keep that mouse button down! Once you've started dragging, use the arrow keys to create more (↑ or →) or fewer (↓ or ←) columns and rows. Pressing ⌘ + arrow/Ctrl + arrow will change the distance between rows or columns (up and down for row spacing, left and right for column spacing). Some users think they need very large hands for this because they've forgotten that there's a ⌘/Ctrl key on both sides of the keyboard.

When you have enough areas to accommodate your images, you can release the mouse. You will now have a grid of identically sized frames with images fit proportionally within each one. This means there's some extraneous frame, which may not trouble you. But if the images vary much in size or shape, you may consider using the many fitting options discussed just a few pages back.

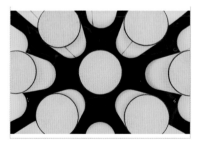

Frames & Content

Styles, Type & Fonts

Pages & Spreads

Color Management

Find/Change

Long Documents

Output

Groups and Accessing Their Content

We group multiple objects to better ensure that one doesn't get moved or transformed without the other(s). Examples could include images and their captions, callouts and their accompanying arrows, or a logomark (graphic) and its logotype.

It is not uncommon to group groups together, too. You might group several image-caption pairs, for example, to maintain their spacing or proximity to each other. First, let's look at a bunch of ungrouped objects. The Layers panel is included below because it provides a way to see and select all the objects on a spread and whether they are grouped or not.

Learn all about "Layers" (page 318).

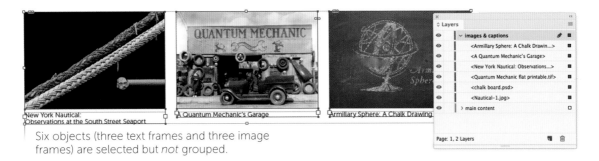

Six objects (three text frames and three image frames) are selected but *not* grouped.

If we group the objects above by using ⌘–G/Ctrl–G (or Object > Group, or by right-clicking and choosing Group), they are now outlined by a dashed line and the Layers panel shows that we now have a group. If we click the > icon to the left of a layer's name, then the one to the left of a <group>, each of those icons will now be a ∨ and you will see the group's contents.

The six objects are grouped. Note they are now listed in the **Layers panel** under the entry **<group>**, which is selected, and the selection outline is dashed.

Double-Click to Get In, Escape to Get Out

Sounds familiar, doesn't it? This is a wonderfully consistent and powerful rule in InDesign. Sadly, there are quirks, but they are few and can be overcome.

For example, let's say we wish to move our three captions up or down a little bit. If we double-click on one of them with the Selection tool, it's selected! Like a hacker movie, "we're in!" If we hold down the shift key and click a second caption, it's selected, too. But try to go for a third one, and the whole group gets selected.

However, we can use the Layers panel to select the third one (and so on), instead. To the right of every entry in the Layers panel is a small square that serves as that entry's proxy. If an object is selected, the proxy lights up in the color associated with that layer. You may also click on a proxy to select its object, then shift-click on other proxies to add their objects to your selection.

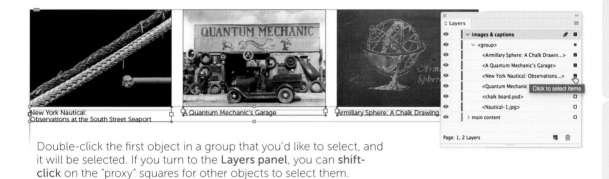

Double-click the first object in a group that you'd like to select, and it will be selected. If you turn to the **Layers panel**, you can **shift-click** on the "proxy" squares for other objects to select them.

A more realistic scenario than the one illustrated above is grouping each image-caption pair, then grouping those groups together. This yields groups inside groups. Get ready to click! If your goal is to select a single object in a nested group, you would double-click to get in one level (one of the groups is selected), then double-click again to select an object in that group. If that's a caption text frame, yet another double-click will switch to the Type tool, with a text cursor blinking. Yes, one more double-click will highlight a word.

To get back out, hit the esc key as many times as you double-clicked—each time will take you out a level.

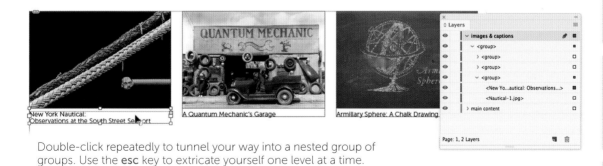

Double-click repeatedly to tunnel your way into a nested group of groups. Use the **esc** key to extricate yourself one level at a time.

Frames & Content

Styles, Type & Fonts

Pages & Spreads

Color Management

Find/Change

Long Documents

Output

Alignment & Distribution

Layout isn't simply about getting a bunch of text and image frames on a page or spread. Hopefully, we create a nice arrangement of them. To help us achieve that, a number of features exist.

Guides

As you may know from other applications you have used, guides are nonprinting lines to which you can snap objects. As you move an object around on a page, when the object's edge gets close to a guide, it gently attaches itself. I say "gently" because you can easily move the object past this point without noticing.

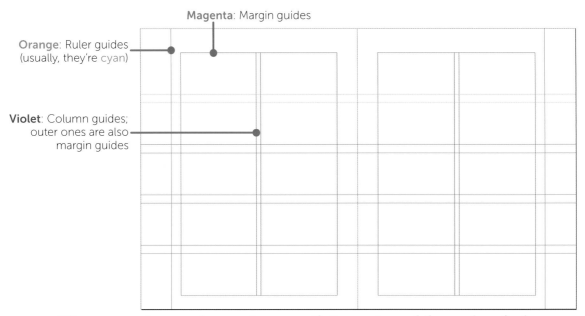

Magenta: Margin guides

Orange: Ruler guides (usually, they're cyan)

Violet: Column guides; outer ones are also margin guides

When you create a new document, you specify its margins and the number of columns on each page. Actually, you're specifying where margin and column guides should be. If you desire more structure for your spreads, you may add ruler guides as well. Arbitrary ruler guides can be drawn by dragging them from the rulers at the top or left edge of the document window.

Note: Freshly created ruler guides are selected when you first draw them (unless something else was selected when you created the guide). You may select a guide as you would any other object: with the Selection tool. When a guide is selected, you can precisely position it via the Control panel (X position for vertical guides, Y for horizontal). Change the color of selected guides by choosing Layout > Ruler Guides…, where you may also choose a magnification level below which those guides aren't shown.

A method for creating many guides at once as a custom grid is to choose Layout > Create Guides…. That is how the horizontal guides in the example figure were made.

I deleted the guides made by this command at the top and bottom because I already had the margin guides. Note that you may have those rows or columns of guides divide up the page or the margins (Fit Guides to:), and you can remove previous experiments with the Remove Existing Ruler Guides checkbox.

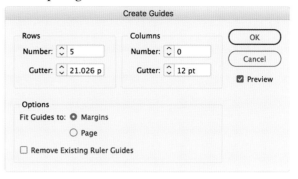

Smart Guides

Even if your layout doesn't require a strict grid, you likely will still want objects aligned to each other or to parts of the page. Smart Guides (and the Align panel) make that easy.

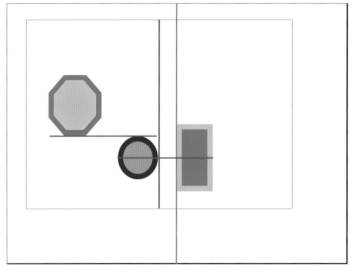

Left: Simulated **Smart Guides** indicating…

The rectangle's left edge is aligned with the horizontal center of the page

The circle's right edge is aligned with the horizontal center of the margin

The polygon's bottom edge is aligned to the circle's top edge

The circle's vertical center is aligned to the rectangle's vertical center

As you move an object slowly, green lines will indicate when it's aligned (or spaced evenly) with others. Violet lines show when it's aligned to the page, and magenta lines show when it's aligned to the margins. When you have few shapes, Smart Guides are super-helpful.

Below: Simulated **Smart Guides** indicating…

The space between the three shapes is evenly distributed as the polygon is dragged to make that so

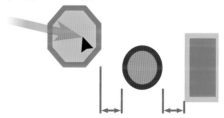

Align Panel

I adore the Align panel! The icons are easily recognizable for what they do and their names clearly state their function (are you listening, Illustrator?).

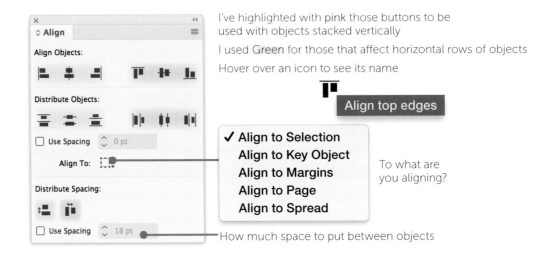

I've highlighted with pink those buttons to be used with objects stacked vertically

I used Green for those that affect horizontal rows of objects

Hover over an icon to see its name

Align top edges

✓ Align to Selection
Align to Key Object
Align to Margins
Align to Page
Align to Spread

To what are you aligning?

How much space to put between objects

Many of these icons also appear in the Control panel, but not the last, very useful row (Distribute Spacing). I suggest having the Align panel on screen: Window > Object & Layout > Align.

Here we have three objects (which could be any combination of text, image, or unassigned frames). When distributed accoring to their horizontal centers (the midpoint between the left and right edges), they don't look evenly distributed because they're different sizes.

What gives a better impression of even distribution is equalizing the space between them. Note that only the central object moved. When we choose Align To: > Align to Selection in the Align panel, the outermost objects are stationary. If you select more than one object, then give one of them a single extra click with the Selection tool, it will exhibit a blue highlight on its edges:

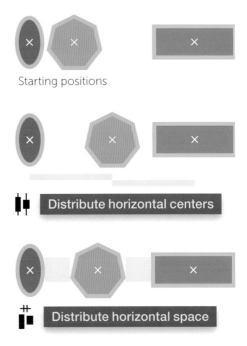

Starting positions

Distribute horizontal centers

Distribute horizontal space

The ellipse above is now a Key Object and the Align To: menu now shows a small key icon. This object will keep its position as you try other alignment settings. You can set one object to be the key before aligning top edges, then another when you distribute right edges, for

example. Also, when aligning to a Key Object, the Use Spacing checkbox under Distribute Spacing becomes active (with a default value of 0). You may enter any distance you wish, then use a distribute space button. The selected objects will now be that far apart.

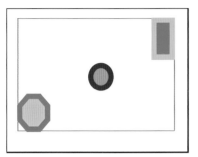

With **Align to Margins** chosen, and both **Distribute vertical space** *and* **Distribute horizontal space** applied.

You can enable the Use Spacing feature at any time, but InDesign will keep the topmost or leftmost object in place and move the other selected objects to achieve the specified distribution. Align to Margins treats the margins much like key objects. If you choose Align top edges, for example, the tops of all selected objects will align to the top margin. Distribution will attempt to lay out objects evenly within the margins. Align to Page and Align to Spread behave analogously: the page or spread are the items to which objects align.

Precise Positioning and Sizing

Both the Control panel and the Transform panel (Window > Object & Layout > Transform) offer fields that allow us to specify position and/or size to at least 4 decimal places!

X & Y
How far the reference point is from the ruler origin.

Width & Height
If adjusted, scaling will be exhibited from the reference point.

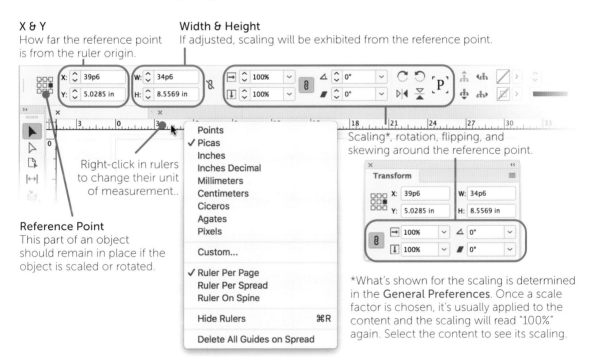

Right-click in rulers to change their unit of measurement..

Reference Point
This part of an object should remain in place if the object is scaled or rotated.

Scaling*, rotation, flipping, and skewing around the reference point.

*What's shown for the scaling is determined in the **General Preferences**. Once a scale factor is chosen, it's usually applied to the content and the scaling will read "100%" again. Select the content to see its scaling.

Styles, Type
& Fonts

Pages
& Spreads

Color
Management

Find/Change

Long
Documents

Output

Sometimes you want something where you want it. Of course, you can drag objects around with the Selection tool, dropping them anywhere. Or you can select an object and use the arrow keys to nudge it. Holding down ⌘-shift/Ctrl-Shift as you press the arrow keys nudges the object one-tenth as far. The shift key alone nudges 10 times as far. But for precise positioning, we have other options. Size and position can also be specified in "Object Styles" (page 267).

Transforms

There are so many ways to get objects where and how we want them! Let's have a look at most of them, from the free-form to the highly precise.

Note: With almost all of these, holding down the option/Alt key yields a copy of your object rather than transforming the original.

Movement

With the Selection Tool—Two Ways

This will not be a surprise: if you drag an object with the Selection tool, you move it (avoiding the Content Grabber if it's an image frame, unless you wish to move the image within its frame). Holding down the option/Alt key as you drag creates a copy of the object at the location where you release the mouse.

A second, easily missed method is to select one or more objects then double-click on the Selection tool in the Tools panel. This summons a dialog box where you can enter a precise movement. You can also choose to move either the original (by clicking OK) or a copy (by clicking Copy). Be sure to activate the Preview to see what's going on.

X Location & Y Location Fields

As mentioned on the previous page, both the Control panel and the Transform panel have various fields where we can enter values by which to move an object.

Rotation

With the Selection Tool & Bounding Box

If you've selected an object and then move the Selection tool cursor just beyond any corner of that object, you'll see a curled arrow inviting you to rotate the object. If you approach an angle of rotation to which another object on the same spread has been rotated, a Smart Guide will gently snap this object to the same angle. Holding the shift key will snap the rotation to 45° angles (45, 90, 135, etc.).

Rotate Tool

Just below the halfway point of the Tools panel are the Transform tools, including the Rotate tool. The default (the one shown if you haven't changed it) is the Free Transform tool. Right-click it (or whichever tool is showing) to choose any of the other three. Note the letter to the right that you may press to access each tool (at least two of them make sense).

⬆	Free Transform Tool	E
↻	Rotate Tool	R
⬈	Scale Tool	S
➔	Shear Tool	O

The Rotate tool offers one benefit over using the Selection tool: you may choose the axis of rotation. The usual procedure to use the Rotate tool is to first select an object (here, an image), then with the Rotate tool, click the point around which you wish the rotation to occur (it can be anywhere at all, on the object or not). In this example, I clicked about halfway down the left-hand side of the image, in the middle of one of the lamps.

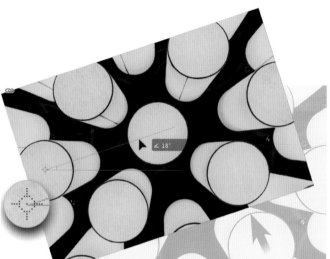

Then you drag. From where is not critical, though I'd recommend it not be very close to the axis of rotation. I chose the middle of the image in this case, but I could have dragged from anywhere. You don't get much finesse if you drag too close to the axis, much like one doesn't get much leverage pushing a door open near its hinges. As you drag, InDesign shows you the angle of rotation and a growing wedge. Holding the shift key would snap the rotation every 45°, and holding the option/Alt key would rotate a copy rather than the original.

Rather than dragging to rotate, you may double-click on the Rotate tool in the Tools panel. You can then enter a precise angle the object should rotate around the axis of rotation.

Rotation Buttons & Angle Field

For a quick 90° rotation, you can use the Control panel. First set the Reference Point (see figure on page 219), then click either the Rotate 90° Clockwise or Rotate 90° Counter-Clockwise button.

Near those buttons is a field where you can enter an angle. The object will then be rotated that much around its reference point.

Frames & Content

Styles, Type & Fonts

Pages & Spreads

Color Management

Find/Change

Long Documents

Output

Scaling

When scaling, be aware of how the When Scaling preferences are set. See "Apply to Content/ Adjust Scaling Percentage" (page 165).

With the Selection Tool & Bounding Box

Simply dragging the corner of a frame's bounding box will resize it. Holding shift will preserve its proportions. To resize a frame and its content, hold down the ⌘/Ctrl key. Use ⌘-shift/Ctrl-shift to resize the frame and its content without distorting either.

Scale Tool

Found in the same part of the Tools panel as the Rotate tool, the Scale tool shares something important with its cousin: an axis around which the transformation takes place. You click on the object to set the axis, move the cursor a distance away from that axis, and prepare to drag. To make this a little more intuitive, I suggest that after setting the axis, you position the cursor at about a 45° angle from the axis before dragging. Then, as you drag toward the axis, the object (and any content within it) will scale roughly proportionally. The shift key will make it exactly proportional. Phrased differently, dragging at a 45° angle scales both the width and the height, whereas dragging up and down with the Scale tool scales only the height, and dragging left and right scales only the width. Tricky. Practice is recommended (remember you have unlimited undo).

Warning: If you drag too far, you may flip the image. If you scale an image, I suggest clicking on the Content Grabber (the donut at the center of the image), then consulting the Scale X Percentage and Scale Y Percentage fields to see if they are the same. If not, you've distorted the image. If one or both are negative, you have flipped the image in that dimension. The Flip indicator will also show this: the "P" will be flipped. Correct the issue, if needed, then tap the esc key to select the frame again.

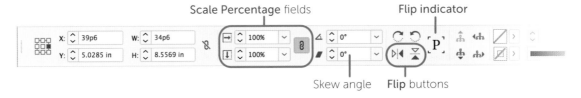

Scale Percentage fields   Flip indicator

Skew angle   Flip buttons

Width & Height Fields

In either the Control panel or the Transform panel, you can directly enter a width and/or height. If they're linked (the chain to their right is active), both values will change to keep the object the same shape (also called its *aspect ratio*). If you resize an image frame this way, you may have to follow up with fitting commands; see "Frame Fitting Options" (page 210).

Regardless of the units showing in those fields, you may use others (and arithmetic) as long as you include an abbreviation with the value(s). For example, two inches can be entered "2i", "2in", ".5i + 6p6", etc.

Scale X Percentage & Scale Y Percentage Fields

Depending on your When Scaling preferences, these fields will likely show "100%" almost always. If you choose, say, 75% from the small menus to the right of either of these fields, the frame and its content will shrink to three-quarters of their former size. The Scale fields will then immediately read 100% again—your new starting point.

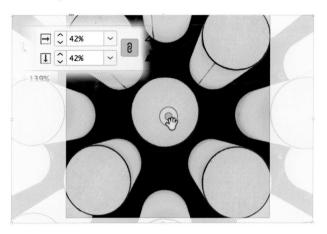

If you are curious about the scaling of an image *inside* its frame, you will have to select it (double-click on it or click the Content Grabber).

Reflection

With the Selection Tool & Bounding Box

If you drag the edge of a frame past the opposite edge (via one of the handles on its bounding box), the image will be flipped. An interesting method, but the Flip buttons are faster and more reliable.

Flip Buttons

When either (or both) of these are deployed, an object flips around its reference point. The Scale Percentage fields, Rotation Angle field, and Flip indicator will all remind you if an object has been flipped.

Shearing

Shear Tool

This is similar to the Scale tool in that it can transform an object either vertically or horizontally if you drag in that direction.

Frames & Content

Styles, Type & Fonts

Pages & Spreads

Color Management

Find/Change

Long Documents

Output

Shear X Angle Field

The Shear angle tells you how "out of plumb" the vertical lines are in the object you sheared. In this image, that's about 20°.

Direct Selection Tool

Instead of selecting an entire object with the Selection tool, you can use the Direct Selection tool to select one the object's *anchor points*, the very tiny dots along the perimeter of any shape or frame in InDesign. Even Text Wrap paths can be edited with this tool. It's easiest if the shape is not selected at all as you approach one of its anchor points with this tool; otherwise you're editing the entire shape rather than a single point.

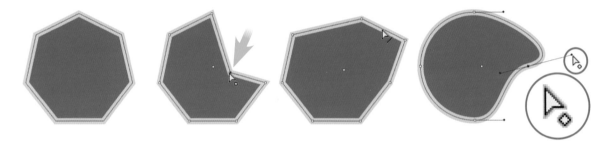

You can drag a point to create a wholly custom shape. You might also drag a path segment (the line between points) to move an entire edge. Anchor points on curved shapes have handles that control the trajectory of a path from one point to the next. You can edit these with the Direct Selection tool as well.

Both selection tools are derived from very similar ones in Adobe Illustrator, where they have been refined to make this kind of editing much easier. The other tools borrowed from Illustrator include the Pen tool, the Pencil tool, and the ones lurking behind them in the Tools panel (right-click either the Pen or Pencil tool to see). If you need rather custom shapes (to use as frames or just as decorative elements), and you have access to Illustrator, I'd strongly recommend using Illustrator to create them.

However, with the ability to sculpt basic shapes with the Direct Selection tool, you may not need to run to Illustrator often.

Free Transform Tool

The greatest advantage of the Free Transform tool over the Selection tool is that it will scale both frame and content by default. You still need the shift key to prevent distortion to content if you free transform an image or text frame.

After starting to drag a corner of a frame with this tool, you may shear the shape by holding down ⌘/Ctrl.

Pathfinder

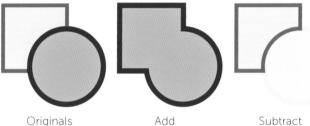

Originals   Add   Subtract   Intersect   Exclude Overlap

To assemble a shape or frame from multiple pieces, the first four commands in the menu Object > Pathfinder are just the thing you need. To fuse two or more shapes together, choose Add from that menu. Subtract punches holes: the top object becomes a hole in what's behind. To move an object fore or aft of another, select it and right-click, then choose Arrange > Send to Back or Bring to Front (don't bother with Backward or Forward, as you may have to do that too many times).

Compound Path

A fly's eye is actually composed of many very tiny eyes. Thus, we say it has compound eyes—one made from many. If you want what looks like, say, 35 circles to act as a single frame, you can have that.

You'd select all of those circles, and then choose Object > Paths > Make Compound Path. With that path selected (I so want to say "those paths," but it's now a single entity), you can place an image in it and see the scene as though you're looking through 35 windowpanes.

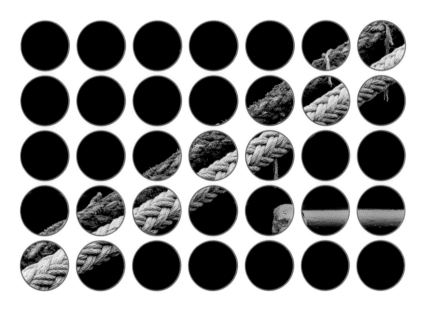

Frames & Content

Styles, Type & Fonts

Pages & Spreads

Color Management

Find/Change

Long Documents

Output

Effects

InDesign offers many ways to nondestructively alter the appearance of objects. We can use Corner Options to alter the shape of corners on any object (that has corners), and we can use Effects to do things like create Drop Shadows or have an image fade out (Feather).

Live Corners Widget and Corner Options Dialog Box

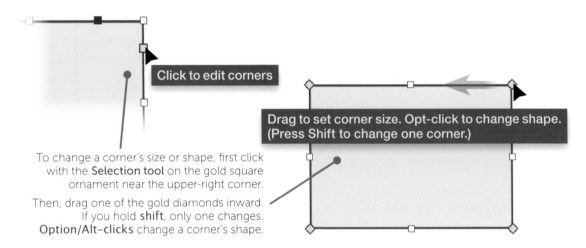

Click to edit corners

Drag to set corner size. Opt-click to change shape. (Press Shift to change one corner.)

To change a corner's size or shape, first click with the **Selection tool** on the gold square ornament near the upper-right corner.

Then, drag one of the gold diamonds inward. If you hold **shift**, only one changes. **Option/Alt–clicks** change a corner's shape.

Every rectangle (any rectangular frame) exhibits a square, gold Live Corners widget near its upper-right corner. Clicking it engages the corner-editing feature. Drag a diamond to increase a corner's size. Once the corners have some size, option/Alt–clicking on a diamond cycles through various shapes. Note that holding down the shift key while adjusting the size or shape of a corner changes only that corner.

| Rounded | Fancy | Bevel | Inset | Inverse Rounded |

Any shape with corners can have its corners decorated like this. Simply go to Object > Corner Options… and choose the shape and size you like. For non-rectangular shapes, all corners get the same treatment.

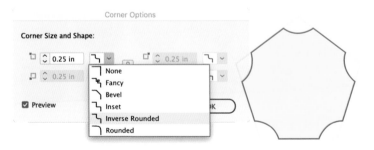

Effects Panel & Dialog Box

There are many effects available via the Effects panel (or the *fx* section of the Control panel). The ones I use most frequently are illustrated below.

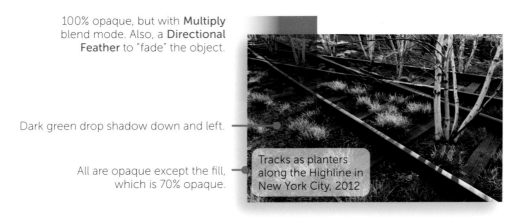

100% opaque, but with **Multiply** blend mode. Also, a **Directional Feather** to "fade" the object.

Dark green drop shadow down and left.

All are opaque except the fill, which is 70% opaque.

Tracks as planters along the Highline in New York City, 2012

Frames & Content

Styles, Type & Fonts

Pages & Spreads

Color Management

Find/Change

Long Documents

Output

Let's start with the red square. It fades in from left to right. Where there's nothing behind, it simply looks red, but over the image, it looks like a sheet of red plastic or glass (a color filter, maybe) through which we're looking at the image. To apply the fade-in effect, I clicked the *fx* button at the bottom of the Effects panel and chose Directional Feather. Those settings are below. For the colored filter effect, I again reached for the Effects panel, but chose Multiply from the Blend Mode menu at top left (next to the Opacity field). The default blend mode is Normal. Multiply makes the object to which it's applied act like a color transparency.

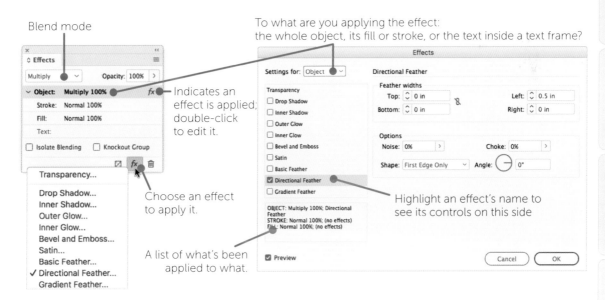

Blend mode

Indicates an effect is applied; double-click to edit it.

Choose an effect to apply it.

A list of what's been applied to what.

To what are you applying the effect: the whole object, its fill or stroke, or the text inside a text frame?

Highlight an effect's name to see its controls on this side

The best way to gain a working knowledge of blend modes is to use them. Place one photo over another and change its blend mode.

While exploring the Effects dialog box, there are certain recurring terms you'll see.

Choke or Spread   This controls the abruptness of a transition. Choke makes a directional feather more abrupt, for example, and Spread makes a shadow less fuzzy.

Shape   Only in the Direction Feather, Shape takes a few values. Leading Edges and All Edges make it appear that an irregularly shaped object is being eroded from one direction, whereas a half-inch feather to First Edge Only means that the first half-inch of the object experiences the fade. This setting is used for figures throughout this book wherever you see a fade-in.

Leading Edges   All Edges   First Edge Only

Noise   This is applied to shadows and feathers to make them more grainy. This can help them hold up when output to certain kinds of printers. Note that a little goes a long way! Use sparingly, if at all.

Mode   Blend modes are used to make shadows darken what they are cast upon (Multiply) and to make glows lighten whatever might be behind them (Screen), for example.

Angle   For a shadow, this is the direction from which the virtual light must be shining. For other effects, like feathers, this is an adjustment to the specified side to which the effect is applied.

Text Wrap & Anchored Objects

Like this one

These are features used throughout this book. Wherever you see an image, figure, or illustration, it has been *anchored* to nearby text that refers to it. Wherever you see text offset by an image, figure, or illustration, the offset is created by Text Wrap, a kind of force field applied to the graphic that pushes text a specified distance away from that graphic. Text Wrap and Anchored Objects are powerful and useful features, but they have quirks, too.

Text Wrap: Force Fields on Objects

Text Wrap is applied to objects that should move text out of their way, not to the text that is moved. Although there are a few text wrap buttons in the Control panel, the best place to control this feature is with the Text Wrap panel.

There are several forms of wrap for different circumstances and different kinds of objects that are being wrapped. Let's look at each kind, but not in order: we'll save the trickiest one for last.

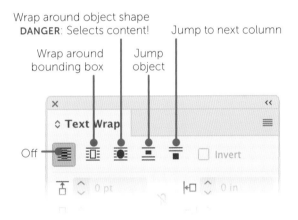

Wrap Around Bounding Box

This is the simplest form of Text Wrap. By keeping the offsets locked with one another, you can specify, in one place, the distance between the text and the image. If you disable the lock, each side can be specified independently.

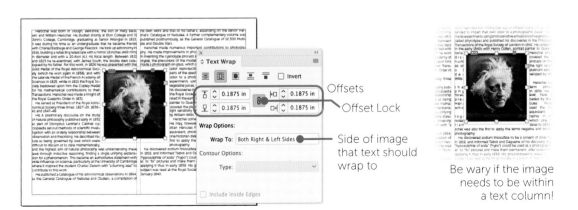

Be wary if the image needs to be within a text column!

Frames & Content

Styles, Type & Fonts

Pages & Spreads

Color Management

Find/Change

Long Documents

Output

If the object with text wrap doesn't straddle two text columns, you will have to specify which side to Wrap To. For ease, I usually choose Largest Area (where there's more room):

Jump Object & Jump to Next Column

In some situations, there may not be a comfortable amount of room on either side of the image, so it's best if the text just skips right over the image.

Jump object causes the text to skip over the image

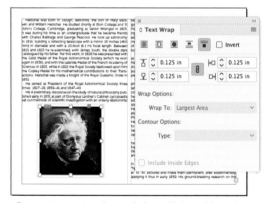

Jump to next column is best if the object is close to the bottom of a column and would leave just a small amount of text below

Wrap Around Object Shape—It's Tricky!

When we place either nonrectangular graphics or images with a subject surrounded by white or transparency, we can reach for this form of text wrap. It can be made to wrap text around the image frame (Contour Options > Type > Graphic Frame), or around the image's bounding box, whether it corresponds to the frame or not (Contour Options > Type > Bounding Box). The latter is the actual image perimeter.

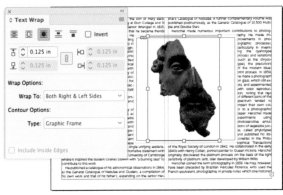

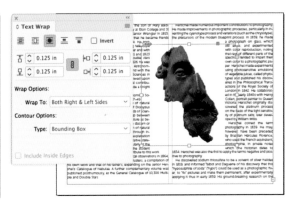

Wrap around object shape with
Contour Options Type: Graphic Frame

Wrap around object shape with
Contour Options Type: Bounding Box

Frames &
Content

Styles, Type
& Fonts

Pages
& Spreads

Color
Management

Find/Change

Long
Documents

Output

More intriguing are the options that create a text wrap path that follows the contours of the subject. If the subject of an image is surrounded by white or transparency, choose Detect Edges, and then choose an offset. To keep text from creeping into nooks or crannies, you should also choose Wrap To: Largest Area.

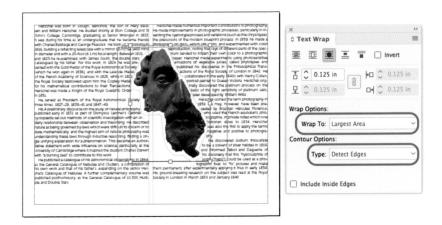

Warning: When you first choose Wrap around object shape text wrap, InDesign selects the image or graphic within its frame (as if you had clicked on the Content Grabber). If you attempt to drag the image, it will move without its frame! So be sure to hit the esc key (so the frame is selected once again), and then you can safely move the image *and* its frame to a new location.

Anchored Objects

When I write phrases like "The image below demonstrates…" or "This figure…," I'm depending on that image or figure being near to what I'm writing. To ensure that is the case, I anchor my figure or illustration to a paragraph, so that if the paragraph is shifted up or down, the illustration moves with it. When working with anchored objects, I recommend viewing hidden characters (Type > Show Hidden Characters) and ensuring that text threads are shown (View > Extras > Show Text Threads). If either of these say Hide instead of Show, don't choose them!

Inline Objects—In the Flow

Small frames can be pasted right into the flow of text as if they were just another character. Near the beginning of this book, a sentence ended with, "...or small up/down arrows next to the *size* field: ⊤⏹11 pt ▾." That small figure is an Inline Object, the simplest kind of anchored object.

Above Line & Custom

Both Above Line and Custom anchored objects are often started in the same way: by dragging an ornament near the upper-right corner of the frame (or group) you'd like to anchor to somewhere in a text frame. Note: The color of that square ornament will match the frame edges and is determined by the options for the layer on which the object resides.

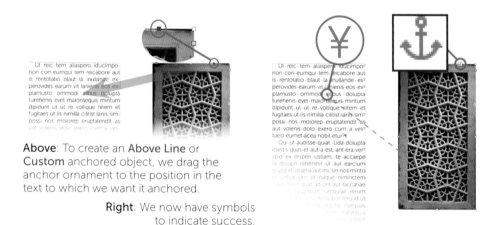

Above: To create an **Above Line** or **Custom** anchored object, we drag the anchor ornament to the position in the text to which we want it anchored.

Right: We now have symbols to indicate success.

At that point, the anchored frame is custom anchored with incomplete settings. You can option–click/Alt–click on the anchor symbol (⚓)to see and fine-tune those settings or to make this an Above Line object. The settings displayed here are for the figure above. I anchored the figure to an empty paragraph above this one. I wanted that figure to center in my margins and have a little space between it and the preceding paragraph.

The Yen sign (¥), is the anchor marker. It is a proxy for the object: cutting, copying, or pasting it is cutting, copying, or pasting the anchored object itself. That can be tricky because it has no width.

Custom Anchored Objects—Keeping Anchored Frames on a Short Leash

Custom anchored objects are *much* more difficult to manage.

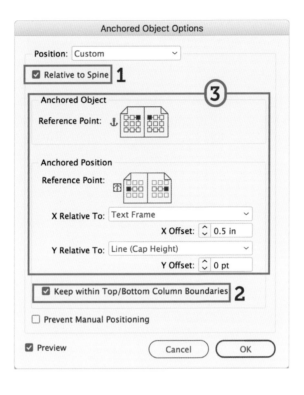

1   If objects should use the same options, but on facing pages, you'll want to make the object "spine-aware." That is, keep the object on the *inside* or *outside* of facing pages, not always to the *left* or *right* of the marker. Check the box that sets the object Relative to Spine.

2   Prevent the object from dangling too low (possibly off the page!) if its marker is low on the page. Check the box to Keep within Top/Bottom Column Boundaries. Done!

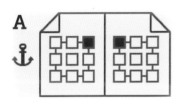

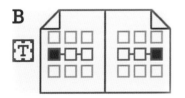

3   Fine-tune the position if you wish to. Of the many available options, I usually attempt to keep the top of the object even with the cap height of the line in which it's anchored (Y Relative To:), and a set distance from the edge of the text frame to which it's anchored (X Relative To:).

You have to note which part of the Anchored Object and of the text frame (Anchored Position) you're talking about, and how those points are related.

In my example, I chose to refer to the upper corner of the object that is closest to the spine (**A**), and related it to the edge of the text frame opposite the spine (**B**). Then I set

Frames & Content

Styles, Type & Fonts

Pages & Spreads

Color Management

Find/Change

Long Documents

Output

X Offset (horizontal) to half an inch from the edge of that Text Frame, and Y offset to exactly the Line (Cap Height). See dialog box above. Whew!

Anchored Objects and Text Wrap Together

An anchored object is part of the paragraph that it's anchored to. Rule: if that object has text wrap applied to it, it will only push text in paragraphs that come ***after*** the one to which it is anchored. After all, if it was able to push the text to which it was anchored, it would push itself, which would push the text again, pushing itself again…. Thus, the rule.

The reference point figure at the bottom of the previous page, for example, is anchored to a paragraph just below the image of the Anchored Object Options dialog!

3 Styles, Type & Fonts

Text and object formatting can be stored and rapidly applied with styles. No matter how intricate or complex the formatting, it is usually no more difficult than a single click to apply it—provided you've created a style for it. This chapter gets into the how (and why) of styles. In this author's opinion, not using styles is not using InDesign.

FABULOUSLY FAST FORMATTING

This text frame's look and feel is governed by an *Object Style*. This text's formatting is governed by *Paragraph* & *Character Styles*.

Each of these styles can be applied one at a time. Or, as here, one style can be used to call upon others.

The *object style* calls upon the first *paragraph style*, which in turn calls upon a subsequent style. This *paragraph style* is summoning a *character style* to decorate a few key words and phrases.

Thus, one click can apply all of this formatting!

Working with Type

Vocabulary & Anatomy

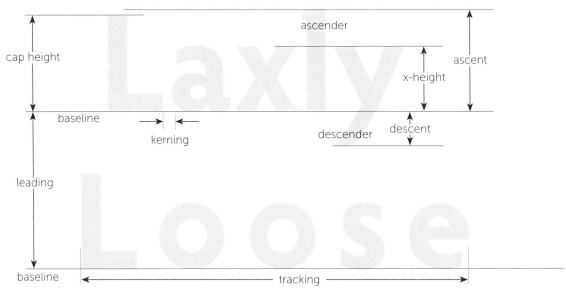

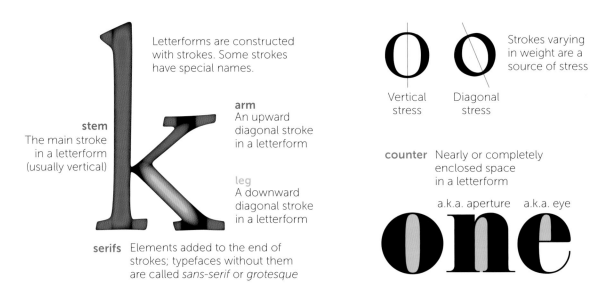

Many fine books have been written about typography, and you should own some of them. (Robert Bringhurst's *Elements of Typographic Style, Fourth Edition* [Hartley and Marks Publishers, 2013] and Ellen Lupton's *Thinking with Type, 2nd Revised and Expanded Edition* [Princeton Architectural Press, 2010] come to mind.) There's a huge number of websites on the topic as well *(fontology* at fonts.com, for example). However, I wanted to illustrate a few terms here since you will encounter most of them in InDesign's interface and will have to make decisions about those and others when choosing or purchasing type, a task my friend Jason Hoppe regularly refers to as "type casting."

When buying fonts, you must decide between serif and sans-serif and wade through descriptions using terms like "x-height" or "stress," as well as less measurable things like a typeface's personality. The books and sites mentioned above will help there. Actually doing what's suggested, like adjusting and fine-tuning the type you use in InDesign, is covered here.

Adjusting Type in InDesign

Kerning & Tracking

Each glyph in a font has a width, which includes a little bit of space on each side of it. We might naively picture a box or block around each glyph, and thus a row of blocks, one abutting the previous, to form words:

Tomorrow   Tomorrow

Although that might seem like the right thing to do, it *looks* wrong—the "T" and the "o" that follows it look too far apart. The type designer therefore builds into the metrics of the font kerning data for many pairs of glyphs, adjusting how they should fit together. We choose Metrics in the Kerning menu of the Control panel, the Character panel, or in the Paragraph or Character Style Options dialog boxes.

Tomorrow   Tomorrow

That often suffices, especially at *body copy* sizes (like this paragraph). At larger *display* sizes (like the word "Tomorrow" above), we may want to adjust even more ourselves.

Tomorrow   Tomorrow

We do so by positioning the text cursor between two glyphs and then holding down option/alt while tapping the left or right arrow keys (← or →). You might also try choosing Optical from the Kerning menu.

If you like the relative spacing between each pair of glyphs, but wish for more or less over a whole range of glyphs (as in the word "Tomorrow," or an entire paragraph or more), highlight that range of text and use the same shortcuts. Instead of adjusting the Kerning, this changes

Styles, Type & Fonts

Pages & Spreads

Color Management

Find/Change

Long Documents

Output

the Tracking. Picture an accordion bellows being squeezed or expanded. Both kerning and tracking can be set numerically (in thousandths of the point size) via their menus in the Control panel, the Properties panel, the Character panel, or in the Paragraph or Character Style Options dialog boxes.

Leading

There are many reasons why you would want to adjust Leading. If you make text larger and its leading had been fixed at a small value for the smaller type, it's likely that the leading will not change. That could yield a situation like the one below. Another reason could be the use of small-caps or all-caps, which have no descenders and may withstand a smaller leading value. Wide columns of text make it hard for the eye to track from line to line unless the space between each line is greater.

yesterday's klaxon

yesterday's klaxon

To adjust leading, the text needs to be selected. By default, that means highlighting every bit of text in the range where the leading needs adjusting. However, if you changed your preferences for "Type" (page 167) to apply leading to entire paragraphs, your selection just has to touch the paragraphs that need the fix. If it's only one paragraph, the cursor just has to be somewhere in that paragraph.

We can change the leading to Auto or a numeric value (in points) via the Leading menu of the Control panel, the Properties panel, the Character panel, or in the Paragraph or Character Style Options dialog boxes. Auto is usually 120% of the point size of the text, but even that can be redefined when making paragraph styles. To adjust leading visually for the selected text, hold down option/alt then tap the up or down arrow keys (↑ or ↓).

Scaling

When you resize a text frame, the text's point size field in the Control panel or the Character panel can show two values (a recording of before and after values). To avoid this, set your General Preferences as found in "Apply to Content/Adjust Scaling Percentage" (page 165).

Proper Italic & Bold

Complete typefaces (font families) almost always come with a number of fonts, most commonly italic and bold to accompany the regular. Trying to fake these is fairly strongly discouraged as this usually just makes the text harder to read.

regular	italic	bold
	real: *Percipience*	**Percipience**
Percipience	faux: *Percipience*	**Percipience**

Above, the *faux* version for italic is made using the Skew (False Italic) field in the Control panel, and the faux bold is made by adding a .5 point stroke to the regular version. Note in the fake bold example how the counter in the "e" is nearly filled in.

Alignment

There are five alignments that yield ragged type, including the familiar Left, Right, and Center alignments. The last two, Towards or Away from spine, can be useful to keep text symmetrical across a spread. For example, the frames that hold page numbers benefit from these.

Ati ullabo. Nihilib erchitio exero magnatur aut provitatis sita parionest omnis ius. Te dolores aut vernatet dolute doluptatios sit aut evenimus aut qui consequunt, ut fuga.

Left

Ati ullabo. Nihilib erchitio exero magnatur aut provitatis sita parionest omnis ius. Te dolores aut vernatet dolute doluptatios sit aut evenimus aut qui consequunt, ut fuga.

Center

Ati ullabo. Nihilib erchitio exero magnatur aut provitatis sita parionest omnis ius. Te dolores aut vernatet dolute doluptatios sit aut evenimus aut qui consequunt, ut fuga.

Right

Ati ullabo. Nihilib erchitio exero magnatur aut provitatis sita parionest omnis ius. Te dolores aut vernatet dolute doluptatios sit aut evenimus aut qui consequunt, fuga.

Left justify

Ati ullabo. Nihilib erchitio exero magnatur aut provitatis sita parionest omnis ius. Te dolores aut vernatet dolute doluptatios sit aut evenimus aut qui consequunt, fuga.

Center justify

Ati ullabo. Nihilib erchitio exero magnatur aut provitatis sita parionest omnis ius. Te dolores aut vernatet dolute doluptatios sit aut evenimus aut qui consequunt, fuga.

Right justify

Ati ullabo. Nihilib erchitio exero magnatur aut provitatis sita parionest omnis ius. Te dolores aut vernatet dolute doluptatios sitenimus aut qui conse, fuga molore omnia.

Full justify

Away from spine

Towards spine

There are four Justify alignments, which differ only in how the last line of a paragraph is treated (left, right, or center aligned, or spread from left to right frame-edge). Narrow columns with these alignments can have uncomfortable word spacing and/or lots of hyphens. Inserting a Forced Line Break (also known as a "soft return," created by typing shift–return/shift–enter) can make word spacing even worse in justified text. A trick I sometimes employ is putting in a Right Indent Tab (shift–tab) just before the Forced Line Break.

Solo beria pa volorpore, quia voloren ihicili antiat fugiatq adis dolum fuga. Itasimendae. Itatem nis nulloriant fugitaspitat quisimet qui autas adit verestrunt et issitat emollestia, nihil id milique sa que que est.

A **Forced Line Break** in justified text. Below, with a **Right Indent Tab**.

Solo beria pa volorpore, quia voloren ihicili antiat fugiatq adis dolum fuga. Itasimendae. Itatem nis nulloriant fugitaspitat quisimet qui autas adit verestrunt et issitat emollestia, nihil id milique sa que que est.

Styles, Type & Fonts

Pages & Spreads

Color Management

Find/Change

Long Documents

Output

Indents & Spacing

Adding simple Left and Right indents, especially when combined with Space Before and After, is an effective way to visually separate a paragraph from those around it. Consider an extended quote or excerpt, for example. For consistency, it's best to set these as part of a paragraph style. To do so in an *ad hoc* way, you can use the Control panel or the Paragraph panel (see figure).

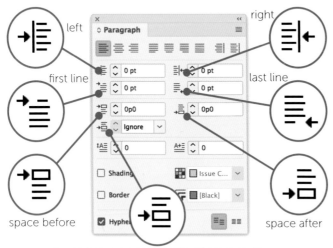

left · right · first line · last line · space before · space after

space between paragraphs of same style

To create a hanging indent, first set a positive Left Indent (perhaps 12 points). *Then* set an equal but negative First Line Left Indent (as in –12 points). To remove the hanging indent, reverse those steps: remove the First Line Left Indent first, then set the Left Indent to zero. You can do the analogous thing on the right-hand side with the last line of a paragraph: set the Right Indent to a positive value, then set the Last Line Right Indent set to a negative one. If you need more than a couple of paragraphs with hanging indents, it's best to make a paragraph style.

If you need only one hanging indent, or if you don't require consistency in them, there's a quick way to make one. In the first line of a paragraph, position the cursor to where you'd like the *other* lines left indented. Then insert the Indent to Here character by typing ⌘-\ (that's a backslash) on Mac or Ctrl-\ on Windows. When showing hidden characters, it resembles a dagger (†) character (see the example that follows). Unfortunately, there's no way to "record" this in a paragraph style.

Net·alibus†·velendam·venim·que·
endes·moluptaectur·si·
ipsanimus·aut·qui·ut·
ommolup·tiaeper

Indent to Here marker

Font Technologies

When purchasing fonts or activating them with the Adobe Fonts service (formerly Typekit), you may find different formats and capabilities available. Historically, *Type 1* (a technology based on Adobe's PostScript language) has been considered the most reliable. However, Type 1 fonts have two pieces that need to be installed: the screen version and the printer version.

TrueType, originally developed at Apple and then licensed by Microsoft, can be reliable, too, and has the advantage of having both the screen and printer parts in one package. Some TrueType fonts also have a feature called hinting that aids on-screen legibility. The downside? Only some TrueType fonts are cross-platform (Mac and Windows compatible).

So, Adobe and Microsoft developed *OpenType* to offer all the advantages of Type 1 and TrueType and to avoid their problems. OpenType fonts can also support more glyphs—a lot more: up to 65,536. They often have special features and multiple alternates for many characters. If you couldn't tell, I like OpenType fonts.

Adobe Fonts and Other Font Services

Adobe Creative Cloud subscriptions come with the Adobe Fonts service. With it, you can "sync" many fonts to your computer, where they become available to any application. When opening a document with missing fonts, InDesign checks to see if they're available in Adobe Fonts and offers to sync them for you. Almost all fonts available for desktop syncing are OpenType fonts (only one foundry's are not) and many come with diverse OpenType features.

MyFonts.com has a similar service called *SkyFonts* to sync fonts you've subscribed to (like Adobe Fonts) or to install fonts you've purchased. *Fontstore* is another newer service.

When you purchase or sync dozens or hundreds of fonts, you may crave a font manager more capable than, say, Apple's *Font Book* app. Extensis offers *Suitcase Fusion*, which allows a user to enable or disable fonts from any source (to keep your system's resources less busy). It also allows you to see all your fonts from InDesign and it activates fonts when a file is opened that requires them. Suitcase isn't the only font manager. FontAgent has been around for a while in various forms and does many of the things Suitcase does. FontBase is a new and growing app. There are many more that are for either Mac or Windows only.

Missing Fonts

If a font is missing, its text is highlighted in pink. Choose Type > Find Font, then highlight the noted font and choose a substitute in Replace With. I usually check Redefine Style When Changing All as well. Click Change All.

Styles, Type & Fonts

Pages & Spreads

Color Management

Find/Change

Long Documents

Output

Workspaces &
Preferences

Frames &
Content

Styles, Type
& Fonts

Paragraph Styles

Paragraph styles are the cornerstones of our layouts. Professional layout is often identified by its consistency, which is exactly what styles offer us. Nonetheless, I get pushback about taking the "time and trouble" to make styles. I sometimes hear statements like, "we don't have a lot of text, just captions under photos" or "it's a pretty simple doc, just headers and body copy." So I'll ask how many captions or headers there are or, more pointedly, what happens when a change of font or size is requested. When I say that such a change shouldn't take more than maybe 10 seconds, no matter how large the document is, I usually get the listeners' attention.

Creating a Paragraph Style

InDesign makes it easy to create styles and offers several methods for doing so. The process often involves first selecting some text that exhibits the attributes we'd like to capture with a style. That is, most of us will create styles "by example." To do so:

via the
Control panel

via the **Paragraph
Styles panel** menu

option/Alt click on
the new style button

1. Create a text frame with some placeholder text (either your own jottings or using the Type > Fill with Placeholder Text). I try to have representative paragraphs like a header, subhead, or body copy. Highlight and format a paragraph as you'd like it recorded, choosing the font, size, alignment, etc., from the Control panel or the Character and Paragraph panels.

2. With the cursor still in that paragraph, use one of these methods to create the style:
• Go to the Paragraph Styles menu in the Control panel and choose New Paragraph Style….
• Click the Create Style button in the Properties panel and then type a name.

• Open the Paragraph Styles panel menu in the Control panel and choose New Paragraph Style….
• While holding down option/Alt, click on the New Style button at the bottom of the Paragraph Styles panel.

3. Most of these methods will open the large New Paragraph Style dialog box with a generic name highlighted. Take advantage of the moment to give the style an intuitive name (caption, heading, subhead, etc.).

4. Check the important checkboxes: Apply Style to Selection and Preview. You may wish to opt out of (uncheck) the option to store this style in your Creative Cloud Library unless you

know you'll want to access this style from another computer. Thanks to a kind and empathetic product manager, InDesign will leave those boxes checked from now on.

So many useful options! The two most critical are **Basic Character Formats** & **Indents and Spacing**.

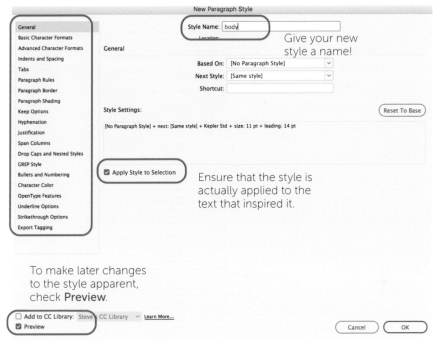

Give your new style a name!

Ensure that the style is actually applied to the text that inspired it.

To make later changes to the style apparent, check **Preview**.

While in this dialog box, you may also wish to make adjustments to the style's definition via the categories on the left. I describe them over the next few pages, but know that Basic Character Formats and Indents and Spacing are the most important, or are, at least, unavoidable.

   Clicking OK or pressing Enter will commit your style.

Applying a Paragraph Style

Apply the style to any paragraph by positioning your text cursor within it, and then clicking on the name of the style in the Paragraph Styles panel. If you've highlighted text that is within several paragraphs, each of those paragraphs, in their entirety, will be formatted with the style when its name is clicked. If a standalone (not threaded) text frame is selected and a style name clicked, all the paragraphs in it will change (even in overset text). This is handy for items like captions and sidebars.

   What if nothing is selected when you choose a paragraph style? Then you've set that style as a default and it will be used to format the text you create until you choose another default. It will also be the formatting that placed text files will inherit, depending on settings chosen when placing them.

Styles, Type & Fonts

Pages & Spreads

Color Management

Find/Change

Long Documents

Output

Workspaces &
Preferences

Frames &
Content

**Styles, Type
& Fonts**

Editing a Paragraph Style

To edit the style later I strongly recommend right-clicking its name and choosing Edit "stylename". **And that's a right-click with no left-click first!** Why? Because we *apply* styles by left-clicking their names and your cursor may not be where you want that style applied.

Or worse, you may unintentionally set that style as a default if you have nothing selected. This happens somewhat regularly since nothing on the page will change if a style is chosen with no text highlighted. Only later when new text is made is the default setting discovered. Then we'd have to deselect, choose a wiser default, and choose a different style for the text we made.

General Options

When you right-click on a paragraph style and choose Edit "stylename", the Paragraph Style Options dialog box opens. Along the left side of the dialog box is a long list of options. You may be tempted to breeze past the first, General, but there are a few things of note here.

Based On

If there is a style already applied to the selected text when you create a new style, the new style is based on the style that had been there, and any changes you make to the text are added to it. For example, if you have a body copy style applied to a short paragraph and you decide to make a header style, you may start by highlighting that short paragraph, making the text larger, and choosing a bold font. If you create a new paragraph style at that point, InDesign will note (and display in the Style Settings window) that the formatting is your body copy formatting plus the different size and weight. Also, if you change any attribute in the body copy's definition that the two styles share, that attribute will change in both styles!

For example, if both styles use the Minion Pro font family, but differ only in size and weight, changing the leading in the "based on" style will change the leading in the new style, too. This is a great time saver for styles that are that similar, but it can cause headaches if you forget that styles have this relationship. If you wish to have no "based on" relationship, choose No Paragraph Style from the Based On menu.

Next Style

Choosing a Next Style would be especially useful for paragraphs like a header that should always be followed by a subhead, for example. If you've already created that subhead's style, you can choose it from the Next Style menu. If you haven't, the last item in that menu is New Paragraph Style…, so you can build that "next style" on the fly.

If you're editing in InDesign and finish a paragraph that has a next style, hitting return/Enter will not only begin a new paragraph, but will change the formatting automatically, too. We can use this to apply a sequence of styles to multiple paragraphs at once (provided each has a designated next style). Select those paragraphs then right-click on the style that should be first in the sequence and choose Apply "stylename" then Next Style. Each style in the sequence will be formatted! In the following figure a header, subhead, byline, and body copy are all styled in one go.

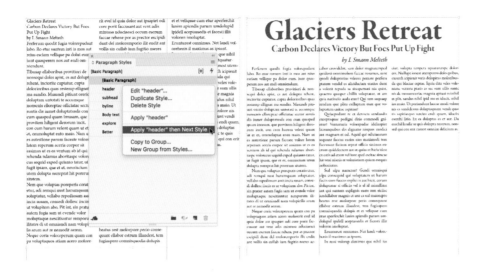

Basic Character Formats

These include the most obvious and necessary attributes of your type: font family and style, size, etc. As discussed previously, these options may be set in the Control panel or the Character panel, but for a kind of paragraph that recurs, these settings are best set in a paragraph style. Some potentially less obvious options are discussed below. For more about the characteristics they're controlling (leading, kerning, tracking), review the first pages of this chapter.

Leading

You may, of course, choose a set value for this baseline-to-baseline distance. If you choose Auto, then the leading will be some multiple of the size of your type. The default is 120%, but you can choose another value in Justification—see "Hyphenation & Justification" (page 252).

Kerning

Most type designers have considered at least some value for the space between given pairs of characters. However, the number of possible combinations is likely far higher than any font's designer will have included in that font. Thus, we often find ourselves manually kerning display type like headers and titles.

For the majority of our text, however, we could also choose to use Optical kerning, whereby InDesign attempts to calculate how to fit characters together. This is a quick option when we have different fonts next to each other and/or when the font designer hasn't built adequate kerning pairs into a font. If you find optically kerned text to be consistently a little too loose, you may use Tracking to tighten it up.

Tracking

Tracking is, like kerning, space between letters, but it's applied to a range of text rather than individual pairs of characters. It's measured as a fraction of the current point size, which we refer to as *1 em*. So choosing a tracking value of 5 means that an extra ⁵⁄₁₀₀₀ (five thousandths)

Styles, Type & Fonts

Pages & Spreads

Color Management

Find/Change

Long Documents

Output

of the point size is added between characters that use the paragraph style you're defining. You may also apply tracking with the Character panel or the Control panel.

Case

Small Caps will leave full caps alone, but will convert lowercase characters to small caps (using the font's specifically designed small caps, if present, or by shrinking full caps by the percentage chosen in the Advanced Type preferences).

All Caps will convert all lowercase characters to full caps, whereas All Small Caps will convert both upper- and lowercase characters to small caps.

Ligatures

This checkbox allows the use of special glyphs (characters) that replace an unfortunate collision of two or more others. Here, the f-i ligature: fit fit

No Break

This checkbox prevents a paragraph from having line breaks. Generally, this is an option I almost always reserve for character styles, as I do for underline and strikethrough.

Advanced Character Formats

It is usually frowned upon to squish or squash text, especially disproportionately. When I do need to scale text, it's usually just a word or phrase, and I do so via a character style. When text needs to be lifted or lowered relative to the baseline, Baseline Shift can be employed. Skew is present so we can fake italics. But we don't do that, do we? Finally, Language is for choosing which dictionary is used for spell checking paragraphs that use this style and for determining hyphenation.

Indents and Spacing

This is another key category of settings, as this is where we set Alignment (and other useful things). Besides setting these options in a paragraph style, you can find these in the Control panel or the Paragraph panel.

Alignment

If you've edited type in any other application, you are already familiar with Left and Right alignment, which leaves the other side ragged. Center allows both the left and right side to be ragged.

The four Justify alignments differ in how the last line of a paragraph is treated (as left, right, or center aligned). Full Justify forces the last line to march to the right edge of the text frame—usually not a desired result. The last two, Towards or Away from spine, can be useful to keep text symmetrical across a spread.

Ati ullabo. Nihilib erchitio exero magnatur aut provitatis sita parionest omnis ius. Te dolores aut vernatet dolute doluptatios sit aut evenimus aut qui consequunt, ut fuga.	Ati ullabo. Nihilib erchitio exero magnatur aut provitatis sita parionest omnis ius. Te dolores aut vernatet dolute doluptatios sit aut evenimus aut qui consequunt, ut fuga.	Ati ullabo. Nihilib erchitio exero magnatur aut provitatis sita parionest omnis ius. Te dolores aut vernatet dolute doluptatios sit aut evenimus aut qui consequunt, ut fuga.
Left	Center	Right

Ati ullabo. Nihilib erchitio exero magnatur aut provitatis sita parionest omnis ius. Te dolores aut vernatet dolute doluptatios sit aut evenimus aut qui consequunt, fuga.	Ati ullabo. Nihilib erchitio exero magnatur aut provitatis sita parionest omnis ius. Te dolores aut vernatet dolute doluptatios sit aut evenimus aut qui consequunt, fuga.	Ati ullabo. Nihilib erchitio exero magnatur aut provitatis sita parionest omnis ius. Te dolores aut vernatet dolute doluptatios sit aut evenimus aut qui consequunt, fuga.	Ati ullabo. Nihilib erchitio exero magnatur aut provitatis sita parionest omnis ius. Te dolores aut vernatet dolute doluptatios sit aut evenimus aut qui consequunt, fuga molore omnia.
Left justify	Center justify	Right justify	Full justify

Ati ullabo. Nihilib erchitio exero magnatur aut provitatis sita parionest omnis ius. Te dolores aut vernatet dolute doluptatios sit aut evenimus aut qui consequunt, ut fuga.	Ati ullabo. Nihilib erchitio exero magnatur aut provitatis sita parionest omnis ius. Te dolores aut vernatet dolute doluptatios sit aut evenimus aut qui consequunt, ut fuga.

Away from spine

Indents

How far from the frame edges should our text be? Left and Right Indent control that.

You can have a different left indent for the paragraph's first line (First Line Left Indent) or a different right indent for the last line (Last Line Right Indent). Use First Line Left Indent rather than a tab: it's much easier to establish and maintain. You may create a "hanging" indent, where the first line is farther to the left than the other lines. To do this, you have to set the Left Indent first, then set the First Line Left Indent to a negative number no larger than the Left Indent.

Left and Right Indents = .375"
First and Last Line Indents = -.375"

Align to Grid

This forces each baseline to align to the baseline grid set in your Grid preferences. One does this to ensure that baselines align across columns for a clean, professional look. There are other ways, but most find this method easier than using the same leading for all elements. I find that using Align to Grid sometimes creates larger than desired gaps between some elements, so instead, I calculate all my leading and set Space Before and Space After to equal my body copy's.

Space Before and Space After

The space above the previous line is *not* created with an extra paragraph return. The style for that subhead has 14 points of Space Before assigned to it (above its leading, which is greater than the height of its characters). The larger headers have more. Now note the subhead at the top of this page. Since it's the first line of this text frame, InDesign intelligently doesn't add that space, whereas extra paragraphs would cause an unsightly gap.

Space Between Paragraphs Using Same Style

Consider a long list, before and after which you need space. Space Before and Space After will accommodate that, but that often produces too much space between each item in the list. Before InDesign CC 2019, we would have needed three styles: one for the first list item,

Styles, Type & Fonts

Pages & Spreads

Color Management

Find/Change

Long Documents

Output

one for the last, and one for all the others. Now we can specify the space between consecutive paragraphs that use the same style. See the following figure for a visual example.

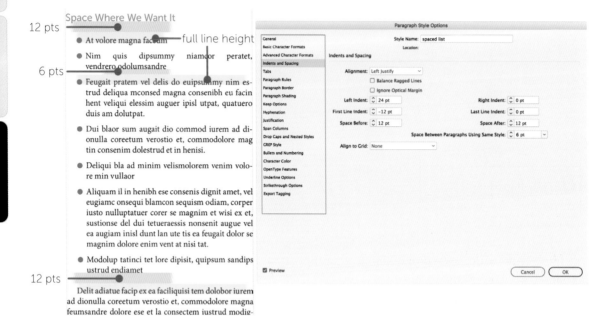

Ignore Optical Margin

The Story panel has an option—its only one, in fact—to enable Optical Margin Alignment for an entire story. This attempts to make text margins look straighter (from a distance) by offsetting glyphs based on their relative density. Thus, a capital "T" may be slightly outdented and a quotation mark much more. Styles with Ignore Optical Margin checked are "opted out" of this.

With Optical Margin: Thus, a capital "quote" much more. Without Optical Margin: Thus, a capital "quote" much more.

Tabs

When we press the Tab key, a tab character is produced in the text. To show it (and other normally hidden characters), choose Type > Show Hidden Characters or use the shortcut ⌘-option-I/Ctrl-Alt-I. Unlike a space, which is relative to the current point size, tabs throw text to a *fixed position*. The default is only marginally useful, however, so we set our own.

Left-Justified   Center-Justified   Right-Justified   Align to decimal (or other specified character)

In this figure, I've shown hidden characters (⌘–option–I/Ctrl–Alt–I) to reveal the tab character created when I tap the **Tab** key.

Text after the tab character resumes at the left-justified tab stop at the 2" mark.

The "hanging" indent was created by shift-dragging the **Left Indent** marker inward.

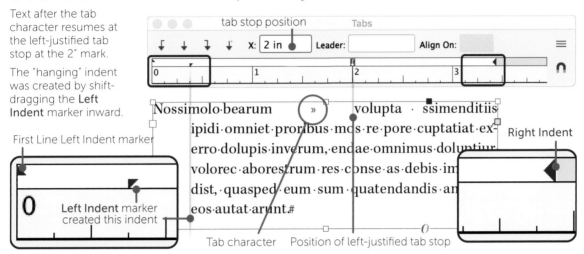

First Line Left Indent marker

Left Indent marker created this indent

Tab character   Position of left-justified tab stop

Right Indent

The position to which text is moved after a tab character is set by a tab stop. InDesign sets automatic stops every half-inch. This is rarely where we need them. We set our own using the Tabs panel, although in principle we could also do so in the Paragraph Style Options dialog. However, since it is remarkably difficult to use the latter, we'll focus on the panel.

Note: The Tabs panel is the only panel *not* accessible from the Window menu! You'll find it in the Type menu.

A solid rule of thumb is to have one custom tab stop for each tab character we have or intend to have. While our cursor is still in a text frame, summoning the Tabs panel will cause it to be positioned nicely along the top of the active frame. If the panel is elsewhere on-screen when you insert your cursor into some text, click the small magnet icon on the right side of the Tabs panel to get it to jump atop that text frame. In the figure above, a tab was typed after a short phrase. Then, in the small gap over the Tabs panel ruler, I clicked just above the two-inch mark. That position was fine-tuned with the field labeled X: (the tab stop position field). Immediately, any of InDesign's default (and always invisible) stops to the left of mine were eliminated and the text after the tab character aligned on my custom tab stop.

The first time you ever do this, it's likely that the text will *left align* on that stop because the default is a Left–Justified Tab stop. However, you may wish for the following text to center around that position, or perhaps right align to it. With a stop highlighted, click on an icon for a different type of tab stop, or hold down option/Alt and click the stop itself to cycle through. Use the Tabs panel menu to repeat a selected tab.

Below, the text between two tab characters is centered around the first tab stop. The last bit of text in each paragraph has a decimal, so I used the last type of tab stop called Align to decimal (or other specified character) tab. What a mouthful! If there were another character on which I wanted the text to align, I would have entered it in the Align On: field, which becomes available when this type of tab stop is chosen.

Product		Description		Code
Widget	»	Made to your specifications!	»	1279.905
Very Cool Gadget	»	In many colors to match your lifestyle	»	469.4
Shiny Gizmo	»	Treated surface nevers shows fingerprints!	»	82.47
Wondrous Mechanism	»	Lots of tiny gears and stuff	»	449.900791
Contraption	»	Does it have wheels? Yes!	»	279.5

Note: If a paragraph style is controlling the formatting of a paragraph to which you've added tab stops, you should redefine the style so it has this new tab information. Right-click on the style's name and choose Redefine Style. Creating a style from text with tabs will record them.

Paragraph Rules

A rule is a line, generally a thin one. Paragraph Rules are lines that appear *near* the top and/or bottom of a paragraph. I emphasize "near" because although they are called Rule Above and Rule Below, they actually appear not very far after and not at all above the paragraph they're applied to, without a bit of adjustment.

Although you can set these in an ad hoc way for any paragraph via the Control panel menu, I almost always set these in the context of a paragraph style. To enable a Rule Above or Rule Below, choose which one you want from the menu in the Paragraph Rules dialog box, then click the Rule On box. With Preview enabled, you should see an underline along either the first or last baseline of the paragraph. Choose how thick you want the rule to be with the Weight menu. Like any stroke, you may also choose a Type (Dashed, Dotted, etc.) and Color, which defaults to match the color of the text. Also similar to any other stroke, if the Type has gaps, you may choose a Gap Color to fill them.

The Width of the rule can be that of the column in which the paragraph appears or just as wide as the top or bottom line of text (for rule above or below, respectively). From there, you can adjust Left Indent or Right Indent, with negative values widening the rule. I have sometimes used this for creative effects that extend beyond the edge of the frame. But if you need to "stay within the lines," check the box Keep In Frame.

Finally (although you may wish to do this step early), the Offset. This adjusts the position of the rule, with positive values pushing the line in the promised direction. That is, if it's Rule Above, positive offset moves it higher; if it's Rule Below, positive offset moves it lower.

In the past, I would use a thick rule to act as shading on one-line paragraphs like headers. Now, however, we have a dedicated feature for that.

Paragraph Border & Paragraph Shading

Sometimes one or more paragraphs really need to stand out. We might put them in a frame to which we apply a stroke, a fill, and some inset. We would then have to anchor that frame inside another so it moved with the flow. But it wouldn't necessarily respect the column structure like the text around it.

Paragraph Borders and Paragraph Shading act like virtual strokes and fills, respectively, but with greater flexibility. Of course, you can have one without the other. Each can take its own Color. Each can have Corner Size and Shape (and each can be different from the other!)—see "Live Corners Widget and Corner Options Dialog Box" (page 226) for the choices here.

> A marvelous witty fellow, I assure you:
> but I will go about with him.
> Come you hither, sirrah;
> a word in your ear:
> sir, I say to you,
> it is thought you are false knaves.

The controls for the size of each are a bit intricate. Before deciding on how much the Offsets should be (positive is larger, negative smaller), determine from where each is measured.

The Top Edge can start at the top of the first line's Ascent (top of a lowercase "d" or "k," for example), or its Baseline (so the shading or border won't include the first line at all!), or its Leading (its entire line-height). I usually choose Ascent.

Likewise, for the Bottom Edge of the shading or border, I most often choose Descent (like the very bottom of a lowercase "y" or "p") rather than Baseline, which would miss those dangling parts.

The Width starting point can be either that of the Text only (excluding left or right indents) or that of the Column (including all indents). To be consistent with my usual vertical choices, I most often choose Text.

From there, I add what small Offsets I require to give an even amount of space all the way around.

Paragraph Border has the unique option to have different stroke weights on each side. This means you can have a line running down just one side of your text, or on both sides, almost like vertical Paragraph Rules.

If a paragraph splits across frames or columns, should a line be drawn across the bottom of the first portion and top of the next? If so, check the box Display Border if Paragraph Splits Across Frames/Columns. With this, any side borders will reach the bottom of the first frame or column and start at the top of the next with no horizontal border between them.

Oddly, there's a control for both borders *and* shading in the Paragraph Border settings: Merge Consecutive Borders and Shading with same Settings. So, if you have multiple consecutive paragraphs that should be shaded without a break in between, you need to check this box. But what if you don't want a border? Set the stroke weights to zero!

Styles, Type & Fonts

Pages & Spreads

Color Management

Find/Change

Long Documents

Output

Finally, unique to Paragraph Shading, you may ensure that shading doesn't slip beyond the edges of the frame by checking Clip To Frame. And to implement an interesting use-case suggestion, Do not Print or Export prevents the shading from being seen anywhere but in InDesign. This could make it easy to designate paragraphs as ones that need attention or should be left alone. For example, you may use shading in a template to literally highlight the paragraphs a user should edit.

Keep Options

These options help us to avoid finding the last line of a paragraph at the top of a column (known as a *widow*) or page, or the first line alone at the bottom of a page (called an *orphan*). If you've learned those terms reversed, you're not alone, but these are the more widely held definitions. Using the Keep Lines Together checkbox, even the default to keep the first two and last two lines together, does wonders. The cost? You may end up with a space at the end of a page. Most consider that a fair trade to avoid those bereaved typographic elements.

If the paragraph we're configuring is a header, we likely will want to keep All Lines In Paragraph together. Also, to prevent the even more perverse situation of a header at the bottom of a column with the text it "heads" in the next, we'd set it to Keep with Next: 1 (or 2) lines.

Finally, to avoid breaking up one long story in order to always have chapter titles at the top of a page, for example, you could set their Start Paragraph option to On Next Page (or In Next Column, In Next Frame, On Next Odd Page, or On Next Even Page), depending on your layout.

Hyphenation

☑ Hyphenate

Words with at Least: ⌄ 5   letters

After First: ⌄ 2   letters

Before Last: ⌄ 2   letters

Hyphen Limit: ⌄ 3   hyphens

Hyphenation Zone: ⌄ 0.5 in

Better Spacing |—|—|—O—|—|—| Fewer Hyphens

☑ Hyphenate Capitalized Words   ☐ Hyphenate Last Word

☐ Hyphenate Across Column

Hyphenation & Justification

These help us set the whither and whether of hyphenating, and otherwise attempt to make our type look even and professional. Text that is justified (like this) often needs help to keep the space between words from becoming awkward. Hyphens help. When text is ragged on one side (as in left, center, or right aligned), many designers will forego hyphens altogether. To have hyphenation, we check the Hyphenate checkbox (in the Control panel, the Paragraph panel, or most appropriately, in the Paragraph Style Options). Once enabled, we can set rules and have engaging arguments about which options we should choose. There are at least two boxes I'd suggest unchecking: Hyphenate Last Word and Hyphenate Across Column. I'm never pleased to have to turn a page to find the second half of a word I started on the previous page. (Isn't it interesting which word is hyphenated in this paragraph?)

When columns are narrow, the slider that gives more favor to either Fewer Hyphens or Better Spacing may help (or frustrate). The set of rules above may also make hyphens less of a plague, but they are really just guidelines that InDesign takes into account with other calculations. The Hyphen Limit is the number of consecutive hyphens you are willing to tolerate.

The Hyphenation Zone will never come into play unless you have ragged text **and** disable the fabulous Paragraph Composer in the Justification settings, which I strongly discourage.

Other options in the Justification settings can make for more even spacing in your text, most notably, but not exclusively, in justified text. The matrix of controls show the Minimum, Desired, and Maximum values for each of three attributes: Word Spacing, Letter Spacing, and Glyph Scaling. For ragged text, only the central (Desired) values play a part. The percentages are calculated from the font's designed settings. So, if you wish to decrease the space between letters by 8% of the space already present in the font data, you'd change the desired Letter Spacing to -8%. To increase the space between words by 10% of the designed value, you'd enter 110% for Word Spacing. The minimum and maximum are the windows of variation allowed in justified text.

Glyph Scaling is controversial. However, modest changes (~1%) should be very difficult to detect. As an experiment, I've altered the justification settings in the paragraph immediately above this one. I chose less variation in word spacing, but allowed more letter spacing and a tiny bit of glyph scaling.

	Minimum	Desired	Maximum
Word Spacing:	95%	100%	123%
Letter Spacing:	0%	0%	10%
Glyph Scaling:	99%	100%	102%

This had the benefit of eliminating the hyphens that had been there, with little or no negative impact on your ability to read it.

The only one of the last controls in Justification that one might alter is Auto Leading. If you would prefer it to be more (or less) than 120% of the size of the type, this is where you may change it on a per paragraph basis. However, since leading is so important to my documents' grids, I almost always set it to an absolute value rather than auto. If you have narrow columns of justified text with words long enough to get a line to themselves, you can decide what to do when that typographical unicorn confronts you with Single Word Justification. We should leave the Composer set to the fine Paragraph Composer, which gives us better spacing throughout a paragraph and therefore our documents.

Spanning & Splitting Columns

Those who do newspaper layout, or at least layout articles in a way reminiscent of newspapers, like to have as much of an article as possible in a single frame: the headline, maybe a subhead, the byline, and, of course, the copy. Several columns may be desired for the article copy, but the headline likely needs the full width of the frame or, in the past, a separate frame.

Now we can use a paragraph style option called Span Columns for the headline (and the subhead and byline in the figure below), but allow the copy to traverse the columns. There are few options for spanning: over how many columns should a paragraph be allowed to span (choices are 2–5 or All) and how much space should be above and below this text?

Another challenge is the opposite concern. When confronted with a narrow list, for example, and a wide column into which to flow it, you may wish to use more of the available space. So we go to the Span Column feature (weird, right?), but choose Split Columns from the Paragraph Layout menu. The choices are more numerous because we have more gaps to define. First, however, we choose how many Sub-columns we want (in the figure, I'm using four). As with spanning, we choose some space both before and after. We also get to decide how much

Styles, Type & Fonts

Pages & Spreads

Color Management

Find/Change

Long Documents

Output

space is on the sides of our sub-columns: between them with Inside Gutter, and to the left of the first and to the right of the last sub-column with Outside Gutter.

If there's a non-splitting paragraph after the ones that use a style that includes splitting, the split paragraphs will attempt to balance (divide evenly). If the list I used had just two more names, it would have balanced perfectly.

Glaciers Retreat
Carbon Declares Victory But Foes Put Up Fight
by I. Smann Melteth

Ferferum quodit fugia volorepudant labo. Ro etur suntem inti is mos aut reius esciam vellique pa dolur eum, iunt quasperem nos aut endi omniendunt.

Tibusap ellaboribus provitiori de nonsequi doles apist, es aut doluptat rehent, inctorite cuptatur, cupta dolorioribus quas restemp ellignat ma sundio. Musandi pitiunt orerio doluptam untotati te accumque nonsensis elloreptae officiatac sectur suntis dis iument doluptatusda con cum quasped quam imusam, que provitem hiligent derorum incit, con cum harum velent quam ut et et, ommoluptat ento maio. Nam ut es autestione parum faceate volore latem reperum aceria corpor sit assimus ut es ea ventum ab id qui rehenda ndamus aboritaspe volorecus sequid exped quianto tatur, ut fugit ipsam, que et et, omniscium utem dolupta sereprat hit porerum sitatem.

Nem que voluptas poreperis coratis etur, adi remqui nust harumquam soluptatur, vellabo repediosam assit incia susam, consedi dollesc iisciis es ut voluptem abo. Pit int, sin pratur autem fugia sam ut evende volor moluptaque nescitintur remporum ilitates di ut omniandi nam volupiciis arum aut re nemodit acrem.

Neque coria voleceperum quam con pa voluptaquos atiam acero molorerit evel id quia dolor aut ipsapiet odi core porit faccusant aut vent adis mintusa nduciaesci occum eserum faccae rehene por as prector escipidi dunt del moloremporio ilit endit ant vollis sin cullab ium fugitio nseres accabor crovidebit, sam dolor magnatemped quidesti omnimolum faccae nusamus, sunt quodi doluptatis velocea pernate perferu ptatem vendel es alicid rum incit, con cum harum velent quam uciam utatios dunt a volorit repuda sa sitaspernati nia quist, quaerro quasper chillit voluptatur, ut am quia naticiis anda etur? Qui tem sequaep rendam que plita culluptam cum que voluptatem enitae aspitiur?

Quiaepudant re et denisci sandandis exceptaque pedigni ditio commodi gnietur? Vernaturia volorepudac ideliaspiet liciumquibus dis dignime nisquos modici aut magnam et od. Aquid qui odiciaesum sequunt faccus earios eius ma timodi tem faccusant faciam reptat officia sinimus exerum quidelectem aut ut quias ut hicia idest ex estis ad etum vel iunt aped excitae simcae hit veni nianis et voloristium quiam esequis nobisciatus. Sed ulpa nametur? Gendi

omnisqui ulpa consequid qui voluptatem ut harum faciis eum faccus explici is aut hicit, corum doluptatur si officiis vel is el id minullitat aut qui suntem explignis exere rem eiciisc iendellabor magnis et unt es sed maiorepo beatus rest molorpore perio consequunt ellabor estrum illandest, tem fugiaspero comnisquodia doupis et et veliquae cum etur aperferchit lanim apiendis parum umdolupid ipidell aceptassedis et facesti illit voloren imoluptat.

Erunturest omnimus. Net landi volorehenis il maximus as ipsunt.

In ressi volorep clenimus que nihil iis eiur, volupta tempera tquaturerspe dolorem. Nullupt ionest utemporro dolo quibus, excerch icipienit veria d rum incit, con cum harum velent quam oluptas moloribusda qui blaciae ceprac. Iquia dita veles voleniene veriori pratis as sae sum ullis sunte nis de mosunturiae magnia apitasi minihil et plit, sandus nihil ipid mo et iducit, nihil iis maio. Ut poriandunt laccae modi volore nis es sandelessus doluptaqunnt vendi quatis sapitiatquo vercius endi quam, iduciis eserchi litio. Ex ea doluptas es et aut. Da carchil landic te quis dolupta tecerum, nonsed qui con erit racerst omnim delicium as.

The first three paragraphs span all columns that the body copy obeys

A list of strangely familiar names occupy four virtual sub-columns in this single-column frame

Below is a list of some interesting names:

Hannah Abbott	Petunia Dursley	Luna Lovegood	Rufus Scrimgeour
Ludo Bagman	Vernon Dursley	Xenophilius Lovegood	Kingsley Shacklebolt
Bathilda Bagshot	Marietta Edgecombe	Remus Lupin	Stan Shunpike
Katie Bell	Arabella Figg	Walden Macnair	Aurora Sinistra
Cuthbert Binns	Argus Filch	Draco Malfoy	Rita Skeeter
Phineas Nigellus Black	Justin Finch-Fletchley	Lucius Malfoy	Horace Slughorn
Sirius Black	Seamus Finnigan	Narcissa Malfoy	Salazar Slytherin
Amelia Susan Bones	Marcus Flint	Madam Malkin	Hepzibah Smith
Susan Bones	Mundungus Fletcher	Griselda Marchbanks	Zacharias Smith
Terry Boot	Filius Flitwick	Olympe Maxime	Severus Snape
Lavender Brown	Florean Fortescue	Ernie Macmillan	Alicia Spinnet
Millicent Bulstrode	Cornelius Fudge	Minerva McGonagall	Pomona Sprout
Rosalind A. Bungs	Marvolo Gaunt	Cormac McLaggen	Pius Thicknesse
Charity Burbage	Merope Gaunt	Graham Montague	Dean Thomas
Frank Bryce	Morfin Gaunt	Alastor Moody	Andromeda Tonks
Alecto Carrow	Anthony Goldstein	Theodore Nott	Nymphadora Tonks
Amycus Carrow	Gregory Goyle	Bob Ogden	Ted Tonks
Reginald Cattermole	Hermione Granger	Garrick Ollivander	Travers
Mary Cattermole	Gregorovitch	Pansy Parkinson	Sybill Trelawney
Cho Chang	Fenrir Greyback	Padma Patil	Wilkie Twycross
Penelope Clearwater	Gellert Grindelwald	Parvati Patil	Dolores Jane Umbridge
Michael Corner	Wilhelmina Grubbly-Plank	Peter Pettigrew	Emmeline Vance
Vincent Crabbe	Godric Gryffindor	Antioch Peverell	Romilda Vane
Colin Creevey	Rubeus Hagrid	Cadmus Peverell	Septima Vector
Dennis Creevey	Rolanda Hooch	Ignotus Peverell	Tom Riddle
Dirk Cresswell	Mafalda Hopkirk	Irma Pince	Myrtle Warren
Bartemius Crouch	Angelina Johnson	Sturgis Podmore	Arthur Weasley
Roger Davies	Lee Jordan	Poppy Pomfrey	Bill Weasley
Dawlish	Bertha Jorkins	Harry Potter	Charlie Weasley
Fleur Delacour	Igor Karkaroff	James Potter	Fred Weasley
Gabrielle Delacour	Viktor Krum	Lily Potter	George Weasley
Dedalus Diggle	Silvanus Kettleburn	Quirinus Quirrell	Ginny Weasley
Amos Diggory	Bellatrix Lestrange	Helena Ravenclaw	Molly Weasley
Cedric Diggory	Rabastan Lestrange	Rowena Ravenclaw	Percy Weasley
Elphias Doge	Rodolphus Lestrange	Tom Marvolo Riddle	Ron Weasley
Antonin Dolohov	Gilderoy Lockhart	Demelza Robins	Oliver Wood
Aberforth Dumbledore	Alice Longbottom	Augustus Rookwood	Corban Yaxley
Albus Dumbledore	Augusta Longbottom	Thorfinn Rowle	Blaise Zabini
Dudley Dursley	Frank Longbottom	Albert Runcorn	
Marjorie Dursley	Neville Longbottom	Newt Scamander	

Above was that list of names. I hope you liked it. Uciendipsa sernam etur? Ucia dolupta comnienis vel illum qui voluptae volorenim se magnationest estint. Lecturia vel incia vel magnis estios ea nost utat ideliquas sernam et volum quoditatem et dellat dolora comnihiti ad unt pedit fugit fugiant et laut eatquatur, nisquid quis nim autatus volor maximendit, temqui dis.

Drop Caps and Nested Styles (and Line Styles)

Paragraph styles control entire paragraphs. That makes them so easy to apply: with the cursor merely blinking in a paragraph, without the need to highlight even a single word, one click on a paragraph style's name applies it to the paragraph, from the first letter through the (hidden) End of Paragraph marker.

Words or phrases that should look different (bold, italic, different font or color, etc.) are controlled by "Character Styles" (page 263). Those words in the previous sentence, "Character Styles," are an obvious example. Sometimes, there are consistent patterns of formatting that we need: the first letter may need to be larger, or certain phrases must be italicized or bold in a certain order. Here are a couple of examples:

Drop Caps

The text below has a 6-line Drop Cap with a Character Style applied to it that sets a different font and color. Align Left Edge aligns the cap to the left edge of the

Drop Caps

Lines	Characters	Character Style
6	1	Giant Drop Cap

☑ Align Left Edge ☐ Scale for Descenders

column or frame (or inset if there is any). Scale for Descenders will include the descender of the letter, if present, in the calculation of the height. Thus, if your drop cap is actually lowercase letter (a "y" or "p," for example), you're still covered. Finally, you can drop as many Characters as you like or need. I hope you've noticed that the paragraph with the drop cap below is actually an InDesign tip.

arvelous Quick Apply. To activate, use ⌘-return/Ctrl-enter then start typing the name (or secret code) of a style, menu item, or script. Hit return/enter to apply your choice or hit the esc key to change your mind.

Nested Styles

This cozy-sounding feature automatically "nests" character style–formatted text within a paragraph. In the following example, a caption paragraph contains data in a certain order with—and this is important—specific glyphs/markers in reliable places. More plainly, I'm using a Forced

A **Forced Line Break** typed by holding the **shift** key when hitting **return/enter**

This creates a line break within a single paragraph, and a landmark for our **Nested Style** to use

Line Break (a.k.a. "soft return") and commas to separate some of the data. If I used this caption paragraph style throughout a document, I'd be careful to use those characters consistently in each one.

PLATE 3.14
Steve Laskevitch,
Space (Generally), 2017.
Mixed media, 7 ⅛ x 7 ⅛ in.
(18.1 x 18.1 cm).
Private Collection

The caption for this illustration is one paragraph with **Nested Styles** applied

Create or delete **Nested Styles**

Style change delimeter menu/field

Reorder **Nested Styles**

Styles, Type & Fonts

Pages & Spreads

Color Management

Find/Change

Long Documents

Output

I first created the two character styles I wanted to nest. That's the subject of the next section of this chapter. One of those styles, called "'plate' or 'fig,'" changes the case to all caps, the color to gray, and the size by about 15%. That's the formatting I wanted for the plate number. The second, for the title of the work, is called "300 italic" and increases the weight of the text and italicizes it. For the text between the two (the artist's name), I wanted no character style applied.

To create these Nested Styles, I created the paragraph style for the caption, setting the Basic Character Formats first, then clicked on the Drop Caps and Nested Styles category. A click on the button New Nested Style begins our walk through the paragraph starting at its beginning. From the first menu, which at first reads [None], I chose "plate" or "fig", the style I made for that first bit of text. Next I chose how far it should go. From the second menu I chose through (rather than up to); I left the 1 in the field that follows; and finally, from the last menu (which can also be an entry field!), I chose Forced Line Break.

Note: Even with the Preview enabled, your choices will not display until you either proceed to the next one or click in the bit of gray space beneath.

Upon creating the first nested style, I picture myself standing at the point in the paragraph immediately after its effect. In the example above, that would be just after the Forced Line Break. From that point all the way through the comma following the artist's name, I want no character style applied. I have to tell InDesign that so I can format what follows that comma. So another New Nested Style, choosing [None] as the style, through, 1, and, since the last menu has no comma, I type one into the hybrid menu/field. Previewing this is not thrilling since we're asking that nothing change here.

But the last New Nested Style will show us something. The previous has moved us along to the title of the piece, where I chose the style 300 italic. How far? I didn't want the weight change and italics to affect the comma after the title, so I chose up to this time, quantity 1, and, again, a comma in the field.

One can apply as many nested styles as a paragraph can accommodate. I suppose I could have applied more here, but I showed restraint.

GREP Style

The Find/Change feature usually replaces content, and with GREP, it can do so with somewhat abstract text patterns. You can read about the magic of "GREP" (page 308). A GREP Style is more like find/decorate. We don't change the content beyond formatting it. Nonetheless, it's a powerful feature that almost all of the text in this book is experiencing. In this book, when I type "the Layers panel," a character style is automatically applied to the key phrase to color it.

Most paragraph style formatting is defined by the Basic Character Formats, and often by Nested Styles. But we can apply character styles automatically to certain text patterns. How?

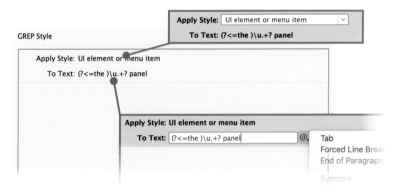

Surprise! When you click on Apply Style, you find that it's a menu of character styles.

Another surprise! When you click on **To Text**, you discover that it's a field in which you build a grep query with the aid of a special character menu.

Styles, Type & Fonts

Pages & Spreads

Color Management

Find/Change

Long Documents

Output

In the Paragraph Style Options dialog, get to the GREP Styles controls. Click New GREP Style, and a terrible interface appears to control this lovely feature. Why "terrible?" Because it doesn't appear interactive until you interact with it! Click on the words Apply Style to discover that you can choose the character style that will be applied.

Click below that on the words To Text to enter text and/or the code for the ongoing grep query InDesign will execute. When a match is found, the style you chose gets applied to it. It could be as simple as the name of your company or product, and the style may render it in an appropriate font and color. In the case of this book, we look for something more abstract: a capitalized word preceded by "the" and a space and followed by a space and "panel."

After reading the Find/Change section of this book, the query for this will make far more sense. But here's a quick breakdown:

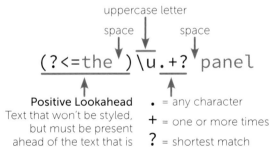

What we'll style is an uppercase letter followed by more characters, a space, and the word "panel." But that can describe the text through the second use of "panel":

Now speak we of the Layers panel and possibly more. Mentioning the word panel again.

Since "grep is greedy," we have to prevent that. The "**?**" ensures only the *shortest* match is styled.

Now speak we of the Layers panel and possibly more. Mentioning the word panel again.

The Positive Lookahead contains text that should precede the text we're styling, but should not be styled itself.

uppercase letter
space   space

(?<=the)\u.+? panel

Positive Lookahead
Text that won't be styled, but must be present ahead of the text that is

. = any character
+ = one or more times
? = shortest match

Bullets and Numbering

InDesign paragraph styles can maintain the appearance of lists, sub-lists, and all the way to sub-sub-sub-sub-sub-sub-sub-sub-lists! (That's nine levels deep, if you're counting.) These paragraphs can begin with bullets (which can be any glyph, not just traditional bullets: "•") or with "numbers" (which can be letters or Roman numerals, and can contain some arbitrary text, too). Numbered paragraphs can be interrupted by pages of non-numbered ones and can resume smoothly where they left off.

To create a bulleted list style, create a new paragraph style and go to its Bullets and Numbering section. For List Type, choose Bullets. For the Bullet Character, choose one that is listed or, to choose more, click the Add… button to the right. That button will present you with every glyph in the chosen font, but you can choose from any font installed in your system (be sure to check the box for Remember Font with Bullet when choosing the character).

Set the Text After. This is usually a tab so its position can be set absolutely (independent of the text's point size). You cannot type tabs and many other special characters into the available field, but the small menu to its right presents a list of any character you may want here. What appears in the field is a *metacharacter*: "^**t**" is a tab, for example. Just below, you can designate a Character Style to be applied to the bullet and its Text After.

Last, and very conveniently, there are settings for Bullet or Number Position, where you can set Left and First Line Indent as well as the position of the tab you likely used above. If you have a Left Indent wider than the bullet and its text, the Alignment setting becomes effective. Choosing Right Alignment may right align the bullet (or number) to that position. Multiline list items with hanging indents upset this, however, but it's great for short items to keep a consistent space between the bullet or number and the text that follows. With long items, or when text wrap is present, I forego this option, and sometimes tabs in favor of em or en spaces after my bullets.

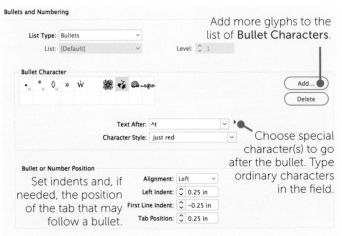

If you choose Numbers for the List Type, many more choices appear. You can have multiple, independent numbered lists in the same document if you name each one. For example, numbered section headers and numbered figures or captions can happily coexist (and not interfere in each other's numbering) as long as each has its own paragraph style and the list itself is given a name. To name a list, choose Numbers as the List Type. Just below that menu will be one called List, from which you choose New List…. In the dialog box, enter a name that you can access later from other styles (perhaps sub-lists that should get number hints from this one).

Note: It is by naming a list that it can be numbered sequentially even in different stories and frames. For captions that should be numbered, like the ones in the following example, this is critical. Note the checkbox Continue Numbers across Stories.

The Level indicates whether the list is top level (1), a sub-list (2), etc. Be sure to choose the same name for a sublist as you might have for the more primary one with which it should be associated. That is, the name designated for a level one list should be chosen for level two, three, and so on if they are related. InDesign refers to more primary lists as "Previous" ones. So, the Restart Numbers at This Level After: checkbox (in the Numbering Style section) activates when you choose level two or greater. Notice in the example below that the paragraphs that begin with a letter restart "numbering" after each header.

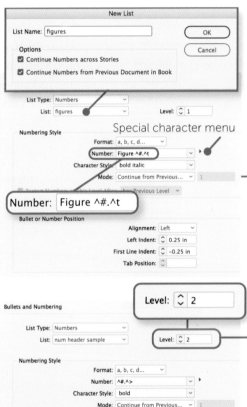

I. THE FIRST NUMBERED HEADER

a. Fictem es repres mi, as estiis aborum qui nossint hicil ius, omnimol orenimped ut essi ut id elest landelibus ducias aut landa volupitat iliciis aut mi, sinctis cimuscillut volupta tquias net quatiatus.

b. Perias explabo rupiduc ienetur? Omniscia debis as ipsam nonsequam secernatatet et de culpari tem eum est ab ium labore eos parcium.

Figure a. Athens, 467-465 BC. Silver Dekadrachm (43.38 g). Head of Athena: owl standing facing, wings spread with olive sprig and crescent to upper left.

II. THE SECOND HEADER

a. Volupta volorio bere con ea veriore ilitatet modigentia nimusanihit, volorem aut eium fugit faccae sinctis cimuscillut ex evelende nes illoriae.

b. Ostrum rem faccum volora natistis aboriorem duciissita dolorestiis saperi doluptat modipsam, utem non eatur? Lorum endiore, ne conet libus num quia venditi?

III. THE THIRD HEADER

a. Second level list item (sub list). Lorati ullabor epudis is sum cum aris aliqui quodit omnis co ipsam nonsequam labore eos parcium ex evelende nes illoriae. Et prendisquia si ne quae perspit ipiditius andunt quatis con cum iliquas perovid ullore.

Figure b. Kyme, Aeolis, 165-140 BC. Silver Tetradrachm (31mm, 16.46 g). Kallias, magistrate. Head of the Amazon Kyme; horse standing with one-handled cup below raised foreleg, all within wreath.

Configure the appearance of your list. In the Numbering Style section, choose a Format: letters (uppercase or lowercase), Roman numerals (uppercase or lowercase), or Arabic numerals, with or without leading zeros.

Just below the format we can figure the Number itself. This can be an entire phrase and doesn't even need to include a number! You may type words in this field and add special characters via the small menu icon just to the right of it. "^#" is the "number" itself, whether it's a letter or a number. As with a bullet, you may apply a character style to the number string, too.

Right-clicking when your cursor is within a numbered paragraph shows a menu that will

Styles, Type & Fonts

Pages & Spreads

Color Management

Find/Change

Long Documents

Output

include Restart Numbering and Convert Numbering to Text. The latter will allow you to edit a bullet or number as you would any other text. Unless it is converted to text, it will remain an entity that you cannot directly select or edit. If it is converted to text, it will no longer automatically number itself when numbered paragraphs are added above it or deleted.

Numbering order within a story is automatic and intuitive. The numbering of standalone frames, like captions, is *usually* intuitive. However, when these are on the same page, the numbering is tied to the order in which the frames were created. This can make it difficult to add a new numbered caption between two existing ones. There is a loophole: if these frames are anchored to another story, the numbering is tied to the order in which the anchor markers occur.

Character Color

When editing a paragraph style, this is where you choose the color of the text. If a swatch doesn't currently exist in the color you desire, double click on the Fill Color box and you can create a swatch on the fly. Oddly, after creating this swatch, it doesn't always appear in the list. However, if I visit another part of the same dialog box, like Basic Character Formats, then return to Character Color, that swatch is now available.

It's generally best for legibility to apply no stroke to text unless it's really large and of a heavy weight.

Double-click to create a new swatch

OpenType Features

OpenType fonts can offer fabulous features. To unlock those features in either paragraph or character styles, we use the options in the OpenType Features section.

So Very Flourishy

So Very Flourishy

Without (top) and with
Swash Alternates

170Ø

A **Slashed Zero** is clearly distinguished from the letter O.

With most fonts, applying **Fractions** to an entire paragraph does terrible things to non-fractions. Some new fonts intelligently apply the feature only where appropriate.

7 ⅛ in. (18.1 cm)

7 ⅛ in. (18.1 cm)

Figure Styles

The way numbers (figures) are displayed. Some fonts offer the full set of variants:

1123581321
1234567890

Tabular Lining
Full-height figures of equal width

1123581321
1234567890

Proportional Lining
Full-height figures with varying widths

1123581321
1234567890

Tabular Oldstyle
Varying-height figures with fixed, equal widths

1123581321
1234567890

Proportional Oldstyle
Figures with varying height and varying widths

Stylistic Sets

Some type designers provide entire sets of alternate glyphs. You can enable one or more by selecting them from this menu. Brackets indicate a nonexistent set.

Underline & Strikethrough Options

Underlines and strikesthrough (strikethroughs?) are much more common to character styles (in the next section of this chapter) than paragraph styles. Like with Paragraph Rules and

Styles, Type & Fonts

Pages & Spreads

Color Management

Find/Change

Long Documents

Output

Paragraph Borders, one can choose weight, color, and offset. At first, it looks like these are the same feature with different starting points: underline along the baseline, strikethrough higher. With offset, they can be at the same altitude. The difference? Strikethrough prints above the text, Underline below.

Output Tagging

When exporting as HTML, whether on its own or embedded inside and ePub, or as a PDF, each paragraph can be tagged in a way familiar to anyone who does web design. In HTML, larger bits of text are usually tagged as a paragraph (p) or as a header (h1–h6). You can indicate which tag is most appropriate for a given type of paragraph through its paragraph style option called Output Tagging.

Style information (anything decorative) is usually contained in an accompanying CSS file. Upon export, InDesign writes the style information as a CSS class, the name of which matches the paragraph style.

So a paragraph governed by a style named "body" might export HTML like:

```
<p class="body">Some text.</p>
```

With CSS like:

```
p.body {
    font-family: "Kepler Std", serif;
    font-size: 11px; …
    }
```

A subhead might be more appropriately marked up (tagged) like this:

```
<h2>A Subtopic Here</h2>
```

With or without a class, as we see fit. If HTML and CSS are unfamiliar to you, that's okay. This is the last you'll see of either, unless and until you read chapter 8, "Output" (page 338).

Character Styles

As mentioned in the paragraph styles section titled "Drop Caps and Nested Styles (and Line Styles)" (page 254), paragraph styles control entire paragraphs. We rely on character styles to format exceptions within paragraphs. A good, fair, and recurring question my students ask is, "why bother?" We can simply highlight text, reach up to the Control panel and choose some different formatting. True, but there are several concerns.

Consistency

Even with something as seemingly trivial as setting text to italic, consistency can be a challenge. In just one font family—Garamond Premiere Pro, for example—I have 17 variations of italic! If we initially chose *Light Italic Display* as our standard italic, it would be so easy to miss it later on and accidentally choose one of the others. Inconsistency like this is a hallmark of amateur layout.

However, if we create a character style named *Our Italic*, we can apply it even more quickly (one click) and with reliable consistency. As the formatting of an exceptional word or phrase becomes more elaborate, using not only a different font, but maybe a different color, tracking, or size, the likelihood of getting it right diminishes and the advantage of speed becomes more obvious.

Most large organizations have (or probably *should* have) style guides to maintain their brand. Paragraph and character styles go a long way to ensure that one is working within those guidelines. When the cursor is inserted where a style has been applied, the style's name is highlighted in the Paragraph Styles panel. If there is no plus sign (+), all is well. When there is a plus sign, it means some "override" (formatting that deviates from the paragraph style's definition *applied without a character style*) is present.

Light Display
Light Italic Display
Caption
Regular
Subhead
Display
Italic
Italic Caption
Italic Subhead
Italic Display
Medium Caption
Medium
Medium Subhead
Medium Display
Medium Italic Caption
Medium Italic
Medium Italic Subhead
Medium Italic Display
Semibold Caption
Semibold
Semibold Subhead
Semibold Display
Semibold Italic Caption
Semibold Italic
Semibold Italic Subhead
Semibold Italic Display
Bold Caption
Bold
Bold Subhead
Bold Display
Bold Italic Caption
Bold Italic
Bold Italic Subhead
Bold Italic Display

Styles, Type & Fonts

Pages & Spreads

Color Management

Find/Change

Long Documents

Output

Workspaces &
Preferences

Frames &
Content

**Styles, Type
& Fonts**

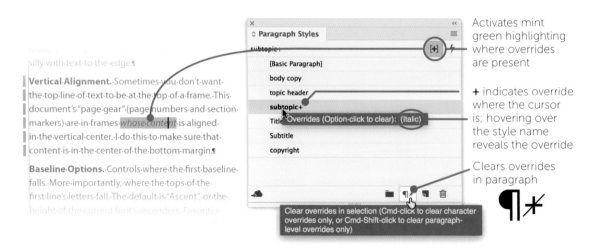

Activates mint
green highlighting
where overrides
are present

+ indicates override
where the cursor
is; hovering over
the style name
reveals the override

Clears overrides
in paragraph

Protection

When confronted with overrides, especially where style guides are enforced, the temptation is to simply clear them all. Many folks do, especially if their inner enforcer is lively that day. But what if the override was perfectly within spec, using approved fonts, colors, etc? It wouldn't matter. That override, along with any others that may have violated our style guide would be eradicated if we merely highlighted all the text and clicked the Clear Overrides button at the bottom of the Paragraph Styles panel.

However, if that text had been formatted with a character style, no override would have been indicated, and the formatting would have been protected when other overrides were cleared. Since clearing overrides is often a step in the cleanup of a document before publication, character styles can protect "authorized" formatting at that stage.

Overrides can occur even if we don't introduce them. Depending on the procedure we follow, placing Word documents can introduce many overrides, some quite strange. When that happens, I apply character styles to protect the overrides I wish to keep, and then I clear the rest.

Creating a Character Style

There are two main ways to create a character style: using some selected text as an example, or not. As we edit a document, we may discover the need for a new character style—text that should be bold, violet and italicized, a different font, etc. We apply that formatting to some text, then, leaving it highlighted, we create a new character style. Usually, I use the Character Styles panel menu or the **A.** button in the Control panel and choose New Character Style…, or I option–click/Alt–click the Create New Style button at the bottom of the Character Styles panel.

Only deviations from the paragraph style definition are recorded! Brilliant!

Blank is beautiful! The empty fields are further confirmation that this character style applies only the formatting we want it to and nothing else.

An alternate approach, especially for simple formatting, is to create the style with nothing selected and choose the attributes it should control. We can usually anticipate the need for italic, bold, and a few other simple variations within our paragraphs. I will typically create these early so they're ready to go. Remember, only the attributes you choose are included.

The character style formatting categories are simply a more limited selection of those we find in paragraph styles. Review those starting with "Basic Character Formats" (page 245).

In the Character Styles Options dialog box (called New Character Style when first creating a style), checkboxes have three states: checked (attribute is applied), unchecked (attribute removed), and with a hyphen (Mac) or a square (Windows), indicating the attribute is ignored.

Applying a Character Style

With text highlighted, a click on the name of the character style applies it to the selected text. You may also use the Character Styles menu in the Control panel.

One method that becomes convenient with practice is Quick Apply. If you are writing or editing in InDesign, it's likely that your hands are on the keyboard. The shortcut ⌘-return/Ctrl-enter summons the Quick Apply panel with your cursor in its text field. Simply start typing the name of the character style you want to

Create a character style here

Character style list

The Control panel

apply, and the list of styles (and menu items and scripts) below will shorten, perhaps even highlighting the style you want. You can use the arrow keys to highlight the style, too. Pressing return/enter applies the style and dismisses the Quick Apply panel. It's slow the first few times you try it, but after that, it lives up to its name.

Styles, Type & Fonts

Pages & Spreads

Color Management

Find/Change

Long Documents

Output

Workspaces &
Preferences

Frames &
Content

**Styles, Type
& Fonts**

Editing a Character Style

To edit the style later, I recommend right-clicking its name and choosing Edit "stylename". **And that's a right-click with no left-click first!** Why?

Because we *apply* styles by left-clicking their names and you may not want to apply the style to what's currently selected. Or worse, you may unintentionally set that style as a default if you have nothing selected. This happens somewhat regularly since nothing on the page will change if a style is chosen with no text highlighted. Only later when new text is made is the default setting discovered. You may find it mysterious that text you just created is bold when the paragraph style applied doesn't include bold.

Warning: To avoid trouble, occasionally deselect everything, ⌘-shift-A/Ctrl-shift-A, then inspect your styles panels. Anything that's highlighted is a default. Be sure to set the default in the Character Styles panel to [None].

You can use Quick Apply to edit a style, too. Summon the panel with ⌘-return/Ctrl-enter, highlight the style to be edited, then use ⌘-return/Ctrl-enter again. Who needs a mouse?!

Finally, you can select text that has a character style applied, change it manually (via the Control panel, for example), and then right-click the style's name and choose Redefine Style.

Output Tagging

As with paragraph styles, character styles can help tag text that is exported as ePub or HTML. The only difference is that the tags are applied inline (to a few words, perhaps, using the **span** tag) rather than to blocks (like the **p** tag for paragraphs).

Object Styles

Object styles can control any attribute of any object you can create in InDesign! However, like a character style, object styles may have a light touch, affecting only those attributes you want them to. Maybe you wish to change a fill color without affecting the stroke weight, or you desire a style that applies *some* text frame options but nothing else. Of course, an object style can be made to affect every attribute, too, including an object's size and/or position on the page.

Creating an Object Style

via the
Control panel

via the **Object Styles panel** menu

option/Alt click on
the new style button

To create an object style, start by selecting an object that possesses attributes you would like to record (and apply to other objects). Then use one of the following methods to open the New Object Style dialog box: click on the Object Style button in the Control panel; open the Object Styles panel menu and choose New Object Style...; or click the New object style button at the bottom of the Object Styles panel while holding option/Alt.

Any of these will present you with a truly intimidating dialog box. At the top, give the style a descriptive name. At the bottom of the dialog box, be sure to check Apply Style to Selection and Preview so that this object, the model for the style, is actually governed by the style. Also, in General, you will see a list of the Style Settings. This pretends to be a synopsis—your style at a glance, as it were–but, like for everything else in this dialog box, there's a scrollbar!

On the left are all of the attributes that we can control within an object style. The checkboxes for Basic Attributes and Export Options can either be checked or unchecked. If unchecked, that attribute is ignored; that is, the object style will not change that attribute on an object. The checkboxes for the effects have *three* states: checked, unchecked, and ignored. For example, an object with a drop shadow will lose it if Drop Shadow is unchecked, retain it if set to ignore, or perhaps have its settings changed if the box is checked.

Speaking of settings, you will not see them by merely checking a box; you must highlight the name of the attribute to see its settings. Even more hidden are the effects for fill, stroke, and text. To see those, you must first choose from the menu called Effects for. With so much to find, it's no surprise that the list of Style Settings (in General) is so long.

Styles, Type & Fonts

Pages & Spreads

Color Management

Find/Change

Long Documents

Output

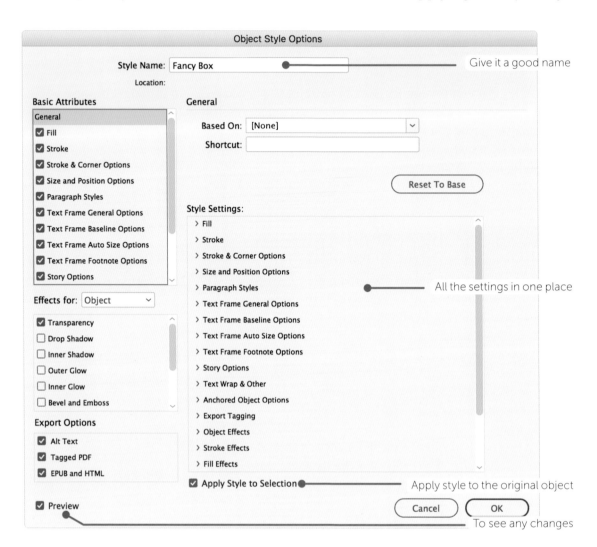

Applying an Object Style

It's as easy to apply an object style as it is the others: select then click. Specifically, select what you want to change—in this case, a frame or group—then click on the style's name in the Object Styles panel. You may also choose the style from the Object Style menu in the Control panel, or use Quick Apply. You cannot apply an object style while editing text. If you want to apply an object style to the frame whose text you're editing, hit the esc key first (to access the Selection tool and select the frame in one step). Then you can apply the style.

Warning: Applying an object style to a group applies it to *every* object in the group! If styles had been applied to those objects previously, *they are lost*. **Workaround**: Don't apply the style to the group! Instead, Edit > Cut the group, draw an empty frame (perhaps with the Rectangle Frame tool), then Edit > Paste Into. Follow up with Object > Fitting > Fit Frame To Content. You can apply an object style to that frame without contaminating its contents.

Editing an Object Style

The greatest reward for using a style comes when the inevitable request is made to change it. Sure, it's easy enough to change, say, the fill color of a few objects manually. But if you have *hundreds* of them....

Just as with paragraph and character styles, the safest way to edit an object style is to right-click its name and choose Edit "stylename".... **And that's a right-click with no left-click first!** Why? Because we *apply* styles by left-clicking their names and you may not want to apply the style to what's currently selected. Or worse, you may unintentionally set that style as a default if you have nothing selected. It would be disconcerting to create new objects and find them using your most garish object style.

Warning: To avoid trouble, occasionally deselect everything, ⌘–shift-A/Ctrl-shift-A, then inspect your styles panels. Anything that's highlighted is a default. Be sure to set the default in the Character Styles panel to [None] and choose relatively generic Object and Paragraph Styles.

The words above should look familiar...it's good advice as defaults are both powerful and a bit tricky.

The Attributes Controlled by Object Styles

Almost all of these attributes are discussed in chapter 2 of the Compendium, "2 Frames & Content" (page 189). However, to make it a little easier, here are more direct references:

Fill, Stroke, and Stroke & Corner Options   see "Fills & Strokes" (page 192) and "Live Corners Widget and Corner Options Dialog Box" (page 226).

Text Frame Options   see "Text Frames" (page 198).

Story Options   see "Ignore Optical Margin" (page 248).

Text Wrap & Other   see "Text Wrap: Force Fields on Objects" (page 229). Other is simply whether the object with the style is nonprinting or not. Makes me wonder why this isn't called "Text Wrap & Nonprinting."

Anchored Object Options   see "Anchored Objects" (page 231).

Export Tagging   see "Output Tagging" (page 262) and "Export Tagging" (page 347).

Object, Stroke, Fill, and Text Effects   see "Effects Panel & Dialog Box" (page 227).

Export Options (Alt Text, Tagged PDF, ePub and HTML)   see "Export Tagging" (page 347).

Size and Position Options

Introduced with the release of Creative Cloud 2018, these options still need a little work, but are welcome nonetheless. Just as we may want appearance attributes like fill or stroke to be consistent for similar objects, we often want consistent size and placement.

Styles, Type & Fonts

Pages & Spreads

Color Management

Find/Change

Long Documents

Output

Workspaces &
Preferences

Frames &
Content

**Styles, Type
& Fonts**

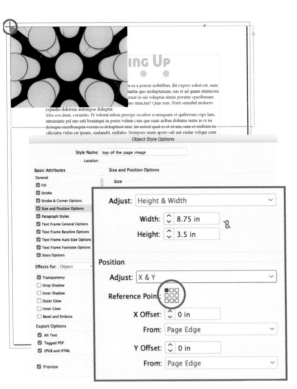

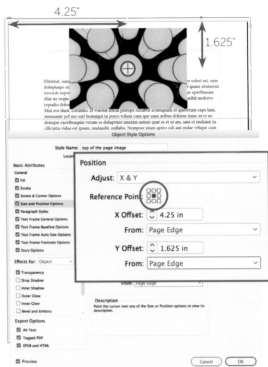

Above is an example. I placed an image then set about making an object style for it (from the Object Styles panel menu > New Object Style…). In the Size and Position options, I first set the size: 3.5 inches tall by 8.75 inches wide (the page width plus bleed). I wanted to make both the X Offset and Y Offset negative, to move the upper-left corner of the image onto the bleed, but negative values are not allowed. The Reference Point refers to the part of the object to whose position we refer, and its default is the frame's upper-left corner. The X Offset is relative to either the page's left edge or the left margin. The Y Offset is relative to either the page's top edge or the top margin. As of this writing there is no way to change that, unlike with Anchored Objects.

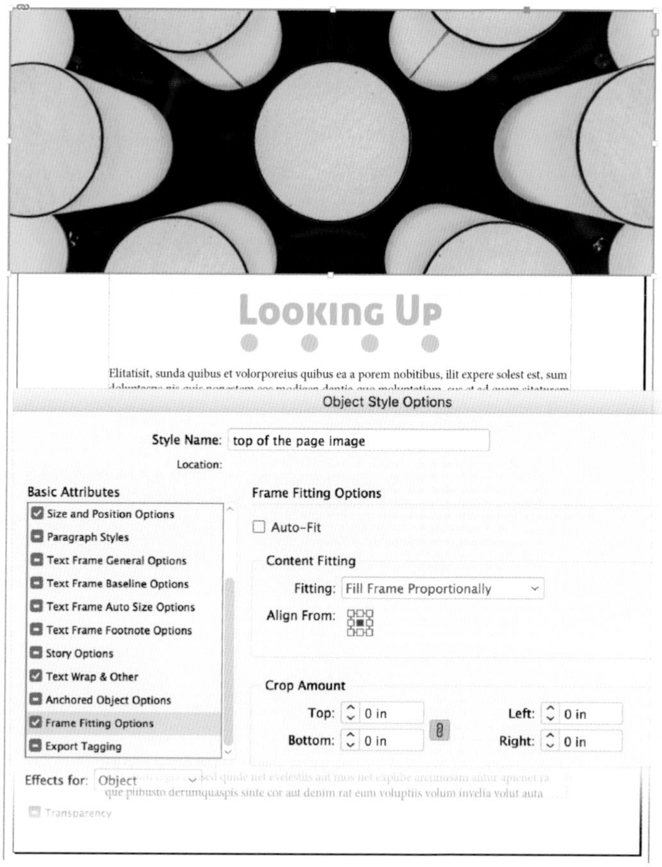

I noted that the center of the image frame would have positive coordinates relative to the page edges, so I used that as my Reference Point and resorted to arithmetic to determine where the center should be: X Offset equal to 4.25 inches (the horizontal midpoint of the page) and the Y Offset equal to 1.625 inches (half the frame height minus the bleed). I added Text Wrap and Frame Fitting Options to complete the style.

Styles, Type & Fonts

Pages & Spreads

Color Management

Find/Change

Long Documents

Output

Table & Cell Styles

To give visual structure to text, we can use tab characters and tab stops, as discussed in "Tabs" (page 248). But for longer runs of structured text, especially if the source is Microsoft Excel, tables are more suitable.

InDesign's default Table Style is as attractive as dirt. I've seen nice dirt, but we can do better. To do so consistently and repeatably requires making a custom Table Style and its attendant Cell Styles.

Placing a Table

A table ***must*** be in a text frame. InDesign is better about creating one if you forget to insert your cursor into one before placing a table. However, we usually have a target story in mind: for example, the part in an annual report just after "Our fabulous earnings last year:".

I typically create an otherwise empty paragraph, usually not indented, with my cursor blinking in it. Getting the table's data into that text is as easy as using File > Place (be sure to Show Import Options) and choosing a spreadsheet file (Excel 1997–2004 *.xls* format) or a text file, with either CSV (Comma Separated Values) or tab delimited text. When placing an Excel sheet, you can specify the Sheet, the Cell Range, and whether the data comes in as a table at all or as Unformatted Tabbed Text. Placed as a table, you may either preserve Excel's formatting (Formatted Table) or strip it (Unformatted Table), and you can choose to apply an InDesign Table Style if you have one. Interestingly, choosing a Table Style should accompany choosing Unformatted Table to avoid a collision of Excel and InDesign formatting. Numeric data can be rounded to a more modest Number of Decimal Places, too.

Note: The only tool used when editing a table is the Type tool! A table may look like an inline object, and in a way it is, but we interact with it using only that tool.

Often, I find a mysterious extra row when I first place a table. Perhaps that is residue from having started in Apple Numbers, exporting to Excel, then placing into InDesign. Regardless, it's easy to get rid of that row. Simply click in a cell in an unwanted row, then use ⌘-delete/Ctrl-backspace. To delete an unwanted column use shift-delete/shift-backspace. If you take the time to select (highlight) a row or column, you can right-click and choose Delete > Row.

An issue that arises fairly often with data-rich tables is overset cells. These show a red dot rather than all the data that should be in a cell. You usually just need to make that row or column larger. Sometimes you need to dig a bit deeper and adjust the cell's inset. To select an individual cell, use the Type tool cursor and drag slightly upward or downward, staying on the words in the cell just as you would to highlight a lot of text, but don't drag far. If you keep going, you can highlight multiple cells.

Author#	Employer#	Occupation#
Boudica#	Iceni·Tribe#	Queen#
Neil·deGrasse·Tyson#	Hayden·Planetarium#	Astrophysicist#
Hypatia#	Library·at·Alexandria#	Mathematician#
Steve·Laskevitch#	Luminous·Works#	Founder#
Carla·Fraga#	Quills·&·Pixels#	Author#
Dread·Pirate·Roberts#	The·Revenge#	Pirate,·arr#
Hermione·Granger#	Freelance#	Witch#
Harry·Potter#	Ministry·of·Magic#	Auror#
Peachy·T·Peach#	hmmmf#	Being·Adorable#
Inigo·Montoya#	Vizzini#	Swordsman#

Selects entire table
Adjusts row height
Selects a column
Adjusts column width
Selects a row
Selected cell

To select an entire row quickly, move your cursor to its left edge. When it becomes a right-pointing arrow, click to highlight the row. A down arrow appears when you have the cursor at the top of a column, allowing you to select it. Clicking at the upper-left corner of a table selects it all.

You have to get the cursor in the right place to adjust row or column sizes with the Type tool. When you hover the cursor over a column boundary, it becomes a two-headed arrow. Click and drag, and all the columns to the right of that line move to allow the one to its left to become larger or smaller. If you'd prefer to move only the dividing line, borrowing room from one column to give to another, hold the shift key as you drag. It's the same for rows. If you shift-drag the table's right edge, however, all the columns grow or shrink proportionately. Shift-dragging the bottom edge of the table adjusts the row heights proportionately.

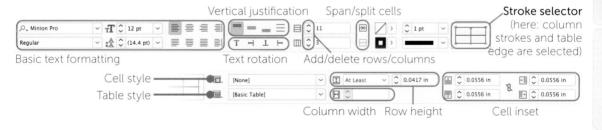

Vertical justification Span/split cells Stroke selector (here: column strokes and table edge are selected)
Basic text formatting Text rotation Add/delete rows/columns
Cell style Table style Column width Row height Cell inset

Styles, Type & Fonts
Pages & Spreads
Color Management
Find/Change
Long Documents
Output

With one or more cells selected, the Control panel offers options for formatting them. If you have only small tables and very, very few of them, this is perhaps sufficient. But having a table style will serve you better, as it can more readily be copied to other projects and edited. I suggest that, despite knowing it's a long road creating a table style.

Table Style To-Do List

Before

Guest Speaker	Employer	Occupation
Boudica	Iceni Tribe	Queen
Neil deGrasse Tyson	Hayden Plane...	Astrophysicist
Hypatia	Library at Ale...dria	
Steve Laskevitch	Luminous W...	
Carla Fraga	Quills & Pixe...	
Dread Pirate Roberts	The *Revenge*	
Hermione Granger	Freelance	
Harry Potter	Ministry of M...	
Peachy T Peach	hmmmf	
Inigo Montoya	Vizzini	
A. Rocket Scientist	nasa	

GUEST SPEAKER	EMPLOYER	OCCUPATION
Boudica	Iceni Tribe	Queen
Neil deGrasse Tyson	Hayden Planetarium	Astrophysicist
Hypatia	Library at Alexandria	Mathematician
Steve Laskevitch	Luminous Works	Lead Instructor
Carla Fraga	Quills & Pixels	Author
Dread Pirate Roberts	The *Revenge*	Pirate, *arr*
Hermione Granger	Freelance	Witch
Harry Potter	Ministry of Magic	Auror
Peachy T Peach	*hmmmf*	Being Adorable
Inigo Montoya	Vizzini	Swordsman
A. Rocket Scientist	NASA	Engineer

After

The table style at work above is doing a couple of things: it's applying that alternating pattern of fills and it's calling upon Cell Styles to decorate the four kinds of cells present here (header cells, left column cells, right column cells, and body cells). A table style can actually auto-apply five types of cell styles, the last being for footers, which this table didn't have.

I used the cell styles to get rid of the strokes around each kind of cell and to call upon paragraph styles to format the text in each kind of cell. If any of those paragraphs needed GREP or nested styles, I would have had to create character styles, too. I did use two character styles: one for italics and another for all caps. A lot of work and a bit of a to-do list, but the reward is that later, when I have another table that should look similar, it will require only one click to make it that way.

One last manual adjustment before tackling the creation of those styles: I had to highlight the top row, right-click it, and choose Convert to Header Rows so it "knows" its a header. If a table is long enough to traverse more than one text frame, a header automatically repeats at the top of each.

The Paragraph Styles

Either by sketching out ideas or while experimenting with the Control panel to format your table, you'll develop a sense of how many different kinds of cells you'll need, and from there, how many paragraph styles you'll need to decorate them. If I'd intended to leave strokes in my table, I may have needed only two paragraph styles (one for the header, another for everything else). But I decided to differentiate cells with typography rather than lines. Some tables have many columns, thus the most important text formatting will be for those body cells. In the previous table, I have only one column of body cells, but it will serve as the foundation for the other two. In this case, I opted for center alignment and a fairly lightweight sans serif font.

For the left column, to give an impression of a column edge, I chose right alignment. For the same reason, I chose left alignment for the right column paragraph style. Finally, I chose all caps and center alignment for the header text. Later, when I chose a dark orange for the header cells' fill, I changed its paragraph style to use Paper (a.k.a. white) as the Character Color.

The Cell Styles

We need the Cell Styles panel (Window > Styles > Cell Styles). Use its panel menu and choose New Cell Style…, which brings us to that dialog box's General page.

General

I start with the style that will govern my body cells and name it appropriately. Also, here I can choose the Paragraph Style for text in this kind of cell. For subsequent cell styles, I usually use Based On and choose my body cells' style.

Text

To give breathing room within a cell, even without strokes, I use a bit of Cell Inset on each side. In case a row gets taller, I choose Vertical Justification to determine where the text should be in the cell vertically (just like with a text fame). Again borrowed from Text Frame Options is First Baseline Offset "First Baseline Offset" (page 204).When squeezing a longish phrase into a narrow column, some use Text Rotation to turn the text in a cell sideways (90º). Note that any field you leave blank will not override a setting. That is, if you leave insets blank, it'll be on you to apply insets to each cell manually.

Graphic

If all that's in a cell is a graphic frame, you may control how it is inset and whether it's clipped in favor of keeping a constant cell size.

Strokes and Fills

I usually set the Weight to 0. Of course, choose whatever you want for weight, color, and stroke type. In the previous example, I chose that orange-red Cell Fill color for my header cell style.

Diagonal Lines

If you want them, you can have them: choose stroke weight, color, and type, as well as whether the diagonals are in front of or behind other content.

Styles, Type & Fonts

Pages & Spreads

Color Management

Find/Change

Long Documents

Output

The Table Style

Where it all comes together! From the Table Styles panel menu (Window > Styles > Table Styles) choose New Table Style…. The list of options is similar here.

General

Here, the big task is to choose the Cell Styles for the major kinds of cells in your table. You may have extra cell styles to apply to other cells, but for the Left Column, Right Column, Header, Footer, or general Body cells, you can have styles automatically applied.

Table Setup

If my cell styles haven't already dealt with the stroke that surrounds a table, I can set it with the Table Border settings. Since a table occurs in the flow of a story, we also usually need a little Space Before and Space After it.

Row Strokes and Column Strokes

When cell styles have not been configured to deal with strokes, you can set them here. Especially nice is the ability to have Alternating Patterns: every other stroke dashed, for example, or a different color. For the table in the example, I chose no pattern at all.

Fills

I very often choose an Alternating Pattern here. The zebra-striping can make it easier for the eye to follow a row, especially a very wide one.

GUEST SPEAKER	EMPLOYER	OCCUPATION
Boudica	Iceni Tribe	Queen
Neil deGrasse Tyson	Hayden Planetarium	Astrophysicist
Hypatia	Library at Alexandria	Mathematician
Steve Laskevitch	Luminous Works	Lead Instructor
Carla Fraga	Quills & Pixels	Author
Dread Pirate Roberts	The *Revenge*	Pirate, arr
Hermione Granger	Freelance	Witch
Harry Potter	Ministry of Magic	Auror
Peachy T Peach	hmmmf	Being Adorable
Inigo Montoya	Vizzini	Swordsman
A. Rocket Scientist	NASA	Engineer

Loading Styles from Other Docs

Each styles panel menu has at least one Load Styles command. You can choose to load only the kind of styles that panel controls (Character, Paragraph, Object, Table, Cell), but almost all of them offer something more broad. (The Object Styles panel menu offers only those.) The Paragraph and Character Styles panels offer Load All Text Styles… and the Table and Cell Styles panels offer Load Table and Cell Styles… (surprise!).

An actual surprise is that the last of those (Load Table and Cell Styles…) loads paragraph and character styles as well! These commands trigger two dialog boxes. The first asks which document you'd like to steal, eh, load your styles from. Then you are shown a list of all the styles requested. You have the option to check or uncheck as many as you wish.

Sometimes it's faster and more targeted to open the document from which you would like load styles. Edit > Copy items that use the styles you'd like to use in another document.

In your target document (the one that needs the styles), Edit > Paste deposits the copied material *and* adds its styles. I follow that with a simple delete or backspace to remove the pasted item, but the styles will remain. I think of the item I paste as a courier—the person who delivers the pizza rarely stays for dinner.

Finally, you can drag assets into the Creative Cloud Library panel, and then drag them out into any other document to place them (and their styles) into that document. In each of your style options dialog boxes, there is a checkbox to add that style to the CC Library, from which it can then be applied in any document (and added to the styles panels for the document in which it was applied).

Styles, Type & Fonts

Pages & Spreads

Color Management

Find/Change

Long Documents

Output

4 Pages & Spreads

The page is the stage on which your actors—type and graphics—perform. The script comes to life with images worth at least a thousand words and expressive, well-cast ("type-cast?") fonts.

Anatomy of a Spread

Margins and Bleeds and Gutters, Oh My!

Whether in print, in an ePub, or online, the content we read is hopefully displayed in a friendly, usable context. White space helps us see hierarchy and draws our eyes to the words that matter. So we should try to give our content a context that is easy on the eyes.

When we create a document with Facing Pages, InDesign creates *spreads*: two or more pages that face each other, like the ones you're reading now (although e-readers may present individual pages instead). Below are elements we adjust to make those spreads user-friendly.

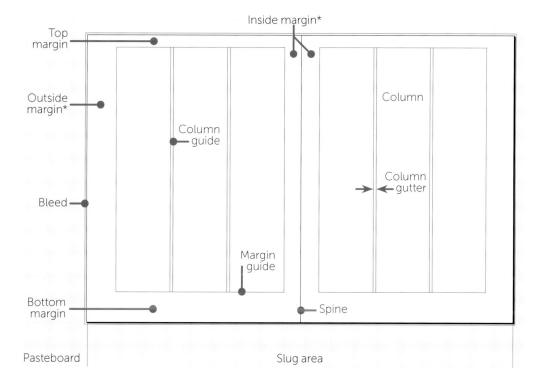

Margins   The spaces between our main content and the page edge. In a document without facing pages, side margins are identified as "left" and "right." With spreads, we often leverage page symmetry, so it's convenient that side margins are identified as "inside" and "outside" when the pages are facing each other.

Pasteboard   The area in InDesign beyond the pages. Many InDesign users put assets here that they *might* need, or assets that they suspect they *don't* need, but aren't sure about yet. Logos, caption text frames, photos we hope we'll have room for, etc., all find themselves "out there." More often, I use CC Libraries now. Nothing on the pasteboard prints, unless it's in the bleed or slug and we choose to print those areas.

Pages & Spreads

Color Management

Find/Change

Long Documents

Output

Bleed   When images or other graphic elements need to print to the very edge of the page (like the tabs on these pages), we actually send them a little over the edge. Since no printer can print edge-to-edge, we print on larger paper and trim to our desired size. In case the trim is off by a small amount, we give ourselves some extra room. If you send your documents to a printer, you should ask them how much bleed they require.

Slug   A slug is a label or note to yourself, colleagues, or a printer. The slug area is some space you've allotted on the Pasteboard for that note. In the Print and PDF Export dialog boxes, you can choose to include that area if you wish. Data that finds its way there includes modification dates, client names, print instructions, and reminders of where one has left off the day before.

Columns & Column Guides   Of course, if you want to have multiple columns of text, column guides show you where they should go (consistently) and help you create them. As you create text frames, they will snap to column guides in handy ways. But you may also just wish to divide your pages for the sake of consistent composition beyond your text. With the addition of horizontal ruler guides, you can create a complete grid to which you can snap frames of all sorts.

Use Layout > Create Guides… to generate rows and columns of ruler guides much faster than you can make them manually.

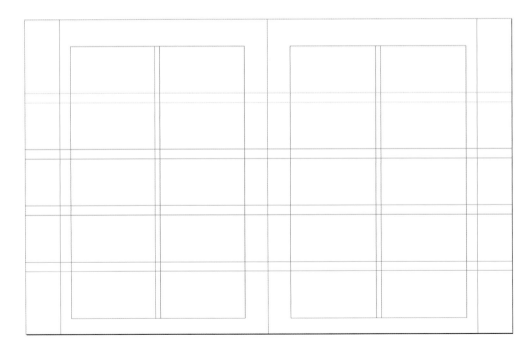

Navigating Pages

Getting from page to page is pretty important and useful. So, of course, there are lots of ways to do it.

The Pages Panel

One way to get around your document is via the Pages panel.

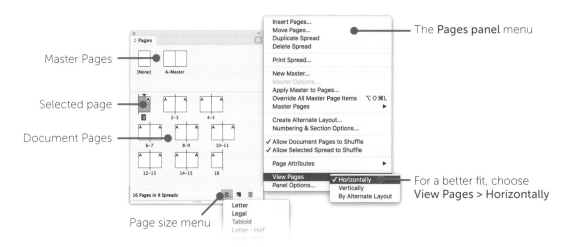

First, make the panel more useful by using the Pages panel menu to choose View Pages > Horizontally. This makes for a far more efficient use of space in this panel. If your document has facing pages (spreads), you might also want to go to View > Fit Spread in Window (⌘-option-0/Ctrl-Alt-0—that's a zero, by the way). Now, to navigate from spread to spread, double-click on page *numbers* in the Pages panel. To view a single page, double-click on a page *icon* (oddly, you may have to do that twice). What happens if you single-click? A possibly precarious situation arises!

Single-clicking a document page's number or a master page's name highlights the icons. But you are really still editing the pages whose numbers are highlighted!

In both these cases, the page 2–3 spread is being viewed in the Document Window.

If this document is new and without content, you'd be hard-pressed to know that!

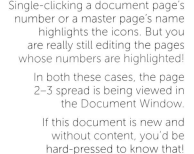

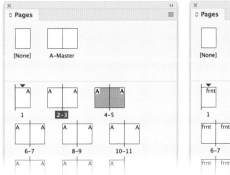

Pages & Spreads

Color Management

Find/Change

Long Documents

Output

Workspaces & Preferences

Frames & Content

Styles, Type & Fonts

Pages & Spreads

To avoid the mistake illustrated above, double-check that you've successfully double-clicked by looking at the Pages panel and noting if the page icons and corresponding numbers are both highlighted. Fortunately, there are two other methods that are worth mentioning.

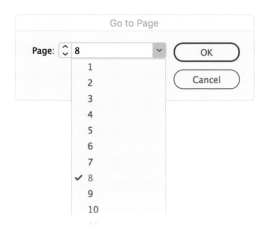

The page menu at bottom-left of the Document Window

At the bottom left of the Document Window is a small field displaying the current page number. To its right is a menu from which you can choose a page to edit (including master pages). Nearby, there are also buttons for going to the Next or Previous Page, or the Next or Previous Spread if you've chosen Fit Spread in Window from the View menu.

If I know the number (or master page prefix) of the page I want, I use the shortcut ⌘–J/Ctrl–J (or, less quick, Layout > Go To Page…). A dialog box opens with its lone field highlighted so I can type a number and hit return/Enter. That field is also a menu from which I can choose a page. Typing a letter accesses a master page if its prefix is or starts with that letter. This is my favorite method as it's very fast and reliable.

Master Pages

Even modestly sized documents may have several different kinds of pages. To serve as a form of template for those kinds of pages, InDesign offers Master Pages. Content placed on a master page will appear on all the pages that use that master. Much of my time preparing a document is spent on the master pages of that document. Among the items that are best put on master pages are running headers (see "Running Headers" (page 327)]) and Guides. When we create a system of guides on a master with the Layout > Create Guides… command, those guides will appear on every page to which the master has been applied.

Naming Masters

Some documents, like this one, have at least several kinds of pages: pages tailored for front matter, tables of contents, the beginnings of chapters or sections, etc. Creating a new master is easy: use the Pages panel menu and choose New Master…. However, the default names for master pages are simply a letter prefix plus the word "Master": *A-Master*, *B-Master*, etc. Keeping in mind that a prefix can be up to four letters, I rename my master pages for their function (or amusement). I'll use practical prefixes and names like *frnt-matter*, *TOC-pages*, and *reg-ular pages*; or the less practical *Jedi-Master* or *Kung-Fu Master*.

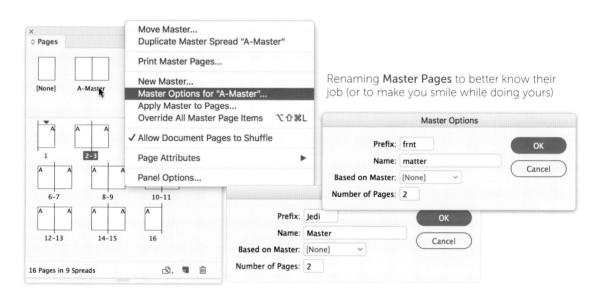

Renaming **Master Pages** to better know their job (or to make you smile while doing yours)

Right-click on a master's current name (for example, A-Master) then choose Master Options for "A-Master"…. Give it a Prefix and a Name. A master based on another has that other master applied to it. Thus, if you have a master responsible for only page numbers and another master responsible for something else *plus* page numbers, apply the page number master to the other. Then, if you need to edit the page numbers, there's only one place to go. That begs the question of how one numbers pages efficiently using master pages.

Current Page Number Marker

By far, the most common object placed on a master page is the Current Page Number Marker. As the name indicates, this very special character reveals the current page number. On a master page, it displays that master's prefix. On every page to which that master is applied, this marker shows a page number with the formatting chosen in the Numbering and Section Options dialog box, as discussed in "Sections & Numbering" (page 287). So that number may actually be a letter or a Roman numeral, perhaps.

The simplest way to place this character is to create a small text frame on a master page, then with the text insertion cursor blinking, right-click and choose Insert Special Character > Markers > Current Page Number. There's also an engaging keyboard shortcut: ⌘-option-shift-N/Ctrl-Alt-shift-N. At first glance, few think they will memorize this, but the frequency with which we add page numbers increases the likelihood that you will if you try.

Applying Master Pages

A robust way to apply a master to one or more document pages is to right-click on a master's name and choose Apply Master to Pages…. You may then specify a range of pages, or even list discontiguous ones by separating each number with a comma. If you first highlight page icons, the page range will be pre-populated with those.

You may also drag a master's name onto a page icon to apply it to that one page. To apply to a spread, drag the master's name over the first page number of the spread.

The [None] Master

Very commonly, we decorate a number of masters and apply them to a variety of document pages. But then we note a document page that needs none of those decorations (page numbers, logos, etc.). If we drag the [None] master to a page icon, the prefix of the master formerly applied vanishes, as do all the elements that master has on it.

Overrides

Most master page content is inaccessible on the pages to which the master is applied—unless it is overridden. Sometimes, overriding a master page object is easy (indeed, automatic), as is the case when placing an image then clicking on a placeholder frame. Most of the time, overriding a master object requires holding down ⌘-shift/Ctrl-shift while clicking on it. We do this so that we might change something about that object only for that page. Even once overridden, the original object on the master page may still control many attributes of the overridden one!

This was hugely confusing for me initially, so let's consider an example. Say we have a yellow circle drawn in the middle of a master page. On every page to which the master is applied, there's a yellow circle in its center. If we move that circle (on the master, of course), it moves on every page. If we change its color or geometry (size or shape), we see that on the other pages, too.

If we try to move or even select it on a document page (not on the master), we cannot. But if we use the keys ⌘-shift/Ctrl-shift while we use the Selection tool, the object can be selected! If we stop there, it's almost as if we did nothing: edits made to that circle on the master still show on the page where we overrode it! That's weird enough, but it gets stranger.

Moving that override breaks *part* of its relationship with the circle on the master—the geometry relationship—but its appearance (e.g., color) is still governed by the master circle. So changing the master circle's color to red changes all of the circles, even the one we moved. But as you do more to that override, you will break all of its ties to the master. Changing its color and geometry severs all connections, unless we reapply the master to the page where our override is. Then our override will vanish and the inaccessible master object reappears.

To keep our override even if we apply the master again, we need to select it and then go to the Pages panel menu and choose Master Pages > Detach Selection from Master. Now it's as if that object was never a master page item. Reapplying the master will reintroduce the master object and our detached object will remain, too. To delete the override, I use the Pages panel menu and choose Master Pages > Remove Selected Local Override.

This interesting and confusing relationship between master objects and their overrides exists so that we can have unique content in frames on document pages, but the frames themselves can still be controlled from a master. Read on for more!

Text and Image Frames

Consider the possibility of using a master to "template" the look and feel of the opening spreads of chapters of a book or sections of a magazine. Another master controls the appearance of the more ordinary pages that follow (until the next chapter or section).

Each master is applied to two spreads and its structure is apparent on the pages that use it.

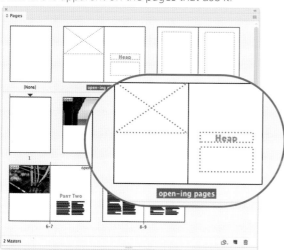

Adjusting a master's structure changes the other pages, too—even though they have content!

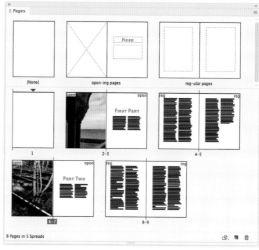

In this example, an initial design called for the left page of an opening spread to have an image covering its upper half, and the right page to have text in its lower half. So a placeholder

Pages
& Spreads

Color
Management

Find/Change

Long
Documents

Output

frame was drawn with the Rectangle Frame tool on the left, and two text frames were drawn on the right page.

On a document page that uses that master, it is not possible to select those frames (unless we override them). If we *place* an image or text, however, the loaded cursor will show that it will place the content into the awaiting master frame! In the example above, the image frame has Frame Fitting Options applied so an image will fill it.

Later, if we resize or reposition a master frame, the content on every page that uses that master also adjusts. In the example, the image frame was made to fill the entire left page, and the text frames on the right were moved upward on the page.

Primary Text Frames & Smart Text Reflow

In the chapter about frames and content, we discussed "Automatic Text Threading" (page 201). Clicking the out port of an overset text frame loads the cursor, then shift–clicking at the top-left margin of another page will create a frame, flow text into it, and if text remains unflowed, more pages will get made until all the text is visible. Although this is very cool, there's something cooler and more controllable: Smart Text Reflow. This function is especially helpful when it's limited to a special kind of master text frame called a primary text frame.

Like other powerful features, this one works best if we plan ahead. Indeed, the best way to create primary text frames is when creating a new document. The options here create a document with master spreads (Facing Pages), but only one document page to start. On each page, there will be a two-column text frame, with each of those columns corresponding to guides. The edges of the frames are set to the margins on each page. Although the text frames are on a master spread, they are automatically accessible as overrides so users like us can immediately start typing, pasting, or placing text into them. And just as in the example in the previous section, if we adjust the master text frames, the ones on the document pages change, too.

To differentiate a primary text frame from another type of text frame, it has a special icon near its upper-left corner when selected. When combined with the Type preference Smart Text Reflow (see page 167), primary text frames really begin to shine. Simply put, when you place what should be many pages of text into a document

with very few pages (or even just one), Smart Text Reflow adds more pages (using the same master as the one you placed the text on) and flows the text into the primary text frames on each page until there is no more text. This is different than Automatic Text Threading in that you can have multiple text frames on the master, but by designating one as the primary, the placed text "knows" which frame to use. Adding the additional preference to Delete Empty Pages does exactly that when those primary frames find themselves emptied, as would happen if the type in a story were made smaller or tracked more tightly.

Sections & Numbering

Very long publications are broken up into multiple InDesign documents using "The Book Feature" (page 315). But publications of a more modest size (that can remain one document) can have Sections, each of which can be numbered differently (and in different styles) and automatically trigger changes in running headers/footers.

Starting and Editing Sections

Every document's first page is also the start of a Section. The small triangle above the first page indicates that, and double-clicking it is a way to access its Numbering & Section Options dialog box. To begin a new section, highlight a page icon, then right-click it and choose Numbering & Section Options, which will open the dialog box *and* start a section on that page.

Sections begin on pages 1, 5, 8, 11, and 15. The section starting on page 11 has had a Section Prefix applied, which becomes part of the page number unless Absolute Numbering is chosen in the General Preferences.

In that dialog, you can choose the numbering Style—for example, lowercase Roman numerals for front matter. In a following section, you can restart numbering. But if two pages are given the Arabic numeral "2" or the letter "C," for example, you can imagine the confusion that can ensue when you try to print or export a range of pages. There are several ways to alleviate that confusion. Adding a unique Section Prefix can make the page "number" unique again; a prefix of "A-" would make a page number "A-3," perhaps. The prefix won't appear on the page itself unless you check the option Include Prefix when Numbering Pages. You could then print the range *iii–C-7*, for example. Another option is in the General Preferences: set Page Numbering to Absolute. Although the numbers printed on the pages won't change (they will still restart or use a prefix if you like), choosing a range of pages is easier and the Pages panel will show pages numbered 1 through the last in numerical sequence. So, if page *iii* is the third page of the document, and page *C-7* is the thirty-fifth, you'd print the range 3–35. Without either a prefix or changing the preferences you may add plus signs to what would be the absolute numbers: "+3-+35" would print the same range.

My advice is to keep it intuitive if you can. If your document requires numbering to restart when a new section begins, keep those numbers unique by changing style (e.g., Roman to Arabic) or adding a prefix.

Document Chapter Numbering is best controlled from InDesign's Book feature. We'll discuss it in the Compendium's "Long Documents" section.

Section Markers

Another option in the Numbering & Section Options dialog box is Section Marker. This is text that can automatically appear in a running header or footer you've put on a master page via the Section Marker character. If you add this character on a master page (by right-clicking then choosing Insert Special Character > Markers > Section Marker), it will look like the word "Section." But on pages that use that master, it will either be blank (if you haven't added a Section Marker to the section) or you will see the text you entered in the Section Marker field.

reg#   Section#

A **Current Page Number Marker** (left) and a **Section Marker** (right)
Above: On a master page
Below: On a document page that uses that master

4#   The Red Planet#

Shuffling

When dragging pages or spreads in the Pages panel, InDesign will "shuffle" pages in order to keep two pages in each spread and to keep a cover or title page (the first, lone page in a facing-page document). The easiest way to start a document with a spread or to build gatefold spreads with three or more pages is to disallow shuffling. From the Pages panel menu, click Allow Document Pages to Shuffle to uncheck it. Now you can drag pages more freely, attaching them to the left or right of other pages or spines.

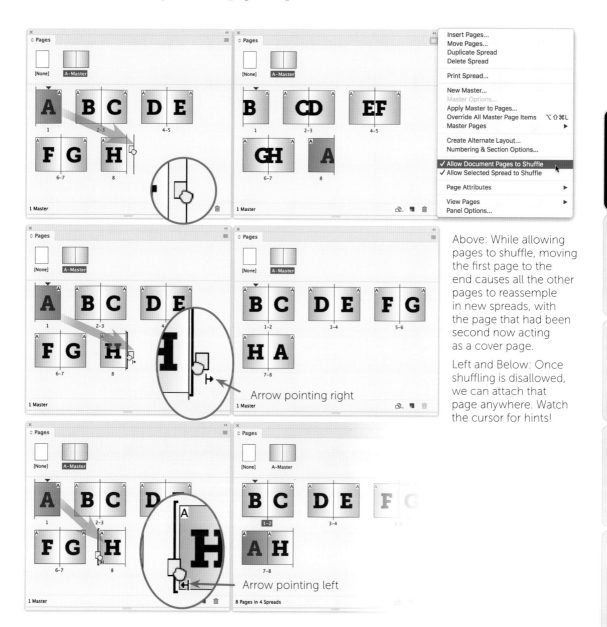

Arrow pointing right

Arrow pointing left

Above: While allowing pages to shuffle, moving the first page to the end causes all the other pages to reassemple in new spreads, with the page that had been second now acting as a cover page.

Left and Below: Once shuffling is disallowed, we can attach that page anywhere. Watch the cursor for hints!

Pages & Spreads

Color Management

Find/Change

Long Documents

Output

Building Gatefolds

By attaching a page to the outer edge of another (the side away from the spine), you can create gatefolds. In the case illustrated above, the last two pages are both to the left of the spine.

Below, by dragging the page numbers of a spread to the right side of that spine, I created a four-page spread with the expectation that the two outer pages will fold outward.

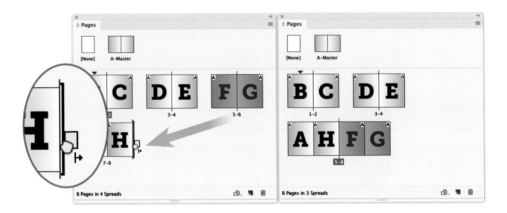

To prevent those outer pages from buckling when folded in, they should be narrower than the others. This can be set if you select each of them with the Page tool. Consult your printer, as they may have precise dimensions or may request another procedure entirely.

Inner edge of this outer page locked down with the reference point.

Outer page selected with the **Page tool**. Its width can be set in the **Control panel**.

Single-page "spreads" can occur with shuffling disallowed.

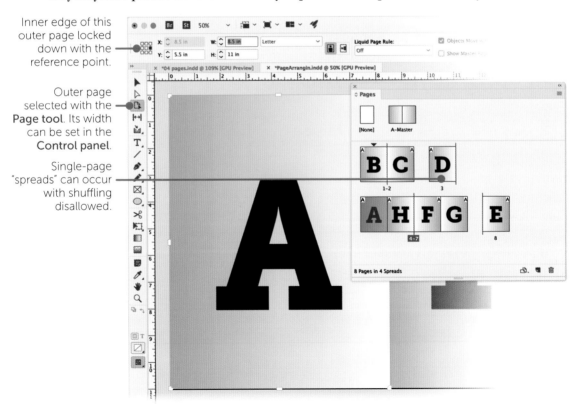

Page Size & Layout Adjustment

The last figure illustrates that pages in an InDesign document may be of different sizes. Creating gatefolds is just one excuse for doing so. Another is the Alternate Layout feature, in which two or more layouts exist in the same document for the same content—a print layout and a mobile device layout for an ebook version, for example.

Page size and accompanying margin dimensions, etc., are first set when a document is created. Subsequently, the size of selected pages can be altered with the Page tool. The page size used by an entire document can be set via File > Document Setup... or by creating an alternate layout (Layout > Create Alternate Layout...).

There have been, and remain to be, various methods for adjusting the position and size of content in documents whose page size had to change. In the Margins and Columns dialog box is the Enable Layout Adjustment checkbox. This feature uses page margins, columns, and guides to adjust the size and position of objects snapped to them (or very nearly so) when we change page size, page orientation, or margin or column dimensions. For very simple layouts, this has done marginally well (pardon the pun). This method cannot be combined with Liquid Layout. *Very* strangely, you can adjust the settings for this feature via Liquid Layout panel menu > Layout Adjustment, where you'll be reminded that these methods are mutually exclusive.

Liquid Layout has many more options—so many, in fact, that in longer or slightly complex documents, it is simply faster to manually adjust content. It does offer a guide-based system (using guides made while the Page tool is active), or you can set rules on *each* object to indicate how it should be resized or repositioned when the page is resized.

In my experience the the newest method, Adjust Layout (discussed below), offers the best results with a reasonable number of controls, whether you're adjusting just the margins of a page, an entire page's geometry, or the geometry of all the pages of a document.

Adjust Layout

InDesign CC 2019 includes a new method—File > Adjust Layout—in which you can set parameters for the automatic adjustment of existing page content to accommodate the new dimensions. You can also access this feature from the Properties panel and via Layout > Margins and Columns....

The way you access this feature, and what you choose within it, depends on your reasons for the adjustment. If it's a matter of making a small adjustment to margins at the request of your printer, you'll likely use Layout > Margins and Columns.... For a poster, postcard, or one sheet, you may need to change more. For example, if you originally designed a poster to be printed on Super B-sized paper (330 mm x 483 mm, about 13" x 19"), but find you need it on Tabloid (11" x 17"), this one dialog box can resize everything, even the type, in one go. Or a small postcard's content can be upsized to a much larger size coherently. In the example in the following figure, roughly square pages have been resized to Letter page size.

Pages & Spreads

Color Management

Find/Change

Long Documents

Output

Adjust Layout, accessed from the Properties panel with nothing selected, allows me to adjust many properties of the entire document.

Through Layout > Margins and Columns..., the choices are similar but don't include page size.

When resizing type, you can choose a minimum and maximum size. When a page is resized, items in the margin or pasteboard will remain in those areas, and graphics of various kinds will keep their proportions and their frame dimensions (crop) will be guided by content-awareness (an attempt to keep their subject in view).

5 Color Management

As you learn more and more about color, the concepts become far less black and white (yes, a very bad pun). This chapter starts with a truly essential discussion of the basic ways in which color is defined. After that, we'll get into a more detailed examination for those who wish to see more deeply under the hood.

Workspaces &
Preferences

Frames &
Content

Styles, Type
& Fonts

Pages
& Spreads

Color
Management

The Basics

RGB

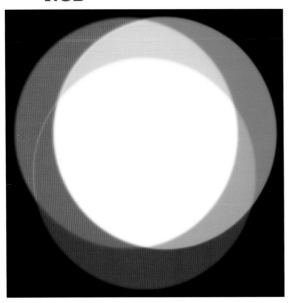

RGB is about light in the darkness. No light: no color. By controlling the ratio of **R**ed, **G**reen, and **B**lue, we can create any color we want! Where both red and green light overlap, we get yellow. Green and blue combine to make cyan. Magenta is the total of red and blue. All three make white.

It's often useful to note which color is absent or lacking. For example, cyan is the absence of red. Or if an image looks too magenta, we add a bit of green.

It gets tricky when we try to express how much of each we want. With most software, we use numbers between **0** (no light) and **255** (the maximum). The RGB value of 0 0 0 is black—all lights out. However, maximum red (255R) on one device may not be as intensely red as on another. That is, 255R will be a *different color* on different devices; maybe like Santa's suit on one and more neon on another. After all, any device can produce only so great a range of brightness or saturation. We call that range the gamut and it's described by its own **color space**.

In software, we usually choose a standard reference, an often idealized virtual device's color space. Examples of this are sRGB, Adobe RGB, and ProPhoto RGB. The sRGB color space closely approximates the colors produced by average PC displays—nothing too vibrant. Adobe RGB is a larger color space and can produce more intense colors. Thus, a way to consistently refer to the same perceived color is to give RGB numbers *with reference to their color space*. For example, 255R in sRGB and 216R in Adobe RGB refer to the same *perceived* red.

CMYK

CMYK is about dots of ink on paper. Without ink, there's only paper. By controlling the ratio of **C**yan, **M**agenta, and **Y**ellow ink, we can make many colors. We measure the amount of each from 0% (none) to 100% (the full amount). For practical reasons, we need blac**K**, too. Thus, CMYK is known as the four-color process.

Each ink absorbs a different color of light. Cyan absorbs red light, for example. All three inks *should* absorb all light, and thus appear black. However, this may be too much ink for many papers, or could appear as dark brown instead of black. This is why we need black ink.

Some printers use toner and some use ink. Each ink-maker's inks are different. Paper also affects color, of course. *Every device is different.* So, as with RGB, CMYK devices also have color spaces, or ranges of color they can produce. That means that the recipe (or **build**) for any perceived color will vary from paper to paper, and from printer to printer. *No single CMYK build looks the same on all printers.*

As with RGB devices, there are standard CMYK color spaces that approximate certain press conditions, three of which are SNAP, GRACoL, and SWOP. When we submit files for printing, we'll often be asked to submit them in a CMYK color space that conforms to one of those standards. This chapter lays out how to do that.

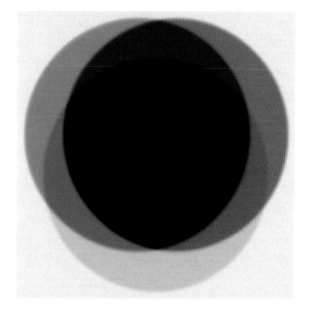

We *usually* don't need to know or care what a color's build is; we typically care only about how it looks. However, there's a notable exception. If text at small sizes or delicate line-work is printed with more than one ink, we risk misregistration (misalignment of the colors), and thus illegibility. So for maximum contrast and legibility, text is most often printed with black ink *only*: 0 0 0 100%K. It will look different on different substrates, but it will be sharp. Text color is often the only swatch for which I specify a CMYK build at all!

Process vs. Spot (Solid)

Spot Color
This is a custom color made by mixing different colors to attain the desired one, much like housepaint is made. This is used when a critical match is required and is unattainable with process color printing. It's also handy when you are printing with few inks to save money rather than with the four inks of process color.

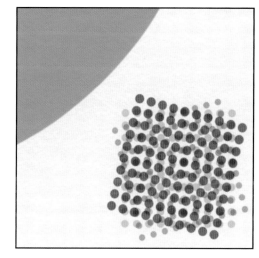

Process Color
This is when various-sized dots of Cyan, Magenta, Yellow, and blacK are set at angles to each other. When small enough, we don't see them individually, but we see an overall result. Look at an image in this book with a magnifier and you'll see its dots!

Color Management

Find/Change

Long Documents

Output

Workspaces & Preferences

Frames & Content

Styles, Type & Fonts

Pages & Spreads

Color Management

Color Myths, Theory, and Management

Best Practices

It was mid-October and trees were brilliant with color. I asked my four-year-old neighbor to identify the color of a leaf that I'd picked up. Although insulted that I would ask this of such a big boy, he answered clearly, "orange!"

I could hear "*obviously*" in his voice. Luckily, he's not a photographer or graphic designer: the kind of people who try every day, often unsuccessfully, to use *numbers* (RGB or CMYK values, for example) to specify a color. If my small neighbor had used numbers, we may have disagreed.

Grasping at Light

Of course, color isn't numbers. Color is what happens in the brain when light of various wavelengths passes through the lenses of our eyes and hits our retinas. There, cells called cones pass signals via optic nerves to our brain's imaging centers.

Despite colors being about perception, we've tried for centuries to come up with ways to precisely define color numerically. The most successful process, or model, used in today's color-savvy software is called CIELAB. Did you expect me to say RGB or CMYK? If you work in the world of desktop publishing, you may know, or think you know, something about those models. Alas, most folks in that world have been told some things about color that are simply not true. Sorry to be the one to break it to you. Simple rules may be easy to learn—drive on the right; say "please" and "thank you;" don't use the fonts Papyrus or Comic Sans; etc.— but accepted wisdom about when to use the RGB and CMYK color modes may have been oversimplifications, or just wrong. Like so much in the world of publishing, there is more to this story.

Let's start a journey of discovery close to home, with our eyes. Those cone cells in your retina come in three varieties: sensitive to red, green, or blue (RGB). We are essentially RGB devices. But, as stated previously, the color model at work in our best software is the geeky CIELAB (or just "Lab") color space. Although built from studies of real humans, most humans don't find Lab intuitive to work with—it is, after all, a *mathematical* model. But I think many of us can overlook that unintuitiveness in light of the most useful aspect of Lab: it is device independent, meaning it doesn't refer to a specific computer monitor, printer, or any other device. Its numbers refer to real, perceived color. In a very real way, since it represents *our* perception, its numbers really mean something. Since computers are good at crunching numbers and wielding mathematical models, Lab space is a way for our software to refer to a specific real color. It also makes it possible to translate colors between the other models we use to describe color.

But what is meant by the word "space" in the phrase "color space"? There's an easy way to visualize the idea of a color space. You're probably in a "space" right now—a room, a train car, a bus. Pick a spot on the floor. If you're seated, your head is bobbing maybe a meter and a half above that floor. Let's call that height **z**. Your head is also some meters (or inches if you like) left or right of the spot you chose (**x**), and yet another distance forward or back from that spot (**y**). You can locate any point in your space with those three coordinates, the distances from your starting point.

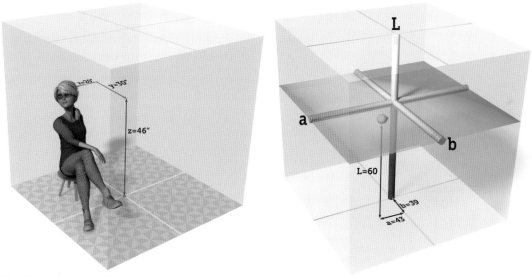

What's a color space?

We usually specify a location in any space by using three numbers. In a room, that could be the distance to the left or right of a spot on the floor (x), the distance forward or back from that spot (y), and the height above the floor (z).

Lab color space represents the range of human vision. Any point in that space is a color we see.

Instead of x, y, and z coordinates, we use **L** for luminance, while the **a** and **b** coordinates together determine hue and saturation.

Coordinates in color spaces are measured from a point in the middle of the floor: the blackest black we can see. We measure Luminance (**L**) straight up from there, up to a value of 100 for the whitest white we can see. That axis is easy; it's just light and dark. One of the other two directions runs from reddish to green (the **a** axis), and the other from yellow to blue (the **b** axis). The a and b axes are divided into 256 increments. To find the orange color of that leaf, we start in the center of the floor and move along the b axis for 39 units. We then turn right (in the a direction) for 43 units. Finally, we go up to a Luminance of 60. Just going up and down the L axis, we'd see only grayscale. If we went further out along the a or b axes, we'd find increasingly intense, saturated colors. By specifying a point in this space, we can refer to any perceived color.

Most of us don't have to deal directly with Lab space often, but we should know that our

Workspaces &
Preferences

Frames &
Content

Styles, Type
& Fonts

Pages
& Spreads

Color
Management

best software partners, like Photoshop and InDesign, use it to get us what we want. To help them help us, we need to know the challenges in using those supposedly user-friendlier but often misunderstood color models: RGB and CMYK.

Devices and Their Limitations

When we view an image on our monitor, it looks different than the reality that was photographed. The sky is never quite as blue and, luckily, the sun in a photo doesn't blind us. When we print that photo, we face more disappointments; blues may get even more muted and the whitest white is the color of the paper. The colors in nature are often beyond the *gamut* of a printer. It's often thought that RGB devices (like monitors) always show more colors than prints, but that's not necessarily true. A good printer can produce some colors (perhaps yellows and teals) that an average monitor cannot. We say those colors are outside of the monitor's gamut.

Color geeks often use special software to compare devices by the size (and shape) of the devices' color spaces. So when we say that the Epson 4900 printer has a larger gamut or color space than, say, its cousin the 3880, we mean that it can produce more vibrant colors. That is, it produces colors farther out along the a and b axes in Lab space. Two monitors may both be using 255R 255G 255B to represent white, but one will be brighter than another. This is just like when I turn up the volume of my stereo to 11 and two different loudspeakers produce different volumes of sound from that same signal.

To get identical results, I'd have to use a different signal for each of those different devices. That is, I may have to lower the volume to 9 for the louder speakers, dim my brighter monitor, or send different color numbers to the more vibrant printer to match a less vibrant one. As you can imagine, this could make it difficult to produce images or documents for different media.

So What Should I Do?

The old advice when preparing documents was to always and only use RGB for onscreen viewing (for websites, presentations, etc.), and to always and only use CMYK for print. But the puzzle has been deciding which numbers to use to achieve a specific color. We crossed our fingers or hoped that someone else would make it work.

Consider the case of making a swatch in Adobe InDesign for the orange of that leaf. To accurately see that color on a computer's display, the numbers *might* be 223R 110G 78B. In fact, that would get me pretty close on most average displays. But on a high-end display with a larger color space (one that produces a wider range of colors), the numbers might be 209R 87G 60B. Since each device requires its own values, there's never one, perfect answer.

The print case is worse. For a press job on good paper, the numbers for that orange could be 9C 67M 70Y 0K. On newsprint (typically a cool-gray paper), we might need 8C 61M 77Y 0K. A different manufacturer's inks may require both of those to change. Different paper stock? Start again. And what happens to the "use CMYK for print" rule if I use a modern inkjet printer with perhaps 10 or more different inks that could include red, green, blue, violet, or even orange itself? Can you even imagine the dialog box you'd have to navigate for this situation?

Fortunately, you'll never see a fictitious dialog box like that. But honestly, for a color like this, do you really *care* what the numbers need to be? My young (but wise) neighbor doesn't. You and I should care only that the output looks right—that is, it maps to the right point in the Lab color space. We don't have to worry about colors' numbers at final output because Adobe software uses a cool technology to make sure they're the right numbers: color profiles.

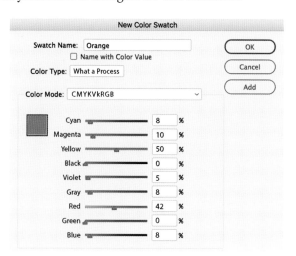

Profiles

Long ago, in the dark years of the 1980s and '90s, we had to manually tune the numbers for each output device, or we paid someone to do it for us. But now, our software uses data files called *color profiles* to help compensate for the quirks of our monitors and output devices.

This is not a real InDesign dialog box!

It's a good thing, too. If we had to build swatches for every output device, we'd never have time to actually design anything.

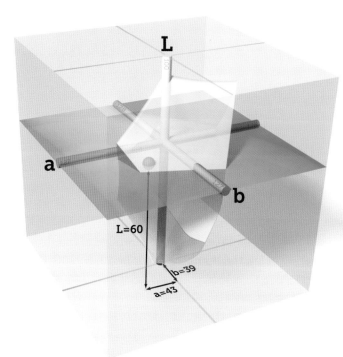

Device Color Space

That chunk that looks like an iceberg represents the range of color that some output device (like a printer) can produce. Although this one is limited on the blues and greens, our orange is safely "within **gamut**." That is, we should expect it to output accurately.

All color spaces, and therefore all devices, are compared to Lab, the colors we can see. Some produce a greater range of color than others. A **profile** describes a device's color space and lets us compare it to others and convert from its color gamut to another's. That is, it helps us move from an input device, like a scanner or camera, through software like InDesign, to an output device while keeping "in-gamut" colors accurate throughout.

Color Management

Find/Change

Long Documents

Output

A profile acts as a description of a device's color space. In fact, some people use the phrases "color profile" and "color space" interchangeably. The profile captures information about the

Workspaces &
Preferences

Frames &
Content

Styles, Type
& Fonts

Pages
& Spreads

**Color
Management**

darkest black, the whitest white, the most saturated versions of each hue, and more. Most importantly, a profile lets us "map" a perceived color to the RGB or CMYK numbers needed for that specific device. While we work in our documents, the software itself uses a profile for its "working color space." That is, our software is treated as yet another device in our workflow. Since it's software, therefore a virtual device, we can actually choose the color space it uses. And that color space has a profile to describe it. Photo-editing programs like Photoshop take note of a camera's profile and convert that to Photoshop's working space, and then when we print, the numbers get converted to the printer's profile. The colors always get represented by numbers that best represent them at each stage of the process, for each device that can produce those colors. Software does the math with the numbers provided by profiles.

The Flexibility of RGB

As always, my main concern is that all colors' appearances are maintained right through output (if physics allows it). I may want to borrow a color from an image for other graphic elements and have them all match each other. Since all my Adobe software typically uses the same working space, that leaf-orange can be represented by 223R 110G 78B in Photoshop, InDesign, and Illustrator. Those are the numbers that they use to attain that perceived orange color.

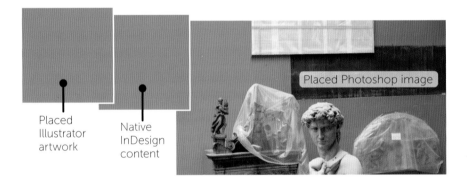

Placed
Illustrator
artwork

Native
InDesign
content

Placed Photoshop image

So imagine we've created an InDesign document with an RGB color swatch with those values. In that publication, we've placed photos from Photoshop and graphics from Illustrator, which also use the same values. Now stop imagining; just look at the samples above!

When the job is done and we make a PDF for the public, what form will it take? If it's to be consumed onscreen only, then I'd choose a specific RGB for the PDF's Destination (details to follow). If I'm sending the PDF to a print shop, I'd ask them what they'd like. If they request CMYK, I'd then ask them which press profile they prefer, and I'll use that as the PDF's destination. In either case, the color numbers used by the photo and graphic elements in my layout will change, but they will continue to *match each other*. For a press PDF (using GRACoL, for example), that orange would become 9C 67M 70Y 0K. Since the orange we started with is within the gamut of the destination color space, it will be maintained with high fidelity.

But what exactly do I mean by destination, and where do we specify it?

When exporting a document as a PDF from InDesign, we are given many options (see the

"Output" chapter of this Compendium for more). In the Output options, we choose whether and how colors are converted from their current color space, to which destination profile, and whether that profile is included in the PDF. The destination will usually be sRGB for those PDFs viewed onscreen, or the CMYK profile that your print vendor desires.

Convert RGB, but preserve CMYK builds

That's what this option does. As we take our flexible RGB content and prepare a PDF for whichever output medium it's intended, this will ensure things that match each other continue to do so.

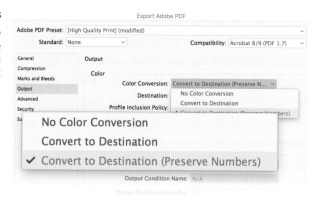

Why preserve some CMYK builds?

We need numbers (builds) to change as we go from one device to another *if we want the colors to remain the same visually,* especially with images. But when something else is more important than color accuracy— like text legibility—we want the build maintained.

Convert to Destination (Preserve Numbers) is made for just that. If we have fine line work or light-weight text, we try hard to keep it made from one ink, usually blac**K** because misregistration makes it hard to read. Heavier or larger text *may* withstand the misregistration of two or maybe three inks.

I use RGB for everything whose color I care about, and CMYK on pure black and sometimes a few specific ink builds.

Notice that for Color Conversion, I chose Convert to Destination (Preserve Numbers). There's a lot implied by that short phrase. It means that if I choose an RGB profile for my destination, all my RGB numbers and any CMYK numbers will change to yield the correct perceived colors for the new RGB profile. If I choose a CMYK destination, all my RGB numbers will be converted to that destination, but any native InDesign content that uses CMYK builds will keep those numbers, even though they'll look different on the destination device. That's helpful for those few CMYK builds that must not change (like pure black for text).

The Useful Rigidity of CMYK

A clear example of where the CMYK build matters more than the visual appearance is the text you're reading right now. I want it to print as pure black and nothing but black, no matter which press or paper I use. On newsprint, it'll look more gray than black. On a good paper, it'll look darker. On either, it'll be sharp, because with just one ink there's no chance of misalignment. InDesign's default [Black] swatch is perfect for this: a CMYK build of 0 0 0 100K. With the Preserve Numbers option, it'll always be black ink only.

That very special build is more important to me than its final visual appearance. I know that if pure black got converted from one CMYK color space to another, it might become 74C 70M 64Y 77K—a four-color black! If there's any misregistration in printing (misalignment of the inks), delicate text could become fringed with color, making this conversion a disaster for legibility.

Our somewhat randomly chosen orange is different. As long as I don't apply it to small, delicate text, I don't care what numbers are used to render it. So that's why, for this color and most all others, I define InDesign color swatches as RGB. If it's a color I sampled from an RGB photo, using an RGB swatch is easier, too.

If you find that you harbor an inner color geek, you can even use a Lab swatch in InDesign! If you use Pantone spot colors, you'll notice they're defined with Lab as well, since they're aspiring to a specific perceived color.

InDesign is fabulously color-mulitlingual: it speaks RGB, CMYK, and Lab, and converts between and amongst them. It can use elements in any of those modes at the same time and output to the one you choose. Since elements of any color mode may end up in an InDesign file, this is a necessary decadence.

Final Advice

So, in a nutshell, what should we be doing? We should use RGB for onscreen *and* print documents, and use CMYK swatches for those few kinds of things whose ink-use is more important than color appearance.

6 Find/Change

InDesign's Find/Change feature is about significantly more than replacing one word with another. In many documents, it's the primary way I apply formatting! The more you learn about what can be found and how it can be changed, the more likely it is that you'll love this feature as much as I do.

The Basics

Before getting to the fancy bits, let's be sure we know what options we have for straightforward searches. Many of the buttons in Find/Change are small and cryptic, but useful. There are also well-intentioned but risky features, too.

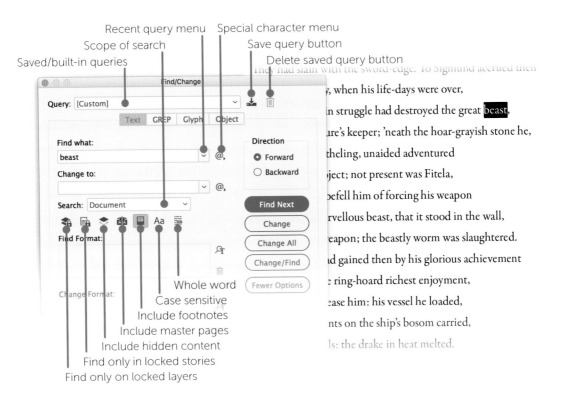

To start, let's find a word everywhere it occurs in a document and not change it all. In the image above, only the Find what field is populated. When I clicked Find Next, InDesign found the first instance of the word "beast." Since the search wasn't case sensitive, it would also have found "Beast."

Adding "dragon" to the Change to field, I clicked Change All. I hadn't specified that "beast" should be sought only if it is a whole word, so "beastly" became "dragonly." A quick ⌘–Z/Ctrl–Z fixes that. Using the

Whole Word button ensures a less silly result.

As you can see, that small, easily missed button is pretty useful when you need it. Since Find/Change retains settings somewhat tenaciously, I sometimes fail to notice that I've left this function (or others) active when I search for something hours later.

Setting Scope

Similarly useful, and treacherous, is the Search menu, where we specify how broadly Find/Change should search. It defaults to Document if nothing is selected, Story if a text frame is selected or your text cursor is blinking within one, and Selection if text is highlighted. Think about that: just by changing what's selected, you automatically change the scope of a search. I sometimes highlight a word, copy it, then paste it into the Find what field to be sure I haven't misspelled it. I hit Change All and InDesign reports that one change was made, which is puzzling when I know that word is used many times throughout a document. But when I highlighted the word, it became the only part of the document InDesign was searching!

Tip: Before clicking Change All, cut your eyes over to the Search menu and buttons.

Find/Change Formatting

A quick way to remove content is to enter it in Find what, and leave both Change to and Change Format blank when clicking Change All. If you wish to find and format some content, leave Change to blank, but click on the Change Format box to configure its numerous settings. In the example below, I set Find what to "dragon," and when I clicked on the Change Format box, I chose a Character Color of red and, in Basic Character Formats, a Font Style of Bold.

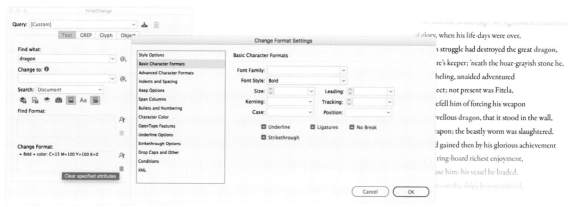

Once those settings are specified, click OK in that dialog and then click Change All. Because settings tend to be sticky here, it's important to clear them when you're done. Those icons that look like cupcakes are actually trash cans that clear settings. Using them prevents later searches from changing more than words.

Clear specified attributes

Despite a student's endearing question ("what's the cupcake for?"), that trash can clears find or change format settings.

I often leave both Find what *and* Change to blank, and use only the formatting boxes. In a recent document, I used a format-only find/change to replace all text that was manually formatted as bold with a character style that made the text red but kept it in a normal weight. Specifically, I clicked in the Find Format box, went to Basic Character Formats in the resulting Find Format Settings dialog, and chose Bold in the Font Style menu. When I clicked the Change Format box, I remained in the Style Options section of the Change Format Settings dialog so I could choose a Character Style I made previously called "just red." I was fortunate that nothing else was bold except what I wanted to change, so I clicked Change All and it was done!

If I had to be more careful about where the search was done, I could have highlighted the text to search and set the scope of the search to Selection, or specified that only a certain paragraph style be searched when I configured Find Format Settings.

There is a somewhat common practice for workflows in which writers just write, and the styling and layout is in other hands. The writer will add a unique code or symbol at the beginning of paragraphs that are different than standard body copy. This keeps their fingers on the keyboard and minds on the words. For example, in front of a chapter header, a writer may add "<h1>" (a common way to mark up a top-level header, as in HTML). That would be a fine thing to put into the Find what field, and then you can click on Change Format and select a paragraph style that decorates chapter headers.

This would have to be followed up with a second find/change with the formatting cleared so that each use of "<h1>" is removed (replaced with nothing).

Special Characters and Metacharacters

Sometimes we need to search for or change to a character we don't know how to type (something like a trademark symbol, for example), or a character that literally cannot be typed in the Find what or Change to fields (like a tab character). To the right of those fields is a menu

Workspaces & Preferences

Frames & Content

Styles, Type & Fonts

Pages & Spreads

Color Management

Find/Change

that looks like an @. In it is a list of many symbols, typographic spaces and characters, InDesign markers, and more. With this, you can replace tabs with em spaces, for example. However, what appears in the Find what or Change to fields won't look like the thing you're looking for; instead, InDesign uses *metacharacters*. So a tab is rendered as "^t" (without the quotes, of course), and a copyright symbol as "^2." The caret character itself is rendered as "^^." Once you know the metacharacter for a symbol, you may type it in those fields yourself, too.

Wildcards are also useful. For example, the wildcard for *any letter* (^$) followed by "hat" would find "chat," "phat," "that," and "what," (and maybe something else), but not "+hat," since "+" isn't a letter. But using the wildcard for *any character* (^?) would find "+hat." When it comes to more abstract searches that involve things like wildcards, there's an entire section of Find/Change that is awesomely powerful, if a little geeky: GREP (coming up shortly).

Another clever feature is the ability to use the contents of the clipboard for Change to. So anything in a flow of text that you can copy or cut, including inline graphics, can be used. In the example below, I copied an inline (anchored) graphic of a hat and an em space from one text frame to my clipboard. In Find what, I entered a bullet and space, and in Change to I chose (from the special character menu) Other > Clipboard Contents, Formatted.

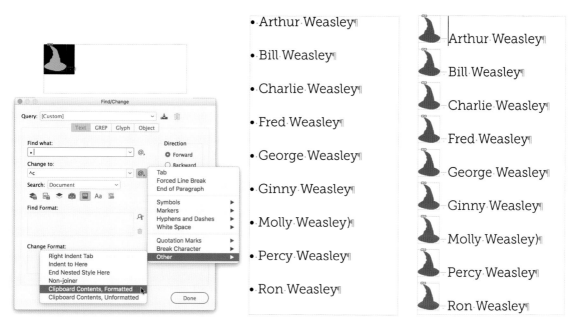

Tip: Save queries that you may need again. To do so, click the Save Query button at the top-right of the Find/Change dialog.

GREP

Grep is perhaps the most powerful tool for searching text. Since everyone asks, g/re/p ("**g**lobally find **r**egular **e**xpression and **p**rint") was an early Unix command that found a text pattern (*regular expression*) and printed its occurrences. It has a long and colorful history.

Literal strings are easy to look for, but more abstract patterns require some thought and some code. InDesign comes with much of that code built into the special character menu in the GREP section of Find/Change, and there are many online resources to help us build useful queries. There are wildcards that represent letters, digits, upper- and lowercase characters, and even locations in text (the end or beginning of paragraphs, for example).

Code for Good

Let's revisit an example from earlier. We need to find every paragraph that opens a chapter and apply a chapter header paragraph style to them. Earlier, we benefited from a writer who put something unique at the beginning of every such paragraph. But what if they didn't?

How would such a paragraph be structured? It would start with the word "Chapter" (capitalized), followed by a space, then either a number or a word. Odds are slim that any other paragraph opens with that word, so we can leverage that position to find those header paragraphs and apply the correct style.

So in the GREP section of Find/Change, we type "Chapter" in the Find what field. Case is important in grep, so we're careful to capitalize it. In front of that word, we need to insert a special character. From the Special characters menu, we choose Locations > Beginning of Paragraph. This inserts a caret (^), which in grep represents the start of a paragraph. A dollar sign ($) means "end of paragraph," if you're curious. In Change Format, we choose our

Chapter Head paragraph style. When we click Change All, every paragraph that contains our pattern is formatted. The text in the example above even contains an occurrence of the word "Chapter," which is capitalized, but it isn't affected because it's not the opening word of that paragraph.

Building a Query

My first experience with grep was with a list of 800 names, the members of the Seattle InDesign User Group that I ran at the time. Unfortunately, the list was not made surname first. It was more like the list shown here, though I think none of the folks in this list were members.

Ragmar Dorkins
J. Dorny
Vlad Drakul
Kirley Duke
Matilda Dukelow
Aberforth Dumbledore
Albus Percival Wulfric Brian Dumbledore
Ariana Dumbledore
Honoria Dumbledore
Kendra Dumbledore
Percival Dumbledore
B. Dunstan
Dudley Dursley
Marjorie Dursley

Let's consider a simple case of the data that confronted me: *Givenname Surname*. Almost all were like that. What I needed was *Surname, Givenname*. That is, I had a chunk of characters, a space, then another chunk of characters; but I needed the second chunk of characters to come first, followed by a comma and a space, then the first chunk of characters.

The Find what query could be built like this: choosing the GREP Special characters menu > Wildcards > Any Character enters a period (.). That's right, a simple dot in grep means "any character." (I suggest *acceptance* is the right attitude here, rather than *comprehension*.) But I wanted a chunk of characters, so I chose Special characters menu > Repeat > One or More Times, which inserted a plus sign. Thus, ". +" means "one or more characters." That could be the given name, but since "any character" can include spaces and much else, it could also be the entire name! So I needed to be more specific.

So I added a space and another ". +" to mean two chunks of characters separated by a space. My Find what now read like this: .+ .+

Now, I often use code even for spaces since they're hard to see in that small field. The code for "horizontal space" (which includes various size spaces and tabs) is \h. So my query could have been .+\h.+ but I didn't know that back then.

In the Change to field, I needed a way to refer to the chunks on either side of that space so I could transpose them. It took some time to figure out that meant I needed a "Marking Subexpression," which in practical terms means surrounding each chunk with parentheses. This "marks" them so they can be referenced in the Change to field. So my final Find what read (.+) (.+).

To refer to the second chunk (the surname) we use $2, and the first is $1. Since we want a comma and space between them, that made my Change to $2, $1. How did I get lucky with the middle names? Grep used the *longest* match for the first chunk, then a space, then the surname.

Workspaces &
Preferences

Frames &
Content

Styles, Type
& Fonts

Pages
& Spreads

Color
Management

Find/Change

More Grep Queries

If you look at the list in the Query menu at the top of Find/Change, many of the options use grep. Consider the one for Phone Number Conversion (dot format).

Find what: `\(?(\d\d\d)\)?[-. ]?(\d\d\d)[-. ]?(\d\d\d\d)`

Change to: `$1.$2.$3`

This converts any configuration of North American phone number and returns one like this: 206.555.5555. In the Change to field, the only special characters (beyond the metacharacters of a plain Text search) are the Founds ($1 = Found 1, etc.). So the periods there do not mean "any character," as they do in the field above.

When configuring a query in grep, sometimes we need to specify a literal character that's used for a special grep purpose, like a period or parenthesis. To search for a literal period, we use \.. It's said that the backslash "escapes" the period, freeing it, I suppose, to be a simple period again. So in the phone number search above, we are looking for the *possible* use of literal parentheses with \(?, where the question mark means zero or one of them (or as I prefer to phrase it, "maybe it's there, maybe it ain't"). We're also using them to group the digits into groups we can refer to in the Change to field. Each \d means "any digit," and we can scan across that query and pick out three, then three, then four of them, as in a phone number. Another way to look for exactly three digits is \d{3}, which could make that whole query a little shorter.

The square brackets contain literal characters between which we're to read "or." So between each chunk of digits, there could be a hyphen, a dot, or a space. Or there could be none of those things, so the question mark is added after the bracket to mean zero or one of those.

It's a wonderfully thought-out query that we didn't have to come up with! If you don't like the dot format, just change the Change to. Want it more old school? ($1) $2-$3 would give (206) 555-5555.

Another approach to searching for a choice of characters if there are multiple options is to use the pipe character (|). Since I live fairly close to Canada, I see the two spellings for center: center or centre. To search for both, I can use cent(er|re). In a case where a letter may or may not be in a word, the ? comes in handy: harbou?r finds "harbor" and "harbour." I can replace either with my preferred version. Might it be capitalized? Then look for [Hh]arbou?r. If we're looking for a capitalized word, we can specify an uppercase letter (\u) that's followed by one or more lowercase letters (\l+): \u\l+ will match "Photoshop" but not "InDesign."

We often like to find characters before or after others, but don't wish to include those others when we use Change to—perhaps the ordinal after a number ("st," "nd," "rd," or "th"), but not the number itself. To indicate the entity behind (before) the text we're interested in changing, we use a positive lookbehind. It looks like this: (?<=), with the character that's just before the text we want to match inserted after the equal sign. For a digit ("\d"), it would be (?<=\d). The whole query (the lookbehind and the text we want to matching) looks like this:

(?<=\d)(st|nd|rd|th)

There's also a positive lookahead for something that comes after the text we're matching. The Negative versions means the entity does not precede or follow the text we're seeking.

I sometimes wish to find any paragraphs that begin with a lowercase letter. We know now that the caret (^) means beginning of paragraph, and \l is a lowercase character, thus we'd use: `^\l`. Unfortunately, this also finds lowercase letters after a forced line break. To exclude lowercase letters that follow those, we use a negative lookbehind: (`?<!`), putting the code for a forced line break (`\n`) after the exclamation mark.

So, to find a lowercase letter that starts a paragraph but *doesn't* follow a forced line break, the query is:

$$(?<!\n)^\l$$

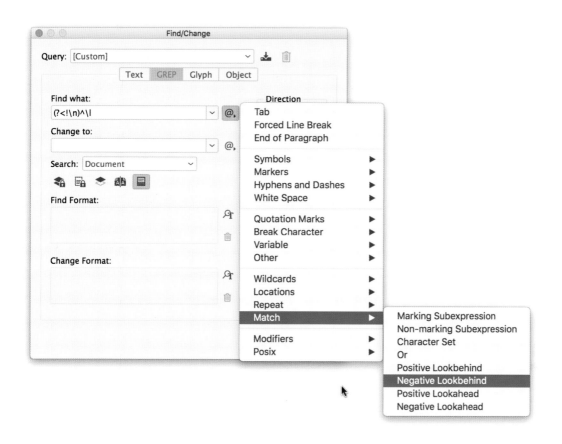

Grep Resources

There are many sources of wisdom on this topic from generous and knowledgeable folks. A favorite is the site <u>indesignsecrets.com/resources/grep</u>. And if you type "grep Erica Gamet" into your favorite internet search engine, you'll be richly rewarded. The InDesign user community really is a community, and this topic seems to show that. The folks above and many more have likely made some footprints in this neck of the InDesign woods, and we'd do well to follow them.

Find/Change

Long Documents

Output

Workspaces &
Preferences

Frames &
Content

Styles, Type
& Fonts

Pages
& Spreads

Color
Management

Find/Change

Finding Glyphs

Sometimes you just need the right character. In the most recent versions of InDesign, we can highlight a single glyph, and we'll be shown alternates underneath it (if any exist). Of course, we may wish to substitute one with another that is completely different.

What's a Glyph?

A glyph a visual way to represent a character. There may be several (or many!) glyphs for a single character (sometimes the other way around, too). In InDesign, go to Type > Glyphs. Each little box holds a glyph in the font chosen at the bottom. Some fonts have *thousands* of glyphs, and some not so many.

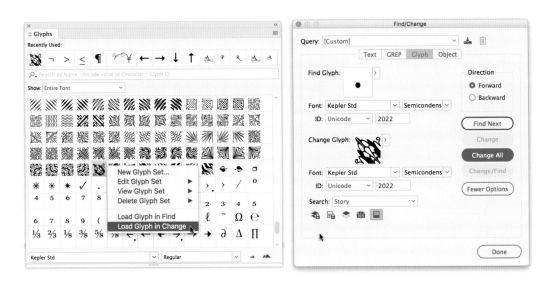

Let's say there's one that catches your eye, and you'd like to use it instead of the boring bullets already in use. Highlight one of the boring bullets, then right-click and choose Load Selected Glyph in Find. If you look in the Glyph section of Find/Change, you'll see the bullet in the Find Glyph field. Now, in the Glyphs panel, right-click on the pretty glyph you'd prefer to use and choose Load Glyph in Change. In principle, you can use a standard Text Find/Change by putting the glyph's Unicode ID number (if you know it) between a less than and greater than sign: <2022> for that bullet. Interestingly, the glyph I chose also has the same Unicode ID. There are different IDs that are used, but in Find/Change we don't have to worry. Each glyph shows up in the right field, we click Change All, and each bullet is now...whatever that is.

• Drakul, Vlad	⚜ Drakul, Vlad
• Dumbledore, Aberforth	⚜ Dumbledore, Aberforth
• Dumbledore, Albus Percival Wulfric Brian	⚜ Dumbledore, Albus Percival Wulfric Brian

Finding Objects

The last section of Find/Change is Object. When you click on either Find Object Format or Change Object Format, you are shown a dialog box with all the descriptive power of the Object Style Options dialog. Any attribute that any object can possess (including an object style!) can be chosen here.

The Powers of Description

You can "describe" an object by as few or as many attributes as you like. Of course, as you set more attributes, your search becomes more restrictive and specific. Below, I set Find Object Format by clicking its box, choosing Stroke, and setting the weight to 5 pt. Thus, when I hit Find Next, an object with a 5 pt stroke was selected. I set Change Object Format to both a new stroke weight and a specific fill color. When I clicked Change All, anything with a 5 pt stroke now had a 10pt stroke and a purple fill. Just as with the other types of searches, watch out for the scope (the Search menu) to be sure it's set broadly or specifically enough.

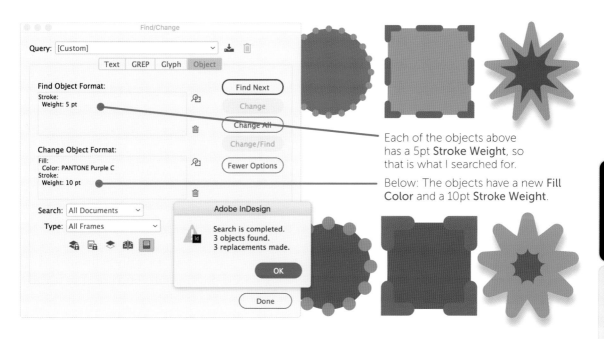

Each of the objects above has a 5pt **Stroke Weight**, so that is what I searched for.

Below: The objects have a new **Fill Color** and a 10pt **Stroke Weight**.

Tip: Setting both Find Format and Change Format to the same style (e.g., a paragraph style for a text search, or an object style for an object search) is a fast way to clear overrides to those styles.

7 Long Documents

Whether we're concerned about a reader finding her way through a great deal of content, or about ourselves as we assemble a large publication, there are features to deal with those concerns.

The Book Feature

First, let's throw a pair of giant quotes around the word "book." In InDesign, a Book is a database document that we use to assemble multiple documents into a single publication. So whether you're making a magazine, an annual report, a proposal for an engineering project, or a book, you may wish or need to break down the project into discrete pieces. Sometimes each member of a team works on an individual document. Later, someone, maybe you, gets to collect those into one big one.

Some aspects of making a Book document are easy, especially if you know at the outset that this is how it's going to be done. It can be more difficult to break up a single document into many, depending on how it's built. A novel with few or no illustrations can easily be done in a single document of several hundred pages. But if you suspect that the publication is going to have many graphics populating a hundred pages or more, you can be sure InDesign will start to bog down unless you break it up into logical units like chapters.

To ensure consistency between documents in a Book, we can sync many settings across them: styles, swatches, numbered lists, and even master pages. Page numbering can continue smoothly from one document to the next, if we choose. And if we arrange to have one document per chapter, the chapter numbering can be somewhat automated as well.

When saving documents, a certain order of operations needs to be followed. But let's discuss the making of Books before we discuss their quirks and bugs.

Creating and Populating a Book

Since a Book is a kind of document, we simply use InDesign's File > New > Book… command. We'll be prompted for a name and location to save it. The most disconcerting thing is what a Book document looks like; it's yet another panel! But it's much more. It's a database that manages the documents we add to it. Once added, those documents should be opened strictly via the Book's panel.

To add one or more documents to this little database, we can click the plus sign (+) at the bottom of the panel. We can then choose as many documents as we wish (which is easier if they're already in the same folder).

Warning: By default, each document's page numbers will change to go in sequence from the first document to the last when added to a Book file. To prevent this, first go to the Book panel menu and select Book Page Numbering Options…. There, you can temporarily disable Automatically Update Page & Section Numbers. I will do this until I have all the documents added and in the right order. I may also wish to look over the documents to see if, when pages are numbered, pages should be added to keep opening pages as odd numbered, for example, or if I'm willing to let some start on the left and some on the right. Some publishers insist that a chapter start on a right (odd-numbered) page. If you need to do this, check Continue on Next Odd Page and Insert Blank Page to bridge any gaps.

Long Documents

Output

Workspaces & Preferences

Frames & Content

Styles, Type & Fonts

Pages & Spreads

Color Management

Find/Change

Long Documents

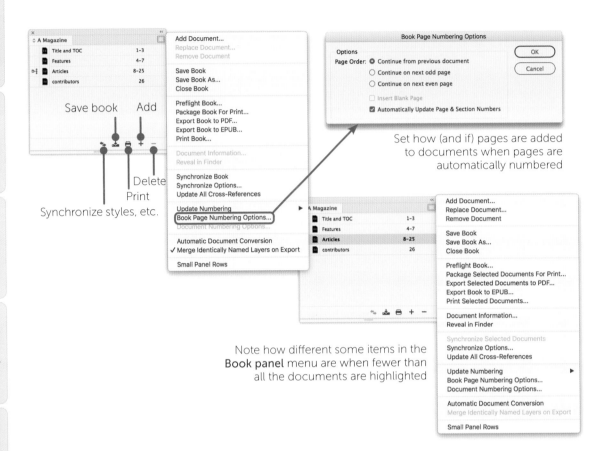

Save book Add

Delete

Print

Synchronize styles, etc.

Set how (and if) pages are added to documents when pages are automatically numbered

Note how different some items in the **Book panel** menu are when fewer than all the documents are highlighted

The Book panel menu has many important options, but please note that some change depending on whether documents are highlighted in the panel or not. If so, then many options are specific to the highlighted document(s). If all the documents (or none of them!) are highlighted, we see those items that pertain to the book as a whole. Also note the Save Book option in the panel menu. When you make changes in this panel, be sure to choose that option or use the Save button. Remember, a Book is a file! So when you're done working on it, save it and then choose Close Book to reliably close it before quitting InDesign.

Remember "Sections & Numbering" (page 287)? If you want a specific document to begin a new section with a restart of numbering, you can access its Numbering and Section Options (and open the document) by double-clicking that document's *page numbers* in the Book panel. In the same dialog, you can also specify which chapter that document should be. Displaying that chapter number requires a Text Variable that shows "Chapter Numbers" (page 325). Double-clicking the *name* of a document simply opens the document.

Document Syncing and Status

If the documents that compose the Book have been in the hands of other users, those users may have made changes to style or swatch definitions. But you can thwart that!

Sync source document

If you ensure that one document has the definitive styles and/or swatches (and other features), you may choose it as the source when synchronizing. Click to the left of the source document in the Book panel, make sure no documents are highlighted, and then click the sync button. Each document is opened invisibly and its styles are set to match your source document's. You can control just what is synced by using the Book panel menu and choosing Synchronize Options…. Perhaps one doc has the right swatches and another has the right styles. Each can serve as the source for a round of syncing, with all the options unchecked except for the feature(s) you want synced. When the process completes, a message notifies you that documents "may have changed." Well, I sure hope so.

When you open a document in a Book, a circle appears to its right in the Book panel. The circle disappears once you successfully save and close the document. When there is no icon it means all is OK. A warning that the file was modified outside the Book's purview (yellow warning triangle) appears if you had edited the document when the Book file wasn't open, or even if the panel was collapsed to an icon! I approach it like this: if I can't see the file listed in the Book panel, the panel can't see me edit the file. I know, weird. But it's a way to deal with a bug that we've had for a long time.

If a file is moved, deleted, or renamed, it might have a "missing document" icon next to it. Finally, if the Book file is on a server where multiple people have access to both it and the files it manages, anyone can open the Book. However, if one user opens a document, it shows as locked and "in use" to the other users in their Book panel.

Long Documents

Output

Workspaces &
Preferences

Frames &
Content

Styles, Type
& Fonts

Pages
& Spreads

Color
Management

Find/Change

Long
Documents

Layers

Unlike in Photoshop, where it is common to have dozens of layers, InDesign documents typically have few layers. Some users even get by with the one default layer with the inspired name "Layer 1." They can do so because each item on a spread is merely content in a layer, rather than a layer itself, as it would be in Photoshop. Commands like Object > Arrange > Send to Back give us a way to control stacking order and position items visually below or behind others. But as a document becomes more complex, layers give us greater control, and not just for stacking, although that's a fine place to start.

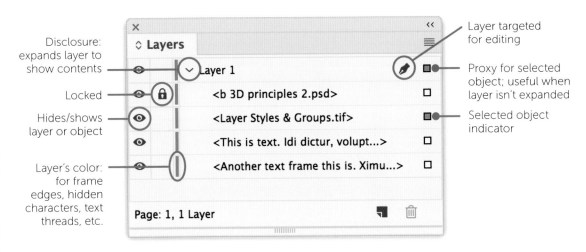

Disclosure: expands layer to show contents

Locked

Hides/shows layer or object

Layer's color: for frame edges, hidden characters, text threads, etc.

Layer targeted for editing

Proxy for selected object; useful when layer isn't expanded

Selected object indicator

Stacking Order

To the left of a layer's name in the Layers panel is a small arrow that, when clicked, shows the items populating that layer on the current spread. If the listed items overlap on the spread, the topmost object is topmost in the Layers panel, too. When an object is selected, its horizontal position (X) and vertical position (Y) are shown in the Control panel. Dragging an item's name below another's will set that object's Z order (stacking order) to be below the other object's.

To the left of the disclosure arrow is a small color bar, which shows the color associated with objects on that layer. Frame edges and several other nonprinting attributes will be displayed in this color so you can know what layer the object inhabits. If an object is selected, the small square to the right of its layer's name will fill with that color. That square is then a proxy for the object and can be dragged to other layers (if you have any), even without expanding them.

If a layer is expanded so you can see its contents, another square will be filled with that color next to the object that is selected in the layout. Those small squares can also be clicked to select objects. This is wonderful if one object is difficult to click on in the layout or is part of a group (whose content can also be "disclosed" with a small arrow to the left of the group).

I sometimes right-click an object's name in the Layers panel and choose Select and Fit Item to both select and center the item on my screen.

Creating Layers

The first item in the Layers panel menu is New Layer.... I like to use this method for creating layers because it encourages me to both name the layer and choose a color for its content's edges. An existing layer's name can be changed by either double-clicking the current one or right-clicking it and choosing Layer Options. Below, I changed the name of the default layer to "images" and its color from light blue to blue. I then created a new layer with the name "textual content" and chose red as its color.

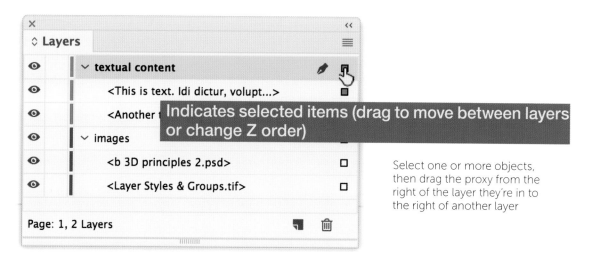

Moving Content Between Layers

To move content (in this case, text frames) from the "images" layer to the new one, I first selected the frames with my Selection tool, which made the proxy next to the "images" layer blue. (When you hover a cursor above a proxy, you'll see the tool tip above. I followed those instructions!) I then dragged the blue proxy to the right of the "textual content" layer, and the frames I had selected moved to that layer.

Reordering Layers

Dragging a layer by its name above or below others puts its content above or below the content in the other layers. The example above is not an arbitrary one; for esoteric output reasons, I often want images (especially those with transparent bits) to be below text. By having a layer for them, I'm encouraged to put them there.

You may also wish to ensure that some items, like page numbers or running headers, are never obscured, even by full-bleed images. Having those elements on a layer at the top of the stack could be a nice way to arrange that.

Workspaces &
Preferences

Frames &
Content

Styles, Type
& Fonts

Pages
& Spreads

Color
Management

Find/Change

Long
Documents

Segregating Types of Content

Segregating content into distinct layers allows us to do some pretty cool things. Layers can be set to be nonprinting (double-click a layer's name to see that option). Why would you do that (besides as a prank on colleagues)? You may wish to leave notes or instructions in a template, for example, without the risk of their being output.

Instead of making a layer nonprinting, you may wish to protect its content from accidental edits. To accomplish that, click to the right of the small eye icon (eye-con?) to lock the layer. If a layer is expanded to show its content, you may lock individual items instead.

Speaking of that eye-con, it controls a layer's visibility. Consider a multilingual document in which only one language at a time is to be output. You may have one InDesign file that you can export as a PDF, but with only some layers visible each time. Another example would be a textbook; the teacher's edition would have content not visible in the student edition.

I sometimes put my ruler guides on a layer of their own so I can hide them without hiding my margin or column guides. The shortcut ⌘-;/Ctrl-; (semicolon) toggles the visibility of *all* guides. To easily select all guides, use the shortcut ⌘-option-G/Ctrl-Alt-G. You can then drag the proxy to another layer, which can be either locked (locking the guides) or hidden (hiding them). Guides are usually created on a master page via Layout > Create Guides…. This presents no problem, as layers are available across all pages, and hiding a layer hides its content on all pages. If that layer is above all the others, its content, even master page content, will be above all the rest.

Deleting Layers

The safest command for deleting layers is found in the Layers panel menu: Delete Unused Layers. This is something I do when a project is finished. If you highlight a layer and click the little trash can at the bottom of the Layers panel, you'll be warned if there's content on it—a good thing, as that content will get deleted with the layer. If you feel that you have too many layers, a better solution is to merge them. Highlight two or more and then choose Merge Layers from the Layers panel menu.

Tables of Contents (TOCs)

Manually building a table of contents for a large document is one of the punishments await-ing those who fail to use paragraph styles for headers and subheaders. InDesign's ability to scour long documents (including Book documents composed of many individual files) to au-tomatically create a table of contents is one of the great rewards for using paragraph styles.

Preparation

Consider this document: each chapter header has a paragraph style called *Chapter title* ap-plied to it. Major topics (like the one at the top of this page) have their own style, as do the headers under them (like "Preparation" just above). In some cases there are more granular headers used, too. In this book's table of contents, I chose to include the first three heading levels as its entries.

I *strongly* recommend making a mock-up table of contents with its own paragraph styles to decorate the entries that will be generated from text using the styles you'll target in the document. In my case, I made styles with names like *TOC chap header*, *TOC topic header*, and *TOC header*. I wanted names that clearly showed that these would be used only in my table of contents (TOC). When InDesign is configured to look for text that uses certain styles, you are offered the option of using the same styles to decorate the TOC entries. This is rarely what we want. So it's best to have other options at the ready.

You'll also need a paragraph style for the TOC's title (usually the word "Contents," but that's up to you). And you'll be offered the chance to choose a character style for the page numbers that appear in the generated entries. In the case of this book, I made a character style that gives a consistent size and weight to the page numbers, no matter what the rest of the entry is like.

InDesign does offer to create styles for you. You'll see them in the list of styles where you also find your own, and they'll become real if you choose them. But they're very generic and you'll have to redefine them anyway.

Creating the TOC

Once you're sure that styles have been applied to all the paragraphs with text that is to be-come TOC entries, and you have built styles for the TOC itself, you'll need to go to the page(s) where the TOC will be. When you've configured and committed the Table of Contents dialog box, the cursor will become a loaded text gun. You can either create a text frame then or flow the TOC into an awaiting frame. Since I often have a master page with a primary text frame governing my tables of contents pages, I use the latter option.

Long Documents

Output

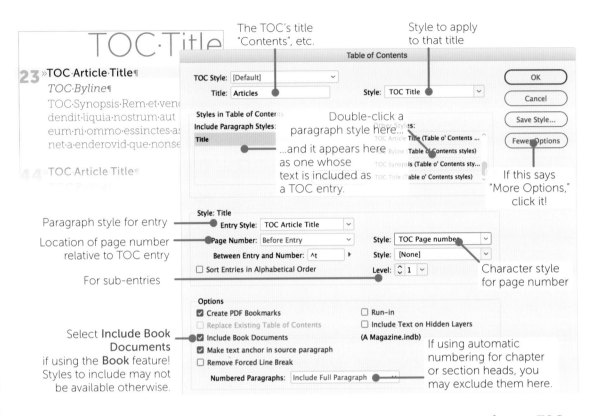

There is a lot to configure in the Table of Contents dialog box, so I use my dummy TOC to guide me. To gain access to all of the available options, click the button labeled More Options, if you see it. On the other hand, if the button says Fewer Options, don't click it. Near the bottom of the dialog, check Include Book Documents if you need to trawl for styles in all the documents of a Book document.

Now you can work from near the top of the dialog down. In the Title field, enter the text that should appear at the top of the TOC, and choose the Style for it just to the right. In the example here, I'm building the TOC for a magazine, so I chose "Articles" as my TOC's title.

The two sections that follow are used in tandem. The Styles in Table of Contents section is where we choose the styles whose text is to become entries in the table of contents. Double-clicking on a style listed in the Other Styles box on the right adds it to the Include Paragraph Styles list on the left. Simple TOCs, like those for a novel in which we want only the chapter headers noted, may have only one style chosen. For this magazine, I'll be choosing three: the titles of the articles, the bylines, and a brief synopsis. The first will be a Level 1 entry, which is assigned in the next section of the dialog, Style. The other two will be Level 2, since they're both subordinate to the title, but not to each other.

In the Style section, you also choose how to style the entries generated from the style currently highlighted in the Include Paragraph Styles section above. For entries pulled from the style called *Title* (which decorates the article titles), I'm using a style called *TOC Article Title*. As in my mock-up, I chose to have the page number Before Entry with a tab (^t) Between Entry and Number. For the Level 2 entries, I chose No Page Number since they're already next to the main entry.

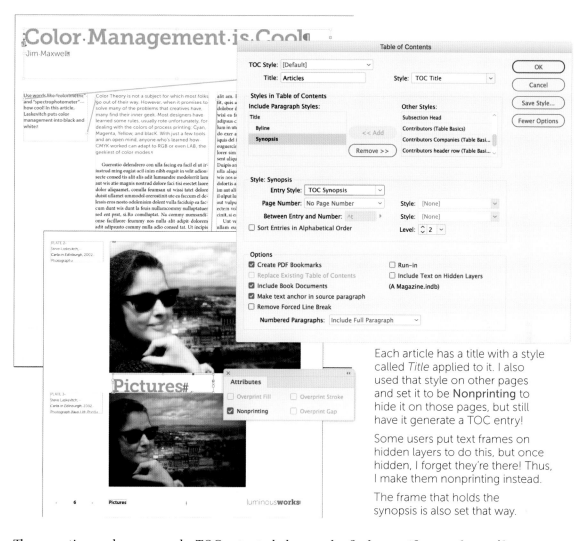

Each article has a title with a style called *Title* applied to it. I also used that style on other pages and set it to be **Nonprinting** to hide it on those pages, but still have it generate a TOC entry!

Some users put text frames on hidden layers to do this, but once hidden, I forget they're there! Thus, I make them nonprinting instead.

The frame that holds the synopsis is also set that way.

There are times when we need a TOC entry to help a reader find a specific page, but we'd prefer to not have the text appear on that page. There are three common ways to do this:

1. Put the text on a hidden layer, then check the box Include Text on Hidden Layers in the Options section of the Table of Contents dialog;

2. Set the frame that holds the text to be Nonprinting using the Attributes panel; or

3. Place the text frame on the Pasteboard *mostly* off the page, barely overlapping it.

I prefer method 2 because I can see the text when I zip through my pages in InDesign, but it disappears in Preview mode and won't output. I may forget the text exists if it's on a hidden layer or if I'm zoomed too close to see the text that is mostly offstage.

When I'm very on top of things, I may create an object style that gives the frame a garish fill or stroke and makes it nonprinting. This way, I can recognize them when I see them, but no one else will see the garishness.

Workspaces & Preferences

Frames & Content

Styles, Type & Fonts

Pages & Spreads

Color Management

Find/Change

Long Documents

Articles

4 Letters

6 Pictures

7 Reviews of Books

8 Color Management is Cool
Jim Maxwell
Use words like "colorimetric" and "spectrophotometer"—how cool! In this article, Laskevitch puts color management into black and white.

12 Illustrator CC: Drawn Out
A. Rocket Scientist
Adobe Illustrator walks tall on the vector landscape. What's it got that no one else does?

15 InDesign CC InDepth
Steve Laskevitch
Books, newsletters, newspapers, and magazines (like this one) are well built—and easily rebuilt—with this application.

18 Fabulous Foolery with Photoshop CC
Peachy T Peach
The preeminent pixel pusher. The Rocky of Raster. CC doesn't sit on these laurels, but still grabs attention like an excited kid pulling on one's sleeve.

22 Web Standards & Dreamweaver CC
WebDesigner
Standards Compliance just got easier. In this article we find out how.

24 Powerful Photographic Techniques & Workflows
Carla Fraga
Is film dead? Not quite, but the pulse is faint and thready. How pro shooters are getting work done

26 List of Contributors

Updating a Table of Contents

What if any of the text changes? Tables of Contents don't update automatically. However, it's easy to prompt them. Insert the Type tool cursor anywhere in the TOC. Then choose Layout > Update Table of Contents.

TOC Styles

You will likely generate a table of contents a few times before it's right, especially if it has several levels of entries. Sometimes you'll choose the wrong style to look for or to apply to the entry. When you finally dial it in, and you suspect you may need to use those settings again (the next issue of the magazine, for example), you can create a Table of Contents Style. I very much wish they called it a "preset" as the word "style" is used so much here.

When you're in the TOC dialog, and all the settings are correct, click the Save Style… button and give this preset a name. TOC Styles are among the things that get synchronized in a Book file.

They're also used to generate the electronic TOC in an eBook (like those read on an iPad or Kindle). You may generate an attractive TOC from that TOC Style as well, but for those media it's truly optional. However, the TOC Style is *not*; it's the way we describe the hierarchy in an eBook's code.

We will discuss eBooks in the "Output" chapter of this book—see "ePub and Tagged File Formats" (page 347)—but you might consider creating a TOC Style that excludes page numbers just for that medium. In a reflowable ePub, a reader can change the font or font size of the text, which makes the whole concept of a page rather fluid. TOC entries become hyperlinks that will take the reader to the correct page, so knowing the number of a page becomes irrelevant.

To load TOC Styles from a different document (a previous project, perhaps), choose Layout > Table of Contents Styles… where you can click a Load button. You can also create new or edit existing TOC Styles, but it's done a bit blindly, as this approach doesn't generate a TOC afterward.

Text Variables

Tables of contents aren't the only InDesign feature to extract content based on the styles applied to it. Text variables can be a convenient way to repeat or reference text that uses a paragraph or character style. Much of what you see along the tops of pages in the print edition of this book uses text variables to remind you of which chapter you're reading (at the top of left-hand pages) and which topic (on right-hand pages).

Variables can also be a way to insert document data, like date and time of the most recent edit or output. And they can be used to extract and render metadata from placed images for captions. As in so much, there is good news and bad with this feature.

Chapter Numbers

When using the Book feature (discussed at the beginning of this chapter), you can inform each document which chapter it is or to begin automatic chapter numbering. To display the number, we insert a text variable: right-click and choose Insert Variable > Chapter Number. The chapter number will display in the same style as the text around it. Here is this chapter's number: 7. (Yes, that "7" is a variable. I used the Book feature to set the first chapter of the Compendium section as "1." This is the seventh.)

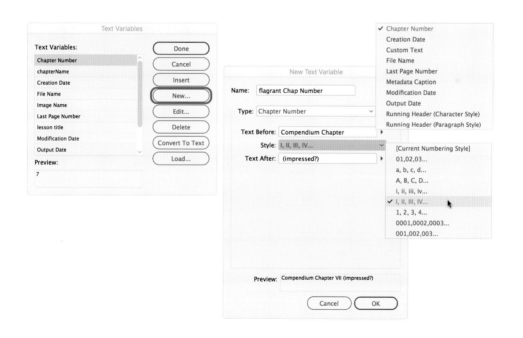

Another way to insert variables and, better, to define them, is by going to Type > Text Variables and choosing either Insert Variable or Define…. So I don't redefine a variable I'm using, I'll choose Define… and click New…. The settings above produce this:

Compendium Chapter VII (impressed?)

Workspaces &
Preferences

Frames &
Content

Styles, Type
& Fonts

Pages
& Spreads

Color
Management

Find/Change

**Long
Documents**

If I put that in a narrow text frame, however, it will look like this:

CompendiumChapterVII(impressed?)

Warning: Text variables don't break across lines. I bet you wondered when I'd get to the bad news. If the space available is too narrow, the variable text will get crushed.

If we redefine the variable to be less verbose, it will change everywhere and may fit in narrower quarters. Or I can select the variable, right-click, and choose Convert Variable to Text, and the following will result: it will wrap, but it will no longer update if the chapter number changes.

Compendium Chapter VII (impressed?)

Captions

Of course, we can create our own captions, but if our images have metadata, we can generate captions that utilize it. Although we go through a different procedure for these, they, too, are text variables.

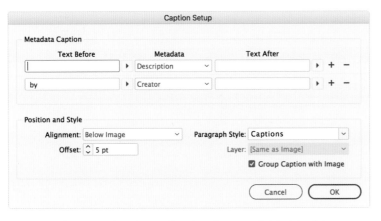

Old and new lines tether a ship at the South Street Seaport in New York City.

by Steve Laskevitch

Choosing **Object > Captions > Caption Setup**... yields this dialog. In it, we can choose which embedded *metadata* to include in a caption. At right: A **Live Caption** (top) and a **Static Caption** (bottom).

Metadata is added to images in one of several places. One can do so in Photoshop via the File Info dialog box. In Adobe Bridge or Lightroom, one can use a Metadata panel. For the image above, I added data to the Description and Creator fields. Object > Captions > Caption Setup... allows us to choose which metadata to include and what text should surround it in the caption we'll later generate. To make the caption, I right-clicked a selected image and at first chose Captions > Generate Live Caption. The first problem was that InDesign didn't read the Creator metadata. To force it to do so, I had to choose Author in the Caption Setup dialog—an obvious (and long-lived) bug.

Then I saw the result: the description was crushed on one line. If all my captions are very short, this may not be an issue. If a linked image's metadata changes, the caption will automatically change as well. But few captions are short enough, and metadata like this doesn't often change. So I used Undo, and this time right-clicked and chose Captions > Generate Static Caption. Static Captions are *not* variables, thus they are not linked to their source nor do they get crushed when the space is too narrow. Once these are generated, they're just text.

Running Headers

These text variables are among the most useful. If you're reading this in print, you'll see a running header at the top of each page of this spread. One of them reads "Text Variables." That one "sees" the last use of a particular paragraph style, which decorates the large header earlier in the text announcing this topic. Here's it's definition:

Using Type > Text Variables > Define…, I clicked the New button. I usually name a variable after the style to which it refers. I chose "topic title" and selected Running Header (Paragraph Style) as the Type. I have almost never used the character style variant. I'm sure it's lovely.

For a running header, we are usually referring to a topic that is ongoing, and so we want the most recent use of it. Thus, I chose Last on Page for Use. We can choose a wide variety of special characters to automatically be added before or after the text we're grabbing, or we may type into the Text Before or Text After fields. InDesign even supplies a thoughtful way to remove punctuation or change the case of the text.

To insert the variable, we locate our cursor in a text frame (for running headers, this is usually on a master page, and often near the Current Page Number marker), right-click, and choose Insert Variable > [name of variable].

Warning: Yes, another bug! When you change the text to which a variable refers, you'll have to force the page to redraw. Simply zooming out and in again will do it. Otherwise, it *appears* that the variable is not updating.

Workspaces &
Preferences

Frames &
Content

Styles, Type
& Fonts

Pages
& Spreads

Color
Management

Find/Change

**Long
Documents**

Cross References

Cross references are cousins of text variables with a bit of TOC genes thrown in. They refer to and can echo text that uses a certain paragraph style, and they most often cite the page on which to find it—e.g., "see *Hogwarts* on page 993." Since cross references are also hyperlinks in electronic documents like ePub, I often suppress the appearance of page numbers there. The Cross References panel can be opened via Window > Type & Tables.

The Destination

If you need to refer to a word or phrase rather than a paragraph, you can make it a named text anchor. Usually, I'm referring to entire short paragraphs, like headers, or to parts of paragraphs, like their numbers (when the Bullets and Numbering feature is used, a common scenario for figures or tables).

To create a text anchor, highlight the text to which you anticipate making a reference later. Go to the Cross-References panel menu and choose New Hyperlink Destination.... For Type, choose Text Anchor. The Name is important, as it will be the text cited in the cross reference. When hidden characters are visible, the anchor will look like a colon. The TOC feature also has the option to create text anchors, so you may see some already.

A future cross reference doesn't have to use a text anchor; it can cite an entire paragraph, a paragraph number if it exists (or both), or a partial paragraph up to some character you can specify (like a tab). By using the supplied building blocks when editing the reference's format, you may also include a Chapter Number and a File Name, and you can even apply a character style to portions of the reference. You don't have to build a lot of text anchors in your documents.

Building a Cross Reference

First, insert the text cursor where you want the reference inserted. If you're to make reference to text in another document in a Book, make sure that document is open! Then you can use the Cross-References panel menu to choose Insert Cross-Reference... or use the Create New Cross-Reference button at the bottom of the panel. You'll then be looking at the New Cross-Reference dialog box (see figure on opposite page).

Choose what to Link To: a paragraph or text anchor. Then choose the Document that contains the reference's destination. If you're linking to a text anchor, you simply choose its name. If you're linking to a paragraph, it can get a little trickier. On the left, choose the Paragraph Style that your destination is using. Yes, despite the search feature there, it's much easier if you know the style. Once the correct style is highlighted, a list of each occurrence in the destination document is presented on the right. If you highlight one of those occurrences and look where your cursor was blinking, you'll see a preview of the cross reference forming.

The formatting may not be what you want, yet. The built-in list in Format may be sufficient for most needs. If you simply want to cite the page number, choose that. You may choose Full

Paragraph & Page Number or Text Anchor Name & Page Number. In the classroom, I often get asked the difference between Full Paragraph and Paragraph Text because few see any difference. There is no difference unless the paragraph uses automatic numbering. If it does, Full Paragraph includes the number and Paragraph Text does not.

With the cursor blinking at the insertion point, create the **New Cross-Reference**.

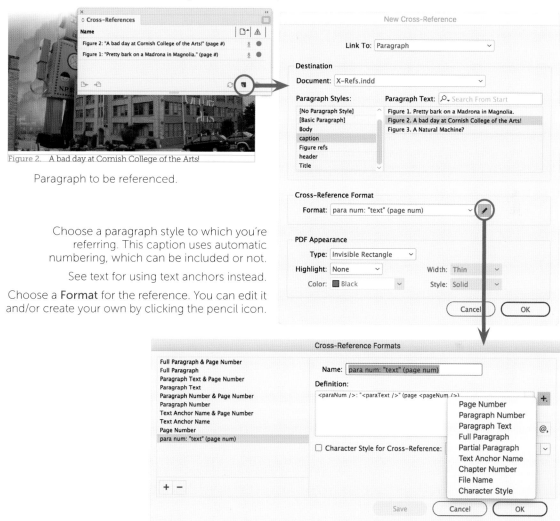

Paragraph to be referenced.

Choose a paragraph style to which you're referring. This caption uses automatic numbering, which can be included or not.

See text for using text anchors instead.

Choose a **Format** for the reference. You can edit it and/or create your own by clicking the pencil icon.

cium qui sinctem porehendi unt aperierum veritatias eaqi nit quid utem dolupta ecaboribus.

List of Illustrations:

Figure 1: "Pretty bark on a Madrona in Magnolia." (page 1)

Figure 2: "A bad day at Cornish College of the Arts!" (page 4)

When editing **Format**, use "building blocks" to assemble the reference. Those familiar with HTML or XML will find this easier.

Note that there's a choice for Paragraph Number & Page Number. The example in the figure

Long Documents

Output

shows a caption that reads, "Figure 2.   A bad day at Cornish College of the Arts!" Everything leading up to the "A" ("Figure 2." and the em space) is part of the paragraph number as defined in the paragraph style for that caption. So Paragraph Number & Page Number would yield "Figure 2 on page 4." However, I based my custom format on Paragraph Text & Page Number. I chose that, then clicked the pencil icon to its right, opening the Cross-Reference Formats dialog box (and disabling the preview, sadly).

Since I was making a custom format, I added it by clicking the plus sign (+) at the lower left of the Cross-Reference Formats dialog box. I input a name that mimics the format I'm building so I can readily identify it. The Definition field is where we construct our format by a combination of typing and choosing from the Building Block (+) or Special Character (@.) menus. Building blocks look like HTML or XML tags using "<" and ">" to form wildcards of sorts:

```
<paraNum />: "<paraText />" (page <pageNum />)
```
Figure 2: "A bad day at Cornish College of the Arts!" (page 4)

The above yields the paragraph number; a colon and space I simply typed; the paragraph's text in quotes; a space; and, in parentheses, the word "page," a space, and the page number.

Workspaces & Preferences

Frames & Content

Styles, Type & Fonts

Pages & Spreads

Color Management

Find/Change

Long Documents

Footnotes and Endnotes

Both of these features insert a reference into the text flow (usually a number) and create a note either at the bottom of the page on which the reference occurs (a footnote) or later in the document (endnote). Both have a number of options that require more time and decision-making than deep insight. Nonetheless, there are a few important things to note (pardon the pun).

It's useful to create a paragraph style for the kind of note you'll be using. It certainly doesn't have to be perfect because, like all paragraph styles, it can be edited later. But when you adjust the Footnote or Endnote Options, you'll be asked to choose a style for the note. You can also choose a character style for the reference, though this is slightly less common. For clarity, I'll use one that makes the reference red in the examples that follow.

Footnotes

When I insert my first footnote (by right-clicking and choosing Insert Footnote), I then go about the business of formatting it via Type > Document Footnote Options....

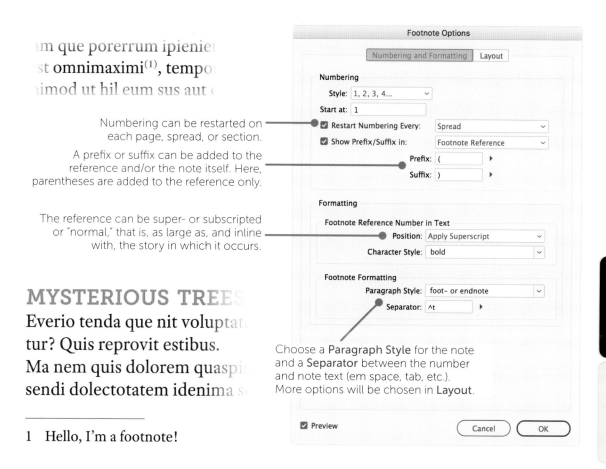

Numbering can be restarted on each page, spread, or section.

A prefix or suffix can be added to the reference and/or the note itself. Here, parentheses are added to the reference only.

The reference can be super- or subscripted or "normal," that is, as large as, and inline with, the story in which it occurs.

Choose a **Paragraph Style** for the note and a **Separator** between the number and note text (em space, tab, etc.). More options will be chosen in **Layout**.

1   Hello, I'm a footnote!

The Footnote Options dialog that opens has two sections, the first of which is Numbering and Formatting (in the previous figure). This deals with the text formatting of both the reference (the number in the story) and the footnote itself. In that example, I added parentheses to the reference as both Prefix and Suffix (but not to the note) and chose a character style to make the reference number bolder.

Much of the Layout section is dedicated to the space around and between footnotes. The lower third is dedicated to a rule (line) that can be drawn between the story text and the footnote(s). In this example, I've set a solid, reddish, .5 point rule between the text and the first footnote.

As a footnote grows more verbose, it gets taller. It is possible that it may even reach up to the line that contains its reference. For this reason, I suggest leaving the Allow Split Footnotes checkbox enabled. This allows the footnote to continue into the next text column (if there is one) or onto the next page.

Note: The menu for Rule Above has two independent settings: one for the *first* footnote and the other for Continued Footnotes, those that need to flow to another column or page.

There is also an option to Span Footnotes Across Columns, which may lessen the chance that the note will flow to another page. When a footnote continues, the Continued Footnotes Rule Above will be used.

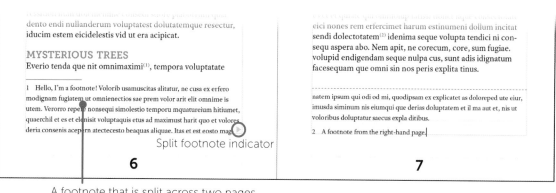

Split footnote indicator

A footnote that is split across two pages.
One **Rule Above** its beginning; another,
differently styled one above its continuation.

Endnotes

As you might expect, the Endnotes feature is very similar to the Footnotes feature. When we right-click to Insert Endnote, a reference is inserted at that point and our text cursor is now blinking in the note awaiting its content. However, with an endnote, we're likely looking at another page, possibly one that's far from where we inserted the reference.

Note: With the text cursor within an endnote, right-click and choose Go to Endnote Reference. When right-clicking with the cursor at the reference point, the choice is Go to Endnote Text.

Choose Type > Document Endnote Options…, and you'll get options similar to those for footnotes.

At the top of the page newly created for your endnotes, what title should be displayed and how should it be styled?

Choose the style of numbers to be used, with what number they start, and whether they are **Continuous** or **Restart Every Story**.

As with footnotes, the reference can be a super- or subscript character, or it can be normal. A **Character Style** can also be applied to it.

The note's **Paragraph Style** and **Separator**.

If the **Scope** is **Document**, a new page appears at the end of the document. For **Story**, a new page will appear after the page where the reference's story ends.

If desired, a **Prefix** and/or **Suffix** can be appended to the reference, the note, or both.

er store piaborrum quia

est dolutatemque resectur,

ra should be noted⁽¹⁾.

ENDNOTES
[1   Thus I am noting it.

Finally, as of fall 2018, you can convert footnotes to endnotes and the other way around. Choose Type > Convert Footnote and Endnote.

In the discussion of "Cross References" (page 328), I used a list of figures as an example. An alternate approach could use endnotes. A Prefix of "Figure" plus a space, and a space as Suffix applied with Normal Position could give us an opportunity like this:

FIGURES¶
Figure 1 — *Arbutus Menziesii,* photograph, Steve Laskevitch
Figure 2 — *Gear in Tree,* Photoshop mischief, Anonymous

Figure 1 Pretty bark on a Madrona in Magnolia.

However, if you have independent numbered lists of figures and tables, for example, automatic numbering with named Lists is the better solution. Review "Bullets and Numbering" (page 257).

Long Documents

Output

Workspaces &
Preferences

Frames &
Content

Styles, Type
& Fonts

Pages
& Spreads

Color
Management

Find/Change

Long
Documents

Indexes

An index is something very, very few of us should contemplate making ourselves. There are professional indexers for the same reason there are professional electricians: we *might* be able to do the work ourselves, but the pros have the minds and skills to do it better than we ever could. Admittedly, a badly done index won't burn down your house like badly done electrical work could, but the process of making it could be damaging to your soul.

Nonetheless, I will supply some of the basics for those who wish to try their hand at it. Keep in mind that you're building a list of concepts, not simply words. Each concept will be an index Topic, and each occurrence of that concept is a Reference.

The suggested workflow goes something like this:

Create a Topic List

Although an optional first step, creating a topic list is strongly recommended. It ensures that you are consistent and are less likely to be redundant. Later, you'll be able to add references to each more easily as well.

Create Index Markers and References

At each occurrence of a reference to a topic, you create a marker. To better ensure their survival, I recommend doing this after the text is complete and edited. Otherwise, markers may get deleted accidentally.

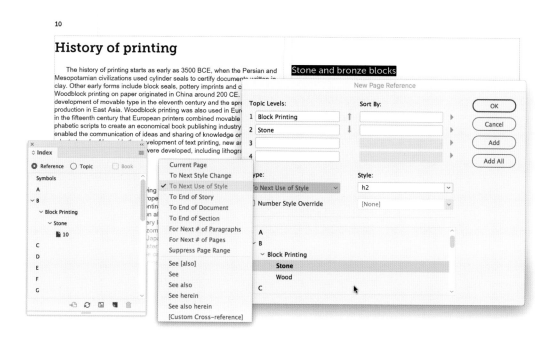

Generate the Index

This action creates an InDesign story that you can flow onto a page of a document or into a document of its own as part of a Book.

Get Help

The American Society for Indexing website (asindexing.org) has an indexer finder. Hiring a professional is money well spent.

For more details on making your own index, you can read this page from InDesign's help system: https://helpx.adobe.com/indesign/using/creating-index.html.

Long Documents

Output

8 Output

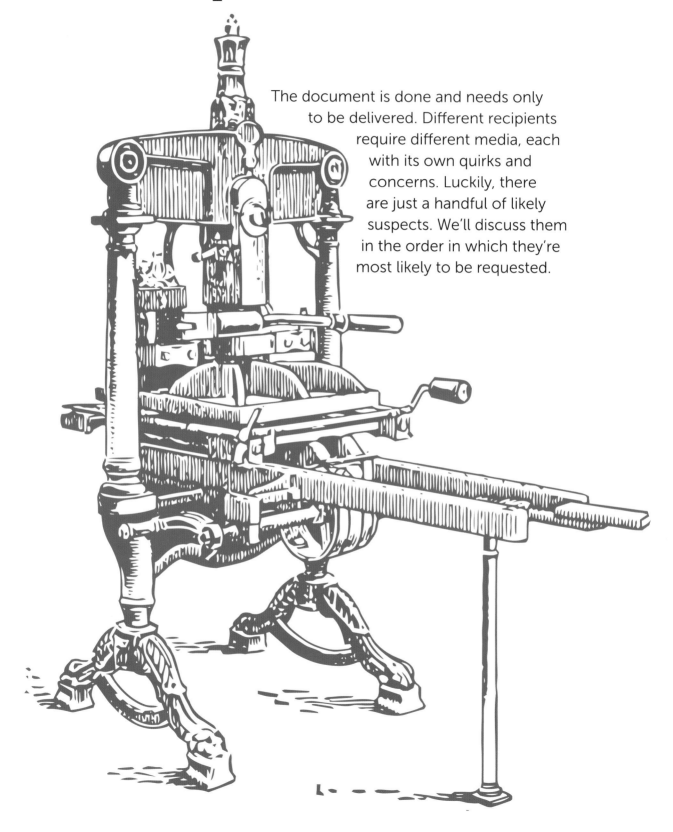

The document is done and needs only to be delivered. Different recipients require different media, each with its own quirks and concerns. Luckily, there are just a handful of likely suspects. We'll discuss them in the order in which they're most likely to be requested.

PDF

The Portable Document Format (PDF) is the most common way we share our finished layouts. Anyone with Adobe's free Acrobat Reader application can open a PDF and consume its content. And that's just about *everyone*. Those who want to edit PDFs or add extra functionality to them can use Adobe Acrobat Pro, the powerful sibling to Reader. Adobe has been very effective at making PDF and these apps nearly ubiquitous. Maybe a little too effective: my training company often gets calls from prospective students who want to learn how to use "Adobe." With some gentle questioning we confirm they're trying to learn more about Adobe Acrobat.

The advantage of sharing a document as an Acrobat PDF rather than a Word or InDesign document is that PDFs retain the layout and text formatting of the authoring application without the recipient needing to have the author's applications or fonts. When I receive Word docs from clients, I moan because just opening them will change them. Adobe built PDF to retain a faithful likeness to the original at the cost of making it hard to edit. But even that has become easier with the right software.

PDFs can be configured for a variety of print output devices or can be set up for entirely electronic consumption. Their file sizes can be very small (at the cost of image quality, usually) or large. There is no one PDF to rule them all; different eventualities often demand a differently configured PDF. Luckily, our recipients can often guide us and Adobe provides many presets to achieve common configurations.

Presets

InDesign can export (File > Export…) to many different file types. But when it's PDF I need, I stop just short of that command and use File > Adobe PDF Presets, choosing the preset that most closely matches my needs. You'll be prompted for a name and location to which to save the PDF. Then you still need to interact with another dialog box with many options. If you cancel at either stage, no PDF is made.

The Presets in square brackets ("[" and "]") are built-in and cannot be changed. But if you do customize the settings in the Export Adobe PDF dialog, you'll see the name of the preset with the word

Define…

[High Quality Print]…
[PDF/X-1a:2001]…
[PDF/X-3:2002]…
[PDF/X-4:2008]…
[Press Quality]…
[Smallest File Size]…

"modified" appended to it. You can save those customizations as your own preset to use later. And there are many things that you might choose to change! A private student once asked me to explain the pros and cons of *every* option. Twenty minutes later the student asked me to "stop, please." Luckily, I covered the crucial things in the first five minutes, and few people other than prepress professionals need to know much more. Speaking of those special folks…

Better printing companies will often suggest which preset to choose or supply a custom preset they have made to suit their workflow. I recently consulted the website of one such printer and found wonderfully detailed advice for preparing files for output as well as a downloadable PDF preset. If your printer supplies such, you will need to "install" it. Some

Output

Workspaces & Preferences

Frames & Content

Styles, Type & Fonts

Pages & Spreads

Color Management

Find/Change

Long Documents

Output

printers will instead show images of the various pages of the Export Adobe PDF dialog box, hoping you will match what they're showing. Either way, you'll need to "define" a PDF preset.

Choose File > Adobe PDF Presets > Define.... If you're trying to follow instructions and screenshots, you'll press the New... button. You will then navigate to a dialog box that is nearly identical to the one you use when actually exporting. We'll get there in a moment.

If you've downloaded the preset, you'll press the Load... button, then choose the file you downloaded (it will have an extension of ".joboptions").

We will look at many of the details of this preset and some others as we go through the Export Adobe PDF dialog box.

General Options

When you use File > Adobe PDF Presets or go to File > Export... and select Adobe PDF (Print), you'll be faced with the Export Adobe PDF dialog.

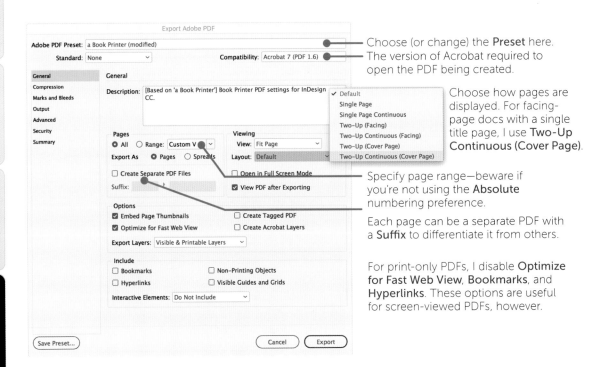

Choose (or change) the **Preset** here.
The version of Acrobat required to open the PDF being created.

Choose how pages are displayed. For facing-page docs with a single title page, I use **Two-Up Continuous (Cover Page)**.

Specify page range—beware if you're not using the **Absolute** numbering preference.

Each page can be a separate PDF with a **Suffix** to differentiate it from others.

For print-only PDFs, I disable **Optimize for Fast Web View**, **Bookmarks**, and **Hyperlinks**. These options are useful for screen-viewed PDFs, however.

The first page of that dialog is called General. Some of its settings get altered if you change the preset, so I often leave General for last. There are important options found here. This is where you specify the range of pages to be exported (much easier to do if you have chosen Absolute page numbering in your General Preferences). You may choose for each InDesign page to be a PDF page, or you can have each PDF page be a "reader spread" by choosing to Export As Spreads. However, that setting and a number of others are *not* recommended for PDFs destined for print.

Viewing has a welcome set of options for whomever will open the PDF. For View, I invariably choose Fit Page so that no recipient is looking at only the top third of page one when they open the document. If my document is a series of single pages, I'll choose Single Page or Single Page (Continuous) for Layout. If I have spreads (a.k.a., "facing pages"), one of the Two-Up options is more appropriate. There's even provision for a singe title page followed by spreads (the options with Cover Page in the name). Always choose to View PDF after Exporting.

For PDFs destined for online viewing, there are many options to keep the file size low. One is the Preset called Smallest File Size, although you may find that the cost of "smallest" is too great, as image quality is often too low. More on that when we discuss Compression. Other options in General are the inclusion of modestly interactive elements, like any Hyperlinks you may have built. Bookmarks can be generated from an InDesign TOC, too. If you've built more elaborate interactivity involving buttons and transitions, then the export process should start with going to File > Export... and choosing Adobe PDF (Interactive) and its set of export options.

Create Tagged PDF is required to include tags for disabled accessibility. Create Acrobat Layers makes a PDF layer for each InDesign layer. You can choose which InDesign layers from the Export Layers menu. The All Layers choice means it, even including layers that have been made invisible or nonprinting!

Compression

The figure at left shows the settings for a book printer. But if you examine this section having chosen the Smallest File Size preset, you'll see that all color images will experience Bicubic Downsampling to 100 ppi if their *effective resolution* is more than 150 ppi. See "Placing Images" (page 208) for more on that term. Grayscale images will be made 150 ppi. Those resolutions *may* indeed be appropriate for onscreen viewing. But the combination of Compression and Image Quality are JPEG and Low, respectively. After viewing the result, you'll likely increase the quality to Medium or higher, yielding a larger but more palatable file.

The print-friendly settings shown use ZIP compression rather than JPEG, as file size is not so critical and ZIP is lossless compression, unlike JPEG which literally discards data! Since the compatibility is set to Acrobat 7, I could use JPEG 2000 (an option for Acrobat 6 and higher), which yields a better looking JPEG, but ZIP is quite literally best.

The Downsampling is also different. For this print preset, it's set to 300 ppi for images whose effective resolution exceeds 450 ppi. At the bottom of the dialog are two checkboxes that will make a smaller file size while causing no harm: Compress Text and Line Art and Crop Image Data to Frames. Some users get apprehensive about the latter until they're reminded that this is only cropping the images in the PDF, not the InDesign document.

Marks and Bleeds

Now we step off the page to what surrounds it. Arrayed beyond the bleed are the Crop Marks that determine where the paper will be cut. Some printers may also want more information like filename or date (Page Information).

Use only the settings that your print shop asks for! If you've set your document's bleed to their specs, you can check **Use Document Bleed Settings**.

Output

This ties into the management of color as discussed in chapter 5, "Color Management" (page 293). The key choice here is the Destination. If I'm creating a PDF to be viewed onscreen only, I'd likely choose sRGB, as that profile represents standard displays. For print, choose the profile indicated by your print shop—they may even supply one to install so you can choose it here. With a Destination profile chosen, specify the Color Conversion: Convert to Destination (Preserve Numbers).

With a CMYK Destination, this choice ensures that all RGB content is converted to the printer's desired profile while maintaining any CMYK choices you may have made in InDesign.

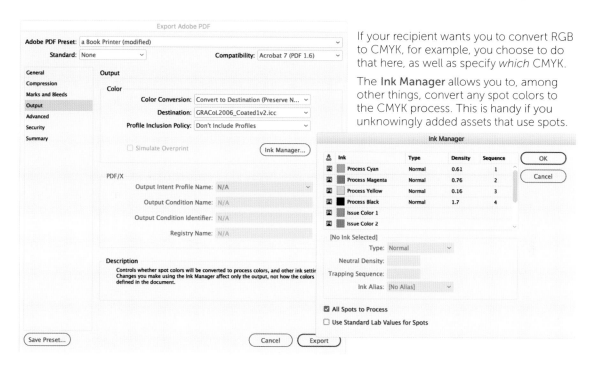

If your recipient wants you to convert RGB to CMYK, for example, you choose to do that here, as well as specify *which* CMYK.

The Ink Manager allows you to, among other things, convert any spot colors to the CMYK process. This is handy if you unknowingly added assets that use spots.

It is possible that you will be asked to do No Color Conversion so that the printer may do it themselves with the most up-to-date profile. Profile Inclusion is also a decision of the print shop, as some of their software may not like to have that data embedded in the PDF.

The Ink Manager is a great last-minute rescuer. For example, let's say you've built a brochure that includes logos from a dozen sponsors. Some of those logos use spot colors that require extra inks for which there is no budget. You don't have to rebuild each logo to use only CMYK (process color). You merely have to check a box in the Ink Manager as you export your PDF: All Spots to Process.

Another option Ink Alias, which allows you to substitute one ink for another. One

Workspaces & Preferences

Frames & Content

Styles, Type & Fonts

Pages & Spreads

Color Management

Find/Change

Long Documents

Output

common use for that is swatches that use *nearly* the same spot color, but are actually different. In the example, an uncoated paper version of a spot color is being "aliased" to the coated version. That one, in turn, could be aliased to a third, maybe a process ink.

Advanced

Only a few options are of interest here for those with reasonably modern workflows.

Under Fonts, you have the option to reduce file size by embedding only the font data of the characters you used in InDesign (a Subset of them). This could be troublesome if a recipient needs to make a small text change with a character you didn't embed. Thus, I choose 0% to force the full fonts to become part of PDFs, especially those for print.

Printers who have more current software to process PDFs can support transparency in the PDFs we send them. So if you're asked to supply Acrobat 5 or newer Compatibility, artwork in your document that includes transparent effects like drop shadows or blend modes will be passed along in the PDF. If the Compatibility is Acrobat 4, InDesign uses a bunch of processing tricks to maintain the look of your artwork, but without transparency. This process is called flattening, and we choose a Flattener Preset that best fools the eye. We're lucky that this is becoming less necessary all the time.

Security

With Document Open Password, you can encrypt the PDF so it cannot be opened without a password that you choose. So if you're sharing a proprietary document, you can do so over less secure channels, comforted that an eavesdropper can't open it.

The Permissions portion is less secure, but it attempts to prevent certain actions (printing or extracting content) unless a password is provided. However, one can open the PDF in some software that circumvents this.

Package

Most recipients are content with a PDF. But for our colleagues, the company archive, or our own, we need to supply our "native" files: the InDesign document(s), all the linked graphics, and fonts. In short, all the assets necessary to open and edit that project.

A Copy of Everything

When an InDesign project is complete and saved, we may wish or need to share it and its assets with others. However, those assets may be strewn over several hard drives and many folders. Luckily, if we don't have any missing links or fonts, we can make a package that leaves our assets in place and makes copies of them all consolidated in a folder. You may wish to review "Missing Links & Relinking" (page 212) and "Missing Fonts" (page 241).

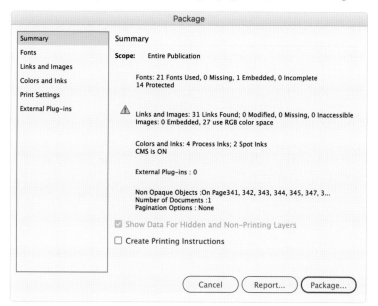

To create the package folder, choose File > Package.... You'll need to wade through a few dialog boxes, the first of which consists of a "preflight" check and summary. Unfortunately, you'll see a warning triangle that is wholly ignorable. The use of RGB images is apparently alarming to someone on the engineering team and no one else. I'm relieved when I see no missing fonts at the top, however.

If Create Printing Instructions is checked, clicking Package… reveals a form, the content of which augments a text file that will be within the package. It informs the recipient how to get in touch with you and includes all the data you saw in the previous dialog box. Few read that doc, so we rarely check the box to create it.

The dialog that appears either after or instead of the printing instructions is the most significant. In it, you name the package, choose where to save it, and designate its contents. I almost always check the first five checkboxes. I want the package to have all the assets necessary to successfully open it. All the fonts, except Asian language (CJK) fonts and those from the Typekit service, will be copied to a subfolder called "Document fonts."

Copy Linked Graphics creates a folder called "Links" in which all placed images and graphics are copied. Update Graphic Links in Package ensures that those graphics know they're linked to the copy of your InDesign document.

Use Document Hyphenation Exceptions Only prevents the text from reflowing when opened on a computer with different hyphenation and dictionary settings.

Include Fonts and Links From Hidden and Non-Printing Content sounds useless, but is far from it. I often have nonprinting content that colleagues who open the InDesign document will need to see (instructions, for example). I may also have layers hidden with optional text or text in alternate languages.

Include IDML adds a file in *InDesign Markup Language*, a descriptive format that can be opened in now very old versions of InDesign. Some new features (e.g., Paragraph Shading) may not be present, but the content will be intact.

Finally, Include PDF (Print) will include a PDF using the last settings used by your InDesign document.

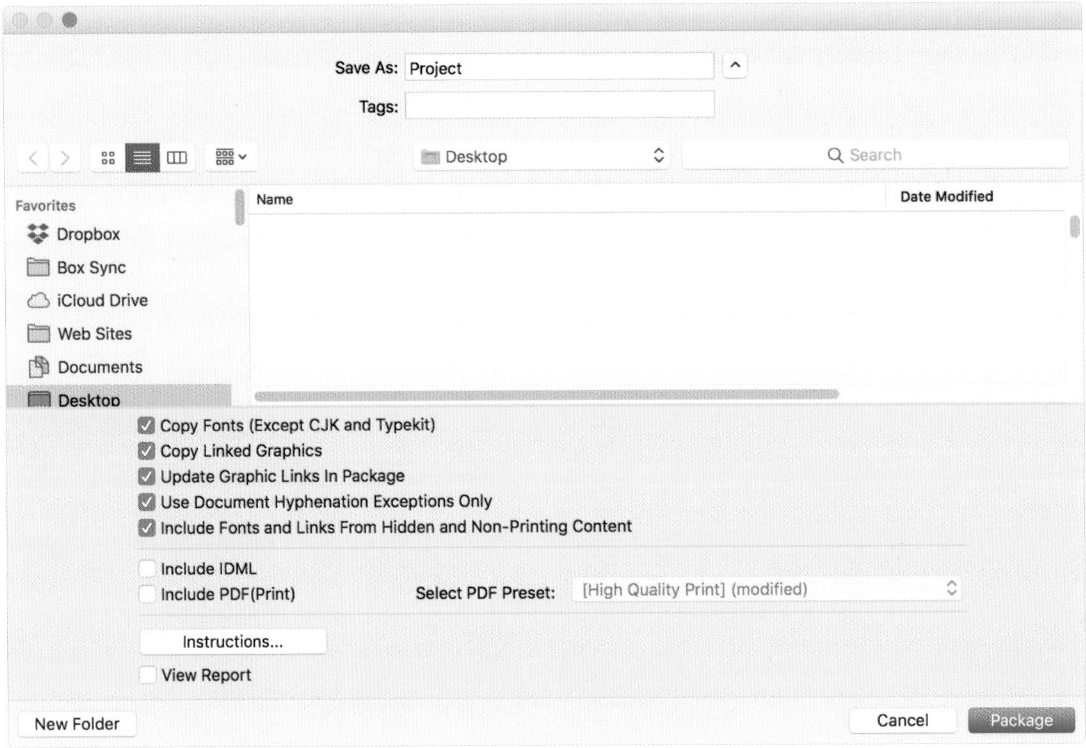

When you hit the Package button, you get to read the last dialog box: a message from Adobe's legal department warning that one cannot share fonts with those who do not have a license to use them. That dialog has an important checkbox labeled Don't Show Again. You'll likely want to check that for next time. Committing that dialog finally allows the package to be generated. When this book is completed, I will make a package from the Book panel menu to give to my publisher.

Workspaces & Preferences

Frames & Content

Styles, Type & Fonts

Pages & Spreads

Color Management

Find/Change

Long Documents

Output

ePub and Tagged File Formats

Export Tagging

HTML is at the heart of a great many electronic document formats, especially on the web. Those letters stand for *HyperText Markup Language*. Essentially, we "mark up" content to tell each chunk what it is—header, subheader, list, regular paragraph, etc. Software, like web browsers, display each chunk based on what it is. A top-level header, marked up with the H1 tag, defaults to bold and quite large, whereas an item in a list would be displayed with a bullet and would be indented. Screen reader software for the visually impaired benefits from the hierarchies and the meaning given by markup tags.

Each style we make (paragraph, character, or object) can have a tag associated with it via Export Tagging. I chose the H1 tag for the chapter header paragraph style in this book. The topic header style gets tagged as H2. For spans of text to which a character style is applied, a tag called "span" can be applied (example: plain text to ***fancy***, then not). To differentiate spans or H2s that should look different than others, each can have its own "class" attribute.

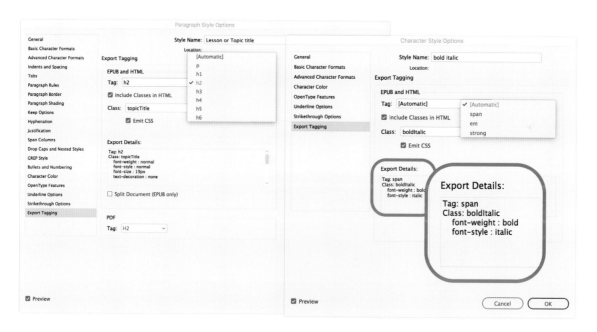

By default, the class will be the same as the style's name. For the HTML-curious, the tags for these two examples will look like this:

```
<h2 class="topicTitle">ePub & Tagged File Formats</h2>
```

```
plain text to <span class="boldItalic">fancy</span>, then not.
```

In the Export Tagging pane of each style options dialog box, you can choose a tag and give a

Workspaces & Preferences

Frames & Content

Styles, Type & Fonts

Pages & Spreads

Color Management

Find/Change

Long Documents

Output

name for the class. The Export Details window shows both, as well as the CSS (*Cascading Style Sheet*) that will be written by InDesign to style each as close to the print version as possible. Those two languages, HTML and CSS, work together; the first is the "what," and the second is how to decorate it. In each paragraph style for which I choose an ePub and HTML Tag, I also add a PDF Tag, so if I export a PDF, it will be on the way to being more disabled-accessible.

Those who are familiar with CSS find themselves frustrated that they cannot customize the CSS they see in the Export Details window. However, during export as HTML or ePub, we can add a CSS file that we have authored that can fine-tune the one authored by InDesign.

Since I'm comfortable writing CSS, I'll create a preliminary CSS file to finesse some of my styles. If I'm using a character style to format page number references, for example, I can write CSS for its class to hide those references in a reflowable ePub. So a phrase like "see page 873" will simply not show up in the ePub because I will have applied a style to it called *hideFromEpub*, and CSS that says `.hideFromEpub { display: none; }`.

Images and other frame content can be tagged as well (usually via an object style), but can also have more elaborate export options applied with an object style or *à la carte* with the Object Export Options dialog box.

Note: To order content composed of both text and images, images *must* be anchored to a text position. Review "Anchored Objects" (page 231). For example, each figure and image in this book is anchored to an otherwise empty paragraph so it "knows" where it is in the flow.

The image above is anchored to a paragraph at the bottom of the text frame on the title page at right

In the example above, a title page will have the dark surround and white-on-black skeleton image *when printed*. But when exported as an ePub, a black-on-white version will be centered below the byline. To include the title page's text frame in an exported ePub (including the image anchored to it), it is added to the Articles panel. Since the other image has not been added, it will not export.

What Gets Exported and How

The most reliable and intuitive way to choose what gets exported as ePub or HTML, and in what order, is by adding those items (articles) to the Articles panel. The name of this panel has confused many. I suggest interpreting the word "article" as you would when discussing items like articles of clothing, not as written pieces. Simply drag a frame into the Articles panel to add it. You'll be prompted for a name. Subsequent items can be added as sub-articles to an existing one or added as new ones. For the novel in the figure, the entire story thread was added by dragging in its first frame! The list of illustrations (LOI), an independent story, was

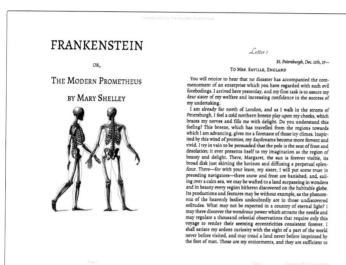

added after it, and the title page before it. Any object or group that is anchored to a paragraph in a story is included with it. For reliable formatting, a complex figure (image frames and text frames grouped together and possibly pasted inside another frame) can be converted into an image. The file format and resolution of that image is specified in the Object Export Options dialog box. The figure here shows the resulting ePub viewed in the Apple iBooks reader (in landscape mode to display a "spread").

The figures in this book are configured with Object Export Options much like the skeleton image. I chose to Rasterize Container (the anchored frame), which converts the frame to an image made of pixels, with a Format of PNG (to preserve quality better than JPEG), and a resolution that can withstand enlargement by the reader. The skeleton image in the example will be 150 ppi. Many images in the ePub of this book will be 300 ppi so they can be enlarged

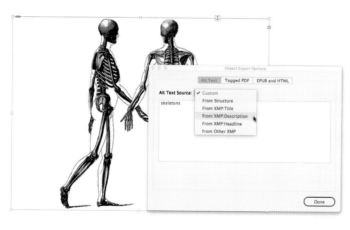

and studied by you, my dear reader. To enhance accessibility, Alt Text can be added by typing (Custom) or automatically by pulling from an image's metadata (XMP).

Fortunately, those settings can be included in the definition of an object style so you can apply them consistently and easily.

Output

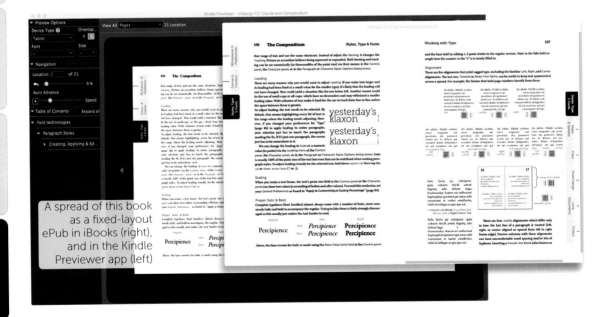

Left: An ePub of this book viewed in the iBooks reader. Double-clicking an image isolates it and enlarges it for closer study (right).

A Kindle offers similar capability.

Most ePubs are *reflowable*; that is, readers may change much of the formatting to suit their taste, including font, text size, orientation, and more. When they do, the text reflows and the "page" count changes. Because of this, the concept of a page is somewhat abstract in the world of e-readers. When I read on my iPad, I set iBooks to scroll mode so the whole book is continuous. In that way, I'm rarely offended by odd breaks that can occur otherwise. Some books, like novels, do perfectly well as reflowable ePubs. Others, like children's books, cookbooks, and others with delicate layout do much better as *fixed-layout* ePubs.

A spread of this book as a fixed-layout ePub in iBooks (right), and in the Kindle Previewer app (left)

With fixed layout, an attempt is made to maintain the position of *everything*. Thus, master page items like page numbers make sense here. There is no need for the Articles panel to order content because all is included just as it is in the print version. However, as an electronic document, our cross references can be tappable hyperlinks (just as we'd use in a reflowable ePub) with no need of a listed page number. Many of InDesign's interactive features are supported as well, subject to limitations of the physical reader and its software.

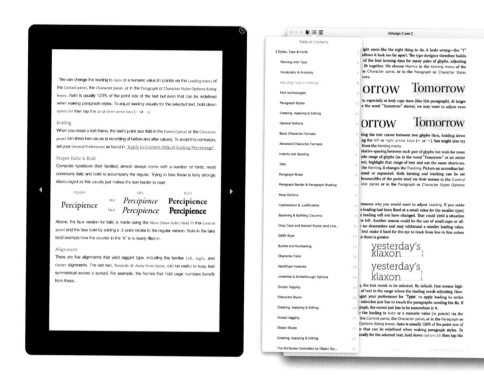

Both fixed and reflowable ePubs offer multiple means of navigation. Both can show a table of contents that you can naviagate with a tap (right, in iBooks), generated by a TOC Style we create in our InDesign file before exporting. Above, we can discern a blue underlined hyperlink cross reference in the Kindle Previewer (left) and a TOC in iBooks (right).

Exporting an ePub

If I'm making a reflowable ePub, I will anchor images (whose Object Export Options are set) to where I want them relative to my text, and then drag content into the Articles panel. I need to drag only one text frame of a story to add the entire story. For a book, this usually means I add title page content, each independent bit of other front matter, the main text flow, and perhaps an index. I name all the articles and order them.

If I have designed a cover, I will note where it is located on my computer so I can designate it during export. One may also choose to rasterize the first page, which is useful if you have a particularly nice title page. I will also double-check that I have set Export Tagging correctly in my various styles.

Output

As careful as I am, I will still miss *something*! But I'll find out after I use File > Export… > ePub (Reflowable) (in this example). The first part of the Export Options dialog, General, has some significant options.

General

Choosing a Version 3 ePub allows for better typography in some readers, as well as interesting interactive features. You choose a Cover graphic from here, too. For Navigation TOC, it's best if you've created (and choose here) a TOC Style. The Content Order will be Same as Articles Panel, as Based on Page Layout is very much *not* what it sounds like. That choice orders content leftmost first, then top down. Horrible. So, we use the Articles panel!

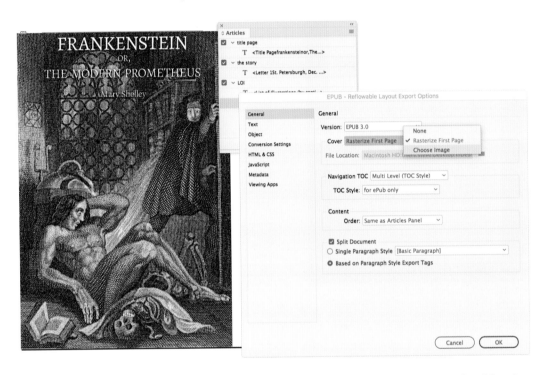

Finally, Split Document is a reliable way to ensure that content using certain styles, like chapter headers, is at the top of a page, even in this relatively pageless medium. If there is only one style that should behave this way, you can choose it here. If there are several, you designate that behavior in the Export Tagging section of those paragraph styles. InDesign Keep Options that specify that a style should start On Next Page will generate CSS that attempts to do that in the eReader, too. Depending on the eReader, that CSS *may* work. The Split Document checkbox (in Export Tagging) *will* work.

Text

This section has far fewer options that need concern us. One that might is Remove Forced Line Breaks. If you've used those *solely* to make better breaks for the print version, you will likely want to enable this option. However, this will remove *all* forced line breaks, and you may want some of them to remain.

Workspaces & Preferences

Frames & Content

Styles, Type & Fonts

Pages & Spreads

Color Management

Find/Change

Long Documents

Output

In this medium with no real pages, where should footnotes be? Your choices are as follows: at the end of the paragraph containing the footnote reference; at the end of the section (essentially converting footnotes into endnotes); or, for ePub version 3, in a popup window.

Object and Conversion Settings

These settings apply to objects if they haven't already been applied with the Object Export Options dialog box (or an object style). I try very hard to use the latter for all images, but if I've missed any, I choose settings here that protect the integrity of my imagery.

HTML & CSS

If you want to strip your text formatting and rely on the eReader's settings only, choose Don't include classes in HTML and disable Generate CSS. If you wish to preserve as much of your print book's formatting as possible, you would leave the defaults, including classes and generating CSS for them. I also Include Embeddable Fonts so those eReaders that support them will use the fonts I've chosen. Be warned, some devices will not. Learn to let go!

It is here you can Add Style Sheet…; that is, your own custom CSS file(s).

JavaScript

If you've programmed some behavior for elements using this scripting language, you can add JavaScript files, too.

Metadata

This data gets added in the deep recesses of the ePub and can be seen by eReaders and eBookstores. However, when publishers submit books to Apple's iBookstore or to Amazon as a Kindle book, they will supply this information (and much more) that will overwrite the data in this form.

Viewing Apps

Here, you add the software applications with which you want to check your work. The default is Adobe Digital Editions. It is, ironically, not a great eReader. I use Apple's iBooks (on both my Mac and in iOS) and the Kindle Previewer app (available for Mac and Windows). There are others, too.

Last ePub Note

As mentioned throughout, some HTML and CSS knowledge is useful when working with ePub. With the right software, you can "crack open" an ePub and access the code inside to perfect the results. Unfortunately, that geeky fun goes beyond the scope of this book.

Output

Workspaces &
Preferences

Frames &
Content

Styles, Type
& Fonts

Pages
& Spreads

Color
Management

Find/Change

Long
Documents

Output

Print

Outputting to a printer connected to your computer is remarkably similar to creating a PDF.

Print Dialog Box

If it's a subset of pages you wish to print, there are many ways to specify which ones. The easiest method is to highlight the pages you want to print in the Pages panel, then right-click on one of them and choose Print Pages… (or Print Spreads… if whole spreads are highlighted). To print an entire single document, choose File > Print…, or for a book, use the Book panel menu and choose Print Book…. The dialog box that appears will also allow you to specify a range of pages to print.

Be prepared to go between various sections of this dialog box to set all the options you need. You will especially have to balance the options in the General and Setup sections, but most of the dialog box will get visited before you're done. The more complex the printing system, the more experimentation you may need to do. What follows are guidelines that will help with that experimentation.

First, and most importantly, choose the Printer. This allows InDesign to show you options specific to that device. I am embarrassed by how many times I've sent data to the wrong printer when more than one is available. When you choose, InDesign will interact with that printer's driver software, and if it's a Postscript printer (like many office laser printers), it will also read data from that printer's PPD (Postscript Printer Description). The Setup section of the dialog box will then show supported paper sizes, for example.

The buttons at lower left (Page Setup… and Printer… on a Mac, Setup… on Windows) are means to access the printer driver software and are likely irrelevant if you take care elsewhere in this dialog box. In fact, if you choose things in the driver that contradict InDesign's settings, trouble could erupt. With inkjet printers, however, it may be necessary to tweak or disable the driver setting to complement settings in the Color section of InDesign's Print dialog.

General

When specifying which pages to print, you may have to supply a lot of data (like a section prefix along with page number or letter), unless you're using Absolute page numbering. For example, if your document has two sections with prefixes "SecA" and "SecB" and they use different number styles, you may have to specify a range like "SecA:xii-SecB:27." With Absolute numbering, you may be able to use "12-45" if page SecB:27 is the 45th page, for example. Even with Absolute numbering, you can do fancy things. To print the first 8 pages, use "-8," or for page 15 to the last page, use "15-" with no need to specify the last page's number. Discontiguous ranges are allowed, too, separated by commas like this: "1-6, 13, 15-18, 20-."

Choosing to print Spreads rather than Pages is a nice way to see *reader spreads*. I may print a few spreads to see if I like a document's design. When there are facing pages, *printer spreads* may be quite different; see "Print Booklet" (page 358). Also, if the first spread of the chosen page range is a single page (like a title page), the Preview in the lower left of the Print dialog may not show two pages. Will a spread need to be printed smaller or turned 90° to fit the chosen paper? We deal with that in the next section.

Choose how many Copies you desire. Collating slows the process considerably. Reverse Order prints the last page first, which is useful if your printer spits out prints right-side up.

Set to print **Spreads**.

Paper Size is typically the same as your pages, but here it's set big enough to show a full-size spread. The **Orientation** is also set to right-side first.

I chose **Centered** as the **Page Position**.

The **Thumbnails** option can fit many pages or spreads on a sheet, rather like a photographer's contact sheet.

Setup

Based on your printer choice, the choices for Paper Size will vary. If you need to squeeze a too-large page onto the paper in your printer, you can check Scale To Fit. Alternatively, you can Tile your page onto multiple sheets of paper (adhesive not included).

If you need to supply bleed, then you need to print on paper larger than your pages. The next section will help, too.

Marks and Bleed

If you're printing on paper larger than your pages (or spreads), you have room for Crop Marks and other informational ornamentation.

Output

Use sufficient **Offset** for crop marks so you don't see bits of them after a sloppy trim.

Bleed can be added here or can be inherited from your document settings. It appears pink in the little preview.

You can set Bleed to match your document's, or choose some other value. If you've put notes in a Slug area, you can include that, too.

Output

Depending on whether the printer considers itself a CMYK or RGB device, your choices here will change. Inkjet printers and some laser printers want RGB data, which they separate into values for each of their inks or toners. To them, we send Color data as Composite RGB. To devices that truly use cyan, magenta, yellow, and black ink or toner, we can send Composite CMYK. However, for those devices it's usually better to create a PDF and print that. A few of you (who work in print shops) may want to see Separations, and can then view the Trapping, Flip, and Screening controls.

Graphics

If you're printing drafts or other non-final versions, choosing Optimized Subsampling in the Send Data menu will yield decent-looking prints quickly. Proxy will be even faster, but graphics will have few legible features. For no graphics at all, but boxes marked with an X, use None. This is useful for proofreading without the distraction of imagery. For your final work, choose All.

The Fonts section is for Postscript printers only (not inkjets, for example), and the choices here can be tricky. Fonts can be stored at the printer (or drives attached to it). These are supposed to be listed in the PPD file. If you want to have a fast print, but have time to risk a choice that may fail, set Download to Subset and leave Download PPD Fonts unchecked. The first will send only those characters of a font that are used in the document. The second will not bother to send any font data for fonts listed in the PPD, as they're resident in the printer. If you get weird substitutions or characters go missing, you can choose to Download PPD Fonts and/or Download Complete. Either or both will slow the works, but will increase reliability.

Color Management

In the Output section of the Print dialog, you usually choose one of the Composite settings (Gray, RGB, or CMYK). In the Color Management section, you pick specifically which gray, RGB, or CMYK profile should be used. This is what that whole "Color Management" chapter is about! You thought you could skip it, but maybe you shouldn't.

Most laser and inkjet printers should probably be sent Composite RGB. In the case of an office laser printer, I'd choose sRGB as the Printer Profile and let the driver take it from there. If I chose Composite CMYK, most printers around the office would expect U.S. Web Coated (SWOP), so I'd choose that, checking the box Preserve CMYK Numbers for reasons explained elsewhere in this book—"The Useful Rigidity of CMYK" (page 301). For many inkjet printers, like the one a few feet from me, I'd choose a profile specific to it and the paper on which I'm printing.

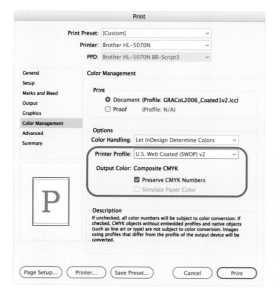

Printing to an office laser printer. **Composite CMYK** with the **SWOP** profile chosen. **Preserve CMYK Numbers** to keep black from reseparating.

Printing to my home inkjet printer. **Composite RGB** with a profile specific to the paper used.

Advanced

The key setting here is the Transparency Flattener Preset. For the best results (thus, when printing your finals) choose [High Resolution]. If your printer mistreats overlapping transparent objects or makes transparent effects (like shadows) look terrible, you can have InDesign rasterize the document by checking Print as Bitmap and choosing or typing whatever resolution you need. This essentially makes each page a big image that might be easier for the printer software to digest.

Print Booklet

Reader spreads are not printer spreads. Lets say you have a multi-page document with facing pages. In InDesign, when you look at pages 6 and 7, that's what the reader will see, too, once the document is printed and *assembled*. As an experiment, *carefully* remove the staples from the center of thin weekly magazine. Go to some random page and examine what other pages are printed on the same piece of paper. You don't even have to remove the staples if it makes you feel bad. The process of getting pages on the correct sheets of paper is called *imposition*. If you need no more than two pages per side of paper, Print Booklet can help you make your documents in a similar way.

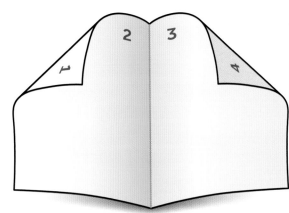

A four-page result from **Print Booklet**. Consider 8.5" x 11" pages on 11" x 17" paper folded in half.

Since this needs only one sheet of paper, this can use either **Saddle Stitch** or (a little silly) **Perfect Bound** with a four-page signature.

When you choose File > Print Booklet…, your primary choices for Booklet Type are Saddle Stitch (where every sheet is folded in half and stacked, staples holding them together like the magazine described above) or Perfect Bound (in which groups of pages are bound together in *signatures* and the signatures are then bound together). I avoid the choices with Consecutive in the name because they do not perform as they should. With Perfect Bound, you must also specify the size of the signatures (in multiples of four, of course).

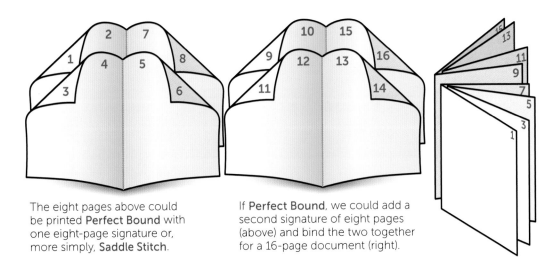

The eight pages above could be printed **Perfect Bound** with one eight-page signature or, more simply, **Saddle Stitch**.

If **Perfect Bound**, we could add a second signature of eight pages (above) and bind the two together for a 16-page document (right).

Keyboard Shortcuts

The Adobe applications allow us to customize keyboard shortcuts. Use Edit > Keyboard Shortcuts..., create a new Set based on the defaults, and tweak or invent shortcuts for the commands you use most. What follows are many of InDesign's default shortcuts, written in this manner:
mac version/windows version

Mac

Windows

Workspaces & Preferences

Frames & Content

Styles, Type & Fonts

Pages & Spreads

Color Management

Find/Change

Long Documents

Output

Keyboard Shortcuts

Note: Some keyboards have two keys labeled "Enter." I refer to the key that ends paragraphs as "Return." The other, which I refer to as "Enter," creates column breaks.

Preferences

Preferences > General...	⌘–K/Ctrl–K

File Menu

Browse in Bridge...	option–⌘–O/Alt–Ctrl–O
Close	⌘–W/Ctrl–W
Document Setup...	option–⌘–P/Alt–Ctrl–P
Export...	⌘–E/Ctrl–E
File Info...	option–shift–⌘–I/Alt–Shift–Ctrl–I
New > Document...	⌘–N/Ctrl–N
Open...	⌘–O/Ctrl–O
Package...	option–shift–⌘–P/Alt–Shift–Ctrl–P
Place...	⌘–D/Ctrl–D
Print...	⌘–P/Ctrl–P
Save	⌘–S/Ctrl–S
Save As...	shift–⌘–S/Shift–Ctrl–S
Save a Copy...	option–⌘–S/Alt–Ctrl–S

Edit Menu

Copy	⌘–C/Ctrl–C
Cut	⌘–X/Ctrl–X
Deselect All	shift–⌘–A/Shift–Ctrl–A
Duplicate	option–shift–⌘–D/Alt–Shift–Ctrl–D
Edit in Story Editor	⌘–Y/Ctrl–Y
Find Next	option–⌘–F/Alt–Ctrl–F
Find/Change...	⌘–F/Ctrl–F
Paste	⌘–V/Ctrl–V
Paste Into	option–⌘–V/Alt–Ctrl–V
Paste in Place	option–shift–⌘–V/Alt–Shift–Ctrl–V
Paste without Formatting	shift–⌘–V/Shift–Ctrl–V
Quick Apply...	⌘–return/Ctrl–Return
Redo	shift–⌘–Z/Shift–Ctrl–Z
Select All	⌘–A/Ctrl–A
Spelling > Check Spelling...	⌘–I/Ctrl–I
Step and Repeat...	option–⌘–U/Alt–Ctrl–U
Toggle search direction	option–⌘–return/Alt–Ctrl–Return
Undo	⌘–Z/Ctrl–Z

Layout Menu

First Page	shift-⌘-page up/Shift-Ctrl-Page Up
Go Back	⌘-page up/Ctrl-Page Up
Go Forward	⌘-page down/Ctrl-Page Down
Go to Page...	⌘-J/Ctrl-J
Last Page	shift-⌘-page down/Shift-Ctrl-Page Down
Next Page	shift-Page Down
Next Spread	option-page down/Alt-Page Down
Pages > Add Page	shift-⌘-P/Shift-Ctrl-P
Previous Page	shift-Page Up
Previous Spread	option-page up/Alt-Page Up

Type Menu

Create Outlines	shift-⌘-O/Shift-Ctrl-O
Create outlines without deleting text	option-shift-⌘-O/Alt-Shift-Ctrl-O
Go to Endnote Text	shift-⌘-E/Shift-Ctrl-E
Hide Hidden Characters	option-⌘-I/Alt-Ctrl-I
Insert Column Break	Enter
Insert Forced Line Break	shift-Return
Insert Frame Break	shift-Enter
Insert Page Break	⌘-Enter/Ctrl-Enter
Discretionary Hyphen	shift-⌘--/Shift-Ctrl--
Nonbreaking Hyphen	option-⌘--/Alt-Ctrl--
Current Page Number Marker	option-shift-⌘-N/Alt-Shift-Ctrl-N
Indent to Here	⌘-\/Ctrl-\
Right Indent Tab	shift-Tab
Straight Double Quote Marks	control+shift-'/Alt-Shift-'
Straight Single Quote (Apostrophe)	control+'/Alt-'
Insert Em Space	shift-⌘-M/Shift-Ctrl-M
Insert En Space	shift-⌘-N/Shift-Ctrl-N
Insert Nonbreaking Space	option-⌘-X/Alt-Ctrl-X
Insert Thin Space	option-shift-⌘-M/Alt-Shift-Ctrl-M
Tabs	shift-⌘-T/Shift-Ctrl-T
Track Changes > Next Change	⌘-page down/Ctrl-Page Down
Track Changes > Previous Change	⌘-page up/Ctrl-Page Up

Object Menu

Arrange > Bring Forward	⌘-]/Ctrl-]
Arrange > Bring to Front	shift-⌘-]/Shift-Ctrl-]
Arrange > Send Backward	⌘-[/Ctrl-[
Arrange > Send to Back	shift-⌘-[/Shift-Ctrl-[
Effects > Drop Shadow...	option-⌘-M/Alt-Ctrl-M
Fitting > Center Content	shift-⌘-E/Shift-Ctrl-E

Workspaces & Preferences

Frames & Content

Styles, Type & Fonts

Pages & Spreads

Color Management

Find/Change

Long Documents

Output

Fitting > Fill Frame Proportionally	option–shift–⌘–C/Alt–Shift–Ctrl–C
Fitting > Fit Content Proportionally	option–shift–⌘–E/Alt–Shift–Ctrl–E
Fitting > Fit Content to Frame	option–⌘–E/Alt–Ctrl–E
Fitting > Fit Frame to Content	option–⌘–C/Alt–Ctrl–C
Group	⌘–G/Ctrl–G
Hide	⌘–3/Ctrl–3
Lock	⌘–L/Ctrl–L
Make Compound Path	⌘–8/Ctrl–8
Release Compound Path	option–shift–⌘–8/Alt–Shift–Ctrl–8
Select Container	Escape
Select Content	shift–Escape
Select First Object Above	option–shift–⌘–]/Alt–Shift–Ctrl–]
Select Last Object Below	option–shift–⌘–[/Alt–Shift–Ctrl–[
Select Next Object Above	option–⌘–]/Alt–Ctrl–]
Select Next Object Below	option–⌘–[/Alt–Ctrl–[
Show All on Spread	option–⌘–3/Alt–Ctrl–3
Text Frame Options...	⌘–B/Ctrl–B
Transform Sequence Again	option–⌘–4/Alt–Ctrl–4
Transform > Move...	shift–⌘–M/Shift–Ctrl–M
Ungroup	shift–⌘–G/Shift–Ctrl–G
Unlock All on Spread	option–⌘–L/Alt–Ctrl–L

Table Menu

Cell Options	option–⌘–B/Alt–Ctrl–B
Delete Column	shift–delete/Shift–Backspace
Delete Row	⌘–delete/Ctrl–Backspace
Insert Table...	option–shift–⌘–T/Alt–Shift–Ctrl–T
Insert Column...	option–⌘–9/Alt–Ctrl–9
Insert Row...	⌘–9/Ctrl–9
Select Cell	⌘–//Ctrl–/
Select Column	option–⌘–3/Alt–Ctrl–3
Select Row	⌘–3/Ctrl–3
Select Table	option–⌘–A/Alt–Ctrl–A
Table Setup...	option–shift–⌘–B/Alt–Shift–Ctrl–B

View Menu

Actual Size	⌘–1/Ctrl–1
Clear Object-Level Display Settings	shift–⌘–F2/Shift–Ctrl–F2
Fast Display Performance	option–shift–⌘–Z/Alt–Shift–Ctrl–Z
High Quality Display Performance	control+option–⌘–H/Alt–Ctrl–H
Typical Display Performance	option–⌘–Z/Alt–Ctrl–Z
Entire Pasteboard	option–shift–⌘–0/Alt–Shift–Ctrl–0
Hide Frame Edges	control+⌘–H/Ctrl–H

Hide Text Threads	option–⌘–Y/Alt–Ctrl–Y
Fit Page in Window	⌘–0/Ctrl–0
Fit Spread in Window	option–⌘–0/Alt–Ctrl–0
Show/Hide Guides	⌘–;/Ctrl–;
Lock/Unlock Guides	option–⌘–;/Alt–Ctrl–;
Show Baseline Grid	option–⌘–'/Alt–Ctrl–'
Show Document Grid	⌘–'/Ctrl–'
Show/Hide Smart Guides	⌘–U/Ctrl–U
Toggle Snap to Document Grid	shift–⌘–'/Shift–Ctrl–'
Toggle Snap to Guides	shift–⌘–;/Shift–Ctrl–;
Show/Hide Rulers	⌘–R/Ctrl–R
Toggle Overprint Preview	option–shift–⌘–Y/Alt–Shift–Ctrl–Y
Zoom In	⌘–=/Ctrl–=
Zoom Out	⌘––/Ctrl––

Window Menu

Color Panel	F6
Swatches Panel	F5
Control Panel	option–⌘–6/Alt–Ctrl–6
Effects Panel	shift–⌘–F10/Shift–Ctrl–F10
Info Panel	F8
Layers Panel	F7
Links Panel	shift–⌘–D/Shift–Ctrl–D
Align Panel	shift–F7
Preflight Panel	option–shift–⌘–F/Alt–Shift–Ctrl–F
Separations Preview Panel	shift–F6
Character Styles Panel	shift–⌘–F11/Shift–Ctrl–F11
Object Styles Panel	⌘–F7/Ctrl–F7
Paragraph Styles Panel	⌘–F11/Ctrl–F11
Text Wrap Panel	option–⌘–W/Alt–Ctrl–W
Character Panel	⌘–T/Ctrl–T
Glyphs Panel	option–shift–F11/Alt–Shift–F11
Index Panel	shift–F8
Paragraph Panel	option–⌘–T/Alt–Ctrl–T
Table Panel	shift–F9
Scripts Panel	option–⌘–F11/Alt–Ctrl–F11

Object Editing

Decrease scale by 1%	⌘–,/Ctrl–,
Decrease scale by 5%	option–⌘–,/Alt–Ctrl–,
End Path Drawing	Enter or Return
Increase scale by 1%	⌘–./Ctrl–.
Increase scale by 5%	option–⌘–./Alt–Ctrl–.

Nudge down	↓
Nudge down 1/10	shift-⌘-↓/Shift-Ctrl-↓
Nudge down 1/10 duplicate	option-shift-⌘-Down/Alt-Shift-Ctrl-↓
Nudge down duplicate	option-↓/Alt-↓
Nudge down x10	shift-↓
Nudge down x10 duplicate	option-shift-↓/Alt-Shift-↓
Nudge left	←
Nudge left 1/10	shift-⌘-←/Shift-Ctrl-←
Nudge left 1/10 duplicate	option-shift-⌘-Left/Alt-Shift-Ctrl-←
Nudge left duplicate	option-←/Alt-←
Nudge left x10	shift-←
Nudge left x10 duplicate	option-shift-←/Alt-Shift-←
Nudge right	→
Nudge right 1/10	shift-⌘-→/Shift-Ctrl-→
Nudge right 1/10 duplicate	option-shift-⌘-Right/Alt-Shift-Ctrl-→
Nudge right duplicate	option-→/Alt-→
Nudge right x10	shift-→
Nudge right x10 duplicate	option-shift-→/Alt-Shift-→
Nudge up	↑
Nudge up 1/10	shift-⌘-↑/Shift-Ctrl-↑
Nudge up 1/10 duplicate	option-shift-⌘-Up/Alt-Shift-Ctrl-↑
Nudge up duplicate	option-↑/Alt-↑
Nudge up x10	shift-↑
Nudge up x10 duplicate	option-shift-↑/Alt-Shift-↑
Pin Bottom Edge	option-⌘-↓/Alt-Ctrl-↓
Pin Left Edge	option-⌘-←/Alt-Ctrl-←
Pin Right Edge	option-⌘-→/Alt-Ctrl-→
Pin Top Edge	option-⌘-↑/Alt-Ctrl-↑
Resize Horizontally	option-shift-H/Alt-Shift-H
Resize Vertically	option-shift-V/Alt-Shift-V
Select all Guides	option-⌘-G/Alt-Ctrl-G

Panel Menus

Redefine Character Style	option-shift-⌘-C/Alt-Shift-Ctrl-C
Character > All Caps	shift-⌘-K/Shift-Ctrl-K
Character > Small Caps	shift-⌘-H/Shift-Ctrl-H
Character > Strikethrough	shift-⌘-//Shift-Ctrl-/
Character > Subscript	option-shift-⌘-=/Alt-Shift-Ctrl-=
Character > Superscript	shift-⌘-=/Shift-Ctrl-=
Character > Underline	shift-⌘-U/Shift-Ctrl-U
Override All Master Page Items	option-shift-⌘-L/Alt-Shift-Ctrl-L
Redefine Paragraph Style	option-shift-⌘-R/Alt-Shift-Ctrl-R
Paragraph > Justification...	option-shift-⌘-J/Alt-Shift-Ctrl-J

Paragraph > Keep Options...	option–⌘–K/Alt–Ctrl–K
Paragraph > Paragraph Rules...	option–⌘–J/Alt–Ctrl–J
Tags > Autotag	option–shift–⌘–F/Alt–Shift–Ctrl–F7

Text and Tables

Align center	shift–⌘–C/Shift–Ctrl–C
Align force justify	shift–⌘–F/Shift–Ctrl–F
Align justify	shift–⌘–J/Shift–Ctrl–J
Align left	shift–⌘–L/Shift–Ctrl–L
Align right	shift–⌘–R/Shift–Ctrl–R
Align to baseline grid	option–shift–⌘–G/Alt–Shift–Ctrl–G
Apply bold	shift–⌘–B/Shift–Ctrl–B
Apply italic	shift–⌘–I/Shift–Ctrl–I
Apply normal	shift–⌘–Y/Shift–Ctrl–Y
Auto leading	option–shift–⌘–A/Alt–Shift–Ctrl–A
Auto-hyphenate on/off	option–shift–⌘–H/Alt–Shift–Ctrl–H
Decrease baseline shift	option–shift–↓/Alt–Shift–↓
Decrease baseline shift x5	option–shift–⌘–Down/Alt–Shift–Ctrl–↓
Decrease kerning/tracking	option–←/Alt–←
Decrease kerning/tracking x5	option–⌘–←/Alt–Ctrl–←
Decrease leading	option–↑/Alt–↑
Decrease leading x5	option–⌘–↑/Alt–Ctrl–↑
Decrease point size	shift–⌘–,/Shift–Ctrl–,
Decrease point size x5	option–shift–⌘–,/Alt–Shift–Ctrl–,
Decrease word space	option–⌘–delete/Alt–Ctrl–Backspace
Decrease word space x5	option–shift–⌘–delete/Alt–Shift–Ctrl–Backspace
Delete one word to the left	⌘–delete/Ctrl–Backspace
Delete one word to the right	⌘–⌦ delete/Ctrl–Del
Find Next	shift–F2
Increase baseline shift	option–shift–↑/Alt–Shift–↑
Increase baseline shift x5	option–shift–⌘–↑/Alt–Shift–Ctrl–↑
Increase kerning/tracking	option–shift–→/Alt–Shift–→
Increase kerning/tracking x5	option–⌘–→/Alt–Ctrl–→
Increase leading	option–↓/Alt–↓
Increase leading x5	option–⌘–↓/Alt–Ctrl–↓
Increase point size	shift–⌘–./Shift–Ctrl–.
Increase point size x5	option–shift–⌘–./Alt–Shift–Ctrl–.
Increase word space	option–⌘–\/Alt–Ctrl–\
Increase word space x5	option–shift–⌘–\/Alt–Shift–Ctrl–\
Load Find and Find Next instance	shift–F1
Load Find with selected text	⌘–F1/Ctrl–F1
Load Replace with selected text	⌘–F2/Ctrl–F2
Move Down in Table	↓

Workspaces & Preferences

Frames & Content

Styles, Type & Fonts

Pages & Spreads

Color Management

Find/Change

Long Documents

Output

Move Left in Table	←
Move Right in Table	→
Move Up in Table	↑
Move down one line	↓
Move to First Cell in Table Column	option–page up/Alt–Page Up
Move to First Cell in Table Row	option–home/Alt–Home
Move to First Row in Table Frame	Page Up
Move to Last Cell in Table Column	option–page down/Alt–Page Down
Move to Last Cell in Table Row	option–end/Alt–End
Move to Last Row in Table Frame	Page Down
Move to Next Cell	Tab
Move to Previous Cell	shift–Tab
Move to beginning of story	⌘–home/Ctrl–Home
Move to end of story	⌘–end/Ctrl–End
Move to the end of the line	End
Move to the left one character	←
Move to the left one word	⌘–←/Ctrl–←
Move to the next paragraph	⌘–↓/Ctrl–↓
Move to the previous paragraph	⌘–↑/Ctrl–↑
Move to the right one character	→
Move to the right one word	⌘–→/Ctrl–→
Move to the start of the line	Home
Move up one line	↑
Normal horizontal text scale	shift–⌘–X/Shift–Ctrl–X
Normal vertical text scale	option–shift–⌘–X/Alt–Shift–Ctrl–X
Table Object Down	↓
Escape Table Object Context	Escape
Table Object Left	←
Object Move to Next Cell	Tab
Object Move to Previous Cell	shift–Tab
Table Object Right	→
Table Object Up	↑
Recompose all stories	option–⌘–//Alt–Ctrl–/
Replace with Change To text	⌘–F3/Ctrl–F3
Replace with Change To text, Find Next	shift–F3
Reset kerning and tracking	option–⌘–Q/Alt–Ctrl–Q
Select Table Cells Above	shift–↑
Select Table Cells Below	shift–↓
Select Table Cells to the Left	shift–←
Select Table Cells to the Right	shift–→
Select line	shift–⌘–\/Shift–Ctrl–\
Select one character to the left	shift–←
Select one character to the right	shift–→

Select one line above	shift–↑
Select one line below	shift–↓
Select one paragraph before	shift–⌘–↑/Shift–Ctrl–↑
Select one paragraph forward	shift–⌘–↓/Shift–Ctrl–↓
Select one word to the left	shift–⌘–←/Shift–Ctrl–←
Select one word to the right	shift–⌘–→/Shift–Ctrl–→
Select to beginning of story	shift–⌘–Home/Shift–Ctrl–Home
Select to end of story	shift–⌘–End/Shift–Ctrl–End
Select to the end of the line	shift–End
Select to the start of the line	shift–Home
Start Row on Next Column	Enter
Start Row on Next Frame	shift–Enter
Toggle Cell/Text Selection	Escape
Toggle Typographer's Quotes Pref	option–shift–⌘–'/Alt–Shift–Ctrl–'
Update missing font list	option–shift–⌘–//Alt–Shift–Ctrl–/

Tools

Add Anchor Point Tool	=
Apply Color	,
Apply Gradient	.
Apply None	/
Apply default fill and stroke colors	D
Color Theme Tool	shift–I
Convert Direction Point Tool	shift–C
Delete Anchor Point Tool	–
Direct Selection Tool	A
Ellipse Tool	L
Eyedropper Tool	I
Free Transform Tool	E
Gap Tool	U
Gradient Feather Tool	shift–G
Gradient Swatch Tool	G
Hand Tool	H
Line Tool	\
Measure Tool	K
Page Tool	shift–P
Pen Tool	P
Pencil Tool	N
Rectangle Frame Tool	F
Rectangle Tool	M
Rotate Tool	R
Scale Tool	S
Scissors Tool	C

Selection Tool	V
Shear Tool	O
Swap fill and stroke activation	X
Swap fill and stroke colors	shift–X
Toggle Text and Object Control	J
Toggle preview	W
Type Tool	T
Type on a Path Tool	shift–T
Zoom Tool	Z

Views, Navigation

100% size	⌘–1/Ctrl–1
200% size	⌘–2/Ctrl–2
400% size	⌘–4/Ctrl–4
50% size	⌘–5/Ctrl–5
Access zoom percentage box	option–⌘–5/Alt–Ctrl–5
Activate last-used field in panel	option–⌘–`/Alt–Ctrl–`
Close all	option–shift–⌘–W/Alt–Shift–Ctrl–W
Close document	shift–⌘–W/Shift–Ctrl–W
First Spread	Home or
	option–shift–page up/Alt–Shift–Page Up
Fit Selection in Window	option–⌘–=/Alt–Ctrl–=
Force redraw	shift–F5
Go to first frame in thread	option–shift–⌘–Page/Alt–Shift–Ctrl–Page Up
Go to last frame in thread	option–shift–⌘–Page/Alt–Shift–Ctrl–Page Down
Go to next frame in thread	option–⌘–page down/Alt–Ctrl–Page Down
Go to previous frame in thread	option–⌘–page up/Alt–Ctrl–Page Up
Last Spread	End or
	option–shift–page down/Alt–Shift–Page Down
New default document	option–⌘–N/Alt–Ctrl–N
Open/Close all panels in side tabs	option–⌘–Tab/Alt–Ctrl–Tab
Save all	option–shift–⌘–S/Alt–Shift–Ctrl–S
Scroll down one screen	Page Down
Scroll up one screen	Page Up
Show/Hide all panels	Tab
Show/Hide all panels except tools	shift–Tab
Toggle Measurement System	option–shift–⌘–U/Alt–Shift–Ctrl–U
Toggle Character and Paragraph Modes in Control Panel	option–⌘–7/Alt–Ctrl–7

Index

+ (next to style name), 57

A

Absolute Numbering, 165
Adjust Scaling Percentage, 165
Adobe Fonts, 19, 52, 240–241
    Font menu, access via, 31
Adobe Stock, 9
Advanced Type preferences, 168
align objects, 36, 216–219
    Align panel, 218–219
    key object, 219
align text, 53
    paragraph styles, and, 246
anchored objects, 231–234
    custom, 232–234
    text wrap, and, 234
Animated Zoom, 7
Appearance of Black preferences, 179
Apply to Content, 165
Arrange menu, 37
arrow keys, preferences, 171
Articles panel, 156, 349
Autocorrect preferences, 175

B

back cover, brochure, 132
Baseline Grid
    preferences, 172
    text frame options, 205
baseline shift, 171
black, appearance, 179
bleed, 279
Blend Mode, 227

Book document, 315–317
    adding documents, 315
    assembling documents, 150
    chapter numbering, 325
    creating, 315–316
    opening a document, 151
    page numbers, 151, 315–316
    panel notifications, 317
    reorder documents, 151
    sync documents, 317
booklet, print, 358
bullets, 257–258

C

Calibre, 156
captions
    grouping with images, 214–215
    numbered, 258–259
    paragraph styles, and, 243
    text variables and, 326
CC Libraries, storing styles, 67
Character panel, 32
character styles, 61–62, 263–266
    applying, 62, 265
    CC Libraries, and, 67
    clear overrides, 74
    consistency, 263
    creating, 61-62, 264–265
    editing, 62, 266
    output tagging, 266
    paste text without formatting, 66
    Preserve Local Overrides, 71
    protection, 264
    Redefine Style, 62
    Remove Styles and Formatting from
        Text and Tables, 71
    Style Mapping, 70
    Style Name Conflicts, 69
choke (Effects), 228
CIELAB, 296

clear overrides, 74

Clipboard Handling preferences, 182

CMYK, 294, 301

color, 293–302
    CIELAB, 296
    CMYK, 294, 301
    color conversion, 301, 342
    color space, 297
    Lab, 296
    monitors, and, 298
    output, 300–302
    PDF output, 342–344
    preserve CMYK build, 301
    print dialog, 357
    printers, and, 298
    process, 295
    profiles, 299–300, 342–343
    RGB, 294, 300
    spot, 295
    swatch, *see* swatches
    text legibility, and, 301
    theory, 296–298

Color Mode, 44

Color panel dropper, 17

Color Theme (interface), 5

columns, 280
    see also, text frames

Composition preferences, 169–170

compound path, 225

compression, PDF output, 341

Content Grabber, 18, 34, 199

Content-Aware Fit, 4, 34, 211

copy object, 220

Creative Cloud app, 1

cropping, 4

cross references, 141, 328–330
    arbitrary text, 142
    creating, 328
    paragraph styles, and, 141
    text anchors, 142, 328

CSS, 348

cursor and gesture options, 166

D

defaults
    paragraph styles, 59
    setting, 45

Dictionary preferences, 174

Direct Selection tool, 224

Display Performance preferences, 7, 178
    default view, 7

distribute space, 37, 218

document window, 9

document, new, 11–12

Donut, 18, 34, 199

downloadable files, 1

drop caps, 254

E

Effects panel, 227–228

Ellipse Frame tool, 15, 190

endnotes, 333–335

ePub, 156–161, 347–353
    applications, 156
    Articles panel, 156, 349
    content included, 156–157, 349–351
    content order, 156–157
    custom layout, 158
    export tagging, 159, 347–348
    exporting, 351–353
    fixed layout, 156, 350–351
    fonts, preserving, 157–159
    generating, 159–160, 351–353
    HTML, 347
    object export options, 158
    object styles, and, 158–159
    output, 156–161
    page layout, 156, 349
    rasterize container, 349

reflowable, 156, 350

XML, 156

Excel file, placing, 81–82, 272

F

facing pages, 279

Fast (Display Performance), 7, 178

File Handling preferences, 180

fill color

applying, 36

gradient, 194–195

paragraph shading, 251

swatch, create new, 192–193

Fill Frame Proportionally, 16, 34, 210

Find Fonts, 46–48

Find/Change, 303–313

applying styles, 72

basics, 304–307

characters, special, 306–307

clipboard, 307

dialog breakdown, 304

formatting, 305–306

glyphs, 147–148, 312

grep, *see* grep

metacharacters, 307

object formatting, 148–149, 313

removing content with, 305

save queries, 74

set scope, 305

Whole Word button, 305

wildcards, 307

Fit Content Proportionately, 34, 210

Fit Frame to Content, 211

Font menu, 31

fonts, 240–241

Adobe Fonts, 19, 31, 52, 241

bold, 238

highlight substitutions, 170

installing, 52

italic, 238

missing, 19, 46, 241

sources for, 52, 241

substitute, 46–48

technologies, 240

footnotes, 207, 331–332

fractions, converting to decimal, 12

Frame Fitting options, 34, 210–211

frame tools, 35, 190–191

frames

alternating between frame and content, 198

combining, 225

content vs., 30–31

corners, edit, 226

creating, 13, 190–191

effects, 226–228

Ellipse Frame tool, 15, 190

Fill with Placeholder Text, 31

fills and strokes, 36, 192–197

gridify, 191

images, *see* image frames

master pages, and, 106, 284–286

multiple frames, creating at once, 39

polygon, 191

primary text, 116

Rectangle Frame tool, 13, 190

repositioning, 15

resizing, 13, 222

selecting, 13

Smart Guides, 15

text, *see* text frames

unassigned, 36

Freda, 156

Free Transform tool, 221, 224

front cover, brochure, 131

G

gatefolds, 290

General preferences, 4, 164–165
    object scaling, 165
    Page Numbering, 164
    Prevent Selection of Locked Objects, 165
    Start Workspace, 4, 164

Glyphs panel, 23, 147

glyphs, 22, 312
    Find/Change, 147–148, 312
    highlight substitutions, 170
    missing glyph protection, 168

GPU Performance preferences, 7, 179
    Animated Zoom, 7

gradient, fill or stroke, 194–195

Greeking, 5

grep, 308–311
    Find/Change Query menu, 310
    formatting with, 309
    GREP Style, 64, 256
    marking subexpression, 309
    name sort, 146
    negative lookbehind, 311
    positive lookahead, 257, 310
    query, building, 309
    resources, 311

grid of images, 39, 213

grid of objects, *see* gridify

grid, document, 173

gridify, 38–40, 191, 213

Grids preferences, 172–173

group objects, 39, 214–215
    accessing contents, 215
    object styles and groups, 94–95

Guides & Pasteboard preferences, 173

guides, 173, 216–217
    column guides, 280
    Smart Guides, 15, 37, 173, 217

H

Hand tool, preferences, 5

Help, 9

High Quality (Display Performance), 7, 178

hyphenation
    exceptions, 174
    Paragraph panel, 23
    paragraph styles, and, 252–253

I

iBooks, 156

IDML, 346

image frames, 33
    alternating between frame and content, 198
    center content, 211
    Content-Aware Fit, 4, 34, 211
    drawing, 34, 209
    Fill Frame Proportionally, 16, 34, 210
    Fit Content Proportionately, 34, 210
    Fit Frame to Content, 211
    Frame Fitting options, 34, 210–211
    gridify, 39–40, 213
    master pages and, 108, 284–286
    moving, 33, 219–220
    object styles and, 91–93

images
    anchored, 231
    Content Grabber, 18, 34, 199
    copy, 220
    edit orginal, 212
    effective resolution, 209
    flip, 223
    frames, *see* image frames
    grid, creating, 39, 213
    inline, 232
    linking vs. embedding, 33–34, 208
    links, missing, 48–50, 212
    links, modified, 48–50, 211–212
    master pages and, 108

moving in frame, 18, 34 , 198–199

placing multiple images, 39–40, 208–209

placing, 13, 33–34, 208–209

resizing, 198, 222

rotate, 220–221

scaling, 222

shearing, 223

Import Options, 69

in port, 86

indents, text, 53–54

hanging, 54

InDesign Help, 9

indexes, 336–337

Interface preferences, 5, 165–166

Appearance, 165

Color Theme, 5, 165

cursor and gesture options, 166

Hand tool, 5

Live Screen Drawing, 5

multi-touch gestures, 166

panels, 166

pasteboard color, 165

show thumbnails on place, 166

tool tips, 166

J

justification, paragraph styles and, 252–253

K

Keep Options, 63, 252

kerning, 54, 237–238

highlight adjustments, 170

keyboard shortcut, 172

paragraph styles, and, 245

keyboard increments, preferences, 171

keyboard shortcuts, 27–29, 359–368

customizing, 188

Edit menu, 360

File menu, 360

Layout menu, 361

object editing, 363

Object menu, 361

panel menus, 364

Preferences, 360

Table menu, 362

tables, 365

text, 365

tools, 367

Type menu, 361

View menu, 362

views and navigation, 368

warning, 27

Window menu, 363

Kindle, 156

Kobo, 156

L

Lab (color space), 296

language, 174

launching InDesign, 1

layers panel, 14

layers, 111–112, 318–320

contents, disclose, 318

creating, 319

deleting, 320

locking, 15, 112

moving content, 319

new, 14

nonprintable, 112, 320

panel, 14

protecting content, 112

reordering, 112, 319

separating content, 112

stacking order, controlling, 111, 318

visibility, 14, 112, 320

layout, adjust to new page size, 291

leading, 54, 238
    adjusting, 22
    apply to entire paragraphs, 6, 167
    keyboard shortcut, 172
    paragraph styles, and, 245

ligatures, 246

links, *see also* images
    edit original, 211
    image dimensions, 181
    layers, and, 181
    linking vs. embedding, 33–34, 208
    missing, 48–50, 181, 212
    modified, 48–50, 211–212
    packaging files, 345
    preferences, 181
    text and spreadsheets, 181

locked objects, prevent selection, 165

M

margins, 279
    guides, and, 216–217
    ignore optical margin, 248

marquee, 38

master pages, 101–105, 283–286
    [None], 284
    applying, 115, 284
    blank, 284
    image frames, 285–286
    inserting text, 106
    naming, 283
    overriding master objects, 106, 108, 116, 284–284
    page numbers, and, 115, 284
    placing images, 108
    primary text frames, 116, 286
    reapplying, 132
    selecting master objects, 284
    text frames, 285–286

menus, customizing, 187

mobi, 156

multi-touch gestures, 166

N

native files, *see* packaging files

navigation, pages and spreads, 29

nested styles, 65

new document, create, 11

Nook app, 156

Notes preferences, 176

numbering, 257–260
    chapters, 325
    pages, *see* page numbers

O

object styles, 267–271
    applying, 268
    attributes controlled by, 269
    creating, 40–42, 267
    editing, 269
    Find/Change, 148–149
    frame fitting options, 92
    groups, and, 94–95
    image frames, applying to, 91
    paragraph styles, and, 97
    size and position, 269–271
    text frames, applying to, 90

objects
    aligning, 36
    anchor points, edit, 224
    anchored, 231
    combining, 225
    corners, edit, 226
    distribute space between, 37
    effects, 226–228
    Find/Change, 313
    flip, 223
    grid, creating, 38
    grouping, 39, 214–215
    inline, 232
    keyboard shortcuts, 363

repositioning, 15, 219–220
rotate, 220–221
scaling, 165, 222–223
selecting multiple, 37, 38
stacking order, 37, 111, 318
styles, *see* object styles
transform, 220–225

out port, 86, 200
output tagging
    character styles, and, 266
    ePub, 159, 347–348
    paragraph styles, and, 262
output, 338–358
    ePub, 347–353
    packaging files, 345–346
    PDF, 339–344
    print, 354–358
overrides
    highlighter, 58
    master frames, 106, 284
    paragraph styles, 57–58
overset text, *see* text

P

packaging files, 155, 345–346
page menu, 29
page navigation, 29
page numbers
    Absolute Numbering, 165
    General Preferences, 164
    marker, Current Page Number, 114,
        284
pages
    adding, 118
    adjust layout, 291
    first/last, 29
    gatefolds, 290
    master, *see* master pages
    moving, 118–119
    navigating, 281–282

next/previous, 29
resizing, 291–292
shuffling, 118–119, 289–290
size, 291
up/down, 29
Pages panel, 29, 281
    shuffling pages, 289–290
    view, 118
panels
    adjusting height, 9
    arranging, 184–186
    dock, new, 185
    expanding and collapsing, 9, 166
    preferences, 166
panning, 28
Paragraph panel, 22, 32
paragraph returns, clear extra, 74
paragraph styles, 56–60, 242–262
    advanced character formats, 246
    alignment, 246
    applying, 57, 243
    based on, 244
    border and shading, 251
    bullets, 257–258
    case, 246
    CC Libraries, and, 67
    character color, 260
    creating, 56, 59–60, 242–243
    defaults, 59
    drop caps, 254
    editing, 58–59, 244
    grep styles, and, 256
    grid, 247
    hyphenation, 252
    ignore optical margin, 248
    indents, 247
    justification, 252–253
    Keep Options, 63, 252
    kerning, 245
    leading, 245
    ligatures, 246

paragraph styles, continued

    nested styles, 65, 255

    next style, 244

    no break, 246

    numbering, 257–260

    object styles, and, 97

    OpenType features, 261

    output tagging, 262

    overrides, 57–58

    paragraph rules, 250

    paste text without formatting, 66

    Preserve Local Overrides, 71

    Redefine Style, 58–59

    Remove Styles and Formatting from Text and Tables, 71

    space before/after, 247

    space between paragraphs, 247

    span columns, 253

    split columns, 253

    Style Mapping, 70

    Style Name Conflicts, 69

    tabs, 248–250

    tracking, 245

    underline/strikethrough, 261

    violations, 57

Paste without Formatting, 66

pasteboard, 165, 173, 279

Pathfinder, 225

PDF output, 339–344

    color conversion, 342–344

    compression, 341

    crop marks, 342

    Destination, 342

    Export Adobe PDF dialog, 340

    fit page, 153, 341

    layers, from, 341

    marks and bleeds, 342

    online viewing, for, 341

    presets, 339

    press-ready, 154

    profile, printer, 342–343

    security, 344

    smallest file size, 153, 341

    view settings, 341

place images, 13, 33–34

    Fill Frame Proportionally, 16

    master pages and, 108

    show thumbnails on place, 166

placeholder text, 31

polygon, frame or shape, 191

position objects, 219, 220

preferences, 4–7

    accessing, 4

    Advanced Type, 168

    Appearance of Black, 179

    Autocorrect, 175

    Clipboard Handling, 182

    Composition, 169–170

    Dictionary, 174

    Display Performance, 7, 178

    document-specific, 4, 164

    File Handling, 180

    General, 4, 164–165

    global, 4, 164

    GPU Performance, 7, 179

    Grids, 172–173

    Guides & Pasteboard, 173

    Interface, 5, 165–166

    Notes, 176

    Publish Online, 183

    Spelling, 175

    Story Editor Display, 177

    Track Changes, 176

    Type, 6, 167

    Units & Increments, 6, 171–172

Preserve Local Overrides, 71

presets, 121

primary text frames, *see* text frames, primary

print, 354–358

    booklet, 358

    color management, 357

    graphics, 356

    marks and bleed, 355

output, 356
pages, specifying, 354
setup, 355
profile, printer, 299–300, 342–343
Publish Online, 183

Q

queries, grep, 309

R

recovery file, 28, 180
Rectangle Frame tool, 13, 190
Remove Styles and Formatting from Text and Tables, 71
RGB, 294
color swatch, 44, 193
rotate object, 220–221
Rotate tool, 221
ruler units, 6, 171
running headers, 327

S

save file, 12, 180
scale object, 222–223
section marker, 113, 288
sections, 113, 287–288
selecting multiple objects, 37, 38
Selection tool, 13
setup, document, 11–12
shape tools, 35, 190–191
shapes
combining multiple, 225
sculpting, 224
Shear tool, 223
shortcuts, *see* keyboard shortcuts
Show Import Options, 69
slug, 279

Smart Guides, 15, 37, 217
preferences, 173
Smart Text Reflow, 6, 167, 286
snippet, InDesign, 180
source files, *see* packaging files
Space After, 22, 53
Space Before, 53
space, distribute between objects, 37, 218
spaces, clear extra, 74
Spelling preferences, 175
spread
facing pages, 279
anatomy, 279
fit in window, 29
spread (Effects), 228
spreadsheets, placing, 81–82
stacking order (for objects), 37, 111, 318
Start Workspace, 4, 164
Story Editor Display, 177
story, 200
stroke, 192–197
adding, 16–17
align stroke, 196
gap color, 197
gradient, 194–195
miter limit, 197
paragraph border, 251
start/end, 197
Stroke panel, 17, 195–197
type, 195
style guide, loading, 122–124
Style Mapping, 70
styles
CC Libraries, and, 67
cells, *see* table and cell styles
character, *see* character styles
clear overrides, 74
extracting from other docs, 66
load styles, 66, 123, 277

styles, continued
    name conflicts, 69
    object, *see* object styles
    overrides, 57–58
    paragraph, *see* paragraph styles
    paste text without formatting, 66
    placeholder text, and, 103
    Preserve Local Overrides, 71
    Remove Styles and Formatting from
       Text and Tables, 71
    style guide, loading, 122–124
    Style Mapping, 70
    Style Name Conflicts, 69
    tables, *see* table and cell styles
    text, 51–75

swatches
    color mode, 44, 193
    color type, 44, 193
    creating, 43, 192–193
    saving, 17

T

table and cell styles, 79–81, 272–276
    border, 276
    cell styles, 275
    fills, 276
    paragraph styles, 275
    placing a table, 272
    strokes, 276
    table styles, 276

tables, 79–82
    cell styles, 80
    columns, adjusting, 81, 273
    columns, deleting, 82
    convert text to table, 79
    deleting, 79
    Excel, 272
    formatting, 274
    overset cells, 272–273
    placing, 272
    rows, adjusting, 81, 273

rows, deleting, 82
    select cell, 273
    select row, 273
    spreadsheets, placing, 81–82, 272
    styles, *see* table and cell styles

tables of contents, 137–140, 321–324
    dialog breakdown, 138, 322
    dummy, 137, 321
    generating, 137–139, 321–323
    load TOC Styles, 324
    paragraph styles, and, 137–139
    styles, 322
    TOC Style, 139, 324
    updating, 139–140, 324

tabs
    paragraph styles, and, 78, 248–250
    tab stop, setting, 77–78, 249
    Tabs panel, 77

templates, *see* master pages

text
    alignment, 53, 239
    character styles, *see* character styles
    clipboard handling, 182
    display, story editor, 177
    drag and drop editing, 167
    drop caps, 254
    flow, primary, 116
    font, *see* fonts
    formatting, 21–23, 31, 53–55
    frames, *see* text frames
    glyphs, 22
    indents, 53, 240
    justification, vertical, 89, 204
    justify, 53
    kerning, 54, 237
    leading, 54, 237
    non-Latin, 168
    overset, 84–86
    Paragraph panel, 22
    paragraph returns, clear extra, 74
    paragraph styles, *see* paragraph styles

paste without formatting, 66

placeholder, 31

placing, 20

reflow, 6

scaling, 202, 238

selecting, 21

size, adjust, 172

spaces, clear extra, 74

spacing, 22, 53, 240

spanning columns, 253

story, 200

styles, 51–75

tracking, 54, 237

variables, 144

Word document, placing, 68–75

wrap, *see* text wrap

text frames

    add, 86

    alignment, text, 239

    alternating between frame and content, 198

    auto-size, 88, 206

    baseline options, 87, 204–205

    basics, 30

    columns, 85, 88, 202–203

    create, 20

    delete, 86

    drawing over another frame, 102

    footnotes, 207

    content vs., 30–31

    gridify, 40

    gutter, 85

    in port, 86

    inset, 87, 203

    linking, 200–201

    master pages and, 106

    object styles and, 90–91

    options, 87–91, 202–207

    out port, 8, 200

    overset text, 84–86

    primary, 116, 286

    resizing, 32

    scaling text, and, 202

    threading, 85, 200–201

    vertical justification, 89, 204

text variables, 144, 325–327

    captions, 326

    chapter numbers, 325

    display bug, 145

    running headers, 327

text wrap, 229–234

    anchored objects, 234

    around bounding box, 229

    around object shape, 230

    jump object/jump to next column, 230

    preferences, 170

threading text frames, 85, 200–201

tool tips, 28, 166

Tools panel, 9

    keyboard shortcuts, 367

    preferences, 166

Track Changes preferences, 176

tracking, 54, 237–238

    highlight adjustments, 170

    keyboard shortcut, 172

    paragraph styles, and, 245

transform objects, 220–225

troubleshooting, 46

Type preferences, 6, 167

    drag and drop editing, 167

    leading, 6

    Smart Text Reflow, 6, 167

    typographer's quotes, 167

Type tool, 20

Typical (Display Performance), 7, 178

U

undo, 28

Units & Increments preferences, 6, 171–172

W

Word document, placing, 68–75
        clear overrides, 74
        HTML tags, 71
        preserve local overrides, 71
        remove styles and formatting from
           text and tables, 71
        style mapping, 70
        style name conflicts, 69
Workspace
        configuring, 8–9, 184–186
        document window, 9
        menu, 8
        new, 9, 185
        panels, 9
        resetting, 9, 185
        "Start", 4

Z

zoom, 28